FINTECH COMPETITION

This open access book is the first to systematically explore competition policy in fintech markets. Drawing from the expertise of law scholars, economists, and social and natural scientists from the EU and the US, this edited collection explores the competitive dynamics, market organisation, and competition law application in fintech markets. It is the 17th volume in the Swedish Studies in European Law series.

Fintech Competition

Law, Policy, and Market Organisation

Swedish Studies in European Law Volume 17

Edited by
Konstantinos Stylianou
Marios Iacovides
and
Björn Lundqvist

•HART•
OXFORD • LONDON • NEW YORK • NEW DELHI • SYDNEY

HART PUBLISHING

Bloomsbury Publishing Plc

Kemp House, Chawley Park, Cumnor Hill, Oxford, OX2 9PH, UK

1385 Broadway, New York, NY 10018, USA

29 Earlsfort Terrace, Dublin 2, Ireland

HART PUBLISHING, the Hart/Stag logo, BLOOMSBURY and the Diana logo are trademarks of Bloomsbury Publishing Plc

First published in Great Britain 2023

A catalogue record for this book is available from the British Library.

A catalogue record for this book is available from the Library of Congress.

Library of Congress Control Number: 2023940000

ISBN: HB: 978-1-50996-334-8
ePDF: 978-1-50996-336-2
ePub: 978-1-50996-335-5

Typeset by Compuscript Ltd, Shannon

Contents

PART III
FINTECH'S INSTITUTIONAL AND REGULATORY SETTING

List of Contributors

Deirdre Ahern is a Professor in Law and Director of the Technologies, Law and Society Research Group at Trinity College Dublin. A member of the League of European Research Universities' Legal Team on Artificial Intelligence, her recent research on crowdlending and on regulatory sandboxes has focused on the regulatory challenges presented by the impact of Artificial Intelligence and other new technologies in the context of fintech.

Liudmila Alekseeva is a PhD candidate in Finance at IESE Business School, University of Navarra. Her work explores the effects of companies' adoption of innovative technologies on labour and productivity. She also studies questions in entrepreneurial finance with a focus on venture capital financing. She has an MSc from Bocconi University in Italy and a BSc from St. Petersburg State University in Russia.

Jonas Valbjørn Andersen is Associate Professor of Digital Methods and Data in Organisations and heads the Information Systems and Digital Innovation research group at the IT University of Copenhagen. He has a background in strategy and IT and holds a PhD in Information Systems from Warwick Business School. His research examines coordination in distributed information systems like blockchains and Distributed Ledger Technologies (DLT), online communities and data ecosystems, as well as organisational processes related to algorithmic decision-making.

José Azar is an economist specialising in antitrust and corporate governance. His work studies the implications for competition of the rise of common ownership of companies by large and diversified asset managers. More recently, he has carried out research on labour market concentration and power. Before joining IESE, he worked at Charles River Associates in the Antitrust Practice. He received his BA from Universidad Torcuato Di Tella in Argentina, and his PhD from Princeton University.

Claire Ingram Bogusz is Associate Professor of Information Systems at Uppsala University, and a research fellow at the Stockholm School of Economics' House of Innovation. She holds a PhD in Business Administration from the Stockholm School of Economics. Her research examines collective organising, particularly when this is mediated or automated using digital artefacts, infrastructures and ecosystems. Her work has examined blockchain and DLTs, as well as gig work and entrepreneurial finance.

Oscar Borgogno is a Research Officer in the International Relations and Economics Department at the Central Bank of Italy, and a teaching assistant at LUISS (Italy). He received his PhD in Law from the University of Turin in 2022 and an MSc in Law and Finance at the University of Oxford. Oscar's research investigates the challenges for competition policy, intellectual property and financial regulation associated with the advent of digital markets.

Lucy Chambers (MA (Cantab), LLM (Harvard), MA (KCL)) is a solicitor and attorney specialising in competition law. She is an Associate in the Competition Group at Slaughter and May based in London and Brussels. Lucy has experience advising multinational companies, including in the financial sector, on mergers and antitrust issues including vertical agreements. Lucy's personal research interests centre on economic analysis of competition law and competition law in the fintech sector.

Iris H-Y Chiu is Professor of Corporate Law and Financial Regulation at University College London. She is Director of the UCL Centre of Ethics and Law, a Research Member of the European Corporate Governance Institute, and most recently, a Senior Scholar at the European Central Bank's Legal Research Programme.

Ryan Clements is an Assistant Professor, Chair in Business Law and Regulation at the University of Calgary Faculty of Law. He is a Member of the New Economy Advisory Committee, Alberta Securities Commission, and of the Investor Advisory Panel, Canadian Securities Administrators. He holds a doctorate in Juridical Science (SJD) and Master of Laws (LLM) Magna Cum Laude from Duke University Law School, and a Bachelor of Laws (LLB), with distinction, and BA Economics (Honours, First Class) from the University of Alberta.

Giuseppe Colangelo is a Jean Monnet Professor of European Innovation Policy and an Associate Professor of Law and Economics at the University of Basilicata. He also serves as Adjunct Professor of Markets, Regulation and Law, and of Competition and Markets of Innovation at LUISS. He is fellow of the Stanford Law School Transatlantic Technology Law Forum (TTLF), the scientific coordinator of the Research Network for Digital Ecosystem, Economic Policy and Innovation (Deep-In), and an academic affiliate with the International Center for Law & Economics (ICLE).

Dean Corbae is the William Sellery Trukenbrod Chair in Finance and a Professor of Economics at the University of Wisconsin–Madison. He is a research associate at the National Bureau of Economic Research. His research on macroeconomics and finance has been published in *Econometrica*, *Journal of Political Economy* and *Review of Economic Studies*, among others. His books include *An Introduction to Mathematical Analysis for Economic Theory and Econometrics* (Princeton University Press, 2009).

Beatrice Crona is a Professor of Sustainability Science, and Science Director at the Stockholm Resilience Center, Stockholm University. She is also Executive Director of the Global Economic Dynamics and the Biosphere Academy programme at the Royal Swedish Academy of Science. Her most recent work focuses on identifying opportunities for financial leadership for climate stability by linking earth system science to ownership and investment patterns.

Pablo D'Erasmo is currently Advisor and Senior Economist at the Federal Reserve Bank of Philadelphia. His research interests are in macroeconomics and industrial organisation, with emphasis on banking. He has published his research in several journals including *Econometrica*, *Review of Economic Studies*, *Journal of Monetary Economics* and *AEJ: Macroeconomics*. Pablo received his PhD in Economics from the University of Texas. He worked as an Assistant Professor at the University of Maryland.

Jens-Uwe Franck is Professor of Law at the University of Mannheim and a Co-Director of the Mannheim Centre for Competition and Innovation (MaCCI). While his main field of research is competition law, research projects regularly address cross-cutting issues and concern banking and securities regulation as well as consumer protection. His research has for some years now focused on competition practice and regulation of digital platforms.

Marios C Iacovides is an Assistant Professor in EU Commercial Law at Uppsala University, Department of Business Studies and a Researcher of the Royal Swedish Academy of Letters, History and Antiquities. His research focuses on competition law and sustainability, the relation between market power and unsustainable business practices and how the Green Deal and the degrowth movement affect EU competition policy. He holds an LLB from King's College London, an LLM from Stockholm University and an LLD (PhD in EU Competition Law and WTO Law) from Uppsala University. He has worked as legal counsel for the Swedish Competition Authority and as Sustainability Advisor for the Hellenic Competition Commission.

Kuan Liu is an Assistant Professor of finance at the Sam M Walton College of Business of the University of Arkansas. His research interests are in financial institutions and markets, with emphasis on banking and macro finance. He has recently published his research in the *American Economic Journal: Applied Economics*. Kuan received his PhD in Finance from the University of Wisconsin–Madison in August 2020.

Youming Liu is a Senior Economist in the Banking and Payments Department – CBDC and FinTech Policy & Research at the Bank of Canada. He received his PhD in Economics from the Boston University. Youming's research focuses on industrial organisation, platform economics and environmental economics. He works on a variety of markets, including payments, automobiles, EV charging stations and music streaming services.

Björn Lundqvist is Professor of Law at the Law Department, Stockholm University. He is the Chair of the Swedish Network of European Legal Studies and the Head of the EU Law Research Group, Director of the European Law Institute, and Director of ASCOLA Nordic. Björn is a well-renowned European competition law scholar and has published extensively on Competition, Data and IP Law-related issues.

Despoina Mantzari is Associate Professor in Competition Law and Policy at University College London. She is Co-Director of the UCL Centre for Law, Economics and Society and Associate Fellow at the Centre for Competition Policy, UEA. Her research combines doctrinal analysis with qualitative analysis and has been funded by the AHRC, the ESRC and the BA/Leverhulme Trust.

Edona Reshidi is a Senior Economist in the Banking and Payments Department – CBDC and FinTech Policy & Research at the Bank of Canada. She is a micro-economist with research interests in payment platforms, vertical markets and search theory. Edona obtained her PhD in Economics from the University of Vienna.

Francisco Rivadeneyra is the Director for CBDC and FinTech Policy & Research at the Bank of Canada. In this role he leads a team developing policy advice in areas of central bank digital currency, electronic money and payments, and the implications for central banks of broader financial innovations. His research focuses on the intersection between technology, payments infrastructures and finance. Francisco holds a PhD in Economics from the University of Chicago.

Konstantinos Stylianou is a Professor of Competition Law and Regulation at the University of Glasgow School of Law. His research focuses on high technology markets particularly as regards policymaking. He has advised governments on competition policy in digital markets, has worked on various projects funded by competition authorities and big tech companies, and is the co-founder of the legal database DB-COMP. He holds an SJD from the University of Pennsylvania, an LLM. from Harvard University and an LLB and LLM from Aristotle University.

Anna Tzanaki is a Senior Lecturer at Lund University's Faculty of Law (Sweden), Affiliate Fellow at the Stigler Center at Chicago Booth Business School (US) and Senior Research Fellow at the UCL Centre of Law, Economics & Society (UK). She is Associate Editor of the *Journal of Competition Law & Economics* (Oxford) and *Competition Policy International* (Boston). Her research focuses on competition law and policy, corporate governance, finance, law and economics, EU and comparative law.

Andrew Usher is a Senior Economist in the Banking and Payments Department at the Bank of Canada. He holds a BSc from the University of Victoria as well as an MA and a PhD from the University of Michigan, all in Economics. He does research in competition and collusion. His work has focused on digital currencies and grocery scanner data.

Simonetta Vezzoso is a legal scholar and an economist. After graduating from the Law Faculty of Milan University, she started a career in private practice. Eventually, she went back to academia and took a German PhD in Economics focusing on innovation and evolutionary theories. Among other things, she is a non-governmental adviser to the International Competition Network and a Researcher and Professor for Competition Policy at Trento University.

Nicolo Zingales is Professor of Information Law and Regulation at the Law School of Fundação Getulio Vargas in Rio de Janeiro, where he heads the E-Commerce Research Group. He is also a Non-Governmental Advisor and a UNDP consultant for the Brazilian competition authority. He holds an advanced law degree from the University of Bologna and a PhD in International law and Economics from Bocconi University.

Part I

Fintech Market Structure and Organisation

1

The Boundaries of Fintech: Data-Driven Classification and Domain Delimitation

CLAIRE INGRAM BOGUSZ AND JONAS VALBJØRN ANDERSEN

I. INTRODUCTION

ALTHOUGH FINTECH HAS been of considerable interest for researchers,[1] policymakers[2] and practitioners,[3] issues remain around how to define what activities and which firms should be considered 'fintech' and which should not. This issue stems partly from a question of whether fintech, or financial technology, is just an instance of digital technologies being used to deliver (new) financial services, or if there is something more to the phenomenon.

At its core, this is a question of boundaries: which services and firms should be included in fintech and how should one decide. Where these boundaries are placed has implications not only for researchers that seek to understand this emerging phenomenon, but also for policymakers – for instance when trying to establish the size and economic importance of fintech, and for regulators when trying to assess whether existing rules apply to fintech organisations, and whether new ones are needed. For authorities interested in competition, the identification of industry boundaries, and the usefulness of existing data for delimiting these boundaries, can help them better define markets or assess the effects of future policies. Boundaries are also of importance when it comes to

[1] See, eg, P Gomber et al, 'On the Fintech Revolution: Interpreting the Forces of Innovation, Disruption, and Transformation in Financial Services' (2018) 35 *Journal of Management Information Systems* 220; and R Teigland et al, *The Rise and Development of Fintech: Accounts of Disruption from Sweden and Beyond* (Routledge, 2018).

[2] See, eg, M Obschonka and DB Audretsch, 'Artificial Intelligence and Big Data in Entrepreneurship: A New Era Has Begun' (2020) 55 *Small Business Economics* 529; D Audretsch et al, 'Innovative Start-ups and Policy Initiatives' (2020) 49 *Research Policy* 104027.

[3] eg, Deloitte, 'Fintech: On the Brink of Further Disruption' (2020), available at: www2.deloitte.com/content/dam/Deloitte/nl/Documents/financial-services/deloitte-nl-fsi-fintech-report-1.pdf; PWC, 'Blurred Lines: How Fintech Is Shaping Financial Services' (2016), available at: www.pwc.com/il/en/home/assets/pwc_fintech_global_report.pdf.

deciding whether policies are needed and what effect they might have. Analysis reliant on registry and panel data is thus done ex ante when considering policy.

How, then, should one distinguish between fintech and adjacent industries like finance and IT? In this chapter, we take an empirical approach to answering that question. Based on a sample of 356 already identified fintech firms in Sweden, we use a supervised machine learning algorithm to (a) derive a dictionary that will allow us to identify 'missing' fintech firms in the Swedish Companies Registry; (b) cluster the resulting firms according to how they describe themselves in order to derive sub-categories or fintech domains; and (c) then compare the resulting fintech firms and their sub-categories against the classification codes used by the Swedish Registries Office, which are built on international standards. This third step is taken to see to what extent existing data can be used to reliably identify fintech firms. Sweden represents a suitable case at it has a considerable fintech ecosystem and follows (European Union) EU data standards, making the method generalisable to at least other EU countries and countries following a similar standard.

Sweden is a good site for a study of this kind, for several reasons. First, Swedish registry data are used frequently in academic and industry research, suggesting that they are extensive and reliable. Second, the country, in addition to an agency tasked with collecting data, Statistics Sweden, has a dedicated agency tasked with conducting analysis for the purposes of guiding policy and facilitating impact and growth assessments, the Swedish Agency for Growth Policy Analysis (Tillväxtanalys). Finally, the country regularly ranks highly in international assessments of its fintech firms, suggesting that there is a population of firms that can be identified in the data.

In so doing, we treat fintech as a phenomenon that spans classifications, specifically finance and information technology, or IT, classifications. Classification-spanning firms and industries present a challenge for policymakers in general because they are poorly understood and hard to identify.[4] For any single area of classification-spanning economic activity, it is hard to identify which firms to include and which to include when conducting analyses – and downstream policymaking. The inability to identify classification-spanning forms calls into question the usefulness of existing data for understanding these new forms, including their impact on productivity and inequality.[5]

II. BACKGROUND: FINTECH AS BOTH A FINANCIAL AND TECHNOLOGICAL PHENOMENON

There are many, though not always compatible, definitions of what fintech is, and thus which firms should be included in a resulting classification. In general,

[4] T Ciarli et al, 'Digital Technologies, Innovation, and Skills: Emerging Trajectories and Challenges' (2021) 50 *Research Policy* 104289.

[5] ibid.

definitions of fintech include two elements: finance, and technology, although they differ in their understandings of which are involved. This has downstream consequences for understanding the different domains or areas of activity within fintech.

Some studies treat fintech as a primarily financial phenomenon empowered by digital technologies,[6] while others – notably including industry analysts – see fintech as something that spans these two classifications, or at least comprises elements of both.[7] Those studies that see fintech as an extension of finance point to the fact that finance and technology have co-evolved:

> [Finance is] … a social technology, based on a system of recording assets and liabilities (credits and debits), which has developed through a series of innovations from coins, through to bills of exchange, double-entry book-keeping, insurance and central banking, all the way to financial derivatives and high-frequency algorithmic trading.[8]

Within this understanding, there is also the observation that technologies 'support and enable' the delivery of financial services,[9] but that while fintech firms are often start-ups, it may also be the case that fintech services are delivered by incumbent actors like banks.

This perspective seems to be consistent with the roots of the term 'fintech'. Schueffel, in 2015, points to the fact that the word 'fintech' was used as early as 1972 to 'stand for financial technology, combining bank expertise with modern management science techniques and the computer'.[10] However, given the advances in technology since then – and in particular the argument that digital technologies have fundamentally changed digital entrepreneurship by decentralising control and making agency unclear,[11] it is entirely possible that the ordinary understanding of the portmanteau may have evolved.

One possible understanding is to emphasise that fintech firms are technology firms first, but that they happen to provide financial services or services to the financial industry. Studies that highlight the importance of the technology in fintech emphasise that 'products and services provided by the industry are financial in nature, the processes and tools are mostly from the technology

[6] eg, E Knight and D Wójcik, 'Fintech, Economy and Space: Introduction to the Special Issue' (2020) 52 *Environment and Planning A* 1490; B Nicoletti, *The Future of Fintech: Integrating Finance and Technology in Financial Services* (Palgrave Macmillan, 2017).

[7] eg, Deloitte, 'Fintech: On the Brink of Further Disruption' (n 3); Gomber et al (n 1); N Wesley-James et al, 'Stockholm Fintech: An Overview of the Fintech Sector in the Greater Stockholm Region' (2015), available at: www.hhs.se/contentassets/b5823453b8fe4290828fcc81189b6561/stockholm-fintech---june-2015.pdf.

[8] Knight and Wójcik (n 6) 1490.

[9] Nicoletti (n 6) 12.

[10] P Schueffel, 'Taming the Beast: A Scientific Definition of Fintech' (2016) 4 *Journal of Innovation Management* 32, 33.

[11] S Nambisan, 'Digital Entrepreneurship: Toward a Digital Technology Perspective of Entrepreneurship' (2017) 41 *Entrepreneurship Theory and Practice* 1029.

industry'.[12] Understandings of fintech within this category build not on which services a firm provides, but rather on the technologies that it uses to provide them – although they do acknowledge that the services themselves need to be offered to customers or other firms in the finance industry. Examples include defining blockchain as primarily a fintech technology[13] and defining wearables that offer payment interfaces, for instance Apple Pay, as also being fintech.[14]

Other, complementary, characteristics of fintech transcend the question of whether finance or technology is more prominent. Instead, they emphasise things like agility,[15] novelty and innovativeness,[16] and the observation that fintech has the potential to, and in the case of for instance cryptocurrencies already does, dissolve physical and geographic boundaries.[17]

A. Domains within Fintech

A significant part of defining what fintech is, therefore, might be thought of in terms of the sub-classifications, or domains, in the larger classification. Again, there are two approaches: one loosely along financial service lines and the other along technology lines.

The approach to defining within-fintech domains along product lines (ie, classify fintech firms in terms of the services that they provide) is taken by Knewtson and Rosenbaum. They argue that fintech can be divided up into four sub-categories (see Figure 1), namely Monetary Alternatives, Capital Intermediation, InvestTech, and Infrastructure. However, one problem with this classification is that it defines financial services very broadly to include not only insurance (InsurTech), but also regulatory services in finance (Financial RegTech). While there are other systems that also have this 'big tent' approach to understanding fintech,[18] others have argued that these are separate areas of economic activity entirely.[19]

[12] HS Knewtson and ZA Rosenbaum, 'Toward Understanding Fintech and Its Industry' (2020) 46 *Managerial Finance* 1043, 1044.

[13] K Leong, 'Fintech (Financial Technology): What is It and How to Use Technologies to Create Business Value in Fintech Way?' (2018) 9 *International Journal of Innovation, Management and Technology* 74.

[14] MA Chen, Q Wuand and B Yang, 'How Valuable Is fintech Innovation?' (2019) 32 *Review of Financial Studies* 2062.

[15] Knewtson and Rosenbaum (n 12).

[16] Chen et al (n 14).

[17] Knight and Wójcik (n 6).

[18] eg, Deloitte, 'Closing the Gap in Fintech Collaboration: Overcoming Obstacles to a Symbiotic Relationship' (2018), available at: www2.deloitte.com/content/dam/Deloitte/us/Documents/financial-services/us-fsi-dcfs-fintech-collaboration.pdf; Deloitte, 'Fintech: On the Brink of Further Disruption' (n 3); and PWC (n 3).

[19] eg, Findexable, *The Global Fintech Index 2020* (2020), available at: findexable.com/wp-content/uploads/2019/12/Findexable_Global-Fintech-Rankings-2020exSFA.pdf.

Figure 1 A financial services-derived classification of fintech domains[20]

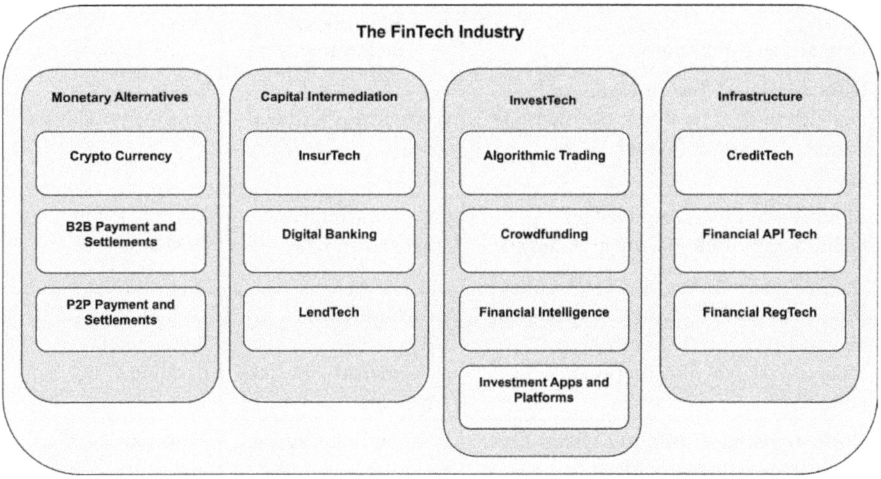

Another alternative is to classify fintech domains along technology lines (ie, classify fintech firms according to the technologies they use). One study that considers how to define fintech along technology lines looks at patent data in order to assess the value of fintech, rooted in an understanding that the technologies are central to the wider phenomenon.[21] Again, this classification of fintech according to key technologies (see Table 1) defines fintech very broadly and includes broader phenomena, for instance, big data, machine learning, and smart devices as being within the ambit of fintech.

Table 1 Definitions and examples of fintech domains in a technology-centric understanding[22]

Domain and definition	Key (digital) technologies	Examples
Cybersecurity: Hardware or software used to protect financial privacy or safeguard against electronic theft or fraud	Encryption, tokenisation, authentication, biometrics	Iris-scanning ATM, Biometric Cards
Mobile transactions: Technologies that facilitate payments via mobile devices, eg, smartphones, tablets, and wearables	Smartphone wallets, digital wallets, near-field communication	Apple Pay, Android Pay, PayPal Venmo

(continued)

[20] Adapted from Knewtson and Rosenbaum (n 12).
[21] Chen et al (n 14).
[22] Adapted from Chen et al (n 14).

Table 1 *(Continued)*

Domain and definition	Key (digital) technologies	Examples
Data analytics: Technologies and algorithms that facilitate transactions data or consumer financial data analysis	Big data, cloud computing, artificial intelligence, machine learning	Credit scoring, sentiment analysis
Blockchain: Distributed ledger technologies used mainly in financial services	Cryptocurrencies, smart contracts	Bitcoin, Ripple, JPM coin
Peer-to-peer (P2P): Software, systems, or platforms that facilitate direct financial transactions between consumers	Crowdfunding, P2P lending, customer-to-customer payments	GoFundMe, Kickstarter, Lending Club
Robo-advising: Computer systems or programmes that provide automated financial advice to customers or portfolio managers	Artificial intelligence, machine learning	Automated investment advice, portfolio placement recommendations
Internet of things (IoT): Technologies relating to smart devices that gather data in real time and communicate via the internet	Smart devices, near-field communication, wireless sensor networks	Smart home sensors, vehicle sensors

These understandings of both what fintech is and which domains are within fintech formed the backdrop for our own empirical study. There are various reasons for individual firms to register as either a financial service or a technology provider, including lower regulatory oversight for technology versus financial service firms, organisational culture and history, and strategic trajectory rather than actual output. Consequently, we used the financial services and technology categories to delineate the population of fintech firms, but opted not to define fintech as being either financial service-first or technology-first. Instead, we defined fintech as a class of firms delivering services that are qualitatively distinct and thus emerge from both categories without necessarily including all firms registered in each category. Therefore, the distinct characteristics of fintech firms is visible in their self-descriptions of their activities rather than in their specific register category. Taking this approach allowed us to build on the understanding echoed in previous studies that fintech combines elements of both finance and digital technologies.

III. RESEARCH DESIGN

There has been considerable enthusiasm from management scholars (and also from other disciplines such as law) in using new, digital methods to advance empirical research, and entrepreneurship research in particular.[23] In the academic and policy realms, much of this analysis is done in order to better understand a phenomenon, for instance to make predictions about sector growth, to infer consumer or investor sentiment, or to develop and text complex models in a data-first way. However, in legal scholarship it has also been suggested that digital empirical methods are not just a method for understanding phenomena, but that they also identify and evaluate unlawful conduct – perhaps even in real-time.[24] Indeed, both private actors and governmental agencies across the globe are creating roles like 'Chief Data Officer' and 'Chief Information Officer' not only to ensure compliance with data privacy laws like the General Data Protection Regulation,[25] but to pioneer and advance data-driven strategies, which typically use advanced analytics like machine learning.[26]

The premise upon which this enthusiasm lies is, first, in the belief that there is an abundance of so-called 'big data'[27] available for complex data-first analysis.[28] Second, proponents highlight that these data have opened the possibility of computational inductive methods[29] and computational theory development.[30]

While it has also been argued that proponents of using these methods of data analysis may misunderstand or oversimplify the processes involved,[31] ignore existing state of the art discussions on quantitative rigour[32] and overestimate the usefulness of the data available for complex analyses, we nevertheless show that, despite these limitations, registry data in conjunction with machine learning methods can provide a useful tool to identify and analyse classification-spanning entrepreneurial firms and associated within-classification economic domains.

[23] eg, M Maula and W Stam, 'Enhancing Rigor in Quantitative Entrepreneurship Research' (2020) 44 *Entrepreneurship Theory and Practice* 1059; Audretsch et al (n 2); Obschonka and Audretsch (n 2).

[24] eg, C Coglianese and A Lai, 'Antitrust by Algorithm' (2022), available at: scholarship.law.upenn.edu/faculty_scholarship/2755.

[25] Regulation (EU) 2016/679 on the protection of natural persons with regard to the processing of personal data and the free movement of such data [2016] OJ L119/1.

[26] In Sweden, for instance, the Swedish Tax Authority boasts an innovation team tasked with exploring how automated and data-driven analyses can improve their service and better detect tax-related crimes. In the United Kingdom, an agency for Government Digital Service was established in 2011, tasked with developing platforms and data-driven methods for improving service delivery.

[27] See R Kitchin, 'Big Data, New Epistemologies and Paradigm Shifts' (2014) 1 *Big Data & Society* 1 for a comprehensive discussion of what big data is, and is not.

[28] After more than a little cleaning, eg, V Mayer-Schönberger and K Cukier, *Big Data: A Revolution That Will Transform How We Live, Work, and Think* (Houghton Mifflin Harcourt, 2013).

[29] eg S Debortoli et al, 'Text Mining for Information Systems Researchers: An Annotated Topic Modeling Tutorial' (2016) 39 *Communications of the Association for Information Systems* 7.

[30] N Berente et al, 'Research Commentary – Data-Driven Computationally Intensive Theory Development' (2019) 30 *Information Systems Research* 50.

[31] D Carter and D Sholler, 'Data Science on the Ground: Hype, Criticism, and Everyday Work' (2016) 67 *Journal of the Association for Information Science and Technology* 2309.

[32] Maula and Stam (n 23).

This work builds on the arguments that (a) using the wealth of data that have become available for social science research should allow researchers to uncover previously complex insights not easily accessible using human intelligence;[33] (b) this should allow researchers to conduct studies on a population, rather than a sample, level;[34] and (c) using digital methods rooted in data could make studies more objective.[35] This enthusiasm extends both to using so-called 'big data' in entrepreneurship research,[36] and to the use of machine learning and artificial intelligence.[37]

A. Context

The choice of Sweden as our reference country is justified on the grounds of being a highly developed economy and one where standardised data is readily available. Sweden typically ranks among the best in the world when it comes to both innovation and good environment for doing business, including a well-established financial centre in Stockholm. According to the Swedish Bankers' Association, the financial industry accounted for 3.8 per cent of total output in Sweden in 2019 and employed around 95,000 people. At the same time, according to Statistics Sweden, 88,200 people, or around 2 per cent of the workforce were employed in finance and 191,100 people, or around 4 per cent of the workforce, were employed in ICT in 2019.

International rankings suggest that Stockholm is the biggest fintech hub per capita in Europe[38] and that Sweden, depending on the definition of fintech and associated metrics, is either seventh in the world[39] or third in the world.[40] At the same time, Swedish state agencies collect extensive data around registered firms, including not only their performance data, but free-text registered descriptions of firms, and registered classifications. We therefore chose to conduct an inductive study of fintech based on Swedish data, with the good quality data making computational analysis viable, and the international rankings indicating that the Swedish population of fintech firms might be considered representative.

[33] ibid.

[34] HJ Miller, 'The Data Avalanche Is Here. Shouldn't We Be Digging?' (2010) 50 *Journal of Regional Science* 181.

[35] D Boyd and K Crawford, 'Critical Questions for Big Data: Provocations for a Cultural, Technological, and Scholarly Phenomenon' (2012) 15 *Information, Communication & Society* 662.

[36] A Schwab and Z Zhang, 'A New Methodological Frontier in Entrepreneurship Research: Big Data Studies' (2019) 43 *Entrepreneurship Theory and Practice* 843.

[37] M Lévesque et al, 'Pursuing Impactful Entrepreneurship Research Using Artificial Intelligence' (2022) 46 *Entrepreneurship Theory and Practice* 803.

[38] Teigland et al (n 1).

[39] Findexable (n 19).

[40] Lucerne University, *FinTech Made in Switzerland: Clouds on the Horizon* (2020), available at: www.hslu.ch/en/lucerne-university-of-applied-sciences-and-arts/about-us/media/medienmitteilungen/2021/03/03/fintech-study-2021.

Swedish data are widely used in entrepreneurship and policy research,[41] making them a credible source of data for an attempt of this kind.

Sweden makes use of the Swedish Standard Industrial Classification (SIC) to classify firms and workplaces according to the industrial activities they carry out. This is based on the EU's recommended standards.[42] As such, then the results of our study can readily be applied to other EU countries and can with few adaptations be applied to other jurisdictions that follow similar standards. To our knowledge, no similar study has been done with SIC classifications. However, a recent study of US patents also made use of machine learning to identify and classify patents that could be considered to be artificial intelligence patents.[43]

B. Data

Our dataset consisted of companies' registry data maintained by the Swedish Companies Registration Office (Bolagsverket, BV) and related data from the Swedish Tax Authority (Skatteverket, SV) for the years from 2002 to 2018. We chose this dataset because it is widely used by policymakers and researchers. Registry data have long been the go-to data for following firms and firms in a particular industry over time, through a large number of repeated measures across different levels of analysis. This allows scholars not only to track firms and industries, but to draw causal inferences and employ multilevel research methods.[44]

As mentioned, Sweden applies the Swedish Standard Industrial Classification (SIC) to classify firms according to their activities. SIC codes are assigned through firm self-selection from a predefined array upon registration. Firms are legally obliged to update them if their industry of operation changes, and these SIC codes are a key way to delineate and classify firms, including entrepreneurial ones. Despite this legal obligation, however, self-identification is not without its problems. The most obvious of these problems is the subjectivity of self-assessment. A further problem, identified through informal conversations with experts, is the suspicion that many firms either register their firms in the broadest possible category to avoid having to change their registered classification later (at a cost), or forget to update their registered category despite the firm

[41] eg, T Ejdemo and D Örtqvist, 'Related Variety as a Driver of Regional Innovation and Entrepreneurship: A Moderated and Mediated Model with Non-linear Effects' (2020) 49 *Research Policy* 104073; or M Grillitsch et al, 'Knowledge Base Combinations and Firm Growth' (2019) 48 *Research Policy* 234.

[42] NACE Rev.2. SNI 2007.

[43] M Miric et al, 'Using Supervised Machine Learning for Large-Scale Classification in Management Research: The Case for Identifying Artificial Intelligence Patents' (2023) 44 *Strategic Management Journal* 491.

[44] K Wennberg, 'Entrepreneurship Research Through Databases: Measurement and Design Issues' (2005) 8(2) *New England Journal of Entrepreneurship* 9.

swinging into a new industry or product, which is commonplace among fintech firms. As becomes obvious below (see section V, Analysis of Results) this may affect the findings.

Some of these problems are, however, mitigated through the use of a second data source. Swedish firms also have the possibility of describing their area of operations in a free text format, usually at the time of registration. These data were also used to create a dictionary for the identification of fintech firms within the broad categories of finance and technology, limiting the effects of outdated or broad SIC category registration.

We delineated our analysis by focusing on firms that had self-selected both of the SIC categories: Technology and Finance. Working from this assumption, we employed a kind of machine learning algorithm, known as natural language processing (NLP), to identify, categorise and analyse patterns of fintech firms.

C. Method and Analysis

Our analysis was conducted in three phases: (i) distinguishing between fintech and non-fintech firms; and then (ii) identifying and categorising fintech firms based on both their free text descriptions and registered description of their activities. Based on this identification and categorisation we then (iii) explored patterns in registry-derived classifications and our NLP-derived classifications to understand if there was a relationship between the two.

i. Defining and Identifying the Fintech Firm Population

We first tried to identify fintech firms from self-reported descriptions in the entire company registry data using neural networks.[45] However, the free-text firm descriptions were too short to yield meaningful categories across the full registry data.

Another approach might be to train a machine learning algorithm, such as a neural network or support vector machine, on some test data to identify fintech firms in the entire population. Having obtained a list of 356 self-identified fintech firms, these test data proved insufficient to train an unsupervised algorithm and obtain useful classifications.

We therefore turned to training an NLP algorithm using a training dataset of 356 confirmed fintech companies provided by the Swedish Agency for Growth Policy Analysis (Tillväxtanalys, TVA). The test data was used to derive vocabularies relating to fintech that we could then apply to identifying fintech firms from the entire population of companies.

[45] CM Bishop, *Pattern Recognition and Machine Learning* (Springer, 2006).

Specifically, we ran the NLP topic modelling algorithm latent dirichlet allocation (LDA)[46] on the most recent free text descriptions of the confirmed fintech firms. LDA determines categories in corpuses of text, in this case specifically firm descriptions, based on term frequency, ie, how many times words appear in the same descriptions. In tuning the LDA algorithm on the training data, we took specific care to determine the right setting of the lambda parameter, which determines the exclusivity of words that are categorised within the same topic. High lambda allows for more topic overlap, and low lambda is more discriminatory and excludes terms that are also prevalent in other categories.[47]

Figure 2 Inter-topic distance map showing fintech related topic cluster

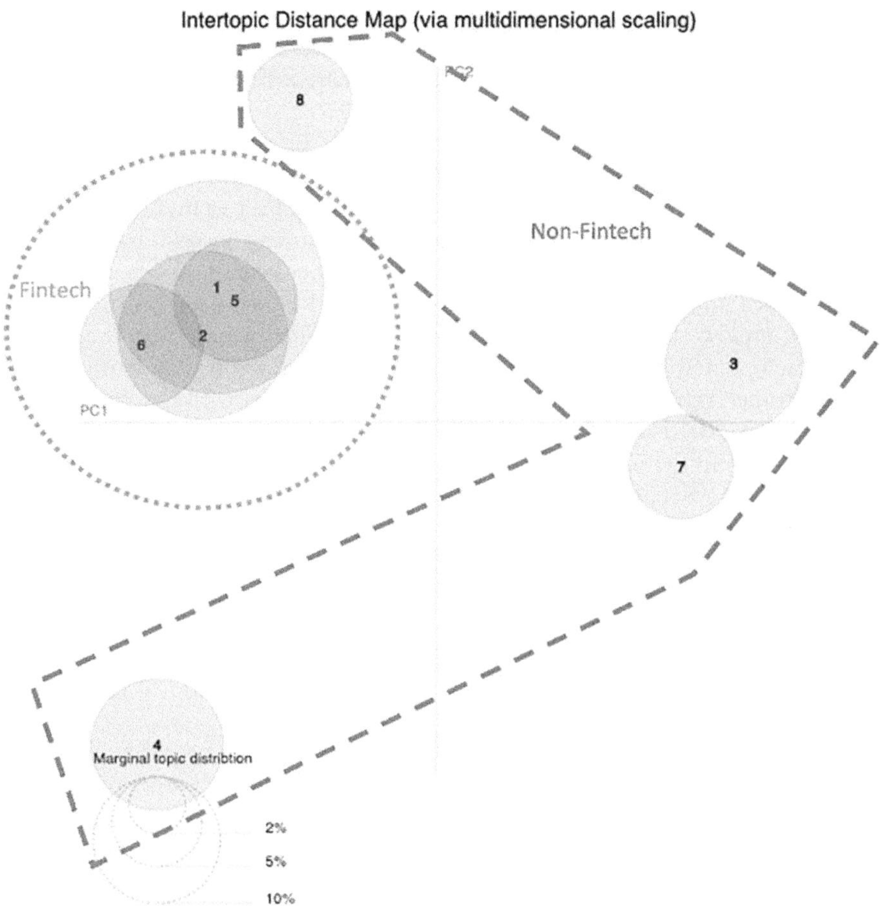

[46] Debortoli et al (n 29); DM Blei, 'Probabilistic Topic Models' (2012) 55 *Communications of the ACM* 77; and DM Blei et al 'Latent Dirichlet Allocation' (2003) 3 *Journal of Machine Learning Research* 993.

[47] Blei (n 46); Blei et al (n 46).

The LDA model revealed clusters of topics with some overlap. Semantically, topic clusters indicated whether a topic was related to either finance or technology. Figure 2 illustrates in a two-dimensional principal component analysis how topics relating to fintech firms are semantically distinguishable as a distinct cluster that separates them from non-fintech topics.

Using this method, we identified two distinct syntactic vocabularies that consistently related to either Technology or Finance. The stemmed terms included in each vocabulary are presented in Appendix A. To ensure the validity of our vocabularies, we manually inspected specific descriptions for prevalence of the selected terms and made minor adjustments.

Having done this, we ran a search algorithm to filter all firms using both Finance and Technology terminology in their free text description. We limited this search to those firms which had registered as being in SIC industries of Finance, Technology, Professional Services, and Other, which included Administrative Services.

We ensured validation of the results in terms of model specification and vocabulary relevance through three steps. First, we fitted the LDA model to the entire dataset and validated the results against the test set to make sure we did not miss any companies (ie, validated for false negatives). Second, based on the initial results, we updated both the vocabularies (ie, lists of words associated with finance and technology) and the LDA model parameters and re-ran the analysis until we had eliminated false negatives. Finally, based on the results from our updated model, we ensured face validity of the results by manually going through the descriptions of identified fintech firms with low frequencies of terms associated with finance and technology to ensure validity in terms of false positives in the included companies (ie, to ensure that we did not include companies that were not fintech). These steps were then also repeated for each category to ensure the validity of fintech firm identification.

In this way, we identified a total of 509 fintech firms through their own descriptions of their operations from the relevant SIC industry codes within the entire Swedish company registry.

ii. Categorising Fintech Firms

The second step involved reapplying LDA to the population of identified firms to discern if there were distinct categories within fintech, both in order to support nuanced policymaking and to relate these categories back to SIC codes. The initial results were manually validated to ensure a meaningful number of categories (represented by LDA parameter k), that each category was distinct and meaningful (LDA parameter λ), and to align the top-level label for each category (but not the content or delineation) with industry nomenclature.[48]

[48] Using Deloitte, 'Fintech: On the Brink of Further Disruption' (n 3) as a baseline.

Thereafter a new LDA analysis was repeated with updated parameter settings. From the resulting topic clusters, we derived distinct vocabularies for each category using a similar method as in step one. By using the topic distribution for each description (θn) resulting from the LDA model, we assigned each firm a score of how strongly it related to each of the categories based on the frequency of word usage associated with each vocabulary divided by the length of each specific vocabulary.

Based on this score, we then assigned each firm a category based on the highest relevance score. To ensure face validity, we again manually inspected the categorisation of specific firms (a) to confirm category fit, especially when there was an identical or similar score in two categories; and (b) to filter out false positives within each category. The result was then validated against the list of fintech firms identified in step 1. To ensure external validity, we asked an external panel of fintech experts to scrutinise our identification and categorisation of the fintech firms. The panel consisted of regulators and industry experts selected by the Swedish Agency for Growth Policy Analysis for their considerable experience in the fintech industry. Each expert was shown the results of the initial LDA topic model and asked to scrutinise the results of the algorithmic categorisation.[49] The panellists' feedback was used to refine and delineate the resulting categories. Following this methodology, we identified 10 categories of fintech firms within the identified 509 fintech firms.

Based on this identification, we also unpacked the firms' year of first registration to see if young (and thus entrepreneurial) firms were overrepresented. We then compared our classification system to the classification system currently in use in Sweden, which corresponds to international standards, to examine how useful existing classification systems are in identifying fintech firms. We then further compared the identified fintech firms and their domains of activity against existing industrial classification codes (SICs) to see the usefulness of these codes in identifying fintech firms. In what follows, we discuss these results.

IV. RESULTS: FINTECH AND ASSOCIATED DOMAINS

In order to derive a definition of fintech based on how fintech firms identified themselves, rather than definitions from academics or policymakers, we relied on the methods and data described above. As fintech represents a new class of industrial activities that are rapidly evolving, transforming, and merging with other classes of industrial activity, general classifications like the one outlined in Figure 1 are never fully up to date nor do they account for the idiosyncrasies of specific jurisdictions at specific points in time. Therefore, more accurate classifications of the fintech must be derived from activities as undertaken by the specific population of fintech firms through self-characterisation or records of

[49] This correspondence is on record with the authors.

business transactions. The task of producing a useful classification of fintech firms therefore involves identification of the population of fintech firms, classification of different sub-categories within the population, and quantitative analysis to identify patterns between sub-categories over time.

Using machine learning techniques, we first identified keywords that characterised how fintech firms described themselves in their registered free-text descriptions. The dictionary of descriptors is contained in Appendix A. For readers who do not speak Swedish we point out that the descriptions of finance included words like 'invest', 'credit', 'market', 'pension', 'transaction', 'advice' and 'pay'. Where they occurred together with IT descriptors like 'application', 'data', 'digital', 'internet', 'software', 'solution' and 'online', we considered those to be good candidates for fintech firms.

We then searched for the firms that contained combinations of both vocabularies and identified 509 firms (including the 356 we used to derive the dictionary). Based on this, we then derived the 10 domains of fintech contained in Table 2 and based on the dictionary of words contained in Appendix B.

Interestingly, the definitions of the 10 categories are very inclusive: they include obvious financial services like credit, payment services and financial management, but also adjacent finance-like services like data and analytics, RegTech (regulation technology), InsurTech (insurance technology) and even digital infrastructures.

There was little or no mention of specific technologies, with the exception of blockchain technologies. These firms were spread across several domains, but were most prominent in the infrastructure domain. This may be a practical choice from blockchain firms, in that they feel that blockchain does not adequately describe their operations. However, it might equally be a strategic decision – to avoid the scrutiny of regulators and similar, given the scepticism with which blockchain has historically been regarded.

Table 2 Descriptions of identified categories, stemmed vocabularies in Appendix B

Category	Count	% cent of total	Category description
Credit	78	15.4	Credit, loans and savings products, including crowdfunding and sales of invoices
Financial management	46	9.0	Financial management services directed towards individuals
Data	23	4.5	Data and analytics
Infrastructure	78	15.2	Technical services sold as products to other firms (typically B2B) to enable financial and fintech activities. Includes security, ERP and some blockchain firms

(continued)

Table 2 *(Continued)*

Category	Count	% cent of total	Category description
Insurance	21	4.1	Applications of fintech specifically within Insurance, includes both insurance firms and firms supporting insurance
Consulting	48	9.4	Consultant firms providing bespoke services (eg, to-order development) within fintech
Payments	77	15.2	Firms offering payments, transactions and remittance services
RegTech	10	1.9	Firms offering compliance and legal (tech) services
Wealth management	62	12.1	Firms offering investment and other wealth management services
Other	67	13.3	Firms that are fintech but not clearly in one of the above categories

A. Grey Areas

Overall, there were considerable grey areas in this analysis. In addition to the 509 fintech firms, we identified a list of 2,247 firms which did not use technology in finance, but rather engaged in both technology *and* finance activities, for instance, by doing both software development and investing in listed and unlisted firms. This suggests that there is considerable untapped potential in the Swedish fintech market given the high number of firms with a good understanding of both finance and technology.

B. Firm Ages

We used the year of first SIC registration as a proxy for year of first registration (as firms register their SIC codes on registration). We can see that 132 firms were registered in 2008 or earlier, and that firm registrations have increased consistently year on year, reaching a peak of about 68 in 2014 (Figure 3). With around 25 per cent of the firms more than 14 years old at the time of writing, this suggests that fintech is by no means a phenomenon that is only being pioneered by entrepreneurs, or new firms.

Figure 3 Number of fintech firms by year and domain

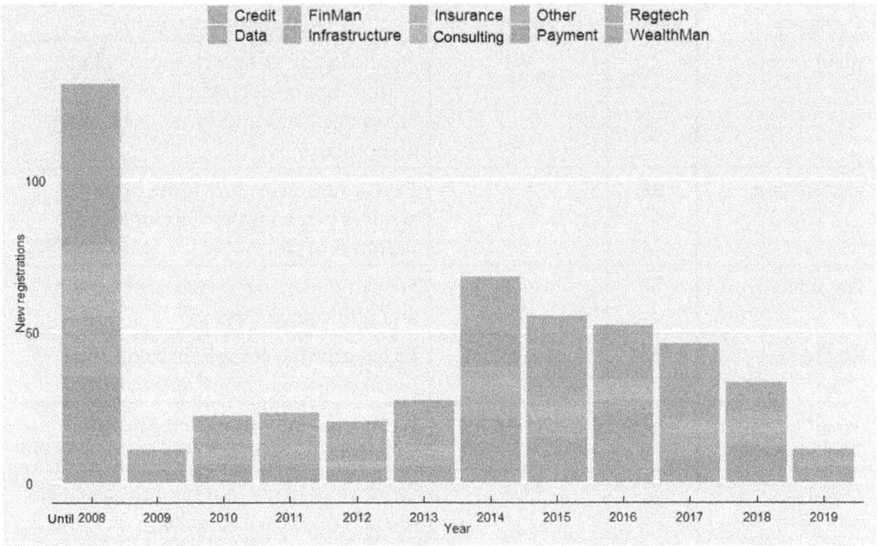

C. Fintech Domains and Industry Classification (SIC) Codes

Based on the identified fintech firms and the resulting fintech domain categories, we now turn to discussing the usefulness of SIC codes in identifying fintech firms. Our hope was that the SIC codes would have some predictive value, given their importance for policymakers and researchers to track industries, draft supportive policies[50] and broadly encourage entrepreneurship.[51]

In particular, our hope was that there would be a relationship between the SIC codes, firm registered descriptions and categorisation. In such a case, a machine learning method like this could then be used to identify other kinds of cross-classification firms, for instance those in AgTech (agriculture), PropTech (property) or similar. Moreover, automated identification and classification of firms could considerably streamline a larger automated process in which analyses of industries and/or industrial sectors could be made. Moreover, such classifications could be used as part of a larger toolbox in ensuring that firms have the correct licences to, for instance, offer credit or financial advice.

Using the most recent SIC codes of the 509 firms, we explored which SIC codes they used to classify themselves. Interestingly, 239 of these (47 per cent)

[50] Audretsch et al (n 2).

[51] Z Acs et al, 'Public Policy to Promote Entrepreneurship: A Call to Arms' (2016) 47 *Small Business Economics* 35; Z Acs et al, 'National Systems of Entrepreneurship: Measurement Issues and Policy Implications' (2014) 43 *Research Policy* 476.

defined themselves as being Tech (IT) companies (SIC group J, 58–63), and only 162 of them (31.8 per cent) described themselves as being primarily finance (SIC group K, 64–68). Almost 15 per cent (14.7 per cent) classified themselves as doing professional work (75 firms, SIC group M, 69–75), while just 33 (6.5 per cent) defined themselves as doing something else (all other SIC codes, including administration and other). A heat map of the number of firms in each fintech category across SIC codes is contained in Figure 4.

Figure 4 Heat map of SIC codes by fintech domain

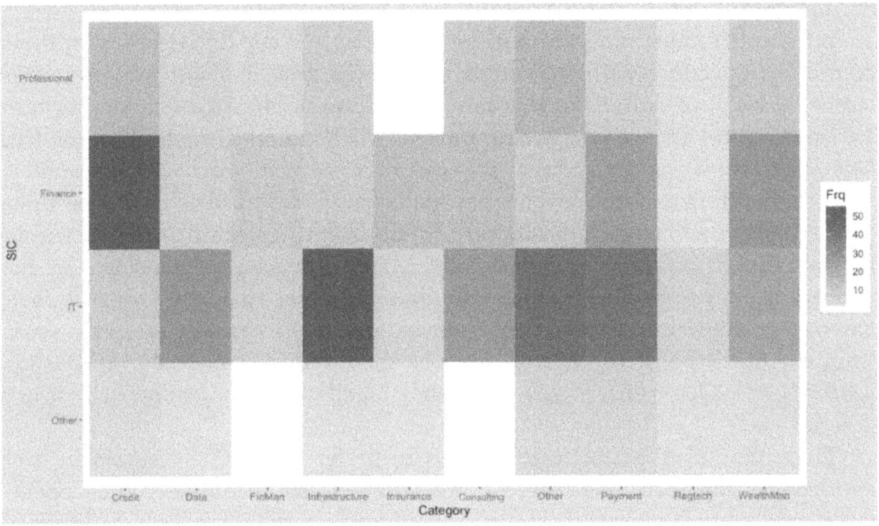

V. ANALYSIS OF RESULTS

In what follows, we discuss some of the key take-aways of this data-first approach to understanding fintech. In particular, we point to how some areas of fintech are more finance oriented (eg, credit), and others more technology oriented (eg, infrastructure), but that broadly fintech is larger than even just finance and technology.

A. Fintech is Broader than Just Finance and Technology

While SIC codes are somewhat limited when it comes to identifying fintech firms in general, they are a better predictor for categories within fintech. Fintech firms that operate in heavily regulated areas of finance, like credit, classify themselves as being financial actors. However, those that operate in tech-heavy areas or which choose to signal that they are technology firms, rather than financial ones, instead choose technology classifications.

Only 73.4 per cent of the firms had a finance or technology SIC code as their primary classification; the rest classified themselves as something different. There are several possible explanations for this.

One possible explanation is that the phenomenon itself is broader than just finance and technology. This idea is supported by the emergence of categories like 'RegTech' and 'consulting' in the analysis. These are not a priori obvious categories in Financial Technology. However, the inclusion of finance-adjacent activities in the definition of fintech is not without precedent: RegTech itself is explicitly included in the definition of fintech by at least one producer of industry reports.[52]

Yet another explanation is that the SIC codes and the free text descriptions do not line up, either with each other, or with the firm's current activities. This might be because either the registered SIC code or the free text description are out of date, or just very broad. Indeed, when manually inspecting the free text descriptions, we noticed that many of them were very broad. For instance, one firm building an international payments network described their firm thus: 'The company will engage in software development, consulting services within IT, own shares in other companies, and related activities'[53] (translated by the authors from Swedish). This is clearly much broader than the scope of their day-to-day activities, although not inaccurate. It also makes strategic sense from the firm's point of view to describe their activities broadly rather than narrowly in order to limit how often they legally have to change their firm's description.

There may also be strategic reasons to prefer one SIC classification over another. For instance, firms may opt for an IT classification when their operations span two classifications, for the simple reason that they are less likely to attract the attention of regulators than in the more heavily regulated realm of finance.

B. Ambiguity and Boundaries in Classifications

Although data like company registry data are thought to present objective and consistent classification and quantification over time, the fact that both free text descriptions and SIC code registrations are self-selections on the part of the firms involved introduces ambiguity, both in the production of unstructured data points such as firm descriptions and in its analysis and interpretation.

[52] eg, Deloitte, 'Fintech: On the Brink of Further Disruption' (n 3); and Deloitte, 'Closing the Gap in Fintech Collaboration' (n 18).

[53] These free text descriptions are publicly available data; also available on request from the authors.

When it comes to the boundaries between finance and tech, it makes sense that as finance becomes more and more technical, it becomes a de facto area of applied IT, in which an IT classification makes the most sense for the firms involved. This is supported by recruitment data that shows that banks are increasingly developing new capabilities and expanding their software portfolios.[54]

When it comes to the boundaries of sub-categories within fintech, our machine learning-generated 'score' which allowed us to place boundaries between different types of fintech also highlighted that the boundaries between the different categories are not sharp. Instead, the vast majority of the firms identified had a dominant or top score, and scores in multiple other areas. However, only eight of the 509 firms had the same score in multiple categories[55] – suggesting that at least a firm's primary area of business is relatively distinct.

One further area of ambiguity lies in the distinction between tech *in* finance (or finance in tech) and finance *and* tech: as mentioned above, in addition to the 509 fintech firms, we identified a list of 2,247 firms which did not use technology in finance, but rather engaged in both technology *and* finance activities. For instance, by doing both software development and investing in listed and unlisted firms. Although registry data are said to track formal developments in economic and industrial activity,[56] it is problematic that this ambiguity exists when it comes to classifications, not least when a classification should be binary.

C. Policy Initiatives to Improve Data

If policymakers at national as well as EU levels want to launch policies that foster and regulate emerging digital entrepreneurship in classification spanning industries, such as fintech, they must first be able to identify and classify firms that participate in these classifications. While it is often the case that legislation itself specifies the kinds of firms to which it applies qualitatively, ex ante analyses of certain industries and industrial sectors are done on the basis of registry data. Registry data are thus used, among others, to conduct ex ante risk and impact assessments.

The data we relied upon in this case were publicly available. This means that an analysis such as this one might not only be used by state agencies interested in understanding new and existing industries, but also by private actors – for

[54] eg R Hendrikse et al, 'The Appleization of Finance: Charting Incumbent Finance's Embrace of Fintech' (2018) 4 *Finance and Society* 159.

[55] Their category was then confirmed by manual inspection.

[56] Acs et al, 'National Systems of Entrepreneurship' (n 51).

instance, companies may use such data to identify competitors. Initiatives by individuals can also benefit, for instance, for a jobseeker identifying potential employers. However, Sweden has a long history of public access to data, and has invested significant resources into collecting and verifying such data. These risks are therefore not new risks, but rather allow for the identification of firms and their classification in new, and perhaps less laborious, ways.

Our large-scale analysis combining supervised natural language processing analysis of known fintech firms and a similar analysis of the company registration database of firms in Sweden confirms that existing industry categories as represented by SIC codes are insufficient to identify fintech firms, and it provides a detailed sub-categorisation of fintech in Sweden as well as details of its economic development in several key dimensions. We believe this method has the potential to serve as a reliable tool for identifying and categorising classification spanning entrepreneurship and their economic impact for both technology and non-technology entrepreneurial activities. As the method is not conditional on the type of entrepreneurial activity, we are confident that it can be applied to a variety of emergent entrepreneurial phenomena including digital and social entrepreneurship as well as emerging ecosystems within, for instance, 'GreenTech' (Green Technology), 'AgTech' (Agricultural Technology), 'SpaceTech' (Space Technology) and others.

VI. CONCLUSIONS

This chapter describes how such classification spanning entrepreneurial firms can be identified and categorised by leveraging existing company registry data. This also provides insights into the structure of the classification-spanning entrepreneurship and its relation to existing industries that is useful for strategically nurturing and regulating these forms of entrepreneurship.

As digital technologies permeate existing industry categories, fintech firms are just one of many classes of new firms that span existing industry classifications. The rise in these kinds of entrepreneurship come against a backdrop of advances in understanding digital entrepreneurship, which has been described as blurring organisational and field boundaries,[57] but which is still emergent. Blurred boundaries are at the core of entrepreneurship, and classification-defying forms of entrepreneurship are a consequence, with associated challenges. Fintech is one kind of new classification-spanning portmanteau.

We hope the method presented in this research note will inspire researchers to apply and validate the method in classification-spanning entrepreneurship beyond fintech and that government agencies and regulators can implement it as a means of identifying, nourishing and regulating emerging entrepreneurial

[57] Nambisan (n 11).

categories. Such implementations may either apply the method in its current form, or with slight adaptations by adding additional textual data sources from a firm's public websites or social media profiles to provide more current and fine-grained classifications. This will not only enhance insights into entrepreneurial activities, but also provide a crucial point of reference for nourishing and integrating firms better with the surrounding economy, thus enhancing the impact and value of emergent entrepreneurship for industry and society at large.

APPENDICES

Appendix A: Stemmed Vocabularies Used to Classify Firms as Fintech/ Not Fintech

Finance	Tech
bank	analys
betal	applikation
bokför	data
crowdfunding	digital
försäkring	finansindustri
invest	hård
kredit	information
lån	internet
marknad	lösning
pension	mjuk
råd	online
räkning	produkt
transaktion	programmering
värdepapper	social
	system
	teknisk
	teknologi
	utveckla
	webb

Appendix B: Stemmed Vocabularies (in Swedish) of Fintech Domains

Insurance	Consulting	Investment	Credit	Payments	Data	Regtech	Infrastructure	Financial management	Other
försäkring	konsult	investera	instrument	betal	data	compliance	identi	privat	inspektion
ansvar	ledning	onoterade	kredit	mobil	analys	juridiska råd	system	översikt	
lösning	planering	rådgivning	lån	program	information	efterlevnad	licens	portfölj	
2004	coaching	försäkring	faktur	betaltjänst	visualis	avtal	säker	jämför	
	strategisk	värdepapper	spar		underlätta	kontrakt	stöd	folkbildning	
	utveckling	valuta			beslut	regel	block	rådgivning	
						signering	valuta	växling	
							växling		

2

Entry Barriers in Fintech

RYAN CLEMENTS

I. INTRODUCTION

THE FINANCIAL TECHNOLOGY (fintech) revolution has created many new possibilities, potential efficiencies and opportunities for enhanced financial consumer welfare.[1] Inherent in fintech's value proposition is the possibility that new firms will use technology to facilitate consumer financial services and transactions, while managing inherent risks and uncertainties in a faster, more cost-effective way than regulated incumbents.[2] Yet breaking into the financial services market as a new fintech firm can be difficult. This chapter identifies core market entry barriers that new fintech firms face when they attempt to provide new technology-mediated financial products and services.

Policymakers have begun studying the forces that affect barriers to entry for new fintech firms and how market dynamics in financial services can generate anticompetitive outcomes.[3] Competition problems in finance are long-standing, as there are relatively 'few incentives for traditional actors to innovate' given high levels of industry concentration, the ability of incumbent firms to extract economic 'rents' and preserve informational advantages while ensuring high consumer 'switching costs'.[4] Fintech-mediated financial services offer the potential for increased efficiency, cost-savings, heightened transparency and financial inclusion, and as a result, policymakers have strong incentives to design regulatory frameworks that maximise consumer benefits, minimise anticompetitive outcomes and ensure appropriate consumer protections and systemic

[1] See generally, HE Jackson, 'The Nature of the Fintech Firm' (2020) 61 *Washington University Journal of Law & Policy* 9, 11–12.

[2] ibid.

[3] A Fraile Carmona et al, 'Competition Issues in the Area of Financial Technology (FinTech)' Policy Department for Economic, Scientific and Quality of Life Policies, European Parliament (July 2018) (EP Study).

[4] C Fracassi and W Magnuson, 'Data Autonomy' (2021) 74 *Vanderbilt Law Review* 327, 331, 335–37; see also O-B Gill and K Davis, 'Empty Promises' (2019) 84 *Southern California Law Review* 1, 10–11 (discussing how incumbent financial institutions can ensure high 'switching costs' on consumers).

risk safeguards.[5] Further, new fintech firms may provide an 'antidote' to the rent-seeking behaviours of incumbent financial institutions and banks.[6]

In July 2018, the European Parliament Policy Department for Economic, Scientific and Quality of Life Policies published a comprehensive report on competition concerns in the fintech sector (the EP Study).[7] The EP Study identified numerous factors in the market for technology-mediated financial services that could create 'anticompetitive behaviours' and barriers to entry for new fintech firms, including network effects originating from platform enterprises, consumer data access silos, and certain anticompetitive practices associated with technology, interoperability and standardisation.[8] These 'competition challenges' emanate from both 'supply-side' perspectives (eg, how certain fintech platforms silo consumer data to ensure competitive advantages) and 'demand-side' variables (eg, how consumers access fintech services, and the use of bundling to ensure high switching costs).[9] Further, the study noted that fintech market evolution has given rise to 'multi-sided online platforms' that service both financial providers and consumers, which in turn create unique barriers to entry and competition challenges.[10]

This chapter complements that study, detailing numerous market and regulatory developments since its publication, including economic factors and barriers to entry originating from decentralised finance (DeFi) applications and protocols, consumer data sharing through 'open banking' regimes, and global trends in entry barrier formation with a focus on anticompetitive forces in the United States (US), the United Kingdom (UK) and the European Union (EU). Despite the potential for diverse consumer welfare-generating outcomes and the establishment of 'new kinds of market transactions' and 'new networks' that may improve traditional payment processes, as well as value transfer and clearing systems, many fintech firms continue to face barriers to entry.[11] The core fintech entry barriers discussed in this chapter are financial and human capital acquisition challenges, market concentration forces, economies of scale and scope, service-bundling, market integration and infrastructure access concerns, network effects from multilayered platform businesses, restrictions in consumer financial data access, portability and control, entry barriers originating from technology infrastructure, standardisation, and interoperability trends, regulatory imposed competition barriers and uncertainties, and consumer perceptions of stability and trust. The chapter concludes by providing recommendations to help global policymakers alleviate fintech market entry barriers while ensuring appropriate consumer and financial system safeguards.

[5] EP Study (n 3) 11.
[6] J Kidd, 'Fintech: Antidote to Rent-Seeking' (2018) 93 *Chicago-Kent Law Review* 165.
[7] EP Study (n 3) 11.
[8] ibid, 11–13.
[9] ibid, 49–51.
[10] ibid, 13.
[11] ibid, 12.

II. DEFINING FINTECH AND TECHNOLOGY-MEDIATED FINANCIAL SERVICES

The term 'fintech' (a popularised phrase for financial technology) has diverse meanings[12] and is the subject of constant evolution.[13] It has emerged as a 'multi-dimensional ecosystem' with a range of participants including large financial market and technology incumbents and new innovations such as decentralised protocols operating on open-source public blockchains with 'no central counterpart'.[14] Widely used, the term fintech generally refers to innovations in financial services that 'could result in new business models, applications, processes, or products with an associated material effect on financial markets and institutions and the provision of financial services'.[15]

Improved efficiency is at the heart of fintech as a value proposition.[16] The EP Study suggested that a 'fintech service' has three primary characteristics: first, it is a 'technology-driven' financial service; second, it results in the provision of a new 'solution', 'business model' or 'alternative' to what currently exists in the incumbent financial system; and third, it creates a 'significant added value' to stakeholders, particularly consumers.[17] Thus, a broad definition of fintech for the purpose of identifying entry barriers encapsulates technology-mediated financial services across a diverse range of product and service offerings, which are either mediated by, or supplemented with, new technological products, processes and infrastructure.[18] These offerings attempt to generate better consumer or firm-level outcomes, including improved incumbent services and products provided by new market entrants.[19] New digital product offerings continue to emerge and evolve in response to consumer demand, the integration of new innovations, and the strategic priorities of new firms.[20] This observation can be seen in the

[12] cp Jackson (n 1) 11; DW Arner, J Barberis and RP Buckley, 'The Evolution of FinTech: A New Post-Crisis Paradigm' (2015) 47 *Georgetown Journal of International Law* 1271, 1272; R Van Loo, 'Making Innovation More Competitive: The Case of Fintech' (2018) 65 *UCLA Law Review* 232, 239; and C Brummer and Y Yadav, 'Fintech and the Innovation Trilemma' (2019) 108 *Georgetown Law Journal* 235, 241; W Magnuson, 'Regulating Fintech' (2018) 71 *Vanderbilt Law Review* 1167, 1174.

[13] WA Kaal, 'Digital Asset Market Evolution' (2020) 46 *Journal of Corporation Law* 909.

[14] J Westmorel, K Andrews Rose and K Kenny, 'Introduction to the Fintech Ecosystem' (2021) 69 *Department of Justice Journal of Federal Law and Practice* 23, 23.

[15] Basel Committee on Banking Supervision, 'Sound Practices, Implications of Fintech Developments for Banks and Bank Supervisors' (February 2018) 8.

[16] C Ancri, 'Fintech Innovation: An Overview, Presentation of Board of Governors of the Federal Reserve System to the World Bank', paper presented to the World Bank by the Federal Reserve Board of Governors (19 October 2016).

[17] EP Study (n 3) 47 (this study also notes seven applicable financial service industries that are impacted by fintech, namely: banking (deposits and lending); payments and foreign exchange; digital currencies; wealth and asset management; personal finance; insurance; and infrastructure related 'enabling' technologies).

[18] R Clements, 'Regulating Fintech in Canada and the United States: Comparison, Challenges and Opportunities' in KT Liaw (ed), *The Routledge Handbook of Fintech* (Routledge, 2021) 418.

[19] ibid.

[20] E Feyen et al, 'World Bank Group Global Market Survey: Digital Technology and the Future of Finance' *World Bank Group Fintech and the Future of Finance Report* (2021).

nascent rise of DeFi applications and protocols and their disruptive impact on securities and derivatives trading, lending, savings, asset-management, insurance and payments.[21] Banks and financial market incumbents also continue to adapt their existing product and service offerings in the digitised space in response to new fintech market entrants.[22] Evidence suggests that underdeveloped markets have experienced particular fintech growth and new firm entry.[23] These markets benefit from greater fintech-driven financial inclusionary forces and increased credit origination for small and medium-sized enterprises.[24] New fintech market entrants can also be found in mature economies like the United States, which is a global leader in fintech venture investing.[25] Consumers in mature markets often report an improved user experience through fintech-originated products and services.[26] Further, mature markets have generated 'strong geographical endogamy' resulting in fintech companies in the United States and Europe often being acquired by larger entities in the same geographic location.[27]

III. IDENTIFYING THE BARRIERS TO NEW FINTECH MARKET ENTRY

A. Financial and Human Capital Acquisition

New fintech firms face steep capital demands (financial, human and 'reputational') to adequately compete in global financial markets that are historically characterised by thin margins, narrow product and service variability, and high consumer switching costs.[28] As a result, access to initial and ongoing capital, and 'strategic capital' from industry-connected venture investors for product development, marketing, operations and scaling is a paramount concern for new fintech firms.[29] A fintech firm that cannot raise sufficient capital to scale will have difficulty competing against well-funded competitors or well-capitalised incumbents.[30] Also, the life cycle of a fintech company, from idea inception and

[21] See generally, D Gogel et al, 'DeFi Beyond the Hype: The Emerging World of Decentralized Finance' Wharton Blockchain & Digital Asset Project, Wharton School, University of Pennsylvania (2021) 9–10, available at: wifpr.wharton.upenn.edu/wp-content/uploads/2021/05/DeFi-Beyond-the-Hype.pdf.

[22] See generally, J Frost et al, 'BigTech and the changing structure of financial intermediation' (2019) 34 *Economic Policy* 761; Bank for International Settlements, 'Big Tech in Finance: Opportunities and Risks' *BIS Annual Economic Report* (2019).

[23] T Didier et al, 'Global Patterns of Fintech Activity and Enabling Factors' *World Bank Group Fintech and the Future of Finance Report* (2021).

[24] ibid.

[25] EP Study (n 3) 11.

[26] ibid, 12.

[27] ibid.

[28] See generally, A Azzuttia, W-G Ringe and HS Stiehl, 'Machine Learning, Market Manipulation, and Collusion on Capital Markets: Why the "Black Box" Matters' (2021) 43 *University of Pennsylvania Journal of International Law* 79, 107.

[29] Richard Harroch, '10 Key Issues For Fintech Startup Companies' *Forbes* (12 October 2019).

[30] EP Study (n 3) 33–40.

proof of concept through to scaled enterprise and mature market penetration will almost invariably involve multiple funding rounds from seed and pre-seed to late-stage venture or initial public offering.[31] For the most part, global fintech venture investing has seen a surge over the last five years,[32] even in crypto-asset and DeFi industry segments that historically have been the source of sustained volatility.[33] Global fintech venture funding has also remained strong despite the Covid-19 pandemic.[34] Fintech worldwide funding trends, as recently documented by researchers at the Bank for International Settlements (BIS), suggest that funding sources for fintech firms are diverse, yet those firms operating in countries with 'more innovation capacity and better regulatory quality' receive higher levels of equity funding.[35] The BIS report also noted that equity funding increased after the introduction of a regulatory sandbox to a geographic location.[36] Research into fintech venture funding also suggests that unregulated fintech start-ups may be more likely to capitalise with debt, rather than equity.[37] Nevertheless, fintech valuations can be difficult to determine, which creates a friction to capital formation.[38]

Perhaps even more challenging than financial capital formation and venture funding for a fintech firm is human capital acquisition and retention, which is also a critical factor when a fintech enterprise is attempting to scale.[39] Talent acquisition shortages and retention challenges are persistent concerns for fintech firms and represent a functional barrier to growth.[40] Fintech founders report

[31] ibid, 41.

[32] Alex Wilhelm and Mary Ann Azevedo, 'The Berserk Pace of Fintech Investing Outshines the Global VC Boom' (*TechCrunch*, 19 January 2022, available at: techcrunch.com/2022/01/19/the-berserk-pace-of-fintech-investing-outshines-the-global-vc-boom/?guccounter=1&guce_referrer=aHR0cH; 'Fintech Investment Smashed All Records in 2021' (*Dealroom.co*, 13 January 2022), available at: dealroom.co/blog/fintech-investment-2021-report; EY, 'Australian Fintech Sector Creating Jobs and Raising Capital, with Sights Set on Overseas Markets' (20 October 2021), available at: www.ey.com/en_au/news/2021/10/australian-fintech-sector-creating-jobs-and-raising-capital; Accenture, '2021 Canadian Fintech Report', available at: www.accenture.com/_acnmedia/PDF-149/Accenture-Fintech-report-2020.pdf.

[33] See generally, Paul Vigna, 'Binance Raises $500 Million Fund for Crypto Investments' *Wall Street Journal* (1 June 2022), available at: www.wsj.com/articles/binance-raises-500-million-fund-for-crypto-investments-11654107370.

[34] Financial Stability Board, 'FinTech and Market Structure in the COVID-19 Pandemic' (21 March 2022) 3, available at: www.fsb.org/wp-content/uploads/P210322.pdf.

[35] Giulio Cornelli, Sebastian Doerr, Lavinia Franco and Jon Frost, 'Funding for Fintechs: Patterns and Drivers' *BIS Quarterly Review* (September 2021), available at: www.bis.org/publ/qtrpdf/r_qt2109c.htm.

[36] ibid.

[37] E Giaretta and G Chesini, 'The Determinants of Debt Financing: The Case of Fintech Start-ups' (2021) 6 *Journal of Innovation & Knowledge* 268.

[38] Jon A Hlafter, Sven G Mickisch and Timothy J Gaffney, 'Valuation Challenges for Fintechs Highlight Legal Considerations in "Down Rounds"' (*Skadden 2020 Insights*, 21 January 2020), available at: www.skadden.com/insights/publications/2020/01/2020-insights/valuation-challenges-for-fintechs.

[39] Deloitte, 'Human Capital Challenges of a Fast-growing Sector: Fintech' (September 2020), available at: www2.deloitte.com/content/dam/Deloitte/uk/Documents/blogs/deloitte-uk-human-capital-challenges-of-a-fastgrowing-sector-FinTech.pdf.

[40] Gazala Anver, 'Talent Shortage Remains Top Concern for Tech and Start-up Communities Amid Change of Government' (*Smart Company*, 2 June 2022), available at: www.smartcompany.com.au/startupsmart/news/talent-shortage-tech-startup-government/.

that salaries alone are not sufficient to retain optimal talent, rather, firm culture, incentives for equity and growth participation, and long-term alignment are also critical factors that a fintech firm must execute correctly in order to compete long term.[41]

B. Market Concentration and Economies of Scale and Scope

Fintech offerings can increase market competition and efficiency in financial services.[42] They also help to reduce costs through the deployment of technology such as streamlined app development, cloud computing, data access through open-banking regimes and application programming interfaces (APIs) for safe consumer financial data sharing, reduced physical branching needs, heightened connectivity infrastructure, and for avoiding regulatory compliance costs by integrating software processes into regulated banking and payments infrastructure (through 'banking-as-a-service').[43] Yet using new digital processes, technological innovations and infrastructure to provide financial products and services can also catalyse market concentration forces and generate 'network effects' for early entry firms, and these forces may serve as 'economic frictions' when subsequent firms attempt to enter the market.[44]

Some fintech firms are able to acquire asymmetrical informational advantages, experience network effects,[45] and economies of scale[46] and scope.[47] Although these are common in the provision of financial services, together they present entry barriers for smaller fintech firms once established.[48] These factors allow incumbent firms and those otherwise possessing significant market share in 'adjacent' technology markets to exact competitive advantages by 're-bundling' product and service offerings given the significant consumer acquisition and search expenses (including marketing, know-your-client compliance,

[41] Deloitte, 'Human Capital Challenges' (n 39).

[42] See generally, J Frost, 'The Economic Forces Driving Fintech Adoption Across Countries' in M King and R Nesbitt (eds), *The Technological Revolution in Financial Services* (University of Toronto Press, 2020).

[43] E Feyen et al, 'Fintech and the Digital Transformation of Financial Services: Implications for Market Structure and Public Policy' (July 2021) BIS Papers No 117, Bank for International Settlements Monetary and Economic Department, 17.

[44] ibid, 8–12.

[45] ibid, 4 ('network effects (or "externalities") are significant in financial services such as payments, where the value of the network to all users (both payers and payees) increases when the number of connected users increases').

[46] ibid, 3 (noting the large fixed costs of traditional financial firms, including back-office systems, physical distribution networks, minimum capital requirements and regulatory compliance programmes that can be amortised over a larger customer base).

[47] ibid.

[48] ibid, i ('[c]lassic economic forces remain relevant even in an age of digital production. Economies of scale and scope and network effects are present in many aspects of financial services production, including customer acquisition, funding, compliance activities, data and capital (including trust capital)').

onboarding, and credit assessment), and product assembly and funding costs faced by new market entrants.[49] Customer acquisition costs are exacerbated by 'user inertia' and high 'switching costs', which are common phenomena in banking and investment management, and yield advantages to the largest firms or those first to market.[50] Switching is also problematic for customers since they must incur time and expense to 'unbundle' their financial product suite and utilise numerous intermediaries, as opposed to a single provider.[51]

Financial firms that build a dominant market position on the basis of data-driven economies of scale, scope and network effects may also be able to use this position to extract economic rents.[52] Dominant firms can leverage 'cross-subsidies' through integrated offerings to deter consumer unbundling and switching, although 'product tying' is an anticompetitive banking practice in many jurisdictions.[53] Large firms can also leverage their market position to enhance their own technology, or proprietary and tailored offerings,[54] or allow new fintech firms to offer products directly to their customers thus becoming 'platform' firms, thereby benefiting from network effects and enhanced data access.[55] The BIS has recently suggested that resulting outcomes in market composition and concentration can yield a 'barbell' comprised of large dominant players, including both financial and tech incumbents, and otherwise 'niche', speciality and 'hyper-focused' firms.[56] The latter are firms obtaining advantages, not due to their market dominance, but rather by becoming 'first movers' in a product or service segment.[57]

Due to operational (and profitability) advantages of legacy financial firms who benefit from economies of scale and scope, 'network externalities', and a relative advantage in greater data resources, incumbent firms have incentives to construct barriers to entry and 'fossilize legacy oligopolistic market structures'.[58] However, competitive pressures are commonly felt by incumbents, since fintech firms can more easily and quickly leverage and integrate with social media platforms and increase market share by providing comparative products and services, without the associated regulatory compliance costs and challenges of being a bank or a large financial institution.[59] Given competitive pressures,

[49] ibid, 1–3, 18.

[50] ibid, 18–20.

[51] ibid, 19–20.

[52] T Rodríguez de las Heras Ballell, 'The Layers of Digital Financial Innovation: Charting a Regulatory Response' (2020) 25 *Fordham Journal of Corporate & Financial Law* 381, 395–96.

[53] Feyen et al, 'Fintech and the Digital Transformation of Financial Services' (n 43) 20.

[54] ibid, 21.

[55] ibid, 1–3, 30–32.

[56] ibid.

[57] ibid, 4.

[58] Rodríguez de las Heras Ballell (n 52) 405.

[59] Shearman & Sterling LLP Perspectives, 'The Changing FinTech Landscape: A Snapshot of M&A Themes and Trends' (July 2021) 3, available at: www.shearman.com/Perspectives/2021/07/Changing-FinTech-Landscape--Snapshot-of-Merger-Themes-and-Trends.

fintech market consolidation opportunities are ripe.[60] The fintech payments and lending space gave rise to consolidation in 2020, including high profile multi-billion dollar deals involving *Ingenico*, *Nets*, *Credit Karma* and *Kabbage*.[61] The Covid-19 pandemic also accelerated the consumer adoption of mobile banking, payments, investing applications and insurance technology ('insurtech'), causing many banks, particularly community and regional US banks, to quickly partner with or acquire fintech infrastructure and solutions providers.[62] Ongoing consolidation, driven by incumbent fears and fintech direct acquisitions to increase market share, could create structural barriers to entry for new fintech firms, changing the composition of the fintech industry away from its historically 'saturated' start-up nature.[63] Rather, it may give rise to firms that are 'undisputed leaders' and, as a result, benefit from scale, cost and perceptional advantages.[64]

Nascent technological innovations, particularly in distributed ledger technology (blockchain) may also give rise to unique concentration factors that impede market entry.[65] For example, 'mining' operations for large proof-of-work blockchain networks (like Bitcoin) are heavily dominated by only a small number of concentrated 'mining pools'.[66] Further, cryptocurrency mining is characterised by high barriers to entry because of economies of scale in computer processing power, energy and electricity access.[67] The market for cryptocurrency exchange platforms is also highly concentrated.[68] The BIS recently noted that DeFi applications, protocols and organisations,[69] create concentration risks – thus exhibiting an 'illusion' of decentralisation – given the nature of governance token distribution and settlement processes on proof-of-stake blockchain consensus mechanisms.[70]

C. Service Bundling, Market Integration and Infrastructure Access Concerns

Financial industry business models and the way that certain products and services are 'bundled' by providers, including integrated fee policies, can also

[60] ibid.
[61] ibid, 4.
[62] ibid, 4–5.
[63] ibid, 5.
[64] ibid, 6.
[65] EP Study (n 3) 67–68.
[66] ibid.
[67] ibid.
[68] ibid.
[69] See generally, R Clements, 'Emerging Canadian Crypto Asset Jurisdictional Uncertainties and Regulatory Gaps' (2021) 37 *Banking and Finance Law Review* 25, 36 ('DeFi generally refers to the use of crypto asset and blockchain open-source technology to provide a financial product or perform a financial transaction or service without a centralized intermediary such as a bank, trust company, investment dealer, stock or derivatives exchange').
[70] S Aramonte, W Huang and A Schrimpf, 'DeFi Risks and the Decentralization Illusion' (December 2020) *BIS Quarterly Review*, available at: www.bis.org/publ/qtrpdf/r_qt2112b.htm.

create entry barriers and anticompetitive pressures in fintech markets.[71] For example, an incumbent wealth or asset manager may engage in a 'blurring of boundaries' and bundle the fees between diverse service offerings like information and research, asset management, and investor advisory, as a means of creating cost barriers to entry for new fintech firms.[72] Another example is when a financial consumer accesses 'bundled' products or services (such as credit cards, savings accounts, investment brokerage, mortgages and bill payment facilitators) at a single institution, enhancing convenience but also presenting 'a large transaction cost for moving to a new bank' that in turn discourages account switching.[73] Industries with high entry barriers can create market conditions for sustainable collusion between incumbent firms, although collusion is less common in 'innovation-driven' markets.[74] High integration can serve as a barrier to new market entry, and this is evident in the US payments space.[75] There have long been concerns over anticompetitive forces in US payments. Over two decades ago, a Southern District of New York court decision concluded that Visa and Mastercard possessed monopolistic power in the payments 'network service market'.[76] New market entrants have also become acquisition targets for payments incumbents (particularly Visa and Mastercard) in an attempt to maintain their integrated dominance in the 'payments supply chain', and enact a 'killer acquisition' strategy.[77] In November 2020, after Visa's proposed acquisition of API provider Plaid,[78] the US Department of Justice filed a suit seeking to block the acquisition, citing monopolistic concerns.[79] This resulted in the abandonment of the intended merger.[80]

The competitive impact of fintech on legacy payment infrastructure can be difficult to ascertain given the emergence of 'two-sided' (also called 'multi-sided') payments platforms as well as 'multilayered' payments transaction facilitators, wherein a payment provider can 'connect' merchants, intermediary service providers and consumers.[81] While 'digitisation' of payment services

[71] EP Study (n 3) 14.

[72] ibid.

[73] Fracassi and Magnuson (n 4) 37.

[74] Azzuttia, Ringe and Stiehl (n 28) 107.

[75] ibid.

[76] *United States v Visa USA Inc*, 163 F Supp 2d 322 (SDNY 2001).

[77] LL Ang, W Taylor and MP Leon, 'Fintech Developments and Antitrust Considerations in Payments' (2021) 35 *Antitrust* 69, 69–70.; see also FM Marty and T Warin, 'Visa Acquiring Plaid: A Tartan over a Killer Acquisition? Reflections on the Risks of Harming Competition Through the Acquisition of Startups Within Digital Ecosystems' (26 November 2020), available at: ssrn.com/abstract=3738299.

[78] Plaid: plaid.com/.

[79] Complaint 76, *United States v Visa Inc & Plaid Inc*, No 3:20-cv-07810, ECF No 1 (ND Cal, 5 November 2020).

[80] Press Release, US Department of Justice, 'Visa and Plaid Abandon Merger after Antitrust Division's Suit to Block' (12 January 2021), available at: www.justice.gov/opa/pr/visa-and-plaid-abandon-merger-after-antitrust-division-s-suit-block.

[81] Ang, Taylor and Leon (n 77) 70.

would imply a higher level of competition and lowered barriers to entry for new firms, high integration at multiple 'functional' levels of the payments supply chain can create entry frictions, especially for payments methods that are widely accepted by merchants and also 'preferred' by customers.[82] As a result, despite an explosion of payments-related innovations over the last two decades, including digitised and contactless payments, the market share for credit transactions of the largest payments providers have remained 'relatively stable' in the United States since 2000.[83]

Reliance on legacy payment systems (or 'rails' as they are also commonly referred to) such as credit, debit card and interbank settlement networks, could perpetuate barriers to market entry for new fintechs in favour of highly integrated firms.[84] New payments infrastructure and 'differentiated rails', such as the Bitcoin and Ethereum blockchain networks and other DeFi value transfer mechanisms may help, however, to decrease incumbent power.[85] Nevertheless, for this to happen there would need to be both widespread merchant and consumer acceptance of crypto-assets and decentralised payment tokens at point of sale. Given their cost-value proposition and high levels of volatility, to date, cryptocurrencies like Bitcoin and stablecoins have largely been held and used for value speculation rather than for payments applications.[86]

Additionally, nascent innovations such as machine learning and artificial intelligence integration into financial products and services, can generate new collusive forces – even 'tacit collusion' given their self-learning dynamic.[87] These collusive forces can impede market entry.[88] For example, researchers have argued that machine learning 'autonomous algorithms', which are being used by financial firms for a variety of investment and decision-making processes including

[82] ibid, 71.

[83] ibid; The competitive landscape of the payments industry is, however, distinct in the EU, where there is evidence that Europeans pay less for payment services than Americans, see 'Bringing European payments to the next stage: a public-private endeavour', Keynote speech by Fabio Panetta, Member of the Executive Board of the ECB, at the European Payments Council's 20th anniversary conference (16 June 2022), available at: www.ecb.europa.eu/press/key/date/2022/html/ecb.sp220616~9f8d1e277b.en.html; A 2020 study on the 'competitive landscape for payments' in Europe also revealed strong competitive dynamics in the payment industry, aided by new technologies such as mobile point of sale, PIN on glass, and tap on phone, and that new entry into the payments space was 'common in practice'. See Oxera Consulting LLP, 'The Competitive Landscape for Payments: A European Perspective' (March 2020), available at: www.oxera.com/wp-content/uploads/2020/03/Competitive-landscape-report.pdf.

[84] Ang, Taylor and Leon (n 77) 71–73.

[85] ibid.

[86] ibid, 72; see generally, Joshua Oliver, 'Bitcoin Has No Future as a Payments Network, Says FTX Chief' *Financial Times* (15 May 2022), available at: www.ft.com/content/02cad9b8-e2eb-43d4-8c18-2e9d34b443fe; Christian Catalini and Jai Massari, 'Stablecoins and the Future of Money' *Harvard Business Review* (10 August 2021), available at: hbr.org/2021/08/stablecoins-and-the-future-of-money; R Clements, 'Built to Fail: The Inherent Fragility of Algorithmic Stablecoins' (2021) 11 *Wake Forest Law Review Online* 131, available at: www.wakeforestlawreview.com/2021/10/built-to-fail-the-inherent-fragility-of-algorithmic-stablecoins/.

[87] EP Study (n 3) 14.

[88] ibid.

algorithmic and high-frequency trading to augment human activity, can lead to 'tacit' collusion between firms (due to correlated and coordinated programming), which has implications for market stability and integrity.[89] Algorithmic deployment into traditional financial products and services may also serve as 'facilitating tools' to implement anticompetitive practices resulting in sub-optimal outcomes for consumers.[90] Algorithms may also play multiple roles in facilitating collusion between market participants.[91]

D. Network Effects and Multi-Level Service Platforms

The unique way that some fintech firms operate may create future market entry barriers for new firms. As noted above, some firms may benefit from 'network effects', where the value of a product, service or platform increases with more users or participants, and as a result some fintech firm's services may become more valuable due to an increase in their user base and the generation of more and superior data.[92] The existence of network effects preserves market power and makes it difficult for new firms to compete.[93] Knowledge of such network effects can deter new fintech market entrants.[94] Advances in technology have allowed for the capture of huge swaths of data and for the emergence of better tools to aggregate, organise, validate, analyse and leverage this data to obtain enhanced consumer insights.[95] Data-driven technological infrastructure, like cloud-based computing, reduces barriers to entry for fintech firms, since they can manage data centres without high cost computer storage and processing facilities.[96] Yet, despite the reduction of initial entry barriers due to cloud computing, many fintech firms are fast transforming into 'platform-based' models where they serve a 'matchmaking' function between different users of their platform.[97] Once achieved, this 'dominant' market position is a significant barrier to entry for new firms.[98]

[89] Azzuttia, Ringe and Stiehl (n 28) 103.

[90] See generally, H Piffaut, 'Algorithms: The Impact on Competition' (2022) 23 *Business Law International* 5.

[91] The Organisation for Economic Co-operation and Development, 'Algorithms and Collusion – Background Note by the Secretariat. Directorate for Financial and Enterprise Affairs Competition Committee' (2017), available at: one.oecd.org/document/DAF/COMP(2017)4/en/pdf.

[92] EP Study (n 3) 13, 51–52, 65–66, 79, 81; see also Tim Stobierski, 'What Are Network Effects?' (*Harvard Business School Business Insights Blog*, 12 November 2020), available at: online.hbs.edu/blog/post/what-are-network-effects.

[93] ibid.

[94] ibid.

[95] Feyen et al, 'Fintech and the Digital Transformation of Financial Services' (n 43) 6.

[96] ibid, 7–8.

[97] K Croxson, J Frost, L Gambacorta and T Valletti, 'Platform-based Business Models and Financial Inclusion' (10 January 2022) BIS Working Papers No 986, available at: www.bis.org/publ/work986.htm.

[98] EP Study (n 3) 13, 51–52, 65–66, 79, 81.

There is some concern in the literature as to whether legacy antitrust frameworks in the United States are 'up to the task' to effectively regulate 'dominant' digital platforms who engage in exclusionary conduct that harms consumers, and whether existing regulatory measures should be strengthened.[99] The potential for market power abuse is particularly acute for fintech digital platforms that interact in 'two-sided markets',[100] and 'provide services for multiple users that interact through the platform and comprise an interdependent network ecosystem'.[101] Their operation as underlying infrastructure has led to suggestions that dominant digital platforms are 'the railroads of the modern era', and require oversight as 'essential facilities'.[102] Assessing the 'essential' nature of a platform technology requires a case-by-case analysis. Some platform technologies (like blockchain-based DeFi ecosystems) are currently in an emergent phase, while others (like BlackRock's *Aladdin* platform as described below) occupy a much more important, and dominant, market position.

Platform firms, which service both sides of a market, are able to leverage the 'connectivity' between different participants and 'package' service offerings while generating network effects for the platform, since more users on a platform leads to better services for all platform participants, and the attraction of more users to the platform because of the enhanced service offerings.[103] As another barrier to entry, dominant platforms may also be able to exert influence over adjacent markets to 'control entry points and protect their core markets from present and future competition'.[104] Increased platform revenue allows for targeted and bespoke products and services for market segments that are not initially serviced by the platform.[105] However, it can also create a 'winner-takes-all' or 'winner-takes-most' scenario where a platform enterprise uses its market dominance to extract rents across its user network.[106] A prominent example of a platform provider experiencing network effects is BlackRock's *Aladdin* investment management technology platform, which is giving rise to several emerging concentration and correlation risks.[107] The phenomenon of network effects is challenging, however, for policymakers because, despite the potential for market

[99] SC Salop, 'Dominant Digital Platforms: Is Antitrust up to the Task?' (2021) 130 *Yale Law Journal Forum* 563.

[100] J-C Rochet and J Tirole, 'Two-Sided Markets: A Progress Report' (2006) 35 *Rand Journal of Economics* 645, 645.

[101] Salop (n 99) 570.

[102] N Guggenberger, 'Essential Platforms' (2021) 24 *Stanford Technology Law Review* 237.

[103] Feyen et al, 'Fintech and the Digital Transformation of Financial Services' (n 43) 7.

[104] F Lancieri and P Morita Sakowski, 'Competition in Digital Markets: A Review of Expert Reports' (2021) 26 *Stanford Journal of Law, Business & Finance* 65, 79.

[105] Feyen et al, 'Fintech and the Digital Transformation of Financial Services' (n 43) 8.

[106] ibid.

[107] See *Aladdin* by BlackRock, available at: www.blackrock.com/aladdin; see also *Financial Times*, 'Aladdin: BlackRock's Fintech Genie Must Shield Funds from Groupthink' (7 April 2022), available at: www.ft.com/content/d2f04390-b76c-41b3-986c-4f8b815d222f?shareType=nongift.

power abuse and anticompetitive behaviours, the platform provides significant value to consumers (and grows more valuable with increased users). There is also emerging evidence that the cryptocurrency market may not exhibit the 'usual implications of network effects', and that this phenomenon may not fully 'define' the nascent cryptocurrency market.[108]

E. Consumer Financial Data Access, Portability and Control

Access to reliable consumer financial data is a critical input in the operating models of many fintech firms since data enhances consumer product offerings and risk profiling.[109] However, it is not certain that a data-driven economy will lead to monopolistic forces in financial services. In fact, some scholars have argued the opposite – that a 'data economy may also lead to more competitive markets with fewer dominant players', since data is a 'tool' that lowers entry costs for smaller firms and start-ups and allows them to compete with larger incumbents[110] and large Wall Street banks.[111] By way of analogy, it was less than two decades ago that social media giants Facebook and Twitter were start-ups themselves.[112]

Nevertheless, once established, large technology firms have significant data generation and access advantages and as they increasingly look to enter the fintech arena, they can utilise their 'vast amounts of data' for anticompetitive practices, including the formation of barriers to entry for new firms.[113] Moreover, the common practice of acquiring at an early stage of growth a much smaller competitor has led to the proliferation of a small number of dominant players in the global technology space, especially in social media.[114]

Certain fintech firms, or incumbent financial institutions, introducing new fintech offerings to existing customers may benefit from superior data access,

[108] K Stylianou, L Spiegelberg, M Herlihy and N Carter, 'Cryptocurrency Competition and Market Concentration in the Presence of Network Effects' (2021) 6 *Ledger* 81.

[109] EP Study (n 3) 87–90.

[110] W Magnuson, 'A Unified Theory of Data' (2021) 58 *Harvard Journal on Legislation* 23, 54–55; see generally, DD Sokol and R Comerford, 'Antitrust and Regulating Big Data' (2016) 23 *George Mason Law Review* 1129, 1136.

[111] See generally, Magnuson, 'Regulating Fintech' (n 12) 1173–87.

[112] See generally, Magnuson, 'A Unified Theory of Data' (n 110) 54–55; Ashlee Vance, 'Facebook: The Making of 1 Billion Users' *Bloomberg* (4 October 2012), available at: www.bloomberg.com/news/articles/2012-10-04/facebook-the-making-of-1-billion-users?leadSource=uverify%20wall.

[113] D Arner et al, 'Governing Fintech 4.0: Bigtech, Platform Finance, and Sustainable Development' (2022) 27 *Fordham Journal of Corporate & Financial Law* 1, 14; see, eg, R Bhadra, 'LinkedIn: A Case Study Into How Tech Giants Like Microsoft Abuse Their Dominant Market Position to Create Unlawful Monopolies in Emerging Industries' (2022) 13 *Hastings Science & Technology Law Journal* 3.

[114] JF Coyle and GD Polsky, 'Acqui-Hiring' (2013) 63 *Duke Law Journal* 281, 283–84; See, eg, Kara Swisher, 'Big Tech's Takeovers Finally Get Scrutiny' *New York Times* (14 February 2020), available at: www.nytimes.com/2020/02/14/opinion/ftc-investigation-google-facebook.html.

generation and control, including organic data generated from operational multi-service platforms, and thereby use data as a source of market power.[115] Data advantages can yield both 'exclusionary conduct', where dominant players prevent data access by competitors, and the practice of 'tying and bundling', which creates leverage for a firm to utilise its market power and impose a wide range of its services on consumers.[116] Despite 'data privacy' concerns garnering significant recent public attention,[117] incumbent banks have historically used consumer 'data silos' to extract rents, inhibit market competition, new firm entry and consumer choice, and offer 'unfavourable rates and inferior products' without customer flight.[118]

Cesare Fracassi and William Magnuson argue that this behaviour occurs because of three broad market failures that inhibit competition in finance.[119] First, because of a 'complex' and 'fragmented' regulatory environment, firms face high compliance burdens and barriers to entry.[120] Second, 'information asymmetries' between the bank and its customers are 'large and hard to resolve' and are compounded by high consumer 'search and switch costs' when comparing competing financial services and products.[121] Third, individuals are not 'rational decision-makers'[122] and thus consumers routinely fail to 'take advantage of simple strategies that could substantially improve their financial positions'.[123]

Further, the way that data has historically been housed at financial institutions is designed to make it as 'private and non-shareable as possible'.[124] Bank control

[115] EP Study (n 3) 83–87.

[116] ibid, 13.

[117] See generally, Sam Schechner and Mark Secada, 'You Give Apps Sensitive Personal Information. Then They Tell Facebook' *Wall Street Journal* (22 February 2019), available at: www.wsj.com/articles/you-give-apps-sensitive-personal-information-then-they-tell-facebook-11550851636; Geoffrey A Fowler, 'I Found Your Data. It's for Sale' *Washington Post* (18 July 2019), available at: www.washingtonpost.com/technology/2019/07/18/i-found-your-data-its-sale/; Stuart A Thompson and Charlie Warzel, 'Twelve Million Phones, One Dataset, Zero Privacy' *New York Times* (19 December 2019), available at: www.nytimes.com/interactive/2019/12/19/opinion/location-tracking-cell-phone.html.

[118] Fracassi and Magnuson (n 4) 331.

[119] ibid.

[120] ibid.

[121] ibid, 331–32.

[122] This notion is supported by a substantial body of scholarship, such as HA Simon, 'Rational Choice and the Structure of the Environment' (1956) 63 *Psychology Review* 129, 129; P Slovic, 'Psychology Study of Human Judgment: Implications for Investment Decision Making' (1972) 27 *Journal of Finance* 779; R Thaler, 'Toward a Positive Theory of Consumer Choice' (1980) 1 *Journal of Economic Behavior & Organization* 39; D Laibson, 'Golden Eggs and Hyperbolic Discounting' (1997) 112 *Quarterly Journal of Economics* 443; K Daniel et al, 'Investor Psychology and Security Under-and Overreactions' (1998) 53 *Journal of Finance* 1839, 1844–45; T Odean, 'Are Investors Reluctant to Realize Their Losses?' (1998) 53 *Journal of Finance* 1775, 1781–95; T Odean, 'Do Investors Trade Too Much?' (1999) 89 *American Economic Review* 1279, 1280–92; D Hirshleifer, 'Investor Psychology and Asset Pricing' (2001) 56 *Journal of Finance* 1533, 1545–46; EJ Elton et al, 'Are Investors Rational? Choices Among Index Funds' (2004) 59 *Journal of Finance* 261, 285–86; D Hirshleifer, 'Behavior Finance' (2015) 7 *Annual Review of Financial Economics* 133.

[123] Fracassi and Magnuson (n 4) 332.

[124] ibid, 327.

of consumer financial data is also historically routed in legal obligations relating to client confidentiality.[125] Open banking, a mechanism whereby consumers can safely access, port and share their financial data through standardised APIs rather than through risky 'screen scraping' technology,[126] is a potential remedy to the closed data-sharing practices of legacy banks.[127] At its core, open banking is about consumer 'autonomy' over how data is controlled, accessed, shared and stored.[128] In theory, it also has the potential to significantly improve consumer financial welfare, since new fintech firms (once they have access to consumer data) can offer a myriad of new product and service offerings.[129] It may also decrease the 'stickiness' of customers to incumbent banks and thereby reduce 'switching costs'.[130]

However, whether 'data portability', a concept largely associated with open banking, will improve competition is contested in the scholarship. The reason is that accommodating regimes are largely focused on consumer switching costs and may not adequately address the barriers to entry created by 'unique data access', network effects and economies of scale.[131] Despite its potential competition enhancing benefits, however, open banking regulatory implementation frameworks around the world have been both slow to manifest, and regionally distinct, including both permissive and mandatory models with distinct eligibility and participation requirements.[132]

[125] H-W Liu, 'Shifting Contour of Data Sharing in Financial Market and Regulatory Responses: The UK and Australian Models' (2021) 10 *American University Business Law Review* 287, 289–90.

[126] ibid, 289–91. See also, Basel Committee on Banking Supervision, Bank for International Settlements, 'Report on Open Banking and Application Programming Interfaces' (2019) 19.

[127] Fracassi and Magnuson (n 4) 332.

[128] ibid, 345–58.

[129] See generally, ibid, 345–46; Bank for International Settlements, 'Report on Open Banking' (n 126) 8–10, 15–16; Open Banking 2019 Review, Open Banking Implementation Entity (2020), available at: www.openbanking.org.uk/news/open-banking-2019-highlights/ (such new services and potential product offerings include faster loan approvals, new or novel credit assessment mechanisms using transaction history for 'thin credit' files, account information aggregation and consolidation services, diverse budgeting and money management applications, payment applications, bespoke and personalised financial services, enhanced investment and wealth management opportunities, account 'assistant' functions; enhanced analytics, credit, investment and wealth management advice and administrative efficiencies such anti-money laundering regulatory compliance).

[130] See generally, Liu (n 125) 291–92; Alasdair Smith, CMA Inquiry Chair, 'Speech at the BBA Retail Banking Conference on Competition and Open Banking' (29 June 2017), available at: www.gov.uk/government/speeches/alasdair-smith-on-competition-and-open-banking.

[131] G Nicholas, 'Taking it With You: Platform Barriers to Entry and the Limits of Data Portability' (2021) 27 *Michigan Technology Law Review* 263.

[132] See generally, Liu (n 125); EMEA Center for Regulatory Strategy, 'Open Banking Around the World', available at: www2.deloitte.com/global/en/pages/financial-services/articles/open-banking-around-the-world.html; Directive (EU) 2015/2366 of the European Parliament and of the Council of 25 November 2015 on Payment Services in the Internal Market [2015] OJ L337/35; Open Banking Implementation Entity, 'UK's Open Banking to Launch on 13 January 2018' (19 December 2017), available at: www.openbanking.org.uk/about-us/latest-news/uks-open-banking-launch-13-january-2018/; Victor Chatenay, 'Australia Has Rolled Out an Open Banking Regime' *Business Insider* (6 July 2020), available at: www.businessinsider.com/australia-open-banking-regime-goes-live-2020-7?r=US&IR=T.

F. Technology Infrastructure, Interoperability and Standardisation

Globally distributed, open-source, programmable blockchain networks function as technological infrastructure for the creation and deployment of new decentralised financial products and applications.[133] The fundamental value proposition of blockchain technology is to 'disintermediate' legacy firms which provide a 'gatekeeper' function, like Wall Street banks, securities and derivatives exchanges, central clearing mechanisms, investment managers, or even central banks in relation to the money supply.[134] In theory, a disintermediated, decentralised market reduces the power of industry 'gatekeeper firms' thereby allowing for greater competition and new market entry.[135]

However, dominant blockchain networks can yield anticompetitive market outcomes if the principles of open access and non-discrimination are not guaranteed and enforced by regulatory authorities.[136] Further, antitrust enforcement may be rendered ineffective given the nature of distributed ledger technology.[137] It has been suggested that large blockchain networks should be regulated using similar strategies as internet regulation, including the 'net neutrality' principle, so as to avoid anticompetitive outcomes.[138] Private, permissioned blockchains, like those being developed by the Depository Trust & Clearing Corporation,[139] may emerge in particular markets like securities and derivatives clearing and settlement, and the firms who control these networks can deny access and exert exclusionary policies,[140] or control standards in a way that discourages competition, including 'paid prioritisation' when recording new transactions on the permissioned blockchain.[141]

Diverse standards and a lack of interoperability can also deter fintech competition and market entry.[142] Incumbent financial institutions have incentives to maintain (or improve) their market share and they could advocate for favourable factors concerning interoperability and standardisation to create barriers to entry for new fintech firms.[143] Standardisation in emerging fintech data-sharing regimes, such as open banking, also has significant competition and

[133] See generally, Clements, 'Emerging Canadian Crypto Asset Jurisdictional Uncertainties and Regulatory Gaps' (n 69); Gogel et al (n 21).

[134] SN Weinstein, 'Blockchain Neutrality' (2021) 55 *Georgia Law Review* 499, 502.

[135] ibid, 514.

[136] ibid.

[137] T Schrepel, 'Is Blockchain the Death of Antitrust Law? The Blockchain Antitrust Paradox' (2019) 3 *Georgetown Law Technology Review* 281.

[138] Weinstein (n 134) 515.

[139] Michael del Castillo, '$11 Trillion Bet: DTCC to Process Derivatives with Blockchain Tech' (*CoinDesk*, 21 December 2017), available at: www.coindesk.com/11-trillion-bet-dtcc-clear-derivatives-blockchain-tech.

[140] Weinstein (n 134) 538–39.

[141] ibid, 515.

[142] EP Study (n 3) 13.

[143] Fracassi and Magnuson (n 4) 353–54.

entry barrier implications.[144] Safe data sharing takes place through APIs, which vary from proprietary forms in a market-driven approach to open banking,[145] to standardised and more formal regulatory models.[146] Proprietary and non-standardised APIs can impose participation cost burdens on new fintech firms, or smaller banks, which desire to participate in an open data-sharing regime.[147] Standardisation is also an important factor in competition policy.[148] Standardisation can cut both ways when it comes to market entry. On the one hand, technological standardisation can lower entry costs since it 'allows firms to compete on more core parts of the service'.[149] Yet it can also yield anticompetitive outcomes and increase barriers to market entry when oligopolistic forces are catalysed, and dominant market participants collude to split market segments in mutually agreeable ways.[150]

Consumer financial data access, sharing, portability and storage is most efficiently facilitated when interoperable standards are used.[151] For example, even under an 'open banking' regime, or broader data access and sharing regime, without interoperable standards, a new fintech market entrant must either rely on costly information 'aggregators', engage in individual negotiations, or incur tremendous ex ante information systems and operational costs to adapt to proprietary access mechanisms, procedures and diverse API standards when attempting to access data at a given institution.[152] This problem is particularly acute in the United States, where there are thousands of different banks and many thousands more insurance, payments and investment companies that also house consumer financial data.[153] The Internet benefited from early

[144] EP Study (n 3) 13.

[145] See generally, Deloitte, 'Creating an Open Banking Framework for Canada, Considerations, and Implications of Key Design Choices' (2020) 45, available at: www2.deloitte.com/content/dam/Deloitte/ca/Documents/financial-services/ca-open-banking-aoda-en.pdf; Kelsey Rolfe, 'Tired of Waiting, Flinks Launches Its Own Open Banking Environment with National Bank' *Betakit* (24 November 2021), available at: betakit.com/tired-of-waiting-flinks-launches-its-own-open-banking-environment-with-national-bank/.

[146] Liu (n 125) 291.

[147] Patrick Barr, 'Open Banking: Designing the future of Finance' *Report To Canadian Credit Union Association* (February 2021) 17, 21, available at: ccua.com/app/uploads/2021/03/Open-Banking-Designing-the-Future-of-Finance-4.pdf; There is some contention, however, on the extent that proprietary or non-standardised APIs create cost or entry barriers for smaller firms given the wide potential ambit of the 'fair use' doctrine established in *Google LLC v Oracle America, Inc*, 141 S Ct 1183 (2021). Here the US Supreme Court held that Google's copying of parts of a Java API in the creation of its Android platform was a 'fair use' as a matter of law and took an 'expansive view of the transformativeness in the fair use analysis', see 'Google LLC v Oracle America, Inc' (2021) 135 *Harvard Law Review* 431. Such an expansive jurisprudential interpretation may not, however, be given in other jurisdictions, and this will also further depend on that jurisdiction's enabling copyright legislation.

[148] EP Study (n 3) 13.

[149] ibid.

[150] ibid.

[151] Fracassi and Magnuson (n 4) 353–54.

[152] ibid, 354.

[153] ibid.

governmental efforts to promote open access, non-proprietary architecture and standardisation, and similar standardisation efforts in the fintech market could yield consumer benefits.[154] Interoperability is supported by standardisation.[155] It also fosters competition,[156] new market and product entry[157] and positive consumer experience.[158] Yet, thoughtful regulatory consideration of standardisation practices is needed, since it may also lead to oligopolistic behaviour and the leveraging of market power by large traditional financial firms which wield significant influence on what those standards are.[159]

G. Regulatory-Imposed Barriers to Entry and Regulatory Uncertainties

Fintech regulatory barriers to entry can take many forms. In the extreme, regulators may opt to ban outright certain types of innovations, like private digital currencies or stablecoins, because of their impact on monetary policy and the regulated banking system, despite their having potential consumer utility.[160] Central banks may also facilitate central bank digital currencies (CBDCs) as a preferred (essentially, a 'permissioned') digital currency, with integration advantages such as legal tender status or bank mandatory uptake.[161] Another regulatory-imposed competition barrier is that extensive initial and ongoing compliance costs, 'diverse regulatory approaches', towards fintech market segments, the overlapping and sometimes fragmentary jurisdiction of domestic agencies, and disparate standards when comparing international regulatory regimes may serve as functional barriers to entry for a firm when entering into a domestic market.[162]

Despite a potential deleterious impact on competition and new firm entry, regulators may also seek to shepherd new fintech innovations into legacy regulatory frameworks – like requiring fintech firms that offer a money substitutable

[154] PJ Weiser, 'The Internet, Innovation, and Intellectual Property Policy' (2003) 103 *Columbia Law Review* 534, 537 ('During the Internet's early years, the U.S. government supported and encouraged a culture of nonproprietary development that self-consciously protected the Internet's open and layered architecture'.)

[155] JG Sidak, 'The Value of a Standard Versus the Value of Standardization' (2016) 68 *Baylor Law Review* 59, 61.

[156] PS Menell, 'Economic Analysis of Network Effects and Intellectual Property' (2019) 34 *Berkeley Technology Law Journal* 219, 226 ('Standardized railroad gauge, for example, supported far-reaching railroad networks, promoted competition in locomotive and railcar markets, and enabled interconnected rail services'.)

[157] See generally, *Rambus, Inc v Infineon Techs AG*, 330 F Supp 2d 679, 696 (ED Va 2004) ('[N]ew producers have easier entry into a market when standards exist').

[158] K Gupta, 'Technology Standards and Competition in the Mobile Wireless Industry' (2015) 22 *George Mason Law Review* 865, 869.

[159] EP Study (n 3) 67.

[160] D Awrey, 'Bad Money' (2020) 106 *Cornell Law Review* 1, 8.

[161] ibid, 14.

[162] EP Study (n 3) 55.

product to obtain a banking licence – thus creating a significant ex ante compliance cost barrier.[163] In the case of money substitutable products such as closed-end peer-to-peer payment systems (like *PayPal*[164] or the now abandoned *Libra* project[165]), crypto-assets, stablecoins or other DeFi payments products, regulatory frameworks may confer 'comparative advantage' on legacy products.[166] This happens when a credibility signal is provided to the market that regulated status equates with greater safety and stability, particularly in the context of volatile and uncertain market conditions.[167]

A more subtle, but arguably much more significant, regulatory barrier to entry for fintech firms is the observation that legacy regulatory policy may favour existing regulated entities like banks and investment companies and disfavour digital innovators in finance.[168] This may take the form of outright barriers to market entry, such as the prohibitively high costs of becoming a bank, or an inability to access critical infrastructure like legacy payment rails.[169] Such dynamics force new fintech firms to partner with banks rather than competing directly against them.[170] Legacy regulatory frameworks may also be ill-suited to the operations of certain digital innovations like DeFi or algorithmic stablecoins,[171] or otherwise leave regulatory 'gaps' that make development and product deployment uncertain or risky from a compliance standpoint.[172] Others may raise barriers to innovation by discouraging regulated entities from promoting or adopting certain innovative business models or new operating segments.[173]

Regulated incumbents operating within the extensive landscape of financial products, processes and services also have incentives to 'push out new fintech services into unaffiliated firms operating beyond the regulated perimeter'.[174] This allows a cost-effective way of retaining customer loyalty and avoiding consumer switching, while providing access to new technologies, 'without assuming full responsibility for custody and other customer protections'.[175]

[163] Awrey (n 160) 8.
[164] D Awrey and K van Zwieten, 'Mapping the Shadow Payment System' (2019) SWIFT Institute, Working Paper No 2019-001, 12–22.
[165] See generally, DA Zetzsche, RP Buckley and DW Arner, 'Regulating Libra' (2021) 41 *Oxford Journal of Legal Students* 80; Timothy G Massad, 'Facebook's Libra 2.0: Why You Might Like It Even If We Can't Trust Facebook' *Economic Studies at Brookings* (June 2020), available at: www.brookings.edu/wp-content/uploads/2020/06/ES-6.22.20-Massad-1.pdf.
[166] Awrey (n 160) 7, 66–67.
[167] ibid.
[168] Van Loo (n 12) 259–61.
[169] EP Study (n 3) 14.
[170] Van Loo (n 12) 259; see also CK Odinet, 'Predatory Fintech and the Politics of Banking' (2021) 106 *Iowa Law Review* 1739, 1744; Brendan Pedersen, 'Why Is It so Hard for a Fintech to Become a Bank?' (*American Banker*, 18 November 2020), available at: www.americanbanker.com/podcast/why-is-it-so-hard-for-a-fintech-to-become-a-bank.
[171] Clements, 'Built to Fail' (n 86).
[172] ibid.
[173] P Treleaven, 'Financial Regulation of FinTech' (2015) 3 *Journal Financial Perspectives* 115, 118.
[174] Jackson (n 1) 14.
[175] ibid.

Thus, a strategic position can be maintained by existing firms that can serve as a functional deterrent for consumers switching their entire account to the new fintech which, in addition to a novel product, is also providing a competing product to the incumbent.[176]

Regulated firms may also have economies of scale that allow them to comply with regulations in a more efficient or cost-effective way. Further, incumbent firms may find it easier to comply with regulations given their familiarity and expertise with compliance frameworks gained through experience and application, as well as an existing working relationship with regulators.[177] There may also be direct regulatory barriers to accessing core financial infrastructure like payments or value transfer systems.[178] As an adaptive response, many fintech firms are avoiding services with extensive regulatory burdens (like depository banking or securities underwriting) and instead focusing on regulatory grey areas or gaps like banking as a service or blockchain-based offerings.[179]

H. The Impact of Consumer Perception and Trust on Fintech Market Entry

Consumer trust is a critical factor in financial services. Historically, banks have served as 'informational intermediaries' whose stability is closely tied to government depositary support, and continual levels of trust and confidence from depositories and borrowers.[180] Consumers want to know that their money and investments are safely custodied and managed, that their desired processes will work as intended, and that they have clear lines of communication and recourse in the event of a problem.[181] Incumbent financial product and service providers, as well as early market entrants, benefit from high levels of brand familiarity and trust.[182] Consumer perception also has a role in crypto-asset market entry, including between digital currencies, stablecoins, trading platforms, wallet providers and DeFi applications.[183]

[176] ibid.

[177] Feyen et al, 'Fintech and the Digital Transformation of Financial Services' (n 43) 21.

[178] ibid.

[179] ibid, 22–23.

[180] B Basarana and M Bagheriaa, 'The Relevance of "Trust and Confidence" in Financial Markets to the Information Production Role of Banks' (2020) 11 *European Journal of Risk Regulation* 650.

[181] ibid.

[182] See generally, R Clements, 'Exchange Traded Confusion: How Industry Practices Undermine Product Comparisons in Exchange Traded Funds' (2021) 15 *Virginia Law & Business Review* 125, 170 (brand trust can also give rise to a consumer 'bias' in favour of an incumbent enterprise known as 'overreliance on salience', that is, a bigger firm is considered more 'trustworthy' simply because of its size); R Stulz, 'FinTech, BigTech, and the Future of Banks' (2019) 31 *Journal of Applied Corporate Finance* 86; Organisation for Economic Co-operation and Development, 'Digital Disruption in Banking and Its Impact on Competition' (2020), available at: www.oecd.org/daf/competition/digital-disruption-in-financial-markets.htm.

[183] EP Study (n 3) 14.

Large technology firms, offering services external to finance, also benefit from a perception of trust given their size and existing user base.[184] This perception can serve as market friction for new fintech firms when attempting to acquire new users.[185] Having a regulated, or licensed, status can also signal trustworthiness. With high initial and ongoing compliance costs such perceptions can be a very steep obstacle for new firms to overcome because existing firms have 'demonstrated their reliability over time'.[186]

IV. CONCLUSION

This chapter has highlighted numerous entry barriers for new firms attempting to offer technology-mediated financial services globally. Regulatory authorities worldwide are tasked with a dynamic responsibility – which must be coordinated across diverse domestic regulatory agencies with varying legal and jurisdictional authority – to 'manage trade-offs',[187] particularly in relation to competition, capital formation, consumer and investor protection, privacy and market stability.[188] Regulators must further evaluate regulatory strategies for their ability to foster 'sustainable development' for communities and environmental stakeholders.[189]

There are several regulatory strategies that can assist in reducing barriers to entry while ensuring adequate consumer protections and financial system safeguards. Regulatory 'sandboxes' and innovation 'hubs' help to support new market entry and enhance competition while ensuring adequate consumer protections and market stabilisers.[190] Regulators may also look to integrate regulatory technology (or 'regtech')[191] for enhanced real-time supervision as a

[184] Feyen et al, 'Fintech and the Digital Transformation of Financial Services' (n 43) 20.
[185] ibid.
[186] ibid.
[187] Brummer and Yadav (n 12).
[188] Feyen et al, 'Fintech and the Digital Transformation of Financial Services' (n 43) 20.
[189] Arner et al (n 113) 48–53.
[190] See generally, Arner et al (n 113) 23–24; L Fahy, 'Regulator Reputation and Stakeholder Participation: A Case Study of the UK's Regulatory Sandbox for Fintech' (2022) 13 *European Journal of Risk Regulation* 138; W-G Ringe and C Ruof, 'Regulating Fintech in the EU: The Case for a Guided Sandbox' (2020) 11 *European Journal of Risk Regulation* 604; RP Buckley, D Arner, R Veidt and D Zetzsche, 'Building Fintech Ecosystems: Regulatory Sandboxes, Innovation Hubs and Beyond' (2020) 61 *Washington University Journal of Law & Policy* 55; A Harriman, 'Playing in the Sandbox: Lessons U.S. Regulators Can Learn From The Successes of Fintech Sandboxes in the United Kingdom and Australia' (2020) 37 *Wisconsin International Law Journal* 615; J Kim, 'Suffocate or Innovate: An Observation of California's Regulatory Framework for Cryptocurrency' (2019) 52 *Loyola of Los Angeles Law Review* 339.
[191] See generally, JW Bagley and NG Packin, 'Regtech and Predictive Lawmaking: Closing the Reglag Between Prospective Regulated Activity and Regulation' (2021) 10 *Michigan Business & Entrepreneurial Law Review* 127.

'new paradigm of technology enabled regulation'.[192] However, the effectiveness of regulatory sandboxes within a particular region may hinge on that nation's 'legal system, regulatory culture and domestic policy economy'.[193]

There are different academic and regulatory schools of thought regarding the consumer benefits of increased competition in financial services.[194] While fintech firms may increase consumer welfare gains and reduce 'rent seeking' of incumbent firms,[195] they may also give rise to heightened instability and decreased consumer choice in some market segments,[196] as well as data vulnerability, hacking and cyber risk.[197] Additionally, legacy antitrust and competitive regulatory safeguards, which focus on consumer pricing and welfare outcomes, may not be well-suited for platform fintech offerings which may eschew short-term profits for greater data control and network effects.[198] Further, increased competition and innovation support can weaken systemic safeguards, particularly in banking.[199] As such, the entry of 'big tech' into finance may require particular entity-based regulation to ensure competitive markets.[200] Big tech integration may also require heightened data reporting requirements given the embedded nature of financial services into non-financial technology applications.[201] Given these complexities, and the various factors identified in this chapter, policymakers must carefully assess the forces affecting barriers to entry for new fintech firms in their jurisdiction, and how market dynamics in financial services may generate anticompetitive outcomes, while ensuring adequate consumer protection, market integrity and financial system stability measures.

[192] C-Y Tsang, 'From Industry Sandbox to Supervisory Control Box: Rethinking the Role of Regulators in the Era of Fintech' (2019) 2 *Illinois Journal of Law, Technology & Policy* 355; GA Walker, 'Regulatory Technology (Regtech) – Construction of a New Regulatory Policy and Model' (2021) 51 *International Lawyer* 1.

[193] C-H Tsai, C-F Lin and H-W Liu, 'The Diffusion of the Sandbox Approach to Disruptive Innovation and is Limitations' (2020) 53 *Cornell International Law Journal* 261.

[194] cp M Amidu and S Wolfe, 'Does Bank Competition and Diversification Lead to Greater Stability? Evidence from Emerging Markets' (2013) 3 *Review of Development Finance* 152 (arguing that competition increases efficiency and leads to better outcomes for consumers); M Keeley, 'Deposit Insurance, Risk and Market Power in Banking' (1990) 80 *American Economic Review* 1183 (arguing that larger banks act more prudently because of their increased equity capital).

[195] Kidd (n 6).

[196] P Foohey, 'Consumers Declining Power in the Fintech Auto Loan Market' (2020) 15 *Brooklyn Journal of Corporate, Financial & Commercial Law* 5 (arguing that market dynamics in fintech originated consumer auto loans is leading to 'power imbalances' between consumers and lenders and reducing net consumer welfare).

[197] CG Bradley, 'Fintech's Promise and Peril' (2018) 93 *Chicago-Kent Law Review* 61.

[198] LM Khan, 'Antitrust Paradox' (2017) 126 *Yale Law Journal* 710.There is some contention, however, as to the unsuitability of 'conventional' antitrust principles to new innovations, and the need to reform this domain, particularly regarding large 'platform' technology enterprises. Other scholars disagree with Khan's assertion and suggest that current antitrust law and enforcement is sufficient to 'properly assess and adjudicate conduct involving digital platforms'. cp JM Yun, 'Does Antitrust Have Digital Blind Spots?' (2020) 72 *South Carolina Law Review* 305; Arner et al (n 113) 26.

[199] GS Steele, 'Banking as a Social Contract' (2021) 22 *UC Davis Business Law Journal* 65, 75.

[200] F Restoy, 'Fintech Regulation: Achieving a Level Playing Field' (2021) FSI Occasional Paper 17.

[201] Feyen et al, 'Fintech and the Digital Transformation of Financial Services' (n 43) 33.

3

Market Concentration in Fintech

DEAN CORBAE, PABLO D'ERASMO AND KUAN LIU*

I. INTRODUCTION

FINTECH IS AFFECTING many areas of financial services, from traditional credit markets to peer-to-peer lending and payment systems.[1] This chapter focuses on the role of fintech lenders in consumer credit markets. We study the evolution of lender concentration in the market for residential mortgages in the United States (the largest consumer loan market) between 2011 and 2019 (ie, after the Great Financial Crisis and before the pandemic).[2] Based on previous research, we classify institutions originating loans on this market into three types: (traditional) banks; non-fintech nonbanks; and fintech nonbanks.[3] Banks are subject to tighter regulations (eg, capital requirements, liquidity requirements), have access to insured deposits and hold a significant fraction of their loan originations on the balance sheet, while nonbanks fund their originations through securitisation financed with short-term securities.[4] As described

* The views expressed in this chapter are solely those of the authors and do not necessarily reflect the views of the Federal Reserve Bank of Philadelphia or the Federal Reserve System.

[1] 'Fintech' is understood here as technology-enabled innovation in financial services, pursuant to the definition of the Financial Stability Board in 'FinTech and Market Structure in Financial Services: Market Developments and Potential Financial Stability Implications' (Financial Innovation Network, 2019).

[2] We focus on the residential mortgage market because we have access to the universe of originations with information on the lender identity and borrower characteristics.

[3] The classification into fintech or non-fintech relies on G Buchak, G Matvos, T Piskorski and A Seru, 'Fintech, Regulatory Arbitrage, and the Rise of Shadow Banks' (2018) 130 *Journal of Financial Economics* 453. Specifically, they classify a lender as a fintech lender if it has a strong online presence and if nearly all of the mortgage application process takes place online with no human involvement from the lender. An institution (or lender) is a bank if it is a depository institution and a nonbank otherwise. While popular literature often calls unregulated, non-depository financial institutions 'shadow banks', we refer to such institutions as 'nonbanks', as classified by the Financial Stability Board (n 1). See section II for further details.

[4] D Corbae and P D'Erasmo, 'Capital Buffers in a Quantitative Model of Banking Industry Dynamics' (2021) 89 *Econometrica* 2975 have studied regulatory arbitrage in a model where big banks with market power interact with small, competitive fringe banks as well as nonbank lenders and showed that regulatory policies can have an important impact on banking market structure.

by others, fintech has a significant presence online and processes mortgages faster than non-fintech lenders.[5]

The period analysed is of particular interest as the Dodd–Frank Act of 2010 (DFA) introduced significant changes to banking regulation. For example, the DFA authorised the Federal Reserve System to impose more stringent capital requirements on banks. Furthermore, the DFA created the Consumer Finance Protection Bureau (CFPB) which has the authority to impose additional compliance requirements on mortgage lenders. In line with evidence in past research, we find that the market share of nonbanks has almost doubled in the last 10 years.[6] There is a significant decline in the loan origination market share among banks. This suggests that technology and regulation might play a role in explaining aggregate dynamics. We document that overall concentration (ie, when concentration is computed using all lenders) in the market for mortgage loans is significant, with the top three lenders taking, on average, 25 per cent of the market.[7] Concentration within the fintech sector is remarkably high, suggesting relatively large entry thresholds and quality differences. Specifically, the top three fintech nonbanks (in 2019: Quicken Loans, Loan Depot, Guaranteed Rate) account for 70 per cent of loan originations within that group. This level of concentration, together with the increase in fintech lending, has led to an increase in overall loan market share among the top three fintech lenders, from 5 to 10 per cent. Other nonbanks have also gained in market share and their concentration has increased; the market share of the top three non-fintech nonbanks (in 2019: United Shore Financial Services, Caliber Home Loans, Fairway Independent Mortgage Corporation) has increased from 2 to more than 10 per cent in the studied period. The mortgage market share of the top three banks (in 2019: Wells Fargo, JP Morgan Chase, Bank of America) has declined from 36 to 16 per cent during the same period. This is explained by a consistent reduction in the market share of banks, together with a reduction in the concentration of the bank sector. We show that most of the change in overall concentration is explained by *within-group* changes in concentration (ie, changes in concentration

[5] A Fuster, M Plosser, P Schnabl and J Vickery, 'The Role of Technology in Mortgage Lending' (2019) 32 *Review of Financial Studies* 1854 showed that fintech lenders process mortgage applications 20 per cent faster than other lenders, controlling for observable characteristics. Fintech lenders adjust supply more elastically than other lenders.

[6] Buchak et al, 'Fintech, Regulatory Arbitrage, and the Rise of Shadow Banks' (n 3); and Fuster et al (n 5).

[7] D Corbae and P D'Erasmo, 'Foreign Competition and Banking Industry Dynamics: An Application to Mexico' (2015) 63(4) *IMF Economic Review* 830 studied concentration within the bank sector and the role the Riegle–Neal Interstate Banking and Branching Efficiency Act of 1994 played in the observed increase in concentration between 1984 and 2018. D Corbae and P D'Erasmo, 'Rising Bank Concentration' (2020) 115(C) *Journal of Economic Dynamics and Control* 103877, also examined the consequences of government policies that promote foreign competition in a concentrated banking industry.

conditional on lender type), not *between-group* changes (ie, lending shifting from banks to the nonbank sector).

We present a simple model with imperfect competition where three types of lenders compete in the loan market, in line with a previous paper.[8] Unlike in that paper, we introduce heterogeneity within each institution type, allowing us to link the model to data on concentration with a particular focus on fintech. The model captures differences in financing costs, lending quality/technology and regulatory pressure.[9] We calibrate our data to match the market structure and dynamics for the period between 2011 and 2019. We estimate that top lenders (when sorted by origination) offer higher quality services than those at the bottom of the distribution, with top banks having the highest quality, followed by top fintech and non-fintech nonbanks. We also estimate that there is a significant improvement in lender quality for nonbanks (fintech and non-fintech) between 2011 and 2019 and this increase is more significant for the top nonbank lenders (fintech and non-fintech). We also estimate a large decline in bank quality, which we link to the reduction in the fraction of consumers that expresses a preference for the person-to-person and branch-based interaction that is at the core of the (traditional) bank business model. According to previous research, a large portion of branches in the United States are old, under-occupied and poorly maintained.[10]

In our main experiment, we show that changes in lender quality, which capture not only consumer preferences regarding the quality of financial services, but also technological advances in the fintech sector, account for more than 50 per cent of the increase in the fintech market share and 40 per cent of the decline in the bank market share. We estimate that changes in overall and within-type concentration are due almost entirely to changes in quality (technology). More precisely, we find that the decline in concentration in the industry between 2011 and 2019 derives from the decline in concentration within the bank sector that is the result of a decline in the estimated quality of top banks. Our main finding is that changes in quality have led to a substantial rise in fintech concentration. This change in concentration in the fintech industry is potentially important for regulatory policy and financial stability. Given that nonbanks' originate-to-distribute loans are implicitly guaranteed by government agencies, there is a

[8] Buchak et al, 'Fintech, Regulatory Arbitrage, and the Rise of Shadow Banks' (n 3).

[9] In line with Buchak et al, 'Fintech, Regulatory Arbitrage, and the Rise of Shadow Banks' (n 3) and Fuster et al (n 5) we understand our estimated differences in quality as capturing relative differences across lenders that derive from technological innovations (eg, impacting processing times); changes in customer accessibility (eg, loan applications that can be completed entirely online and expand access to some borrowers); and the provision of a more comprehensive customer service.

[10] J Frederic et al, 'Reimagining the Bank Branch for the Digital Era' (McKinsey & Company, 6 December 2017), available at: www.mckinsey.com/industries/financial-services/our-insights/reimagining-the-bank-branch-for-the-digital-era.

potential moral hazard problem along the same lines as for deposit insurance in traditional banks. Thus, growing concentration in fintech nonbanks could lead to a too-big-to-fail problem in that sector of the mortgage market, similar to that for traditional banks.

Our chapter is related to previous work on the roles of nonbanks and fintech lenders on credit markets.[11] The most closely related papers study fintech lending and how technology changes shaped the evolution of the industry in the last decade.[12] We use the same definition of fintech lenders as those papers and similar data sources, contributing to the literature by looking at how technology and entry costs affect lending concentration in the overall market for consumer mortgages and importantly, concentration *within* lender type.[13]

Past research has investigated the connection between bank capital regulation and the prevalence of nonbanks in the US corporate loan market.[14] Others have studied fintech lending to small businesses and found that fintech tends to replace loans from large banks rather than those from small banks.[15] Along the same lines, it has been shown that finance companies and fintech lenders replaced lending from banks to small businesses after the 2008 financial crisis.[16] One paper provides evidence on the terms for direct lending by nonbanks in the market for business credit.[17] Our chapter also contributes to this broader literature by looking at credit markets and the role of nonbank lending.

II. EVIDENCE ON FINTECH MARKET CONCENTRATION

In this section, we describe the datasets used in this chapter and present the main facts.

[11] See T Adrian and AB Ashcraft, 'Shadow Banking: A Review of the Literature' in G Jones (ed), *Banking Crises: Perspectives from The New Palgrave Dictionary* (Palgrave Macmillan, 2016) for a review of the literature on credit intermediation outside the bank sector.

[12] Buchak et al, 'Fintech, Regulatory Arbitrage, and the Rise of Shadow Banks' (n 3); and Fuster et al (n 5).

[13] J Jagtiani, L Lambie-Hanson and T Lambie-Hanson, 'Fintech Lending and Mortgage Credit Access' (2021) 1 *Journal of FinTech* 2050004, studied whether the growth of fintech lending in mortgage markets results in expanded credit access. G Buchak et al (2020) 'iBuyers Liquidity in Real Estate Markets', available at: ssrn.com/abstract=3616555, studied technological disruptions in the real estate market and the emergence of iBuyers.

[14] RM Irani, R Iyer, RR Meisenzahl and JL Peydró, 'The Rise of Shadow Banking: Evidence from Capital Regulation' (2020) 35 *Review of Financial Studies* 2181.

[15] T Balyuk, AN Berger and J Hackney, 'What is Fueling FinTech Lending? The Role of Banking Market Structure' (2020) *mimeo*, available at: ssrn.com/abstract=3633907.

[16] M Gopal and P Schnabl, 'The Rise of Finance Companies and FinTech Lenders in Small Business Lending' (2022) 35 *Review of Financial Studies* 4859.

[17] S Chernenko, I Erel and R Prilmeier, 'Why Do Firms Borrow Directly from Nonbanks?' (2022) 35 *Review of Financial Studies* 4902; J Murfin and R Pratt, 'Comparables Pricing' (2019) 32 *Review of Financial Studies* 688 present evidence on the financing of durable goods through captive finance subsidiaries.

A. Sample Description

We constructed our main sample using the Home Mortgage Disclosure Act (HMDA) loan origination dataset.[18] Our sample period was 2011 to 2019. We included all loans, ie, both purchase and refinance as well as non-conventional loans. Adopting a classification previously used by others, we sorted financial institutions into three types: banks, non-fintech nonbanks and fintech nonbanks.[19] An institution (or lender) was characterised as a bank if it was a depository institution, otherwise it was a nonbank. A lender was considered a fintech if it had a strong online presence and if nearly all of the mortgage application process took place online with no human involvement.[20] An updated classification included some fintech banks (ie, banks that switched from a more traditional application procedure with significant person-to-person interaction to one similar to that of nonbank fintech lenders).[21] No bank fitted the fintech definition prior to 2017. Since the adoption of a fintech application procedure is relatively recent, we decided to continue with the original three-type classification for the analysis in this chapter.[22]

We focused on the top 200 lenders in each year's HMDA data throughout our sample period since this facilitated a connection between the simple model (see section III) and the data and reduced the measurement error derived from unclassified institutions (ie, institutions not included in the original sample).[23] On average, the top 200 lenders accounted for 70 per cent of total originations by volume. Among them, we called the ones we identified from the previous classification as 'matched' institutions, while those that were not identified were called 'unmatched' institutions. 'Matched' institutions accounted for, on average, 80 per cent of the total lending in this group. They corresponded to 110–32 institutions out of 200 in any given year. HMDA provides information on the regulatory status of each institution, so we could classify 'unmatched' institutions by their bank/nonbank status based on their regulatory agency code. To complete the classification of all institutions in the top 200, we placed 'unmatched' nonbank

[18] Buchak et al, 'Fintech, Regulatory Arbitrage, and the Rise of Shadow Banks' (n 3). The data are publicly available at: www.consumerfinance.gov/data-research/hmda/historic-data/.

[19] We manually matched lenders in HMDA in 2019 using lender names to the updated list that Buchak et al, 'Fintech, Regulatory Arbitrage, and the Rise of Shadow Banks' (n 3) have provided (published in 2019). We were able to match 391 of the 566 unique lenders on the list. Complete matching was not possible, as some of the institutions in their list had changed names, merged with other lenders, or were no longer active in 2019 (ie, they might have existed in previous years, but not in 2019). Once lenders were matched, we kept the type of the given lender constant for the length of our sample. Additionally, we classified Better Mortgage Corporation as a fintech lender, following the discussion in Jagtiani et al (n 13). See the updated list from Buchak et al, 'Fintech, Regulatory Arbitrage, and the Rise of Shadow Banks' (n 3) here: sites.google.com/view/fintech-and-shadow-banks.

[20] Buchak et al, 'Fintech, Regulatory Arbitrage, and the Rise of Shadow Banks' (n 3).

[21] ibid.

[22] See also Fuster et al (n 5); and Jagtiani et al (n 13) for a similar three-type classification.

[23] Buchak et al, 'Fintech, Regulatory Arbitrage, and the Rise of Shadow Banks' (n 3).

institutions in the non-fintech bin. Since most of the 'unmatched' institutions were relatively small, this assumption provides a conservative (lower bound) estimate for fintech market shares and concentration. Our sample included 29 unique fintech lenders.[24] Table 1 presents the list of fintech lenders active in 2019, their origination volume, market share within Top 200 lenders, and entry date (or when first observed in our sample of top 200 lenders).

Table 1 Fintech lenders in 2019 (top 200 lenders HMDA)

Fintech Lender Name	Fintech Start	Volume (MM)	Market Share
Quicken Loans	2011	141,639	7.61%
loanDepot LLC	2011	44,870	2.41%
Guaranteed Rate Inc.	2011	27,556	1.48%
Guild Mortgage Company	2011	21,269	1.14%
MOVEMENT MORTGAGE, LLC	2011	16,695	0.90%
PENNYMAC LOAN SERVICES LLC	2014	13,796	0.74%
Provident Funding Associates	2011	11,361	0.61%
Eagle Home Mortgage, LLC	2011	9,993	0.54%
Cardinal Financial Company LP	2011	9,702	0.52%
Amerisave Mortgage Corporation	2011	4,919	0.26%
Impac Mortgage Corp. dba CashCall Mortgage	2012	4,474	0.24%
SWBC Mortgage Corporation	2011	3,704	0.20%
Better Mortgage Corporation	2019	3,568	0.19%
LendUS LLC dba RPM Mortgage	2017	3,519	0.19%
NFM, Inc.	2017	3,271	0.18%
PARAMOUNT EQUITY MORTGAGE, LLC	2011	2,451	0.13%
MORTGAGE INVESTORS GROUP	2011	2,008	0.11%
First Savings Mortgage Corporation	2011	1,999	0.11%

Note: Loan level data from HMDA. Classification based on latest version of lender classification data.[25] Fintech start corresponds to the year the lender first was classified as fintech or the initial year in our HMDA sample. MM stands for millions.

In addition to the HMDA sample, we used data from Fannie Mae and Freddie Mac. These datasets provided information on interest rates and performance on a subset of 15-year and 30-year, fully amortising, full documentation, single-family, conforming fixed-rate mortgages. This loan level data contained

[24] The updated list contains 51 fintech nonbanks, while the original list contained 12 fintechs in HMDA (all nonbanks).

[25] Buchak et al, 'Fintech, Regulatory Arbitrage, and the Rise of Shadow Banks' (n 3).

geographical information and some important borrower characteristics, such as borrower credit scores. We linked this dataset to the classification described above in order to analyse differences in loan interest rates across institution types. The combination of Fannie Mae and Freddie Mac data covers the majority of conforming loans issued in the United States.

B. Main Findings and Fintech Concentration

In this section, we describe the evolution of the mortgage market since 2011. Subsection II.B.i presents aggregate dynamics and the evolution of market shares by lender type. Subsection II.B.ii describes the evolution of lender concentration with a focus on fintech lending. Subsection II.B.iii provides a decomposition of lender concentration to help understand the dynamics.

i. Mortgage Market Size and Aggregate Level Concentration

We start by documenting aggregate dynamics in our sample. Our findings are in line with those in previous research.[26] Figure 1 presents the volume of loan originations (in $ trillion) among the top 200 lenders (by value of loan originations). Loan originations increased by more than 80 per cent between 2011 and 2019.

Figure 1 Total loan originations (volume, $ trillion, top 200 lenders)

Note: Loan level data from HMDA. Our sample period was 2011 to 2019. We included all loans (both purchase and refinance as well as non-conventional loans).

[26] Buchak et al, 'Fintech, Regulatory Arbitrage, and the Rise of Shadow Banks' (n 3); Fuster et al (n 5); and Jagtiani et al (n 13).

Figure 2 shows the evolution of market shares by lender type between 2011 and 2019. The market share of nonbanks more than doubled during this period, from 24 to 55 per cent (Figure 2 panel (iii)). There was also an increase in the number of nonbank lenders (from 90 to 111), but the growth in the number of institutions was not as strong (a 23 per cent increase). This suggests that a large portion of the increase in the nonbank market share derived from the growth of incumbent nonbank lenders. Within the nonbank sector, both non-fintech and fintech firms showed considerable growth. The non-fintech nonbank lenders' market share increased from 16 to 37 per cent, while fintech nonbanks' market share increased from 8 to over 17 per cent. The counterpart of the increase in nonbank lending market share was the decline in the presence of traditional banks. The market share for the bank sector fell from 76 to just above 45 per cent. The growth of the nonbank sector was not confined to a specific segment of the residential market. Previous research shows that while the growth of nonbanks was more significant in the conforming loan segment, there was also considerable growth in the segment of Federal Housing Administration mortgages.[27]

Figure 2 Market shares and number of lenders (by lender type)

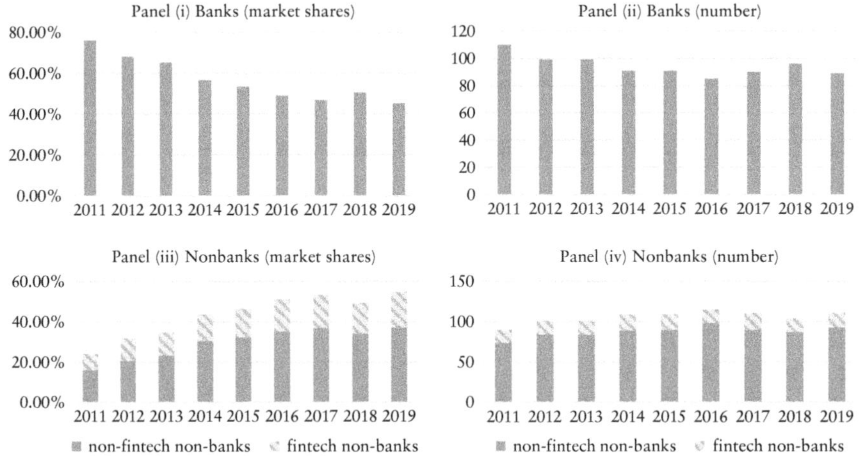

Note: Loan level data from HMDA. Our sample period was 2011 to 2019. We included all loans (both purchase and refinance as well as non-conventional loans). Classification was based on the latest version of lender classification data.[28] Market shares corresponded to shares of originations among the top 200 lenders.

The financing structure of loan originations differs significantly between banks and nonbanks. The share of bank loans held on balance sheet is 31 per cent on average (see Table 1, panel B).[29] In the case of nonbanks, the average is 7.5 per cent, with non-fintech lenders at 6.8 per cent and fintech lenders at 10.5 per cent.

[27] Buchak et al, 'Fintech, Regulatory Arbitrage, and the Rise of Shadow Banks' (n 3).
[28] ibid.
[29] ibid.

A large portion of the loans originated by nonbanks are sold to banks, government-sponsored enterprises or insurance companies. Previous research has shown a dramatic increase in the role that government-sponsored enterprises play for fintech lenders; in 2015, nearly 80 per cent of loans which originated in this sector were financed by some underlying government guarantee.[30]

Figure 3 focuses on fintech lending during the period. The market share of fintech lenders increased from close to 8 to more than 17 per cent. Fintech lenders grew more slowly than the non-fintech nonbanks during the early years, translating to a decline in their share of nonbank originations between 2012 and 2014. This trend changed, and by 2019 they had recovered some of the lost share of nonbank lending. The number of nonbank fintech lenders (among the top 200 lenders) fluctuated between 16 and 20.

Figure 3 Fintech lending (market shares)

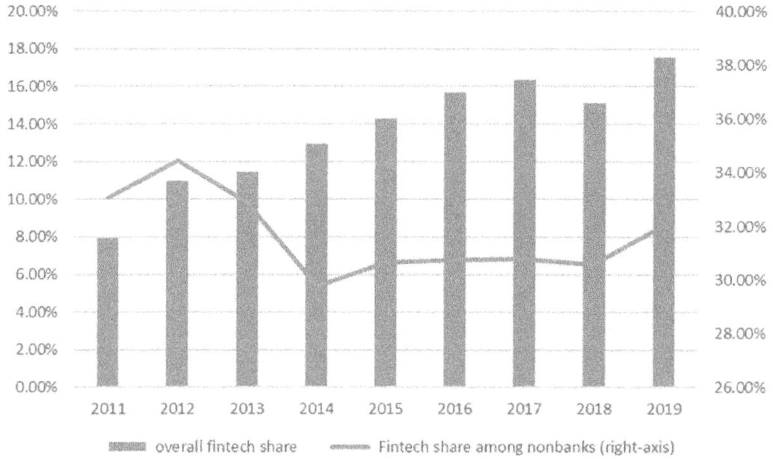

Note: Loan level data from HMDA. Our sample period was 2011 to 2019. We included all loans (both purchase and refinance as well as non-conventional loans). Classification was based on the latest version of lender classification data.[31] 'Overall fintech share' refers to the share of fintech lending in total lending by top 200 lenders. 'Fintech share among nonbanks' refers to the share of fintech lending in total nonbank lending (also restricted to top 200 lenders).

Figure 4 shows the evolution of three measures of market concentration at the national level: the Herfindahl-Hirschman Index (HHI) (defined as $HHI_t = \sum_{i=1}^{N} s_{i,t}^2$, where $s_{i,t}$ corresponds to the market share of lender i (in per cent) in period t), the market share of the top three lenders (C3), and the market share of the top 10 per cent lenders (when sorted by originations).[32] The figure shows that there was a decline over

[30] ibid, Figure 4.

[31] ibid.

[32] The HHI is a widely used measure of market concentration and can assume values between $\left[\frac{1}{N}, 10{,}000\right]$, where N is the number of lenders in the industry. See, eg, E Rossi-Hansberg, PD Sarte and N Trachter, 'Diverging Trends in National and Local Concentration' (2021) 35 *NBER Macroeconomics Annual* 115.

time in the degree of market concentration (consistent across the three measures).[33] The HHI dropped from 570 in 2011 to 236 in 2019 (an almost 60 per cent decline). The market share of the top three lenders (C3) declined from 36 to 20 per cent. There was also a (less pronounced) decline in the market share of the top 10 per cent lenders (when sorted by originations), from 61 to 52 per cent. Together with the decline in concentration, this created a shift in composition. As we showed in Figure 2, there was a shift towards nonbank lending (fintech and non-fintech). This compositional change was also reflected at the top of the distribution. For example, all the top three lenders in 2013 were banks (Wells Fargo, JP Morgan Chase Bank, Bank of America). During the period from 2014 to 2018, only two of the top three are banks (Wells Fargo, JP Morgan Chase) with the third being a fintech lender (Quicken Loans). In 2019, JP Morgan Chase dropped from the top three lender list to be replaced by a nonbank lender (United Shore Financial Services) and Quicken Loans replaced Wells Fargo at the very top. We have explored these compositional effects and changes in concentration by type below.

Figure 4 National level concentration (all loans/all lender types)

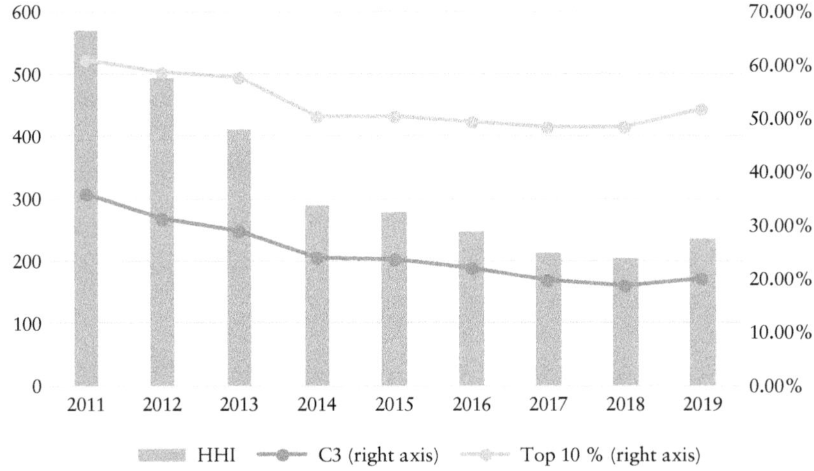

Note: Loan level data from HMDA. Our sample period was 2011 to 2019. We included all loans (both purchase and refinance, as well as non-conventional loans). Classification was based on an existing classification system.[34] The Herfindahl-Hirschman Index (HHI) equals $\sum_{i=1}^{N} s_i^2$, where s_i corresponds to the market share of lender *i*. C3 refers to the market share of the top three lenders in the market. Top 10 per cent corresponds to the market share of the top 10 per cent lenders when sorted by originations (since we studied the top 200 lenders, this corresponds to the top 20 lenders).

[33] Figure 4 shows three measures of concentration at the national level. Figure 9, below, shows that these dynamics were consistent with data aggregated from smaller markets (county level). In that respect, the evidence for mortgage origination appears to show a different pattern from any of those described in Rossi-Hansberg et al (n 32) for other industries.

[34] Buchak et al, 'Fintech, Regulatory Arbitrage, and the Rise of Shadow Banks' (n 3).

Table 2 presents the changes in market share by lender type. Most of the gain in the nonbank sector is accounted for by the largest lenders (non-fintech and fintech). In the bank sector, most of the decline is accounted for by banks in the top three of the loan distribution. This suggests that concentration has declined in the bank sector and increased in the nonbank (fintech and non-fintech) sector. Next, we will study the dynamics of lender concentration.

Table 2 Changes in market shares (by lender type)

	Market share changes 2011–19			
Lender Type	**Largest**	**2nd Largest**	**3rd Largest**	**Non-top 3 Rep.**
Banks	−12.67%	−4.61%	2.70%	−0.03%
Nonfintech Nonbanks	4.99%	1.60%	1.49%	0.10%
Fintech Nonbanks	4.81%	1.03%	0.74%	0.17%

Note: Loan level data from HMDA. We included all loans (both purchase and refinance as well as non-conventional loans). Classification was based on an existing classification system.[35] Market share changes corresponds to the percentage point change in overall market share for a given lender type between 2011 and 2019. The 'non-top three rep'. refers to the change in market share for the representative non-top three lender in the relevant group.

ii. Fintech Concentration

We start this subsection by exploring how the compositional changes in the industry affected the evolution of market concentration. Figure 5 shows the HHI (panel (i)), C3, and the market share of the top 10 per cent lenders (panel (ii)), when separating lenders by whether they are a bank or not. Both panels show consistent trends. The bank sector appears to be more concentrated than the nonbank sector on average, but differences decrease towards the end of the period. The HHI for bank lenders is 2.5 times larger than that of nonbank lenders in 2011, but only 25 per cent larger in 2019. A similar dynamic can be observed for C3 and the market share of the top 10 per cent lenders. The dynamics of concentration conditional on bank status are explained by a significant reduction in concentration in the bank sector (recall also the decline in their overall market share), together with an increase in concentration in the nonbank sector. For example, the HHI for the nonbank sector increased by more than 50 per cent between 2011 and 2019, while the HHI for banks declined by 44 per cent during the same period. This increase in concentration in the nonbank sector derives from significant growth at the very top of the distribution.

[35] ibid.

Figure 5 Concentration by bank status

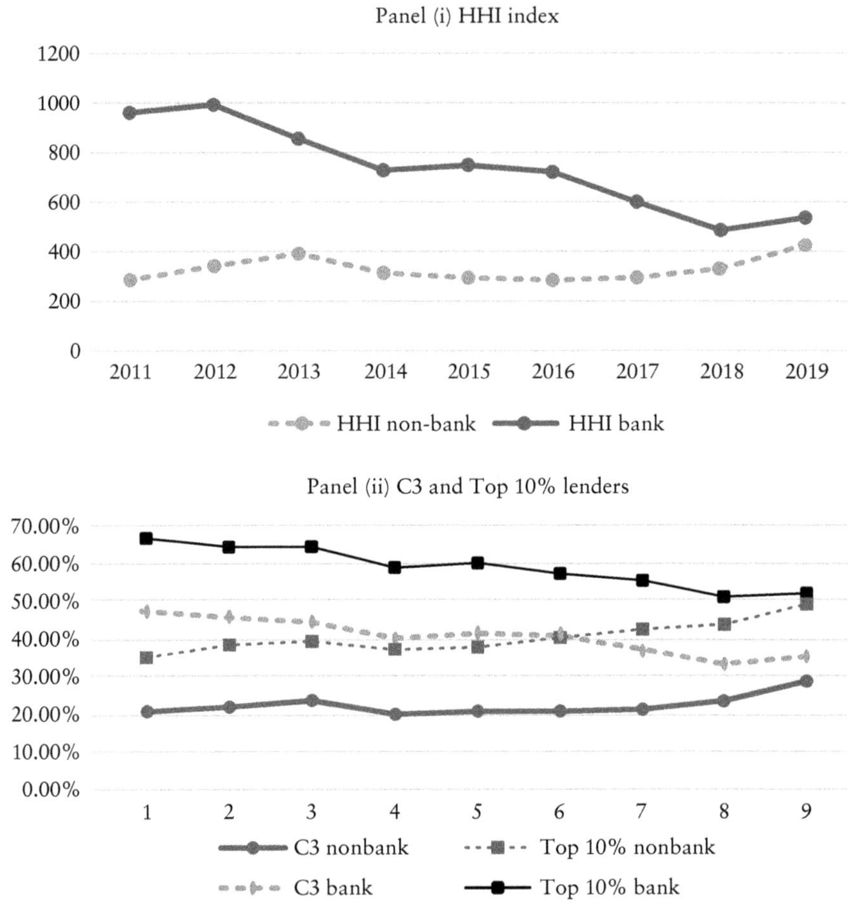

Note: Loan level data from HMDA. Our sample period was 2011 to 2019. We included all loans (both purchase and refinance as well as non-conventional loans). Classification based on latest version of lender classification data.[36] The Herfindahl-Hirschman Index (HHI) equals $\sum_{i=1}^{N} s_i^2$, where s_i^2 corresponds to the market share of lender *i*. C3 refers to the market share of the top three lenders in the market. Top 10 per cent corresponds to the market share of the top 10 per cent lenders when sorted by originations (since we studied the top 200 lenders, this corresponds to the top 20 lenders).

[36] ibid.

Figure 6 Concentration by fintech status

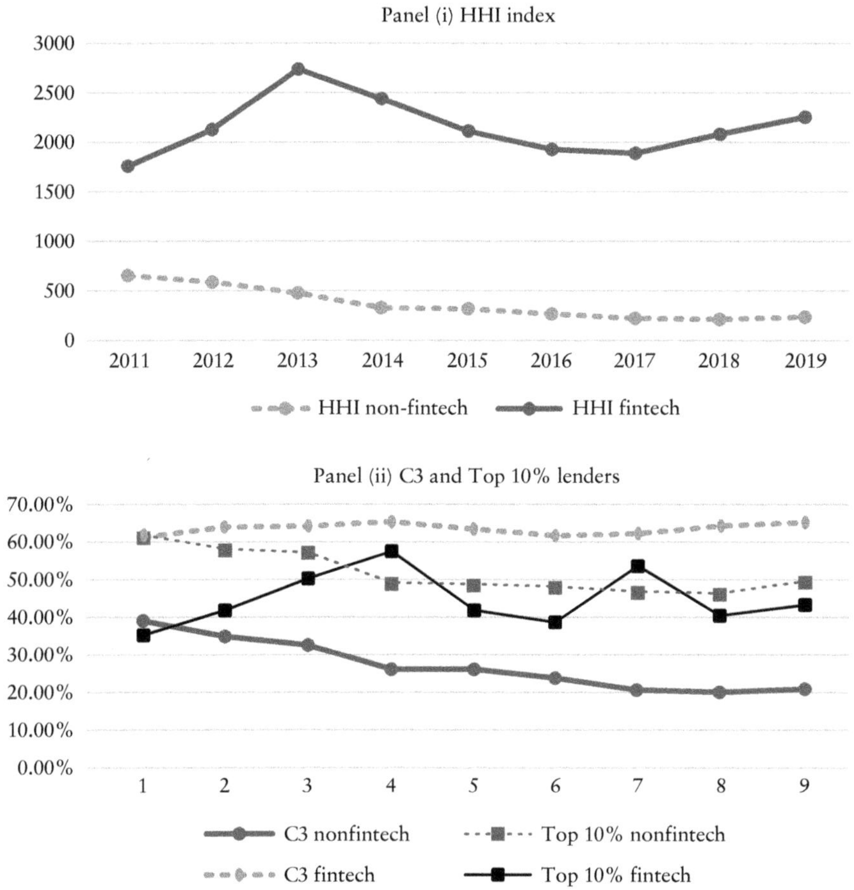

Note: Loan level data from HMDA. Our sample period was 2011 to 2019. We included all loans (both purchase and refinance as well as non-conventional loans). Classification based on latest version of lender classification data.[37] The Herfindahl-Hirschman Index (HHI) equals $HHI = \sum_{i=1}^{N} s_i^2$, where s_i^2 corresponds to the market share of lender *i*. C3 refers to the market share of the top three lenders in the market. Top 10 per cent corresponds to the market share of the top 10 per cent lenders when sorted by originations (since we studied the top 200 lenders, this corresponds to the top 20 lenders).

[37] ibid.

Now, we focus on market concentration by fintech status. Figure 6 shows the HHI (panel (i)), C3, and market share of the top 10 per cent lenders (panel (ii)) when separating lenders into fintech and non-fintech (banks and nonbanks). Fintech lenders were significantly more concentrated that non-fintech lenders. The HHI for fintech lenders was 2–7 times larger than that of non-fintech lenders. The number of fintech lenders in the sample (top 200 lenders in HMDA) was 16–20. The HHI and C3 reflect the fact that most lending by fintech lenders was done by a handful of institutions (C3 was 62–66 per cent), while lending in the non-fintech sector was more equally distributed across more institutions (between 180 and 184 entities). The decline in concentration for non-fintech lenders derived from the decline in the bank sector. The market share of the top 10 per cent lenders appeared to be lower for fintech than for non-fintech. It is relevant to note that lending by the top 10 per cent lenders in the case of non-fintech lenders corresponded to lending by around 18 lenders, while this corresponded to two lenders at most for fintech lenders. Thus, while the top 10 per cent lenders accounted for a similar fraction of lending in both sectors towards the end of the period, the non-fintech sector needed 5–6 times more lenders to achieve the same market share.

The patterns described in Figures 5 and 6 (higher concentration in the fintech and bank sectors relative to non-fintech and nonbanks, with concentration declining in the bank sector and increasing in the nonbank sector) were also evident when we looked at concentration measures in relation to our three-type classification of lender originators: commercial banks, non-fintech nonbank, fintech nonbank. Figure 7 shows the HHI (panel (i)), the market share of the top three lenders (panel (ii)), and the market share of the top 10 per cent lenders (panel (iii)).

Figure 7 also helps explain the dynamics of the industry. On the one hand, as the market share of nonbank increases, the overall level of concentration declines. On the other hand, as the market share of fintech lenders increases, concentration will tend to increase as well. In the period from 2011 to 2019, the shift towards a less concentrated nonbank sector dominated, but the second force appeared to gain strength towards the end of the period, explaining the uptick in overall concentration in 2018 and 2019 (see Figure 4).

iii. Market Concentration Decomposition

We conclude this section by presenting a decomposition of market concentration. This decomposition provides intuition for the pattern described in Figure 7. We decompose the HHI (one of our measures of concentration) as follows:

$$HHI_t = \left(S_t^B\right)^2 HHI_t^B + \left(S_t^{NF}\right)^2 HHI_t^{NF} + \left(S_t^F\right)^2 HHI_t^F,$$

where S_t^j and HHI_t^j denote the market shares and the HHI, respectively, within type $j \in \{B, NF, F\}$ (ie, when the market is defined using loans from lenders

Figure 7 Concentration by lender type

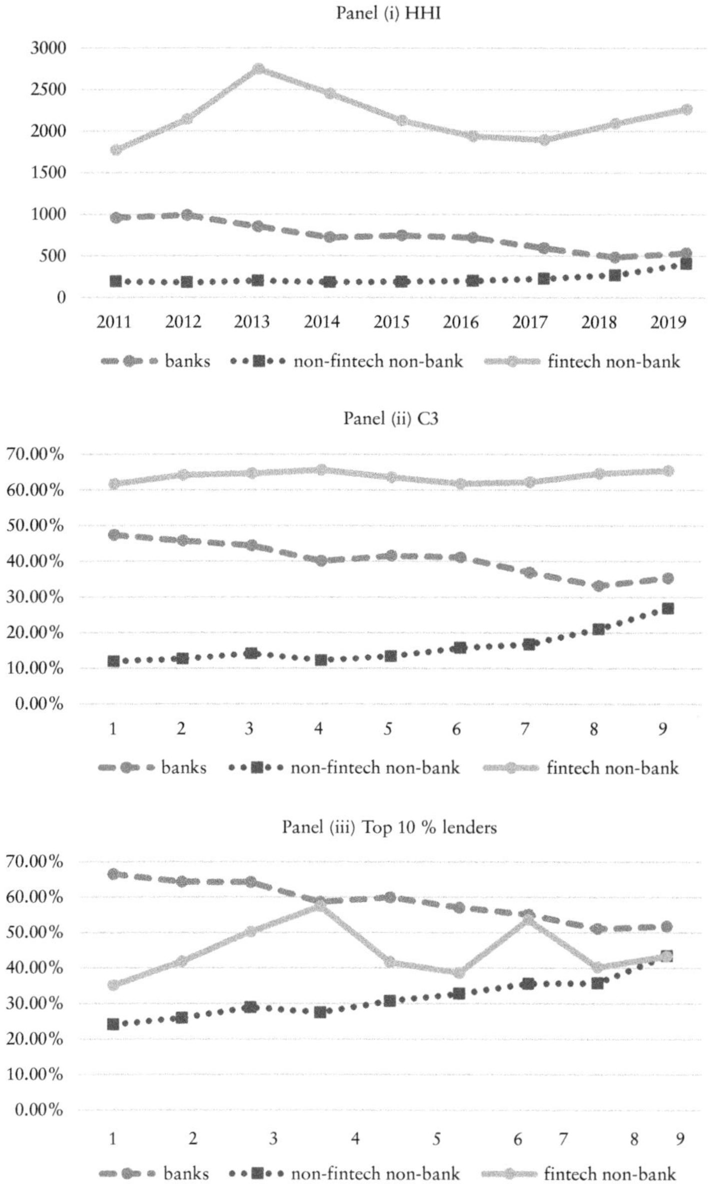

Note: Loan level data from HMDA. Our sample period was 2011 to 2019. We included all loans (both purchase and refinance as well as non-conventional loans). Classification based on latest version of lender classification data.[38]

[38] ibid.

of type *j*).[39] Expanding the overall HHI in this way shows how changes in concentration in each group contribute to changes in overall concentration. In addition, changes in overall concentration between period t and any period τ can be decomposed into changes between groups (ie, changes derived from redistribution of market shares across types) and changes within groups (ie, changes due to changes in concentration within groups). More specifically, we can write:

$$\Delta HHI_t = \sum_{j \in \{B,NF,F\}} \Delta\left(S_t^j\right)^2 HHI_t^j - \sum_{j \in \{B,NF,F\}} \left(S_\tau^j\right)^2 \Delta HHI_t^j,$$

where $\Delta HHI_t = \text{HHI}_t - \text{HHI}_\tau$. We call the first term in the previous equation 'ΔHHI_t between' and the second term 'ΔHHI_t within'. Panel (i) in Figure 8 presents the evolution of the overall HHI, 'ΔHHI_t between' and 'ΔHHI_t within' when looking at changes between year t and 2011 (the initial year in our sample). Using this decomposition, we can estimate how much of the overall concentration change is explained by changes in concentration within group. Figure 8, panel (i) shows that most of the change in overall concentration is explained by within-group changes (the contribution is most significant towards the end of the period). In other words, the evolution of the concentration within lender type appears to be the main determinant of concentration in the market for residential mortgages. Within-group changes in the HHI explain 30–75 per cent of the overall decline in concentration. For example, in 2019, the overall decline in the HHI was 334 and the decline in 'ΔHHI_t within' was 237 (71 per cent of the overall decline). It is possible to show that these dynamics derive mostly from the decline in concentration within the bank sector (see Figure 7).

To explore this further, panel (ii) in Figure 8 shows the evolution of the individual terms $\left(S_t^j\right)^2 HHI_t^j - \left(S_\tau^j\right)^2 HHI_\tau^j$ for $j \in \{B,NF,F\}$. We observed that changes associated with the bank sector explained the total change in the overall HHI. Concentration within the nonbank sector has increased, with fintech increasing slightly more than non-fintech.

To complete the analysis of concentration and to complement the insights we gathered from looking at the HHI, we computed C3 and the market share of the top 10 per cent lenders. We also created a Lorenz curve (a measure of lending inequality) using originations from all lenders and conditional on lender type. Lorenz curves are one of the main ways in which household income and wealth inequality are measured. Like the HHI, the Lorenz curve allows us to look at the

[39] Rossi-Hansberg et al (n 32). See Appendix VII.A for the derivation of this decomposition.

Figure 8 HHI decomposition

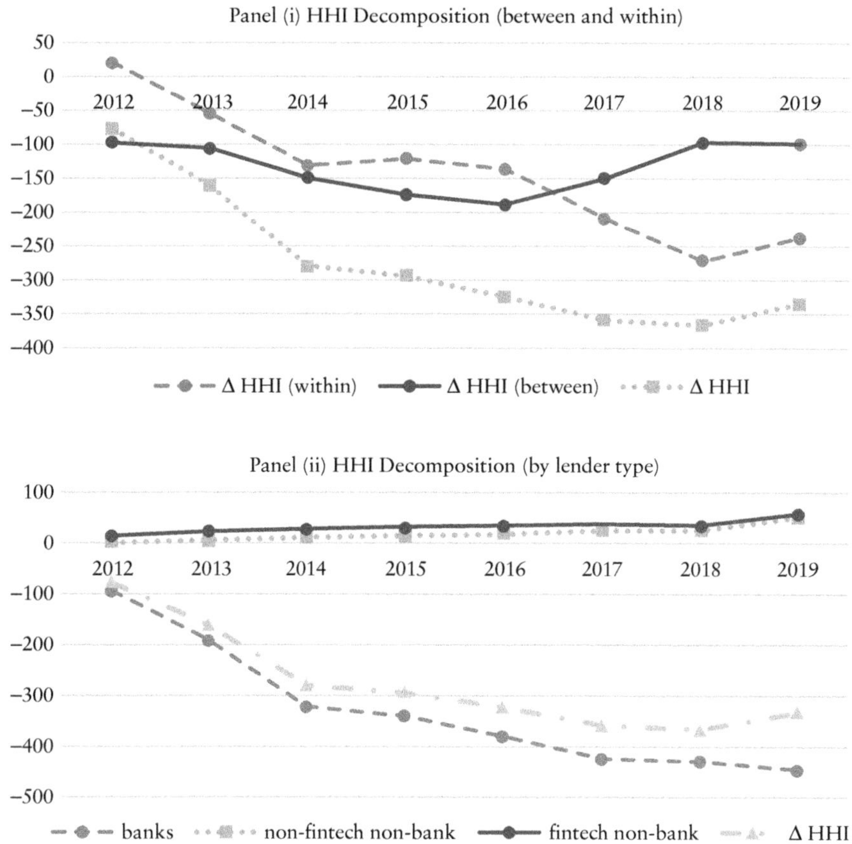

Note: Loan level data from HMDA. Our sample period was 2011 to 2019. We included all loans (both purchase and refinance as well as non-conventional loans). Classification based on latest version of lender classification data.[40] In panel (i), 'ΔHHI_t between' equals $\sum_{j\in\{B,NF,F\}}\Delta\left(S_t^j\right)^2 HHI_t^j$ and 'ΔHHI_t within' equals $\sum_{j\in\{B,NF,F\}}\left(S_\tau^j\right)^2 \Delta HHI_t^j$ with τ equal to 2011. In panel (ii), each of the lines plots the corresponding value of $\left[\left(S_t^j\right)^2 HHI_t^j-\left(S_\tau^j\right)^2 HHI_\tau^j\right]$ for $j\in\{B,NF,F\}$ (banks, non-fintech nonbanks, fintech nonbanks, respectively).

entire distribution. Figure 9 presents the comparison of Lorenz curves for 2011 and 2019. Panel (i) shows that concentration has declined, when all lenders are included (a shift of the curve towards the 45-degree line implies a reduction in concentration). This is consistent with the evidence presented in Figures 4 and 8.

[40] Buchak et al, 'Fintech, Regulatory Arbitrage, and the Rise of Shadow Banks' (n 3).

Figure 9 Lorenz curves loan origination

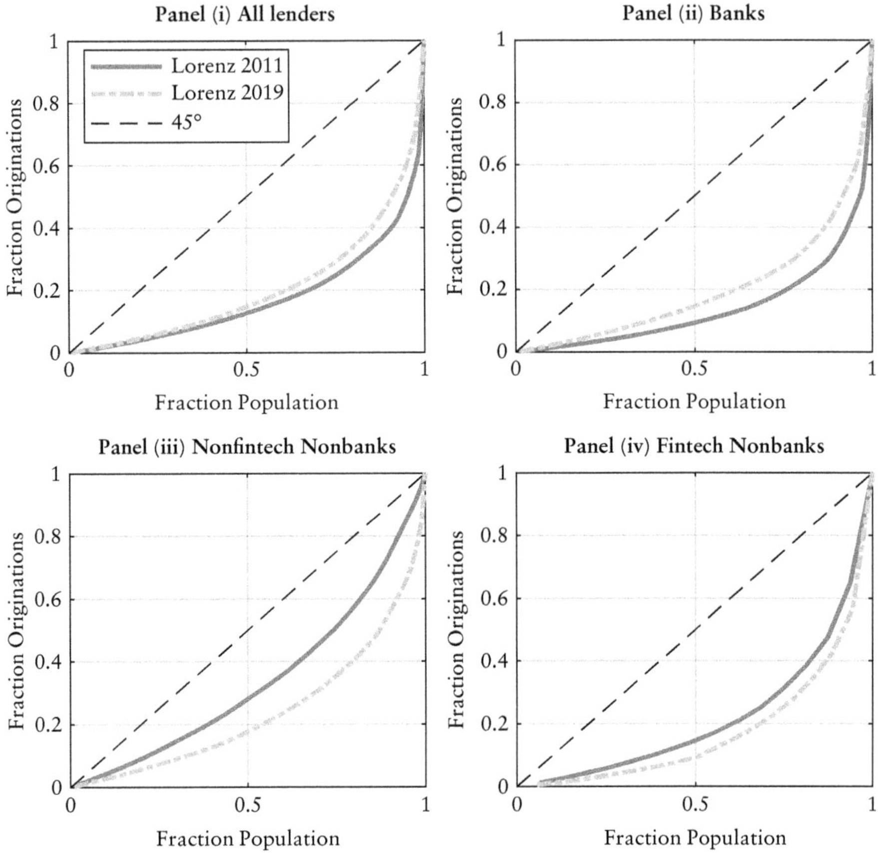

Note: Loan level data from HMDA. Our sample period was 2011 to 2019. We included all loans (both purchase and refinance as well as non-conventional loans). Classification based on latest version of lender classification data.[41]

Interestingly, panels (ii)–(iv) show that while concentration declined for banks, it increased for non-fintech and fintech nonbanks.

We also studied the evolution of market concentration using the HHI at the county level. Figure 10 shows the (loan-weighted) average of the US county level HHI for all lenders ('all lenders') and within bank type. As in the case of the national level estimates, we found that there was a decline in concentration during the period and that the fintech sector was significantly more concentrated

[41] ibid.

than the non-fintech nonbanks and banks. There was significant heterogeneity across counties, with some counties serviced completely by traditional banks and some completely by fintech lenders.[42] Other researchers have found that having a zip code level HHI greater than 625 (the 90th percentile value) is associated with a 3.7 percentage point greater fintech loan share.[43]

Figure 10 Local market concentration (overall and by lender type)

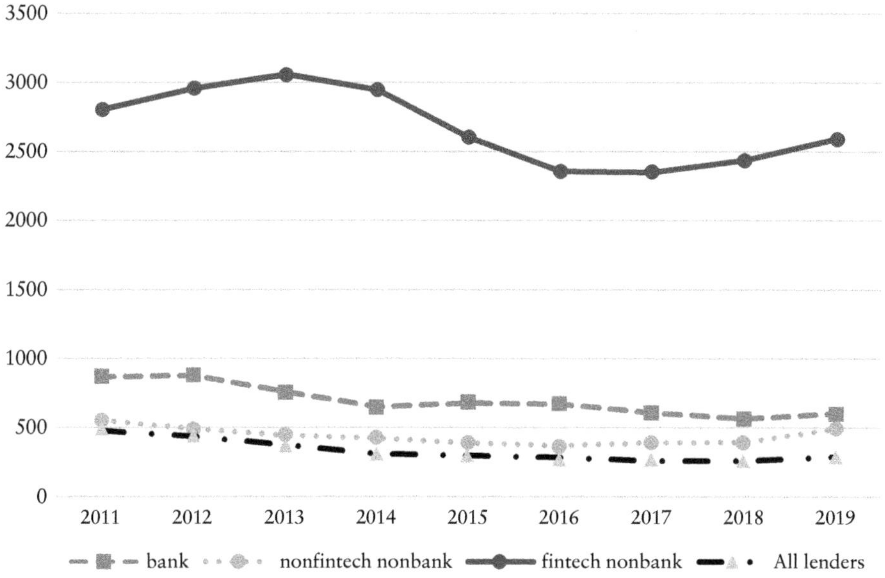

Note: Loan level data from HMDA. Our sample period was 2011 to 2019. We included all loans (both purchase and refinance as well as non-conventional loans). Classification based on latest version of lender classification data.[44] 'All lenders' refers to the HHI computed using all lender types. 'Bank', 'fintech nonbank' and 'non-fintech nonbank' correspond to the HHI within lenders classified as banks, fintech nonbanks and non-fintech nonbanks, respectively. The figure shows the loan-weighted average of the county level HHI.

We now turn to the analysis of mortgage interest rates. Using the Fannie Mae and Freddie Mac loan data for 2011–19, we tested differences between the interest rates charged by different bank types. We extended an existing approach to include dummies for the largest banks in each sector and focus on the

[42] eg, in 2016 Boyd County, Nebraska, was completely serviced by fintech lenders while Hooker County, in the same state, was completely serviced by traditional banks.

[43] Fuster et al (n 5) also show that loans originated in census tracts that are included in fewer than 10 banks. Community Reinvestment Act (CRA) assessment areas are more likely to be fintech compared with loans originated in tracts with more assessment areas.

[44] Buchak et al, 'Fintech, Regulatory Arbitrage, and the Rise of Shadow Banks' (n 3).

conforming loan sample reporting FICO scores.[45] We estimated the following regression:

$$rate_{ijzt} = \beta_1 FintechB_j + \beta_2 NonFintechNB_j + \beta_3 FintechNB_j + \beta_4 Largest_j + \beta_5 2nd\ Largest_j + \beta_6 3rd\ Largest_j + Z_j'\Theta + X_i'\Gamma + \delta_{zt} + \epsilon_{ijzt},$$

where an observation is a mortgage i, originated by lender j, in zip code z, in quarter t. The dependent variable $rate_{ijzt}$ is the mortgage rate in percentage points. $Fintech\ B_j$ corresponds to a dummy variable that takes value 1 if the lender is a fintech bank. Similarly, $NonFintech\ NB_j$ takes value 1 if the lender is a non-fintech nonbank, and $Fintech\ NB_j$ if the lender is a fintech nonbank. The rank dummies $Largest_j$, $2nd\ Largest_j$ and $3rd\ Largest_j$ represent whether lender j is the largest, second largest or third largest by loan amount in its sector, respectively. The vector Z_j' contains interacting terms between lender type dummies and lender rank dummies. We included borrower (mortgage) characteristics in X_i' and zip-time fixed effects in δ_{zt}.

Table 3 shows our results. The base group in the regressions in columns (1) and (2) is (traditional) banks, so the coefficients reported in these columns are relative to banks. For instance, the coefficient of the dummy 'nonbank' in column (1) shows that interest rate in a loan originated by a nonbank lender was, on average and after controlling for borrower and regional differences, 3.93 basis points higher than that of a traditional bank. Thus, nonbank lenders charged slightly higher interest rates than banks. When looking within this group along the lines of our lender classification (as in column (2)), we found that fintech lenders charged higher interest rates than non-fintech nonbanks, which charged higher interest rate than banks. This is consistent with previous evidence.[46] There is no evidence that fintech lenders originated riskier mortgages, suggesting that risk does not play a role in interest rate differentials.[47] The base group in columns (3) and (4) is non-top three banks, so coefficients in these columns are relative to this group. We found that interest rates increased with bank size, with the top three banks charging higher interest rates than others, but decreased with nonbank lender size, with lenders in the top three charging lower interest rates than banks and other nonbanks (column (3)). Column (4) shows that this was driven mostly by non-fintech nonbanks, while there was also evidence of fintech nonbanks charging lower interest rates. Focusing on size differences among nonbanks, column (6) shows that fintech lenders at the very top appeared to charge higher rates than non-fintech and smaller fintech lenders.

[45] ibid.

[46] ibid. A different sample that includes Federal Housing Administration loans shows that nonbank lenders charge higher interest rates on conventional loans but lower rates on Federal Housing Administration loans. See Buchak et al, 'Fintech, Regulatory Arbitrage, and the Rise of Shadow Banks' (n 3); and Fuster et al (n 5).

[47] Fuster et al (n 5).

Table 3 Interest rates by lender type

	Interest rate					
	All lenders				Non-Banks	
Lenders	(1)	(2)	(3)	(4)	(5)	(6)
Non-Bank	0.0393*** (0.0011)		0.0563*** (0.0015)			
Non-Fintech Non-Bank		0.0176*** (0.0013)		0.0628*** (0.0015)		
Fintech Non-Bank		0.0606*** (0.0013)		0.0325*** (0.0024)	0.0403*** (0.0014)	–0.0235*** (0.0019)
Largest			0.0279*** (0.0012)	0.0277*** (0.0012)		–0.0445*** (0.0022)
Second Largest			0.0619*** (0.0014)	0.0618*** (0.0014)		–0.0234*** (0.0026)
Third Largest			0.0331*** (0.0034)	0.0323*** (0.0034)		0.0137*** (0.0019)
Nonbank × Largest			–0.0042** (0.0019)			
Nonbank × Second Largest			–0.0617*** (0.0021)			
Nonbank × Third Largest			–0.0289*** (0.0037)			
Nonfintech Nonbank × Largest				–0.0799*** (0.0022)		
Nonfintech Nonbank × Second Largest				–0.0851*** (0.0031)		
Nonfintech Nonbank × Third Largest				–0.0206*** (0.0037)		
Fintech Nonbank × Largest				0.0518*** (0.0029)		0.1138*** (0.0033)
Fintech Nonbank × Second Largest				–0.0232*** (0.0027)		0.0614*** (0.0032)
Fintech Nonbank × Third Largest				–0.0223*** (0.0044)		–0.0098*** (0.0029)
Borrower and loan controls	Yes	Yes	Yes	Yes	Yes	Yes
Zip – Quarter FE	Yes	Yes	Yes	Yes	Yes	Yes
Adj R2	0.7051	0.7055	0.7058	0.7068	0.7087	0.7101

(continued)

Table 3 *(Continued)*

	Interest rate					
	All lenders				Non-Banks	
Lenders	(1)	(2)	(3)	(4)	(5)	(6)
Within Adj R2	0.4644	0.4652	0.4658	0.4675	0.4556	0.4581
Period	2011–19	2011–19	2011–19	2011–19	2011–19	2011–19
Num Observations	6,947,858	6,947,858	6,947,726	6,947,726	2,448,142	2,448,142

Note: Loan level data from Fannie Mae and Freddie Mac. Our sample period was 2011 to 2019. This sample included conforming loans only. Classification based on latest version of lender classification data.[48] Standard errors in parentheses. $^{*}p < 0.10$, $^{**}p < 0.05$, $^{***}p < 0.01$.

III. A SIMPLE MODEL

In this section, we present a simple model that allowed us to analyse the role of technology in explaining the concentration dynamics that we described in the previous section. The model environment closely follows the environment described elsewhere.[49]

A. Environment

There are three types of lenders that compete for a mass B of mortgage borrowers: (traditional) banks b, non-fintech nonbanks n and fintech nonbanks f. There are N_b number of banks, N_n non-fintech nonbanks, and N_f fintech nonbanks. Within each type, there are four heterogeneous lenders. The first three lenders of a type correspond to the largest, second largest and third largest lender, by loan amount, of that type in the data. We think of the fourth lender within a type as representative of the non-top three institutions. We denote lender types by $\tau \in \{b,n,f\}$ so that the number of the non-top three representative lenders of each type is equal to $N_\tau - 3$.

i. Demand

Lenders in the model are indexed i and offer mortgages at interest rate r_i. Borrower b's utility from choosing a mortgage from lender i is

$$u_{ib} = -\alpha r_i + q_i + \epsilon_{ib} \tag{1}$$

Borrower utility declines with the mortgage rate with $\alpha > 0$ measuring interest rate sensitivity. Borrowers also derive utility from nonprice attributes of lenders: $q_i + \epsilon_{ib}$. We think of q_i as the quality of financial services provided by lender i

[48] Buchak et al, 'Fintech, Regulatory Arbitrage, and the Rise of Shadow Banks' (n 3).
[49] ibid.

(eg, technological innovations that affect processing times, customer accessibility, the clarity of information provided to the customer, and the provision of a more comprehensive customer service). The rest of a borrower's utility from lender i is captured by ϵ_{ib}, an independent and identically distributed taste shock that we assume follows a type one extreme value distribution.

ii. Supply

Lenders differ in quality of service q_i and in the marginal costs of providing a mortgage ρ_i, which can reflect their external finance costs. Operating within a market entails a fixed entry cost c_i, such as the cost of basic regulatory registrations, offices and support staff. Note that lenders within a type τ are also heterogenous, so that the lender side of the economy is parameterised by each type's qualities $\{q_{\tau 1}, q_{\tau 2}, q_{\tau 3}, q_{\tau 4}\}_{\tau=b,n,f}$, funding costs $\{\rho_{\tau 1}, \rho_{\tau 2}, \rho_{\tau 3}, \rho_{\tau 4}\}_{\tau=b,n,f}$ and fixed entry costs $\{c_{\tau 1}, c_{\tau 2}, c_{\tau 3}, c_{\tau 4}\}_{\tau=b,n,f}$.

In addition to changing a bank's marginal cost, regulatory burdens may also reduce traditional banks' activities on the extensive margin. For example, binding capital requirements raise the cost of making loans. Our model captures this type of regulatory burden through parameter γ_b. If lender i is a bank, its probability of lending to a specific borrower is scaled by a factor γ_b. A higher γ_b captures a relatively unconstrained bank, a lower γ_b captures a relatively constrained bank. Throughout the model, we assume that nonbanks are not subject to such regulatory burdens, so we set $\gamma_n = 1$ and $\gamma_f = 1$. If the market share a bank would have obtained without regulatory burdens is s_i, then the actual market share is $\gamma_b S_i$.

Conditional on being present in a market, a lender sets its interest rate r_i to maximise its expected profit:

$$\pi_i = (r_i - \rho_i)\gamma_i s_i F - c_i \qquad (2),$$

where F is the total face value of loans in the market (ie, size of the mortgage market). A lender only operates in a market as long as $\pi_i \geq 0$.

iii. Equilibrium

An equilibrium is a market structure comprising the number of lenders of each type N_τ, the pricing decisions of lenders $r_{\tau i}$ and the market shares of lenders $s_{\tau i}$ such that:

1. Borrowers maximise utility in equation (1), taking market structure and pricing as given.
2. Lenders set interest rates to maximise profits, taking market structure and the pricing decisions of other lenders as given.
3. There is free entry: the number of firms of each type N_τ is set such that profits of all firms are zero. (Eq (2) equals zero for all lenders i).

Given the type one extreme value distribution of idiosyncratic taste shocks ϵ_{ib}, consumers' optimal choices result in standard logistic market shares:

$$s_i\left(r_i, q_i; \{r_j, q_j\}\right) = \frac{\exp(\alpha\, r_i + q_i)}{\sum_{j=1}^{N}\exp\left(\alpha\, r_j + q_j\right)},$$

where N is the total number of lenders in the economy. That is, $N = N_b + N_n + N_f$.

Given regulatory burdens γ_i, the actual market shares of a lender i of type τ is given by:

$$\hat{s}_{i\tau}\left(r_{i\tau}, q_{i\tau}; N_\tau, N_{-\tau}\right) = \frac{\gamma_\tau \exp(\alpha\, r_{i\tau} + q_{i\tau})}{\sum_\tau \sum_{j=1}^{N_\tau}\gamma_\tau \exp\left(\alpha\, r_j + q_j\right)}.$$

The total market share of a type τ is the sum of individual lenders' market shares within the type, which is given by:

$$S_\tau = \sum_{i=1}^{N_\tau} \hat{s}_{i\tau}\left(r_{i\tau}, q_{i\tau}; N_\tau, N_{-\tau}\right).$$

The solution to the lender's profit-maximisation problem over interest rate choice gives the standard expression for markup over funding costs as a function of market share:

$$r^*_{i\tau}\left(N_\tau, N_{-\tau}\right) - \rho_{i\tau} = \frac{1}{\alpha}\,\frac{1}{1 - \hat{s}_{i\tau}\left(r_{i\tau}, q_{i\tau}; N_\tau, N_{-\tau}\right)} \tag{3}$$

Equation (3) makes it clear that the more inelastic/insensitive demand is to interest rates (ie, the smaller the α), the higher the markup, and the greater the market share of a particular bank of type τ (ie, the higher the $\hat{s}_{i\tau}$), the higher the markup of the bank (ie, the higher the $\left(r^*_{i\tau}\left(N_\tau, N_{-\tau}\right) - \rho_{i\tau}\right)$. Lastly, zero-profit conditions pin down the number of banks of each type τ:

$$\pi_i\left(N_\tau, N_{-\tau}\right) = \left(r^*_{i\tau}\left(N_\tau, N_{-\tau}\right) - \rho_{i\tau}\right)\hat{s}_{i\tau}\left(r_{i\tau}, q_{i\tau}; N_\tau, N_{-\tau}\right)F - c_{i\tau} = 0$$

B. Calibration

In order to quantify the contribution of lender quality to changes in market share and concentration in the industry, we needed to calibrate the parameters of the model. We allowed the parameters to change from year to year to give the model enough degrees of freedom to exactly match the data on interest rates, market shares, the size of the market and the number of lenders by lender type. More specifically, we used the data presented in section II to obtain values for the sequence of parameters $q_{i\tau}, \rho_{i\tau}, c_{i\tau}, \alpha$, and γ_b between 2011 and 2019. For each year, we observed the number of lenders by type $N_{i\tau}$, the market share of each lender $\hat{s}_{i\tau}$, the loan interest rates $r_{i\tau}$ and the total size of the market F. We used a strategy similar to that described elsewhere and made the following identifying assumptions:[50]

Assumption 1: funding costs are measured relative to 10-year US treasury yield (ie, $\tilde{\rho} = \rho - r^{10}$).

Assumption 2: quality and funding costs are relative to non-top three banks (a normalisation):

$$\tilde{\rho}_{4b} = q_{4b} = 0.$$

Assumption 3: $q_{4b} - q_{4n}$ is constant. That is, the difference in service quality between non-top three banks and non-top three non-fintech nonbank is constant.

Assumption 4: in the first year in our sample (ie, 2011), $\gamma_b = 1$.

Table 4 shows the calibrated values for 2011 and 2019 by lender type.[51] Our calibrated parameters imply that in 2011, top lenders offered higher quality services than lenders not in the top three, with the top banks having the highest quality, followed by fintech and non-fintech nonbanks. The ranking was similar across lenders not in the top three, with non-fintech nonbanks offering the lowest quality lending services. The data show that between 2011 and 2019, quality improved for most lenders (except top banks) and that the largest gains were in the top non-fintech nonbanks, followed by fintech nonbanks. The changes are significant, but not large enough to reverse the original ranking completely, with the top fintech moving from fourth place to second place in the ranking. We linked the estimated reduction in bank quality to the reduction in the fraction of consumers that expressed a preference for the person-to-person and branch-based interaction that is at the core of the (traditional) bank business model. Technology and advertising make consumers more aware of options and more likely to search and find better alternatives.[52] The increase in estimated fintech quality can be associated with fintech technological innovations that reduce the cost of applying for a loan and involve no human loan officer. The experiments presented in the following section study the role of these quality changes in explaining the changes in lender market shares and the dynamics of concentration.

[50] ibid. See Appendix VII.B for more details on the calibration strategy.

[51] Appendix VII.B presents the full-time series of the estimated parameters by lender type.

[52] E Honka, A Hortaçsu and MA Vitorino, 'Advertising, Consumer Awareness, and Choice: Evidence from the US Banking Industry' (2017) 48 *Rand Journal of Economics* 611.

Table 4 also shows that there is a relatively homogeneous decline in funding costs (with the smallest decline for the top bank and the largest for the top fintech and non-fintech nonbanks). As stated in identifying Assumption 2 above, we normalised the funding cost spread for non-top three banks to zero, so changes in funding costs for this group displayed in Table 4 correspond one-to-one to changes in the 10-year US treasury yield. That means that the table also reveals a significant variation in terms of entry costs. In 2011, top lenders (across all types) showed the highest cost, with entry into banking being more costly than entry into fintech and non-fintech nonbanking. In 2019, in line with changes in market shares, the top fintech lender showed the highest entry cost. All lenders except the top bank had an increase in entry costs between 2011 and 2019, with the largest increase happening at the very top of the distribution of nonbanks.

Table 4 Calibrated parameters (2011 and 2019)

	Lender Type	q			ρ (%)			c (bn $)		
		2011	2019	Δ	2011	2019	Δ	2011	2019	Δ
B	Largest	3.97	2.99	–0.98	2.52	2.03	–0.49	3.02	2.64	–0.38
B	Second largest	3.27	2.66	–0.61	2.72	2.11	–0.61	1.29	1.82	0.53
B	Third largest	3.00	2.62	–0.38	2.72	2.08	–0.64	0.99	1.77	0.78
B	Non-top three	0.00	0.00	0.00	2.78	2.14	–0.64	0.05	0.13	0.08
N	Largest	0.78	2.36	1.58	2.79	2.04	–0.75	0.10	2.27	2.16
N	Second largest	0.49	1.40	0.91	2.82	2.14	–0.67	0.07	0.82	0.75
N	Third largest	0.42	1.34	0.92	2.85	2.18	–0.67	0.07	0.76	0.69
N	Non-top three	–0.57	–0.57	0.00	2.84	2.20	–0.64	0.03	0.11	0.09
F	Largest	2.10	2.68	0.58	2.86	2.10	–0.77	0.36	3.03	2.67
F	Second largest	1.36	1.51	0.15	2.84	2.17	–0.67	0.18	0.91	0.73
F	Third largest	0.72	1.01	0.29	2.82	2.16	–0.66	0.09	0.55	0.46
F	Non-top three	–0.46	–0.30	0.16	2.81	2.17	–0.64	0.03	0.15	0.12

Note: Calibrated parameters using loan level data from Fannie Mae and Freddie Mac and HMDA. Our sample period was 2011 to 2019. This sample includes conforming loans only. Classification based on latest version of lender classification data.[53] Lender type 'B' refers to banks, 'NF' to non-fintech nonbank and 'F' to fintech nonbank.

IV. MAIN EXPERIMENTS AND RESULTS

We used the model to perform our main experiments. The goal was to understand the impact of technology (lender quality) and costs on the dynamics of lender market shares and concentration.

[53] Buchak et al, 'Fintech, Regulatory Arbitrage, and the Rise of Shadow Banks' (n 3).

In our first experiment, and to set a baseline, we analysed the evolution of the industry if the calibrated parameters $\{\gamma_j, q_j\}$ had remained constant at their 2011 levels and the fixed operating cost c_j and the funding costs ρ_j had evolved as shown in Table 3.[54] We called this experiment 'costs', as it captures the effect of changes in the estimated lenders' cost structure. As pointed out by others, changes in the fixed operating cost c_j are partly induced by increased regulatory burdens after the 2010 Dodd–Frank Act.[55] The solution to this experiment provides a path of interest rates, market shares and number of banks consistent with a counterfactual world where only costs change between 2011 and 2019.[56]

We found that changes in costs explained about a quarter of the increase in the market share of non-fintech nonbanks and only a tenth of the increase in fintech lending (Figure 11). Changes in funding costs were relatively homogeneous among nonbanks, with an average and median reduction of 68 basis points. They were about 10–25 basis points smaller for banks than for nonbanks, with larger differences observed at the very top of the distribution, explaining the changes in market shares and number of lenders. Figure 10 shows changes in concentration for the entire market and by lender type. Changes in overall concentration were significant in the data (and our calibration), but almost none of those changes derived from changes in costs (as the overall change in HHI under 'costs' was negligible).

This result hides important heterogeneity within type. Both bank and fintech concentration increased due to changes in costs (non-fintech lenders' concentration declined slightly). In the case of banks, the increase in concentration derived from the reduction in operating costs for the very top bank (versus an increase for all other bank lenders, which saw operating costs more than double between 2011 and 2019). This led to a significant decline in market share for banks not in the top three (about 70 per cent of their overall reduction in lending between 2011 and 2019) and a decline in the number of non-top three banks (28 banks exited the market in the counterfactual experiment). In the case of fintech nonbanks, the increase in concentration derived from the larger reduction in funding costs, mitigated to some extent by the increase in operating costs for the top nonbanks that resulted in an increase in market share for top fintech lenders. In this experiment, our measure of within-group HHI variation was positive, as there was an increase in the HHI for banks and fintech nonbanks. Figure 12 shows that the overall change in the HHI in the 'costs' experiment was almost null, implying that, in this case, the within-group variation was fully

[54] The parameter that controls the demand elasticity α also evolves in step with the calibrated values. We assume that entry costs for top lenders of each type adjust so there is at most one lender as the largest, one as the second largest and one as the third largest for each type.

[55] K Liu, 'The Impact of the Dodd–Frank Act on Small US Banks' (2022) *Mimeo*, available at: ssrn.com/abstract=3419586.

[56] The solution sets a baseline, as our second experiment incorporates changes in quality in addition to changes in costs. The effects of changes in quality correspond to the differential effect between the result of that experiment and this baseline.

compensated by the between-group HHI variation, driven by the decline in the market share of banks.

Figure 11 Changes in market shares and number of lenders

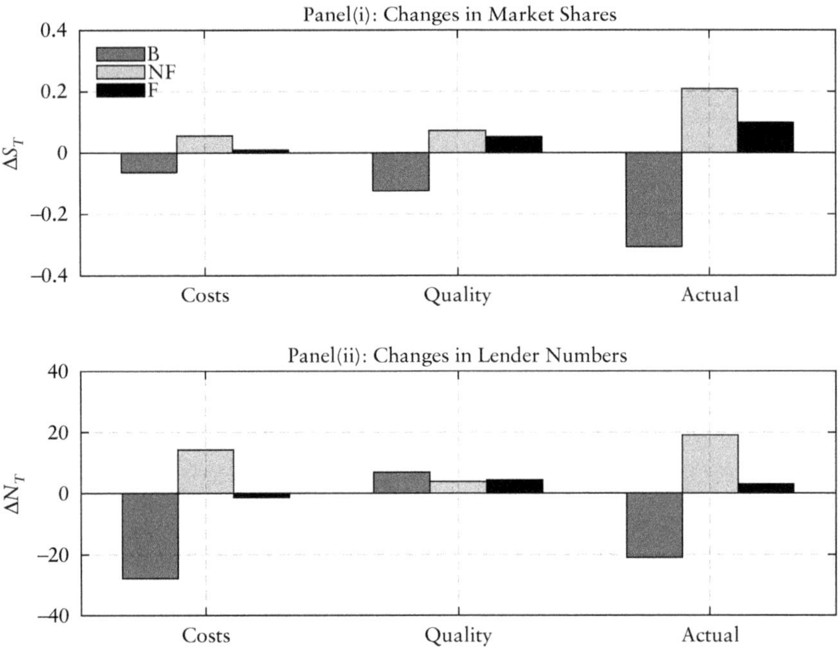

Note: Counterfactuals for the change in lender market shares and number of lenders implied by our model. 'Costs' refers to the counterfactual that evaluates changes to operating and funding costs only. 'Quality' refers to the counterfactual that evaluates changes to the lender quality parameters only. 'B' refers to banks, 'NF' to non-fintech nonbanks and 'F' to fintech nonbanks.

In our second experiment, we analysed how changes in lender quality (technology) affected the equilibrium outcome. We called this experiment 'quality' and it captured changes in consumer preferences toward non-traditional lenders as well as fintech technological innovations that reduced friction in mortgage lending.[57] In particular, we solved the equilibrium of the model keeping the value of γ_j constant at the calibrated value in 2011 and used the calibrated sequence of $\{c_j, p_j, q_j\}$. The difference between the outcomes in this experiment and that in the baseline experiment ('costs') allowed us to quantify the impact of lender quality and technology.

[57] As analysed empirically in Fuster et al (n 5) and Buchak et al, 'Fintech, Regulatory Arbitrage, and the Rise of Shadow Banks' (n 3). Fuster et al (n 5) document that fintech lenders process mortgages faster than traditional lenders and that fintech lenders respond more elastically to changes in mortgage demand.

Figure 11 shows that changes in quality explained 40 per cent of the decline in bank market shares, 35 per cent of the market share gain of non-fintech nonbanks, and more than 50 per cent of the increase in the market share of fintech nonbanks. As described in the previous section, the calibrated parameters showed a significant decline in q_j for banks (a 13–25 per cent reduction) and an increase for all nonbanks (slightly more pronounced for non-fintech). These quality dynamics explained the decrease in the bank market share with most of the effect deriving from the intensive margin (ie, lending activity by incumbent banks) at the top of the distribution. Top banks reduced their lending by up to 10 per cent. The number of banks (not in the top three) increased (+7), but the change was not large enough to compensate for the lending reduction by large banks. In the case of nonbank lenders (both non-fintech and fintech), the increase in quality resulted in positive changes along both the intensive and the extensive margin (ie, changes in the amount of lending by incumbent lenders and changes in the number of lenders, respectively). The portion of the total change explained by quality changes in the fintech sector in our experiment was consistent with previous results.[58] With a smaller increase in quality, most of the change in fintech lending derived from the extensive margin (the number of fintech lenders almost doubled).

Figure 12 shows that the dynamics of lender quality have important implications for overall and within-group lender concentration. This experiment explained 97 per cent of the overall change in the HHI with the reduction in the bank HHI more than explaining the overall change (as previously described, the 'costs' experiment reversed some of this decline). With a completely different outcome, we observed that the increase in quality concentrated in the top nonbanks (fintech and non-fintech) resulted in a large increase in concentration of nonbanks. The results showed that the 'quality' experiment more than explained the total change in concentration within the nonbank sector (as measured with both the HHI and C3).

In summary, we found that quality (or technology) improvements in the nonbank sector explained most of the variation in market shares and concentration observed in the data. In the case of market shares, it explained 40, 35 and 53 per cent for banks, non-fintech nonbanks and fintech nonbanks, respectively. In the case of concentration (when measured using the HHI), quality explained almost all of the overall variation. In the cases of banks and non-fintech nonbanks, quality explained more than the total variation in concentration observed in data.[59] As Table 4 shows, this was the result of the significant changes in quality observed at the very top of the distribution in both the bank

[58] Buchak et al, 'Fintech, Regulatory Arbitrage, and the Rise of Shadow Banks' (n 3).

[59] This means that changes in quality alone generated a larger change in non-fintech nonbank concentration than what was observed in the data. The changes arising from the 'costs' experiment offset this effect of quality changes.

and the non-fintech nonbank group. Finally, quality explained 43 per cent of the changes in fintech concentration. While there are important changes in quality at the top of the distribution, we estimated quality changes to be more homogeneous among fintech nonbanks.

Figure 12 Changes in concentration (HHI and C)

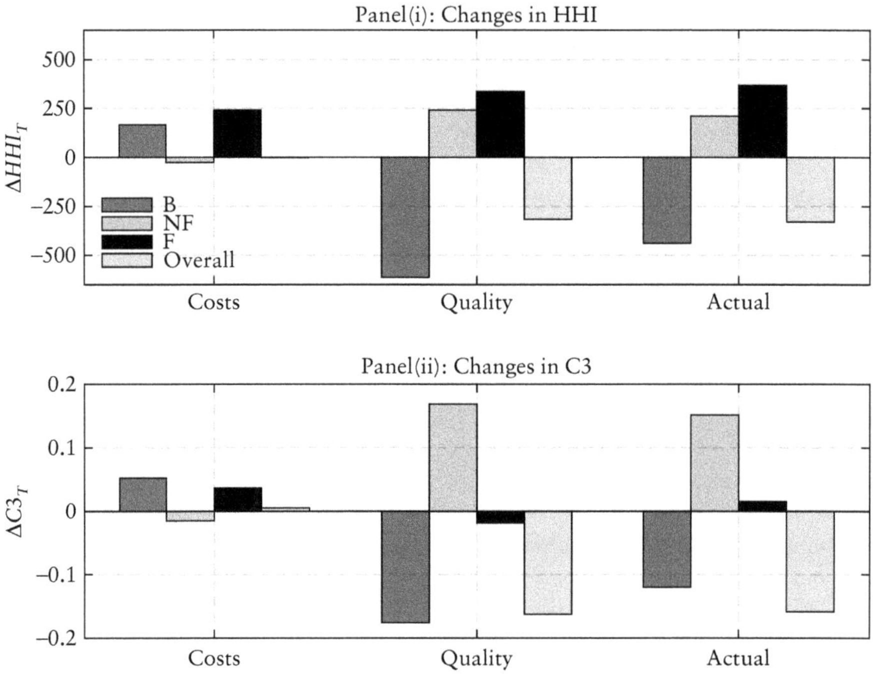

Note: Counterfactuals for the change in lender market shares and number of lenders implied by our model. 'Costs' refers to the counterfactual that evaluates changes to operating and funding costs only. 'Quality' refers to the counterfactual that evaluates changes to the lender quality parameters only. 'Overall' corresponds to measures of concentration computed using all lenders, 'B' refers to banks, 'NF' to non-fintech nonbanks and 'F' to fintech nonbanks.

V. FINAL REMARKS AND DIRECTIONS FOR FUTURE RESEARCH

This chapter presents evidence on concentration in the residential mortgage market and the role of fintech lenders. Consistent with previous literature, we find that the industry is shifting towards nonbank lenders. In addition, we describe in this chapter that fintech lending is significantly more concentrated than bank and other nonbank lenders. We used our model to show that changes in lender quality and technology play a crucial role in explaining the dynamics of the market and the evolution of concentration over time.

There is a key trade-off to be considered when analysing the observed changes in concentration. On one hand, as we estimate, one of the drivers of the shift towards nonbank fintech lenders (and the implied effect on concentration) is the increase in lender quality, which reflects that consumers derive higher benefits from their borrowing activity. On the other hand, a shift towards a lender sector (nonbank fintech) with higher concentration has negative implications for competition and consumer surplus. Moreover, it is important to consider that nonbanks do not rely on insured deposits. Therefore, their increased participation might not be problematic so long as they do not pose a risk to financial stability (ie, risk to other financial institutions or systemic risk). The model in this chapter is not well suited to quantify the relative magnitudes of these effects; thus, we leave this interesting analysis for future research.

The focus of our chapter has been concentration in the fintech industry and the role of changes in lender quality and technology. We also leave for future research the role of regulatory changes, such as capital and liquidity requirements. Further, we plan to study the role in promoting market concentration of the originate-to-distribute model that derives from the implicit guarantee that government agencies offer and its associated moral hazard problem, similar to deposit insurance. This business model is prevalent among nonbanks and, especially, fintech lenders.

APPENDIX I

A. HHI Decomposition

Let l_i denote loans originated by lender *i* and *L* the total value of loans originated. Total loans originated by banks (B) are denoted by L^B, total loans originated by non-fintech nonbank L^{NF}, and total loans by fintech nonbanks L^F. Then, we can decompose the HHI as follows:

$$HHI_t = \sum_{i=1}^{N} s_{i,t}^2 = \sum_{i=1}^{N_t} \left(\frac{l_{i,t}}{L_t} \right)^2$$

$$= \sum_{i \in B} \left(\frac{L_t^B}{L_t} \right)^2 \left(\frac{l_{i,t}}{L_t^B} \right)^2 + \sum_{i \in B} \left(\frac{L_t^{NF}}{L_t} \right)^2 \left(\frac{l_{i,t}}{L_t^{NF}} \right)^2 + \sum_{i \in B} \left(\frac{L_t^F}{L_t} \right)^2 \left(\frac{l_{i,t}}{L_t^F} \right)^2,$$

$$= \left(S_t^B \right)^2 HHI_t^B + \left(S_t^{NF} \right)^2 HHI_t^{NF} + \left(S_t^F \right)^2 HHI_t^F$$

where S_t^j and HHI_t^j denote the market shares and the HHI, respectively, within type $j \in \{B, NF, F\}$ (ie, when the market is defined using loans from lenders of type *j*).[60] Expanding the overall HHI in this way shows that changes in overall concentration between periods *t* and any period τ can be decomposed in changes between groups (ie, changes derived from changes in market shares)

[60] As seen in Rossi-Hansberg et al (n 32).

and changes within groups (ie, changes derived from changes in concentration within groups). More specifically, we can write:

$$\Delta HHI_t = HHI_t - HHI_\tau = \sum_{j\in\{B,NF,F\}} \left(s_t^j\right)^2 HHI_t^j - \left(s_\tau^j\right)^2 HHI_\tau^j$$

$$= \sum_{j\in\{B,NF,F\}} \Delta\left(s_t^j\right)^2 HHI_t^j - \sum_{j\in\{B,NF,F\}} \left(s_\tau^j\right)^2 \Delta HHI_t^j .$$

We call the first term 'ΔHHI_t between' and the second term 'ΔHHI_t within'.

B. Calibration Details

In this appendix, we present further details of the calibration strategy. The calibration process is as follows. Using the optimal pricing equation (ie, Eq. (3)) of non-top three banks and data on the average interest rate and market shares of non-top three banks, we pin down α:

$$\alpha = \frac{1}{r_{4b}} \frac{1}{1-\hat{s}_{4b}}.$$

This gives a common (across-lender) value of α that varies from year to year.[61] To calibrate the service quality of the non-top three non-fintech nonbank, q_{4n}, we first take the ratio of market shares between the non-top three non-fintech nonbank and the non-top three bank in 2011 (when $\gamma_{4b} = \gamma_{4n} = 1$):

$$\frac{\hat{s}_{4n}}{\hat{s}_{4b}} = \frac{\exp(\alpha r_{4n} + q_{4n})}{\exp(\alpha r_{4b} + q_{4b})}.$$

Rearranging the terms in this ratio and using the assumption that $q_{4b} = 0$, we solve for the value of q_{4n} in 2011:

$$q_{4n} = \alpha(r_{4n} - r_{4b}) + \ln\left(\frac{\hat{s}_{4n}}{\hat{s}_{4b}}\right).$$

Based on *Assumption 3* above, q_{4n} stays constant over the sample period. Therefore, once we know q_{4n} in 2011, we also know q_{4n} for all later years.

[61] Using the optimal pricing equation of non-top three banks is convenient as ρ_{4b} is normalised to zero, so we do not need to set a value for ρ to solve for α.

Similarly, we may solve for $q_{i\tau}$ for the top three banks by taking the ratios of their market share to the market share of non-top three banks (since $q_{4b} = 0$ and γ_b is the same across banks, it is straightforward to solve for q_{ib}). Having obtained q_{4n}, we solve for q_{in} and q_{if} by taking the ratios of their market shares to the market share of the non-top three non-fintech nonbanks $(\hat{s}_{4n})$. Using data on interest rates and market shares, we obtain a sequence of $q_{i\tau}$ for every year in the sample.

Next, we calibrate the funding costs for each lender. Inverting the optimal pricing equation (Eq (3)), and with the value of α at hand, we solve for the funding cost spread (over the 10-year treasury rate) for lender i of type τ at year t as follows:

$$\tilde{\rho}_{i\tau} = (r_{i\tau} - r^{10}) + \frac{1}{\alpha}\frac{1}{1-\hat{s}_{i\tau}}.$$

Having obtained $q_{i\tau}$ for all lenders in all years, we are also ready to solve for the regulatory burden faced by banks – γ_b – by taking the ratio of the market share of any bank and the market share of any nonbank. The value of γ_b is then obtained by rearranging items in that ratio:

$$\gamma_b = \alpha(r_{ib} - r_{in}) + \ln\left(\frac{\hat{s}_{ib}}{\hat{s}_{in}}\right) + q_{in} - q_{ib}.$$

Finally, we pin down the fixed costs of lenders by solving for $c_{i\tau}$ using the free entry condition:

$$c_{i\tau} = \left(r_{i\tau} - \tilde{\rho}_{i\tau} - r^{10}\right)\hat{s}_{i\tau}F.$$

Table 4 in the main text presented the value of the estimated parameters for 2011 and 2019. In this appendix, we complete the description of our calibration by showing the full time series. Figure A.1 shows the value of α_t. The average value is 0.597, with a minimum of 0.449 and a maximum of 0.832. Figures A.2–A.4 present the estimated lender qualities (q_τ), entry costs (c_τ) and funding costs (ρ_τ), respectively, by lender type in each year from 2011 to 2019. Panel (i) shows the corresponding values for banks, panel (ii) the values for non-fintech nonbanks and panel (iii) the value for fintech nonbanks.

Figure A.1 Demand elasticity

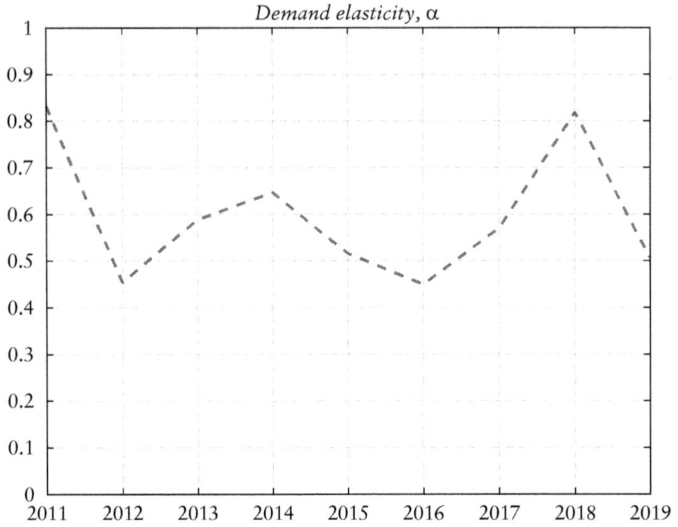

Figure A.2 Lender quality q_τ (by lender type)

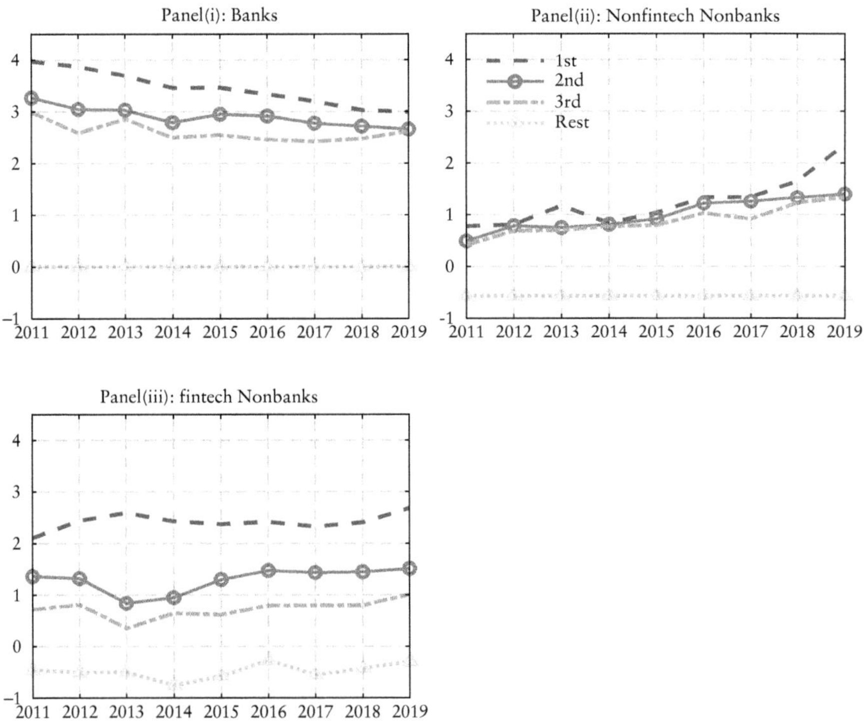

Figure A.3 Lender entry cost c_τ (in billions \$, by lender type)

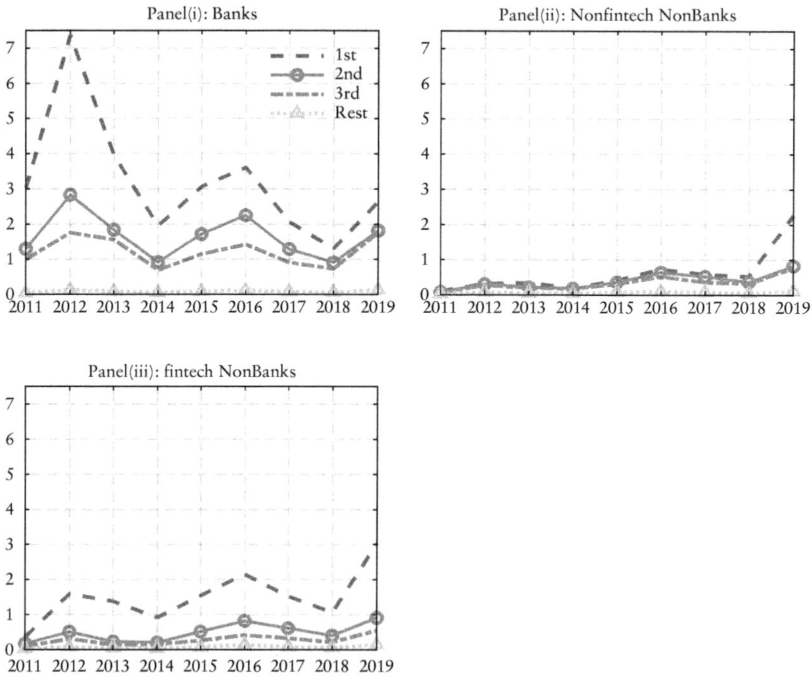

Figure A.4 Funding costs ρ_τ (in %, by lender type)

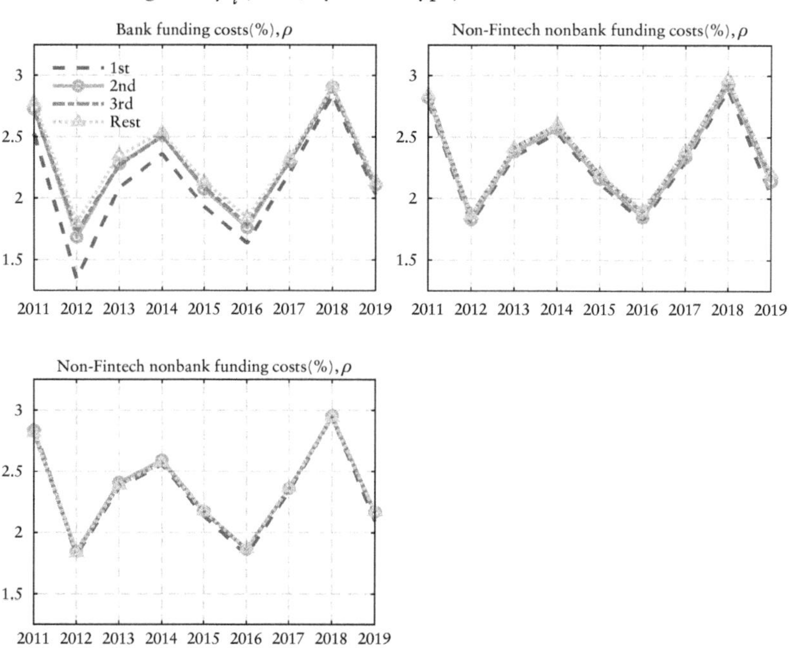

4

Common Ownership in Fintech Markets

ANNA TZANAKI, LIUDMILA ALEKSEEVA AND JOSÉ AZAR

I. INTRODUCTION

IS COMMON OWNERSHIP in fintech companies an empirically significant phenomenon? What impact does it have on competition and innovation in fintech markets and what implications does it carry for competition law enforcement? This chapter studies these questions, providing evidence and insights regarding the extent of common shareholdings held by different types of investors in different types of firms and the likely concerns in selected fintech market segments and countries. It also comments on how the specific ownership and governance structures of fintech firms may materially influence the magnitude and systemic nature of effects associated with common ownership.

Fintech markets differ in a number of important ways from traditional markets, which are usually less dynamic. Fintech firms are seldom publicly listed companies, for which the common ownership phenomenon has been more extensively empirically studied. This affects the empirical and theoretical dimensions of potential competitive effects. On the other hand, it also creates distinct challenges and opportunities for competition law enforcement, which have thus far been under-theorised and under-appreciated. By shedding light on these novel issues surrounding common ownership in fintech as well as the complex relationships between fintech competition, innovation and investment, this chapter aims to deepen the analysis of the implications of common ownership for the operation of firms and markets. As such, it also aims to provide useful guidance to antitrust policymakers for appropriate future action.

The structure of the chapter is as follows. Section II presents empirical evidence on the extent of common ownership in fintech markets across various types of firms, investors and countries. Section III studies the potential impact of common ownership on fintech firms' behaviour and market competition. Section IV discusses the implications of the findings for competition law enforcement. Section V concludes by summarising the key takeaways of the chapter.

II. COMMON OWNERSHIP IN FINTECH MARKETS

Common ownership, the simultaneous ownership of minority shares in competing firms by institutional investors, has recently been the subject of novel economic theory and empirical studies suggesting potential effects on competition and innovation.[1] Most empirical evidence gathered thus far focuses on US markets and publicly listed firms, in which a small group of large institutional investors such as mutual and index funds have extensive common shareholdings.[2] The issue has gained significant attention given the meteoric rise of index funds and their asset managers – the so-called 'Big Three' (BlackRock, Vanguard, State Street) – in light of the recent increasing growth of portfolio diversification and passive investment strategies.[3] Scholars have specifically linked the recent rapid and significant increase in common ownership in public markets to the enormous success of passive index funds as an easier and cheaper means of portfolio diversification and the dramatic growth of (quasi) indexing, including index-tracking exchange-traded funds (ETFs) and quasi-indexer mutual funds.[4] In turn, this unprecedented capital concentration has triggered discussions about the potential implications for competition and consumers of institutional common ownership in multiple rival firms within the same industry (and often the largest ones).[5]

[1] Organisation for Economic Co-operation and Development (OECD), 'Common Ownership by Institutional Investors and Its Impact on Competition' (2017) DAF/COMP(2017) 10 (summarising the literature).

[2] J Azar, MC Schmalz and I Tecu, 'Anticompetitive Effects of Common Ownership' (2018) 73 *Journal of Finance* 1513; J Azar, S Raina and M Schmalz, 'Ultimate Ownership and Bank Competition' (2022) 51 *Financial Management* 227; M Torshizi and J Clapp, 'Price Effects of Common Ownership in the Seed Sector' (2019) 66 *Antitrust Bulletin* 1; M Backus, C Conlon and M Sinkinson, 'Common Ownership and Competition in the Ready-to-Eat Cereal Industry' (2021) NBER Working Paper 28350; A Banal-Estañol, M Newham and J Seldeslachts, 'Common Ownership in the US Pharmaceutical Industry: A Network Analysis' (2021) 66 *Antitrust Bulletin* 68; J Xie, 'Horizontal Shareholdings and Paragraph IV Generic Entry in the US Pharmaceutical Industry' (2021) 66 *Antitrust Bulletin* 100.

[3] LA Bebchuk and S Hirst, 'The Specter of the Giant Three' (2019) 99 *Boston University Law Review* 721; J Azar, 'The Common Ownership Trilemma' (2020) 87 *University of Chicago Law Review* 263.

[4] Azar, 'The Common Ownership Trilemma' (n 3); J Fichtner, EM Heemskerk and J Garcia-Bernardo, 'Hidden Power of the Big Three? Passive Index Funds, Re-Concentration of Corporate Ownership, and New Financial Risk' (2017) 19 *Business and Politics* 298; J Harford, D Jenter and K Li, 'Institutional Cross-Holdings and their Effect on Acquisition Decisions' (2011) 99 *Journal of Financial Economics* 27; M Backus, C Conlon and M Sinkinson, 'Common Ownership in America: 1980–2017' (2021) 13 *American Economic Journal: Microeconomics* 273; JC Coates, 'The Future of Corporate Governance Part I: The Problem of Twelve' (2018) Harvard Public Law Working Paper No 19-07. Azar, ibid, 269 and Fichtner et al, ibid, 304 note that more than 80% of the equity assets of each of the Big Three asset managers comprises of index funds. According to Azar, it is this that has led to the Big Three's growth and concentration, which collectively have an 81% share of index funds assets, and their extensive common shareholdings in almost all publicly listed firms in the US.

[5] OECD, 'Common Ownership by Institutional Investors' (n 1); Federal Trade Commission, 'US FTC Hearings on Competition and Consumer Protection in the 21st Century, Panel #8: Common Ownership' (6 December 2018).

However, common ownership is a broader phenomenon that is not limited to a specific type of common shareholders, such as the Big Three, or to a specific type of commonly held firms, such as publicly traded companies or firms in direct competitive relationship.[6] But so far, there has been little evidence provided on common ownership in private or closely held companies, which is the most common form for start-ups and fintech firms. Although the presence of large investment funds is less pronounced in countries outside the United States, there is emerging evidence that common shareholding is as prevalent in Europe and Australia, making politicians and competition law policymakers attentive to the evolution and impact of this new phenomenon.[7] It is also well understood that the (degree of) common ownership and its likely effects may vary across different markets[8] and depend on the type of common (and non-common) investors and commonly held firms, ie, the specific ownership and governance structures in place in each individual case.[9] Importantly, common ownership has been shown to have potentially opposing effects on competition (negative) and innovation (positive) within a given industry (intra-industry) and further potential beneficial effects across industries (inter-industry).[10]

[6] A Tzanaki, 'Varieties and Mechanisms of Common Ownership: A Calibration Exercise for Competition Policy' (2022) 18 *Journal of Competition Law & Economics* 168; J Azar and X Vives, 'Revisiting the Anticompetitive Effects of Common Ownership' (2022) European Corporate Governance Institute – Finance Working Paper No 827/2022.

[7] N Rosati et al, 'Common Shareholding in Europe' (Publications Office of the European Union 2020) EUR – Scientific and Technical Research Reports (JRC121476); S Frazzani et al, 'Barriers to Competition through Joint Ownership by Institutional Investors' (2020) Study for the Committee on Economic and Monetary Affairs, European Parliament, Luxembourg; N Rosati, P Bomprezzi and M Martinez Cillero, 'Institutional Investors and Common Ownership in the European Energy Sector', available at: papers.ssrn.com/abstract=4046563; Monopolkommission, 'Hauptgutachten XXIV: Wettbewerb 2022' (5 July 2022); Monopolkommission, 'Biennial Report XXII: Competition 2018' (3 July 2018); Competition and Markets Authority (CMA), 'State of UK Competition Report 2022' (29 April 2022); Note by the United Kingdom, 'OECD Roundtable on Common Ownership by Institutional Investors and its Impact on Competition' (2017) DAF/COMP/WD(2017) 92; Parliament of the Commonwealth of Australia, 'Report on the Implications of Common Ownership and Capital Concentration in Australia' (2022) House of Representatives Standing Committee on Economics.

[8] MC Schmalz, 'Recent Studies on Common Ownership, Firm Behavior, and Market Outcomes' (2021) 66 *Antitrust Bulletin* 12; M Patel, 'Common Ownership, Institutional Investors, and Antitrust' (2018) 82 *Antitrust Law Journal* 279; J Seldeslachts, M Newham and A Banal-Estañol, 'Changes in Common Ownership of German Companies' (2017) 7 *Economic Bulletin – DIW Berlin* 303; O Eldar, J Grennan and K Waldock, 'Common Ownership and Startup Growth' (2020) Duke Law School Public Law & Legal Theory Series No 2019-42.

[9] MC Schmalz, 'Common-Ownership Concentration and Corporate Conduct' (2018) 10 *Annual Review of Financial Economics* 413; Tzanaki, 'Varieties and Mechanisms of Common Ownership' (n 6); J Azar and A Tzanaki, 'Common Ownership and Merger Control Enforcement' in I Kokkoris and C Lemus (eds), *Research Handbook on the Law and Economics of Competition Enforcement* (Edward Elgar Publishing, 2022); CS Hemphill and M Kahan, 'The Strategies of Anticompetitive Common Ownership' (2020) 129 *Yale Law Journal* 1392.

[10] ÁL López and X Vives, 'Overlapping Ownership, R&D Spillovers, and Antitrust Policy' (2019) 127 *Journal of Political Economy* 2394; M Antón et al, 'Innovation: The Bright Side of Common Ownership?' (2018) IESE Working Paper, available at: papers.ssrn.com/abstract=3099578; Azar and Vives, 'Revisiting the Anticompetitive Effects of Common Ownership' (n 6); J Azar and X Vives, 'General Equilibrium Oligopoly and Ownership Structure' (2021) 89 *Econometrica* 999.

Some economic studies present an empirical account of common ownership in the banking sector in a number of important jurisdictions with different characteristics.[11] There is also some very limited scholarship on the magnitude and implications of common shareholding among fintech firms associated with ride-sharing platforms with overlapping investors in Southeast Asia.[12] However, there is no systematic or comprehensive account of the extent of common ownership in fintech markets more generally. Providing this is the aim of this chapter.

A. The Global Fintech Landscape

The empirical analysis that follows focuses, for the most part, on start-ups and private fintech companies, which represent the vast majority of the fintech firms worldwide[13] and have not yet been subject to rigorous study regarding the state of common ownership. For completeness and comparison, this analysis is supplemented with data on a smaller sample of fintech firms that have successfully gone public following an initial public offering (IPO) and are present in public markets.

We gathered data for the analysis from the Crunchbase database (as of February 2022). Crunchbase is one of the most popular databases used for the analysis of venture capital (VC) and private equity investments. Since most of the fintech companies that we analysed are private, this database can provide us with the richest information about the equity investments in such firms. We collected information about all companies with the industry classified as 'fintech' and the earliest company formed dating back to 1995. The company data contain name, date of founding, location, product market description, activity status (active or closed), as well as estimates of revenue and number of employees. In addition, we collected information about all the financing rounds received by these companies, showing round-by-round funding amounts each company had raised and the investors that participated in each round. The information we obtained about investors includes names, location and type (VC, angel, private equity, corporation, etc). The analysis only includes fintech companies classified as active and for which there were data on financing rounds and participating investors that allowed us to identify common owners and estimate investors' ownership shares. Overall, our data contains information about equity financing in almost 6,800 fintech companies from 113 countries. Note that fintech companies in our analysis are young, with nearly 90 per cent of the fintech companies in our sample founded after 2010 and almost 50 per cent of companies founded after 2016.

[11] A Banal-Estañol, N Boot and J Seldeslachts, 'Common Ownership Patterns in the European Banking Sector – The Impact of the Financial Crisis' (2022) 18 *Journal of Competition Law & Economics* 135; Azar, Raina and Schmalz (n 2).

[12] S Van Uytsel, 'Horizontal Shareholding Among Fintech Firms in Asia: A Preliminary Competition Law Assessment' in M Fenwick, S Van Uytsel and B Ying (eds), *Regulating FinTech in Asia: Global Context, Local Perspectives* (Springer, 2020).

[13] According to Crunchbase data.

Figure 1a shows the countries included in the analysis ranked by the total number of fintech companies. The largest fintech market by the number of companies is the United States (2,375), followed by the United Kingdom (765), China (400), India (380) and Canada (215). Figure 1b shows the total amount of capital invested in fintech companies in these countries. Again, the United States is the largest market ($99.1 billion), followed by China ($45.3 billion), the United Kingdom ($29.4 billion), India ($17.5 billion) and Germany ($9.1 billion). If Europe is taken as a whole, it will be the second largest market in both figures with 1,820 fintech firms and $54 billion invested.

Figure 1 Number of fintech companies and amounts invested in them, by country

Figure 1a **Figure 1b**

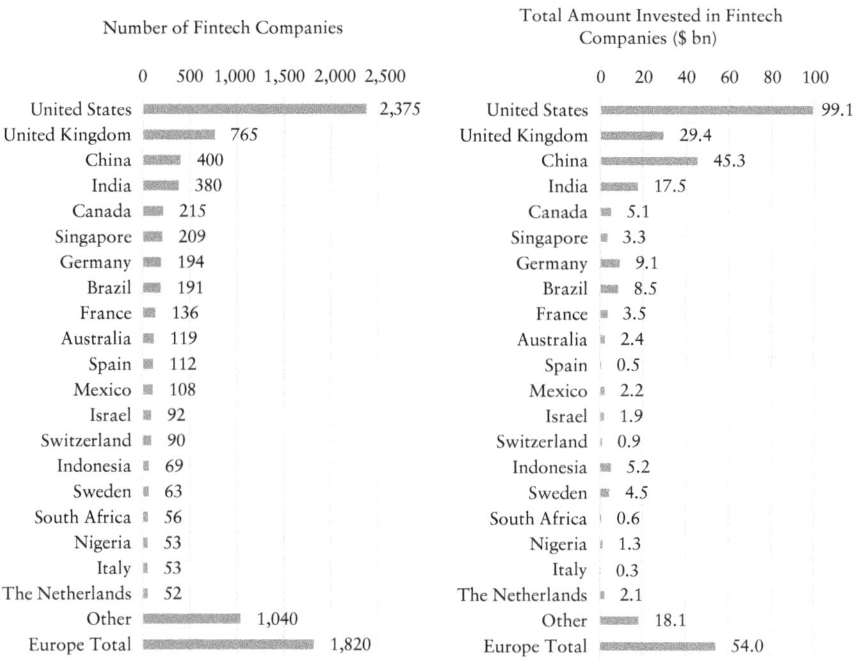

Table 1 shows the top 10 investors, ranked by the share of total dollar investment in fintech companies worldwide.[14] The columns show each investor's name, type, the number of fintech companies in which the investor has minority

[14] The ranking of top investors worldwide (Table 1) and the rankings by country (Table 2 and Table 3) presented later are based on estimated ownership of investors according to the method described in section III.B. Due to differences in how some financing rounds' details are recorded in different databases, the estimations of the dollar amounts invested and the calculated ranks occasionally differ from the presented estimates when datasets other than Crunchbase are used. Importantly, the main conclusions drawn from the presented results are not affected by such potential discrepancies.

ownership, and the percentage of capital contributed by the investor in the total amount invested in fintech companies worldwide. The total number of fintech companies with minority ownership represents the number of unique fintech companies in which at least one of the top 10 investors holds shares (the reported investors can hold minority shares in the same firms). As can be seen in this table, the overwhelming majority of the largest global investors in fintech are VC or private equity firms. However, we can also observe JP Morgan among the largest investors in fintech companies, suggesting that established financial institutions such as investment banks are also active in the financing of young innovative fintech companies.

Table 1 Top 10 fintech investors worldwide

Investor name	**Investor type**	**Number of fintech companies with minority ownership**	**Investor's share of total worldwide $ investment %**
Softbank	Venture capital	70	2.39
Sequoia	Venture capital	115	2.07
Tiger Global Management	Private equity firm	102	1.48
Temasek Holdings	Private equity firm	26	1.10
GIC	Private equity firm	25	1.04
JP Morgan	Investment bank	49	0.99
The Carlyle Group	Private equity firm	10	0.99
General Atlantic	Private equity firm	24	0.96
Ribbit Capital	Venture capital	61	0.93
Warburg Pincus	Private equity firm	14	0.82
Total		**382**	**12.77**

Figure 2 illustrates the share of dollar investment in fintech companies worldwide by investor category. This illustration confirms that the largest financial investors in fintech start-ups, which are typically early-stage private companies, are venture capitalists and private equity investors. However, other investor types, such as investment banks, angels and corporate VC units, also have an important presence in the fintech industry. At the same time, it is also notable that large asset managers such as the Big Three in the United States represent a minor share of investments in fintech start-ups worldwide (around 2 per cent in total). That is, large asset managers may invest in small private fintech companies through their active investment portfolios and are found here to do so to a limited extent. The market conditions (illiquidity of assets, frictions, lack of perfect public information regarding start-up valuation) as well as legal constraints (restrictions on the level and type of pension fund investments) in private markets may explain the low percentage of this group of institutional investors in common shareholdings in privately held fintech firms.[15] Besides, the total investment share and common ownership by the Big Three asset managers in private fintech firms is unlikely to have the systemic character or extensive scope they are observed to have in publicly listed firms (including fintech) for yet another reason: by definition, passive index funds, which represent the vast majority of the assets under management of the Big Three, exist only in the context of public capital markets.[16]

Nevertheless, one should note that our data may underestimate the extent to which large asset management firms invest in fintech companies as such investors often engage in private equity markets indirectly, ie, through participation in VC and private equity funds as limited partners. This means that these institutional investors may provide capital to the funds but are not participating in their management. For example, according to data in Pitchbook, a popular database on private equity investments, Blackrock has acted as a limited partner in nearly 80 VC and private equity funds since 2001. Most of these funds include between 20 to 200 other limited partners, depending on fund size, and such limited partners' investments are passive. Thus, as a rule (to retain their limited liability status) limited partners shall not participate in the funds' day-to-day activities or actively influence the funds' portfolio companies.[17] Yet, in recent years, large asset management firms have started directly investing in private markets, typically by participating in the later stages of VC financing. According to our Crunchbase dataset, Blackrock invested in 20 fintech companies and State Street in four, whereas the Vanguard Group has not invested in fintech companies as a direct investor. However, the number of investments in private early-stage firms by asset managers, including in industries other than fintech, has been growing quickly in the last three years. Therefore, it is expected that the share of traditional large asset managers as fintech investors will increase in the coming years.

[15] OECD, 'Annual Survey of Investment Regulation of Pension Funds and Other Pension Providers' (2021), available at: www.oecd.org/finance/private-pensions/annualsurveyofinvestmentregulationof-pensionfunds.htm.

[16] See above (n 4).

[17] M Steindl, 'The Alignment of Interests between the General and the Limited Partner in a Private Equity Fund – The Ultimate Governance Nut to Crack?' Harvard Law School Forum on Corporate Governance (11 March 2013), available at: corpgov.law.harvard.edu/2013/03/11/alignment-of-general-and-limited-partner-interests-in-pe-funds/; W Magnuson, 'The Public Cost of Private Equity' (2018) 102 *Minnesota Law Review* 1847.

Figure 2 Fintech investment by investor category worldwide

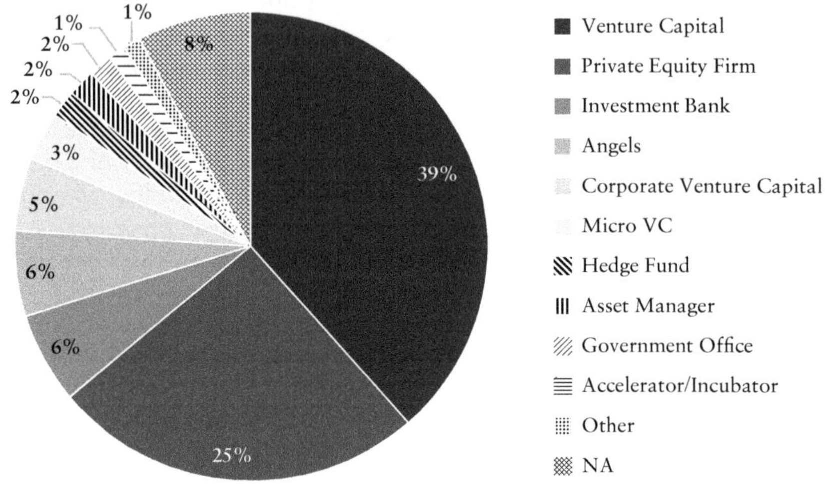

B. Top Common Investors in Fintech by Country

In this section, we provide more granular data on the fintech investment landscape broken down by country and region. Table 2 below reports the top 10 investors in each country, focusing on a selection of European markets (the United Kingdom, Spain, Sweden, Ireland). The columns show each investor's name, type, the number of fintech companies in which the investor has minority ownership, and the percentage of capital contributed by the investor in the total amount invested in fintech companies in the country. Investors are ranked based on the proportion of total dollar investment in fintech companies in the country.

In most European markets, private equity and VC are the largest and most common fintech investors. The notable outlier is Ireland, where the government has a very strong presence as a common investor of fintech companies, and investment banks also provide a considerable share of investment. Of the four European fintech markets that we have presented in detail, Ireland has the highest aggregated share of top 10 investors that provide financing in the country's fintech market. The United Kingdom has the lowest collective share of top 10 investors' fintech financing, with some common ownership observed. Blackrock is present in Sweden among the largest investors, but with investments in only two fintech companies. All in all, the number of fintech companies that are commonly held by each of the top 10 fintech investors in each of the four markets is limited.

Table 2 Top 10 fintech investors by country (European markets)

Investor name	Investor type	Number of fintech companies with minority ownership	Share of total country's investment %
UK			
Tiger Global Management	Private equity firm	9	3.35
Motive Partners	Private equity firm	2	2.47
CPP Investments	Asset manager	1	2.38
Softbank	Venture capital	5	1.91
Accel	Venture capital	11	1.75
DST Global	Private equity firm	4	1.42
GIC	Private equity firm	2	1.21
Target Global	Venture capital	5	1.20
Toscafund Asset Management	Hedge fund	2	1.08
Capability and Innovation Fund	Government office	16	1.08
Total		**43**	**17.86**
Spain			
Prime Ventures	Venture capital	1	7.42
Rinkelberg Capital	Venture capital	1	4.70
Credit Suisse	Investment bank	1	4.70
Crowdcube	Venture capital	9	4.37
ING Group	Investment bank	1	3.86
National Health Forecast (PSN)	Corporate venture capital	1	3.86
Greycroft	Venture capital	1	2.73
Spark Capital	Venture capital	1	2.51
All Iron Ventures	Venture capital	2	1.87
Encomenda VC	Micro VC	6	1.66
Total		**19**	**37.66**
Sweden			
Commonwealth Bank of Australia	Corporate venture capital	1	7.00
Northzone	Venture capital	3	4.18

(continued)

Table 2 *(Continued)*

Investor name	**Investor type**	**Number of fintech companies with minority ownership**	**Share of total country's investment %**
HMI Capital	Venture capital	2	3.47
BlackRock	Asset manager	2	2.91
Chrysalis Investments	Venture capital	1	2.91
Dragoneer Investment Group	Private equity firm	1	2.59
Alma Mundi Ventures	Venture capital	1	2.35
WestCap	Private equity firm	1	2.35
Softbank	Venture capital	1	2.35
Raison Asset Management	Private equity firm	1	2.35
Total		**5**	**32.46**
Ireland			
Allied Irish Banks	Investment bank	1	16.56
ING Group	Investment bank	1	11.52
Enterprise Ireland	Government office	23	8.92
Frontline Ventures	Venture capital	2	6.36
Disruptive Technologies Innovation Fund	Government office	1	5.20
Act Venture Capital	Venture capital	2	3.34
Trinity Ventures	Venture capital	1	3.34
Covid-19 Credit Guarantee Scheme	Government office	1	2.86
Octopus Ventures	Venture capital	1	2.74
Lifeline Ventures	Micro VC	1	2.01
Total		**29**	**62.87**

Table 3 presents the top 10 investors in other selected countries outside Europe (the US, Brazil, China, Indonesia). The columns show each investor's name, type, the number of fintech companies in which the investor has minority ownership, and the percentage of capital contributed by the investor in the total amount invested in fintech companies in the country. Again, investors are ranked based on the proportion of total dollar investment in fintech companies in the country.

The total number of fintech companies with minority ownership represents the number of unique fintech companies in which at least one of the top 10 investors holds shares (the reported investors can hold minority shares in the same firms).

The US has the lowest collective investment share of its 10 largest investors (11.04 per cent). On the other hand, all top US fintech investors have a large number of common shareholdings, and each of them holds minority shares in at least 10 fintech companies. In contrast, the other markets are considerably more concentrated when looking at the top 10 investors' total share of the country's fintech financing. But they have rather limited common ownership considering the number of rival fintech companies in which those largest investors hold minority interests. One noteworthy exception is the VC firm Sequoia in China, with 22 investments in fintech companies. Again, the largest and most common categories of fintech investors are venture capitalists and private equity firms. At the same time, we also observe some large investment banks among the top fintech investors. Distinctively, in Indonesia, corporate VC has a significant presence.

In addition, we can observe from Table 2 and Table 3 that the reported top investors often do not hold minority shares in the same group of firms (ie they have limited company overlaps). Both tables show that the total number of unique fintech companies with minority ownership by at least one of the top investors in most cases significantly exceeds the number of fintech companies held by each of the top investors. For instance, as Table 2 shows, in the United Kingdom, 43 unique companies have minority ownership by at least one of the top 10 investors, while the largest number of companies held by an individual investor (Capability and Innovation Fund) is 16. This is unlike public markets where several large asset management firms tend to have common minority shareholdings in virtually all companies comprising the same index of publicly listed firms (ie, they have extensive if not perfect company overlaps).

Table 3 Top 10 fintech investors by country (other markets)

Investor name	Investor type	Number of fintech companies with minority ownership	Share of total country's investment %
United States			
Sequoia	Venture capital	37	1.88
Tiger Global Management	Private equity firm	36	1.52
Andreessen Horowitz	Venture capital	56	1.32
Ribbit Capital	Venture capital	29	1.30
Softbank	Venture capital	24	1.07

(continued)

Table 3 *(Continued)*

Investor name	Investor type	Number of fintech companies with minority ownership	Share of total country's investment %
DST Global	Private equity firm	16	0.89
Coatue	Private equity firm	27	0.82
Insight Partners	Private equity firm	22	0.79
ICONIQ Capital	Private equity firm	10	0.75
Accel	Venture capital	34	0.71
Total		**218**	**11.04**
Brazil			
JP Morgan	Investment bank	2	23.83
Advent International	Private equity firm	1	5.07
Softbank	Venture capital	6	4.29
Propel Venture Partners	Venture capital	2	4.22
Goldman Sachs	Investment bank	4	3.56
MSA Capital	Private equity firm	1	2.95
Berkshire Hathaway	Investment bank	1	2.95
Sands Capital Ventures	Private equity firm	1	2.95
Kaszek	Venture capital	12	2.79
Ribbit Capital	Venture capital	7	2.30
Total		**26**	**54.88**
China			
Sequoia	Venture capital	22	4.66
China Creation Ventures (CCV)	Venture capital	2	4.62
The Carlyle Group	Private equity firm	2	4.49
Warburg Pincus	Private equity firm	2	3.27
Credit Suisse	Investment bank	3	3.25
General Atlantic	Private equity firm	2	3.25
GIC	Private equity firm	3	3.21
Primavera Capital Group	Private equity firm	5	3.19
Khazanah Nasional	Private equity firm	2	3.18
Temasek Holdings	Private equity firm	2	3.16
Total		**29**	**36.29**

(continued)

Table 3 *(Continued)*

Investor name	Investor type	Number of fintech companies with minority ownership	Share of total country's investment %
Indonesia			
Alibaba Group	Corporate venture capital	2	28.12
Softbank	Venture capital	5	9.09
EV Growth	Venture capital	5	7.42
Sinar Mas Group	Corporate venture capital	1	3.83
Google	Corporate venture capital	1	3.36
Temasek Holdings	Private equity firm	1	3.36
The Silverhorn Group	Venture capital	1	2.40
Sequoia	Venture capital	7	2.31
SCB Group	Corporate venture capital	1	1.92
Ant Group	Corporate venture capital	1	1.92
Total		**13**	**63.72**

Table 4 below shows the combined share of dollar fintech investments by the top 10 investors in each country, for a wide variety of countries. The columns show the country, the total number of fintech companies in the country and the total share of dollar investment in fintech companies by the top 10 investors. Only countries with at least 30 fintech companies in our data are reported. Countries are ranked by the number of fintech companies within each geographical area (ie, Europe, Americas, Asia, Australia, Middle East, Africa).

Table 4 Combined investment share of 10 largest investors

Country	Number of fintech companies in the country	Top 10 investors' combined ownership in country's fintechs %
Europe		
UK	765	17.86
Germany	194	23.36
France	136	27.07

(continued)

Table 4 *(Continued)*

Country	Number of fintech companies in the country	Top 10 investors' combined ownership in country's fintechs %
Spain	112	37.66
Switzerland	90	34.49
Sweden	63	32.46
Italy	53	55.71
The Netherlands	52	62.61
Ireland	46	62.87
Estonia	40	56.55
Denmark	31	66.05
Americas		
US	2,375	11.04
Canada	215	24.48
Brazil	191	54.88
Mexico	108	45.08
Colombia	48	41.64
Chile	38	54.29
Argentina	37	61.81
Asia		
China	400	36.29
India	380	33.87
Singapore	209	20.81
Indonesia	69	63.72
Japan	50	51.41
South Korea	42	68.52
Australia	119	36.11
Middle East		
Israel	92	25.30
United Arab Emirates	52	46.02
Turkey	35	69.91
Africa		
South Africa	56	44.09
Nigeria	53	60.01
Kenya	34	73.76

The main conclusion that may be drawn from Table 4 is that across the three leading regions (Europe, Americas and Asia), a higher combined investment share by top 10 investors is observed in those fintech markets where the number of fintech companies is smaller. It is also interesting to note that as Table 2 and Table 3 illustrate, the level of dollar investment by each of the top 10 fintech investors across countries does not necessarily correlate with the number of companies in which they have common shareholdings. This may be explained by the fact that larger dollar investments are typically undertaken in fintech companies at later stages of their development, when companies might be reluctant to accept financing from an investor who has other investments in competing fintech companies.[18]

C. Common Ownership Networks in Fintech Markets

This section provides an illustration of common ownership connections between rival fintech firms and the interpretation of their associated network graphs. Figure 3 shows the common ownership networks of fintech companies active in the market for payments only in two selected countries, ie, Sweden and the United Kingdom in Figure 3a and Figure 3b respectively. The countries were chosen to contrast payment markets of a different size, with the United Kingdom being the largest European payments market and Sweden a relatively small market.[19] The size of the dark circles in the graphs is a proxy for the firm size in terms of employment and the size of light circles is a proxy for the size of investors in terms of their total dollar fintech investments worldwide. Clearly, the most notable difference between the two markets is the size of the networks. The Swedish market is characterised by just a handful of fintech companies active in payments, each having its own group of investors that is largely unconnected to others. Here, the largest group of investors is backing Klarna (large dark circle at the centre of the graph). Generally, in this market, there is a low overlap of investors across firms.

In contrast, the UK market seems significantly more interconnected, at the first sight. We can observe a large number of companies and investors, with visible links between companies and groups of their investors. More specifically,

[18] In fact, among investors with the largest number of common holdings in fintech companies, we often observe investors focusing on very early-stage start-ups, ie, incubators, accelerators, angel investors, VC specialising on early-stage investments. Such investors seem to engage in a 'spray and pray' investment strategy by investing small amounts in a large number of early-stage fintech firms. For instance, accelerators Y Combinator in the US and Techstars in the UK have the largest number of fintech holdings (with 165 and 50 investments respectively). At the same time, Y Combinator is ranked only 46th in the US and Techstars is ranked 244th in the UK in terms of their shares of the country's total amount invested in fintech.

[19] We did not choose even smaller markets due to a low number of observations.

the UK market is characterised by the presence of a core group of larger fintech companies (Monzo, Revolut, Wise, Checkout.com, represented by the larger dark circles at the centre of the graph) as well as a few smaller companies (eg, Divido, Currencycloud, GoCardless), each of which is funded by large groups of investors that tend to have at least one other payments company in their portfolio. However, with a closer look, we can observe that beyond the core group of firms and investors shown to be concentrated in the centre, there are many payments companies with investors that tend not to have other investments in the industry. Importantly, there are few investors that hold more than two competitors in their portfolio simultaneously. Specifically, 79 per cent of all investors in the UK payments market have only one such portfolio company; 11 per cent of investors hold two payments fintech companies; and only the remaining 10 per cent have more than two payments companies in their portfolio at the same time, while only four investors hold 10 or more payments companies in their portfolios.

Thus, although more common ownership may seem to exist in the United Kingdom given that Figure 3b shows more connections between payments fintech companies, this does not necessarily mean that the network is denser. Indeed, as we show later when estimating the likely impact of common ownership (lambdas), the UK's payments market is characterised by a lower measure of common ownership. For this reason, one should be careful with interpreting or drawing inferences from network graphs alone, since visually it may be difficult to understand the extent of the likely concerns associated with common ownership.

Figure 3 Network graphs (payments market only)

a. Sweden b. UK

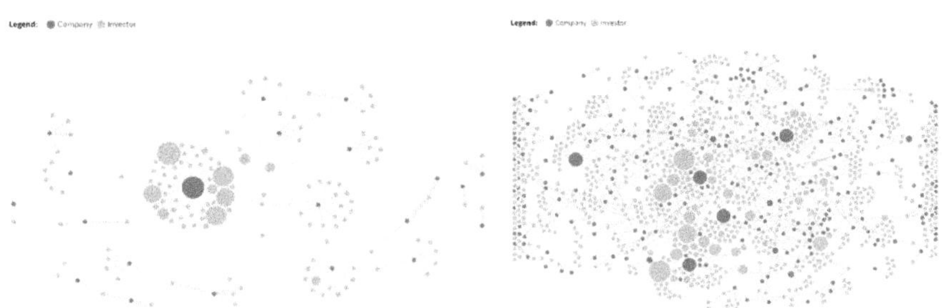

III. IMPACT OF COMMON OWNERSHIP IN FINTECH MARKETS

The above empirical analysis clearly shows that the span of common ownership varies widely across different geographies, fintech markets and investor types. But what is the likely impact of common ownership? Economic theory suggests that common ownership may have both negative and positive effects on market competition and innovation, depending on the circumstances.[20] A critical component in the competition analysis is estimating the 'common owners' weights' (or 'lambdas'), which serve to assess the magnitude of the likely effects of common ownership based on a unilateral effects analysis. In addition, it is important to consider the parallel existence and interplay of cross-ownership and common ownership structures when evaluating competition effects. This may occur in the context of mergers and acquisitions of fintech companies by investors that may have common shareholdings across other firms in the target's market and/or may themselves be in a competitive relationship with the acquired target company. The following sections expand on these considerations.

A. Theories of Harm and Efficiencies

Common ownership among horizontal competitors, or 'horizontal shareholding',[21] may have adverse effects on competition in the form of increased prices and/or reduced quantities, choice, quality or innovation, as seen in unilateral and coordinated effect theories of harm.[22]

i. Unilateral Effects

Unilateral effects arising from horizontal common ownership have been the focus of most economic research to date. It has been shown that common ownership may lead to lessened incentives to compete,[23] innovate[24] or enter[25] product markets, by means of various mechanisms.[26] The basic assumption that drives these results is that 'under common ownership in oligopoly, "atomistic"

[20] López and Vives (n 10); X Vives, 'Common Ownership, Market Power, and Innovation' (2020) 70 *International Journal of Industrial Organization* 102528; AJ Gibbon and JP Schain, 'Rising Markups, Common Ownership, and Technological Capacities' (2022) *International Journal of Industrial Organization*, available at: doi.org/10.1016/j.ijindorg.2022.102900.

[21] E Elhauge, 'Horizontal Shareholding' (2016) 129 *Harvard Law Review* 1267.

[22] OECD, 'Common Ownership by Institutional Investors' (n 1) 16–21 (summarising the main theories on the effects of common ownership and early criticisms).

[23] Azar, Schmalz and Tecu, 'Anticompetitive Effects of Common Ownership' (n 2); Azar, Raina and Schmalz (n 2).

[24] On unilateral effects based on reduced innovation incentives, see the European Commission's merger control enforcement practice in Case M.7932 *Dow/DuPont*, Commission decision of 27 March 2017, Annex 5, paras 56–60; and Case M.8084 *Bayer/Monsanto*, Commission decision of 21 March 2018.

[25] Xie (n 2); M Newham, J Seldeslachts and A Banal-Estanol, 'Common Ownership and Market Entry: Evidence from the Pharmaceutical Industry' (2018) DIW Berlin Discussion Paper 1738; A Ruiz-Pérez, 'Market Structure and Common Ownership' (2019), available at: www.cemfi.es/~ruiz-perez/alexandro_ruiz_perez_JMP_nov2019.pdf.

[26] E Elhauge, 'The Causal Mechanisms of Horizontal Shareholding' (2021) 82 *Ohio State Law Journal* 1; Tzanaki, 'Varieties and Mechanisms of Common Ownership' (n 6); M Antón et al, 'Common Ownership, Competition, and Top Management Incentives' (2023) 131 *Journal of Political Economy*, available at: doi.org/10.1086/722414.

firms and shareholders cannot be assumed, which in turn leads to theories about an altered objective function of the firm (portfolio value maximization)' and altered unilateral competitive incentives (across-firm internalisation of profits).[27] In essence, if 'a firm is exactly a set of assets under common ownership' (eg, following a merger or majority acquisition),[28] it is questioned whether and to what extent assets under partial common ownership belong to only one or another firm, neither or both,[29] especially when based on minority shareholdings.[30] Yet, a 'blurred firm boundary effect' has been empirically found for example in the presence of common VC investors – a common set of investors in fintech firms.[31] In practice, unilateral effects theories suggest that even without any communication or coordination, commonly held firms may have a reduced tendency to expand output or lower prices in order to gain market shares, since this may come at the expense of industry rivals in which the common owners may have extensive, albeit minority, parallel shareholdings.[32]

The theory underlying the commonly held firms' altered market conduct and increased market power is that common ownership affects the incentives and behaviour of the managers of those firms. That is, managers of commonly held firms are thought to maximise the total portfolio profits of their common shareholders, taking into account their parallel holdings in rival firms in the same industry. In an environment of oligopolistic markets where firms strategically interact, aggressive competition – or targeted governance that improves individual firm performance – imposes negative externalities on the commonly held firms and their common shareholders.[33] Therefore, the latter have an incentive to internalise those externalities and in given circumstances, they may also have the power to influence firm management and implement their preferences.

[27] Tzanaki, 'Varieties and Mechanisms of Common Ownership' (n 6) 178–79. On the origins of the economic theory of partial ownership (of which common ownership is a special case) and its more recent extensions, see DP O'Brien and SC Salop, 'Competitive Effects of Partial Ownership: Financial Interest and Corporate Control' (2000) 67 *Antitrust Law Journal* 559; J Azar, 'Portfolio Diversification, Market Power, and the Theory of the Firm' (2016), available at: papers.ssrn.com/abstract=2811221; J Azar and RM Ribeiro, 'Estimating Oligopoly with Shareholder Voting Models' (2022), available at: papers.ssrn.com/abstract=3988265.

[28] B Holmström and J Roberts, 'The Boundaries of the Firm Revisited' (1998) 12 *Journal of Economic Perspectives* 73, 77 (describing as a black box both the market in transaction costs economics and the firm in neoclassical microeconomic theory, and the advantages of the modern property rights approach pioneered by Grossman and Hart that showcases the costs and benefits of integration independently of the presence of a market).

[29] Schmalz, 'Common-Ownership Concentration and Corporate Conduct' (n 9) 418.

[30] Tzanaki, 'Varieties and Mechanisms of Common Ownership' (n 6) 178 (discussing how legal and economic theory on the boundaries of the firm fail to capture partial common ownership in the form of diffuse, minority shareholdings and the significant implications for antitrust analysis).

[31] L Lindsey, 'Blurring Firm Boundaries: The Role of Venture Capital in Strategic Alliances' (2008) 63 *Journal of Finance* 1137.

[32] Schmalz, 'Common-Ownership Concentration and Corporate Conduct' (n 9) 417.

[33] Antón et al, 'Common Ownership, Competition, and Top Management Incentives' (n 26) 28; M Condon, 'Externalities and the Common Owner' (2020) 95 *Washington Law Review* 1.

The control or influence mechanism over managers is clear in the case of 'active' investors and fund managers (eg, through the exercise of voice, exit or engagement).[34] This is particularly so for 'concentrated' common owners with significant stakes, board seats and a dominant voting position in the governance of at least one of their commonly held firms.[35] The same is true for private commonly held companies, where the control dynamics may be more easily and directly observable in practice. For instance, control in a given company may be specified according to provisions in their charter, bylaws or shareholder agreements that may provide for special control rights and governance structures (eg, class-voting rights or dual-class shares).[36] VC investors that extend significant financing to start-ups might contractually agree for additional and direct control rights (eg, veto, board representation) compared with those automatically granted by law based on their minority shareholder status.[37] Although it may be challenging to generalise on the control dynamics for the universe of private companies, one is usually able to observe the specific control arrangements in place in individual firms. In this sense, one may be also able to observe the relative power and potentially active influence of common investors in private firms in concrete cases.

Still, alternative channels of control may exist based on passive mechanisms: when there are no other dominant shareholders in corporate governance, especially in widely held public companies, even perceived 'passive' common institutional investors may be able to realise their collective interests and relative power in pursuit of portfolio value.[38] Such control is de facto and shared among common owners (and possibly with corporate managers) rather than formal and stand-alone.[39] Principal-agent conflicts that are typical in large public corporations with a dispersed ownership structure are factored into the latest economic models and estimations. However, the likely anticompetitive effects of common

[34] B Charoenwong, Z Ni and Q Ye, 'Active Mutual Fund Common Owners' Returns and Proxy Voting Behavior' (2022), available at: papers.ssrn.com/abstract=4184584; Schmalz, 'Common-Ownership Concentration and Corporate Conduct' (n 9).

[35] Tzanaki, 'Varieties and Mechanisms of Common Ownership' (n 6).

[36] Gl Rauterberg, 'The Separation of Voting and Control: The Role of Contract in Corporate Governance' (2021) 38 *Yale Journal on Regulation* 1124 (discussing the differences between the three instruments and noting that private companies need not publicly disclose any shareholder agreements).

[37] Some VC investors in start-ups publish their model Term Sheets as a matter of good business practice even if they are not legally required to do so. These contracts are subject to negotiation and may also change over time (eg, when there are multiple investors in later and larger rounds). On the process of negotiating boards in start-ups and contractually separating control from ownership, see E Pollman, 'Startup Governance' (2019) 168 *University of Pennsylvania Law Review* 155, 181–83.

[38] Tzanaki, 'Varieties and Mechanisms of Common Ownership' (n 6); Anna Tzanaki, 'The Passive Mechanisms of Common Ownership' (*ProMarket*, 5 May 2022), available at: www.promarket.org/2022/05/05/passive-mechanisms-common-ownership/.

[39] Tzanaki, 'Varieties and Mechanisms of Common Ownership' (n 6).

ownership persist, though they are observed to be limited in magnitude.[40] This means that managers may not fully internalise the anticompetitive incentives of common owners as theoretical models predict, but only partially, due to the presence of (some) managerial agency costs.[41] As a result, contextual and empirical analysis may be necessary in each individual case, to approximate the actual effects of common ownership in a given setting.

Furthermore, quantification measures of common ownership such as the modified Herfindahl–Hirschman Index (MHHI)[42] or the common owners' weights (lambdas)[43] rely on theoretical scholarship based on unilateral effects. The former estimates the level of additional market concentration and 'effective' market power due to common ownership, whereas the latter estimates the degree of internalisation of rivals' profits relative to own firm profits by the firm manager in its objective function due to common ownership.[44] Ultimately, both methods aim to capture the increased unilateral pricing incentives produced by common shareholdings in rival firms.[45] In addition, both measures incorporate the common investors' financial interests (profit share) and degree of influence (control share) in each competing firm in the same industry, in order to quantify those unilateral anticompetitive incentives.

[40] Azar and Ribeiro (n 27); Backus, Conlon and Sinkinson, 'Common Ownership and Competition in the Ready-to-Eat Cereal Industry' (n 2); Antón et al, 'Common Ownership, Competition, and Top Management Incentives' (n 26).

[41] Tzanaki, 'Varieties and Mechanisms of Common Ownership' (n 6) 223; Azar, 'The Common Ownership Trilemma' (n 3) 286–93.

[42] TF Bresnahan and SC Salop, 'Quantifying the Competitive Effects of Production Joint Ventures' (1986) 4 *International Journal of Industrial Organization* 155; O'Brien and Salop (n 27).

[43] Backus, Conlon and Sinkinson, 'Common Ownership in America' (n 4) (who call this measure 'kappa' instead of lambda); Vives (n 20); Azar and Tzanaki (n 9).

[44] Backus, Conlon and Sinkinson, 'Common Ownership in America' (n 4) 275: 'All of these measures – profit weights, MHHI, and alternatives – agree on the broad trend in Figure 1. However, the profit weights approach, which starts with the objective function of the firm, is the only one that offers a fully general path forward for empirical study of the common ownership hypothesis. We emphasize that while we are the first to construct our measure – the common ownership profit weights – at this level of breadth, neither the innovation nor their use in empirical work is novel here. The theory goes back as far as Rotemberg (1984), is implicit in the MHHI measure of Bresnahan and Salop (1986), has been applied to cross–ownership in O'Brien and Salop (2000), and has seen application in various tests of the common ownership hypothesis (Kennedy et al, 2017; Gramlich and Grundl, 2017; Boller and Morton, 2019)'.

[45] The profit weight approach that we employ in this chapter to measure the impact of common ownership is the one that is increasingly being used in the literature since it is more tractable and reliable as a stand-alone measure. The early empirical papers showing anticompetitive effects of common ownership in the airline and banking industries have been partially criticised for using the MHHI to regress the price effects due to endogeneity concerns (although those papers did use additional tests and alternative specifications to address such concerns). For an overview of the critiques, see DP O'Brien and K Waehrer, 'The Competitive Effects of Common Ownership: We Know Less Than We Think' (2017) 81 *Antitrust Law Journal* 729; TA Lambert and ME Sykuta, 'The Case for Doing Nothing About Institutional Investors' Common Ownership of Small Stakes in Competing Firms' (2018) University of Missouri School of Law Legal Studies Research Paper No 2018-21; MB Fox and MS Patel, 'Common Ownership: Do Managers Really Compete Less?' (2022) 39 *Yale Journal on Regulation* 136; Patel (n 8); and for a reply to those critiques, see J Azar, MC Schmalz and I Tecu, 'The Competitive Effects of Common Ownership: Economic Foundations and Empirical Evidence: Reply', available at: papers.ssrn.com/abstract=3044908.

The degree of control that the common owners have materially affects their ability to impact outcomes in corporate governance and market competition. For instance, if the common owners have no control or influence, common ownership will have zero effects. Firms will act independently in the market, as they will continue to maximise their own individual firm value. Typically, most theoretical and empirical economic literature assumes 'proportionate control' – that is, control weights are assumed to be equal to profit weights. Some models check this basic assumption against alternative control scenarios for robustness and still find anticompetitive effects flowing from common ownership.[46] On the other hand, in the absence of other dominant shareholders and special governance structures and given the often relatively large size, systemic presence and potentially cumulative influence of institutional shareholders, common owners may de facto have disproportionate corporate power and thus may substantially affect market outcomes.[47]

Yet, most of the empirical literature on common ownership using different control assumptions to estimate its competitive effects has focused on publicly listed companies commonly held by large institutional investors. Private firms and start-ups, which are more likely (commonly) owned by other types of investors such as VC, have hardly been subject to empirical scrutiny. Importantly, the governance landscape of private firms may differ dramatically from that of public firms. Besides, the specific governance structures in place may vary among private companies (eg, when rights of control or corporate decision-making are allocated based on and governed by tailored shareholder agreements)[48] or between other types of private companies and start-ups (as a special species of entity that defies the public–private company dichotomy and has particular characteristics such as a focus on innovation and financial backing by VC investors who may have a dual role as shareholders and directors on the board of their financed firms).[49] For these reasons, it is crucial that the analysis focuses on the real-life setting in which common ownership is observed, including the specific ownership and governance structures of the commonly held firms (type, size and distribution of shareholders, legal environment and any special contractual

[46] Azar, Schmalz and Tecu, 'Anticompetitive Effects of Common Ownership' (n 2); Schmalz, 'Common-Ownership Concentration and Corporate Conduct' (n 9).

[47] Tzanaki, 'Varieties and Mechanisms of Common Ownership' (n 6); Schmalz, 'Common-Ownership Concentration and Corporate Conduct' (n 9).

[48] Shareholder agreements may alter the default allocation of control based on statutory corporate law, eg, shareholder control rights as a function of their voting power. On the prevalence of this contractual technique especially among private (but also public) companies and the implications, see the seminal analysis by Rauterberg (n 36); J Fisch, 'Stealth Governance: Shareholder Agreements and Private Ordering' (2022) 99 *Washington University Law Review* 913.

[49] Fisch (n 48) 915 ('the term startup [is used] to describe the growing category of innovative venture-funded companies that defy the traditional categories of public and private companies'); Pollman (n 37) (offering a new illuminating account of the governance complexity and particularities of start-ups, given the innovative and evolving nature of their business and capital structure, which are characterised by heterogenous shareholders, overlapping governance roles and often board monitoring failures).

arrangements shaping corporate governance) as well as the relevant market structures (concentrated markets with oligopolistic competition, structural and personal links among the commonly held firms).[50]

ii. Coordinated Effects

Common ownership may also affect competition in product markets by means of coordinated effects. Theories of harm relating to coordinated effects suggest that common ownership may increase the likelihood for either explicit coordination among commonly held firms or tacit collusion under conducive market conditions and other surrounding conditions.[51] Either way, the market conduct of the firms changes in a coordinated fashion, as does the industry equilibrium, with the goal of maximising joint profits and gaining monopoly rents. Besides, non-commonly held rival firms in the oligopoly may have aligned interests to achieve a coordinated outcome, as they may share in the supracompetitive profits.[52]

Common shareholders may facilitate explicit or implicit coordination through various means. First, common owners may act as 'cartel ringmasters' or 'instigators' by having an active and leading role in orchestrating anticompetitive coordination among their portfolio firms.[53] This could be achieved through common owners' active discussions and engagement with corporate management or boards, with a view to influence the companies' long-term strategies,[54] during private meetings or during earning calls where investors are present and firm and industry profitability are discussed.[55] As relatively large minority shareholders, common owners may have privileged access to management and more generally they may have more control than their formal equity share suggests.[56] Like an industry association or a non-rival (consulting) firm that could serve as a

[50] Tzanaki, 'Varieties and Mechanisms of Common Ownership' (n 6); GC Means, 'The Separation of Ownership and Control in American Industry' (1931) 46 *Quarterly Journal of Economics* 68.

[51] EB Rock and DL Rubinfeld, 'Common Ownership and Coordinated Effects' (2020) 83 *Antitrust Law Journal* 201; Patel (n 8) 49; A Tzanaki, 'The Regulation of Minority Shareholdings and Other Structural Links between Competing Undertakings: A Law & Economics Analysis' (PhD thesis, UCL (University College London) 2017); Tzanaki, 'Varieties and Mechanisms of Common Ownership' (n 6) 206; L Boller and F Scott Morton, 'Testing the Theory of Common Stock Ownership' (2019) NBER Working Paper No w27515.

[52] Rock and Rubinfeld (n 51) 226; Boller and Scott Morton (n 51) 38.

[53] For a comprehensive overview of coordinated effects theories, see Rock and Rubinfeld (n 51) who 'identify five scenarios, based on antitrust case law and enforcement experience, in which common ownership could plausibly increase the potential for coordinated conduct in concentrated markets'. Common owners acting as a 'cartel ringmaster' or initiator is one of these scenarios: eg, the 'frackers hypothetical' the authors analysis has a loose basis on an actual case reported in the business press when large common shareholders met with the aim to get frackers to cut output and boost profits.

[54] Case M.7932 *Dow/DuPont*, Commission decision of 27 March 2017, Annex 5, para 19.

[55] Rock and Rubinfeld (n 51).

[56] Case M.7932 *Dow/DuPont*, Commission decision of 27 March 2017, Annex 5, §3 and 4; Tzanaki, 'Varieties and Mechanisms of Common Ownership' (n 6).

'cartel facilitator', common owners may promote explicit agreement or information-sharing regarding important competitive parameters among industry rivals and thus actively and in full knowledge contribute to the implementation and maintenance of a cartel.[57] Indeed, there is some evidence that rival firms with common ownership links may explicitly conclude anticompetitive agreements to raise prices (and profits), restrain output[58] and prevent or delay entry (eg, settlement agreements between commonly held brand and generic drug manufacturers that aim to withhold generic entry into pharmaceutical markets).[59]

Furthermore, common owners may serve as a conduit of communication or a channel for access to and transmission of information among the commonly held firms.[60] Information exchanges, especially private ones, 'can help to provide focal points and more generally solve the coordination problem that arises in a prisoner's dilemma setting',[61] but also fill in the gaps in a real-world 'incomplete cartel contract' that is legally unenforceable, by ensuring monitoring and compliance among the cartelising firms (and avoiding misinterpreting rival moves as deviations due to a changing environment).[62] In this way, common ownership links may help align incentives among the commonly held firms and thus enhance the transparency and credibility of communications regarding their competitive strategies.[63] Even public statements or unilateral disclosures expressing the common shareholders' strategic preferences regarding the future conduct of their portfolio firms in the market may under certain circumstances potentially be considered anticompetitive.[64] Besides, common ownership is shown to increase voluntary disclosure of strategic information that promotes coordination between firms.[65]

Common owners may also encourage adoption of executive compensation packages tied to rival or industry performance and designed to align incentives

[57] Cartel facilitators are sanctioned under EU competition law as long as they qualify as 'undertakings' even if they are not active in the same market(s) where the cartel takes place. A Vallery and C Schell, 'AC-Treuhand: Substantial Fines for Facilitators of Cartels' (2016) 7 *Journal of European Competition Law & Practice* 254.

[58] Bradley Olson and Lynn Cook, 'Wall Street Tells Frackers to Stop Counting Barrels, Start Making Profits' *Wall Street Journal* (13 December 2017), available at: www.wsj.com/articles/wall-streets-fracking-frenzy-runs-dry-as-profits-fail-to-materialize-1512577420.

[59] J Xie and J Gerakos, 'Institutional Cross-Holdings and Generic Entry in the Pharmaceutical Industry' (2020) 110 *AEA Papers and Proceedings* 569.

[60] Rock and Rubinfeld (n 51); Patel (n 8) 52.

[61] Rock and Rubinfeld (n 51) 234.

[62] M Motta, 'Review of Michael Whinston, Lectures on Antitrust Economics (MIT Press, 2006)' (2007) 3 *Competition Policy International* 316.

[63] EU Horizontal Merger Guidelines, recitals 47–48; Rock and Rubinfeld (n 51).

[64] ibid; OECD, 'Unilateral Disclosure of Information with Anticompetitive Effects' (2012) Policy Roundtable DAF/COMP(2012) 17; I Lianos and F Wagner-von Papp, 'Tackling Invitations to Collude and Unilateral Disclosure: The Moving Frontiers of Competition Law?' (2022) 13 *Journal of European Competition Law & Practice* 249.

[65] A Pawliczek, AN Skinner and SLC Zechman, 'Facilitating Tacit Collusion through Voluntary Disclosure: Evidence from Common Ownership' (2022), available at: papers.ssrn.com/abstract=3382324.

between common owners and managers of their portfolio firms.[66] Inducing agreement on common facilitating practices such as incentive schemes is another means of facilitating coordination.[67] Indeed, common ownership as cross-ownership may in itself be an anticompetitive facilitating practice.[68] It has been also claimed that common ownership may be a substitute for explicit collusion in certain industries.[69]

Even without any explicit agreement or communication, common ownership may be able to induce and sustain tacit collusion by altering the incentives of portfolio and rival firms to collude or compete, and their relative gains and losses.[70] However, economic research on market-wide tacit collusion in the abstract is inconclusive. On the one hand, common owners may increase the likelihood and success of collusion by increasing firms' incentives to collude and the discount rate for managers of their portfolio firms.[71] This, in turn, increases their long-term gains from cooperation and decreases the incentives and likelihood of defection. On the other hand, common ownership may render punishment softer and less costly for deviating firms. This is because, when competition reverts to the pre-existing non-collusive level at the punishment stage, firms may earn higher profits if common ownership generates unilateral effects.[72] This increases the incentive to deviate and makes collusion harder to sustain.

In short, common ownership may have a coordinating, signalling or monitoring and deterring function, enabling coordinated market outcomes. These effects and functions of common shareholders among competitors, and related antitrust risk, may be exacerbated if common ownership (structural links) is coupled with interlocking directorates (personal links).[73] In such case, common investors may be able to appoint the same person(s) as a director on the board of

[66] Rock and Rubinfeld (n 51); W Neus, M Stadler and M Unsorg, 'Market Structure, Common Ownership and Coordinated Manager Compensation' (2020) University of Tübingen Working Papers in Business and Economics No 133; W Neus and M Stadler, 'Common Holdings and Strategic Manager Compensation: The Case of an Asymmetric Triopoly' (2020) 39 *Managerial and Decision Economics* 814.

[67] SC Salop, 'Practices That (Credibly) Facilitate Oligopoly Coordination' in JE Stiglitz and GF Mathewson (eds), *New Developments in the Analysis of Market Structure* (MIT Press, 1986).

[68] Tzanaki, 'The Regulation of Minority Shareholdings and Other Structural Links between Competing Undertakings' (n 51); D Gilo, 'Partial Ownership as a Strategic Variable to Facilitate Tacit Collusion' (1995) 10/95, revised 4/97 John M Olin Program in Law, Economics, and Business, Harvard Law School, Discussion Paper No 170.

[69] Banal-Estañol, Newham and Seldeslachts (n 2) 98.

[70] Rock and Rubinfeld (n 51); Patel (n 8).

[71] Boller and Scott Morton (n 51) 38.

[72] Patel (n 8) 52–53. Yet the collusion analysis and the underlying economic incentives are complex as Patel notes. For economic models showing under what conditions partial ownership may hinder or faciliate collusion, see respectively DA Malueg, 'Collusive Behavior and Partial Ownership of Rivals' (1992) 10 *International Journal of Industrial Organization* 27; D Gilo, Y Moshe and Y Spiegel, 'Partial Cross Ownership and Tacit Collusion' (2006) 37 *Rand Journal of Economics* 81.

[73] Y Nili, 'Horizontal Directors' (2020) 114 *Northwestern University Law Review* 1179; J Azar, 'Common Shareholders and Interlocking Directors: The Relation Between Two Corporate Networks' (2022) 18 *Journal of Competition Law & Economics* 75; Eldar, Grennan and Waldock (n 8); OECD, 'Antitrust Issues Involving Minority Shareholdings and Interlocking Directorates' (2009) Policy Roundtable DAF/COMP(2008) 30.

multiple competing firms in which they have common shareholdings. Similarly, if common owners are also common creditors in rival firms, the likelihood of collusion is increased.[74]

iii. Efficiencies and Procompetitive Effects

Common ownership of horizontal competitors may also generate procompetitive efficiencies and other beneficial effects for consumers and society.[75] Efficiencies that enhance the commonly held firms' abilities and incentives to compete or innovate, for instance by realising cost savings or innovation synergies, may outweigh any negative effects on competition and benefit consumers, leading to lower prices, higher quality, new or improved products and services and/or more choice.[76] These are favourably viewed by antitrust enforcers and policymakers. While common ownership may produce additional and substantial benefits for corporate governance and the operation of capital markets (eg, minimising managerial agency costs, greater diversification, lower cost of capital, increased liquidity) that result in profit for shareholders and investors, consumers do not generally stand to gain.[77] Competition policy does not trade off such efficiencies against competition and consumer harms. These are disregarded by antitrust enforcers as 'out-of-market' efficiencies,[78] since competition enforcement is in principle 'market-specific'.[79]

An important parameter of competition in fintech markets, which are generally more dynamic in nature, is innovation. Several theoretical and empirical economic studies indicate that common ownership in both publicly traded and private firms (start-ups) may have positive effects on innovation under specific circumstances. These effects are particularly pronounced in high-tech or highly innovative industries that are subject to large innovation and technological and informational spillovers.[80] Indeed, it has been shown that common ownership

[74] DD Sokol, 'Debt, Control, and Collusion' (2022) 71 *Emory Law Journal* 695.

[75] OECD, 'Common Ownership by Institutional Investors' (n 1) 28–29 (summarising the literature on potential benefits from common ownership).

[76] Azar and Tzanaki (n 9) 275.

[77] Tzanaki, 'Varieties and Mechanisms of Common Ownership' (n 6) 170, 204, 217; OECD, 'Common Ownership by Institutional Investors' (n 1) 28–29; JB Baker, 'Overlapping Financial Investor Ownership, Market Power, and Antitrust Enforcement: My Qualified Agreement with Professor Elhauge' (2016) 129 *Harvard Law Review Forum* 212, 227–31 (noting, however, that within-industry diversification benefits to financial investors holding shares in competitors are limited because industry profits and equity values are highly positively correlated; besides, if common ownership lessens competition this increases the positive correlation and further lessens the diversification benefits).

[78] Azar and Tzanaki (n 9) 276; Patel (n 8) 56.

[79] Tzanaki, 'Varieties and Mechanisms of Common Ownership' (n 6) 204 ('competition enforcement is "market-specific" in that only efficiency gains within the same relevant market [and for the same group of consumers] may offset potential anticompetitive unilateral effects [consumer harm] found in that market').

[80] López and Vives (n 10); Antón et al, 'Innovation' (n 10); Eldar, Grennan and Waldock (n 8); J González-Uribe, 'Exchanges of Innovation Resources inside Venture Capital Portfolios' (2020) 135 *Journal of Financial Economics* 144; Gibbon and Schain (n 20).

by VC investors is blurring firm boundaries, solving incomplete contracting and information problems, a (welfare increasing) effect that is particularly important to the success of young firms.[81] However, depending on the specific type of common investors (eg, large asset managers and institutional investors or venture capitalists, focused or long-term financial investors), the magnitude of efficiencies and the means through which these are attained may differ.[82] Accordingly, the innovation implications of common ownership may differ depending on the specificities of the particular industries, firms and investors.[83] For these reasons, the analysis of the innovation effects of common ownership needs to be case-specific, like the analysis of the competition effects.

The rationale for bringing about these welfare-enhancing effects is of the same logic as that underlying unilateral and coordinated theories of harm: (i) common owners are interested in maximising their total portfolio profits and in doing so, they will induce corporate managers to internalise *positive* externalities among their portfolio firms;[84] or (ii) common owners may have the incentives and abilities to induce *beneficial* coordination and facilitate information flows among their portfolio firms.[85] In the case of VC investors, 'active' mechanisms due to strong control rights and board representation across commonly held rival firms may provide a more straightforward and observable means of effectuating such effects.[86] Furthermore, it is suggested that common ownership in private markets may counterbalance any short-term anticompetitive effects of common ownership among public firms, as the former may encourage entrepreneurial activity and entry of innovative, high-growth start-ups into dormant industries and thus disrupt larger firms that may be commonly owned and have limited incentives to compete.[87]

More generally, common ownership may mitigate firms' disincentives to innovate and invest in cost-reducing research and development (R&D) by solving the technological spillover problem among portfolio firms.[88] Moreover, common institutional ownership may improve innovation productivity as well as rationalise and minimise wasteful duplicative efforts.[89] Common institutional owners may also increase innovation incentives by attenuating the career risks of corporate managers.[90] Besides, they may be able to play a more active monitoring role

[81] Lindsey (n 31).

[82] P Borochin, J Yang and R Zhang, 'The Effect of Institutional Ownership Types on Innovation and Competition' (2018) Working Paper, available at: papers.ssrn.com/abstract=3204767.

[83] López and Vives (n 10); Eldar, Grennan and Waldock (n 8).

[84] López and Vives (n 10); Vives (n 20).

[85] J He and J Huang, 'Product Market Competition in a World of Cross-Ownership: Evidence from Institutional Blockholdings' (2017) 30 *Review of Financial Studies* 2674.

[86] O Eldar and J Grennan, 'Common Ownership and Entrepreneurship' (2021) Duke Law School Public Law & Legal Theory Series No 2021-25 3.

[87] ibid.

[88] López and Vives (n 10).

[89] He and Huang (n 85).

[90] P Aghion, J Van Reenen and L Zingales, 'Innovation and Institutional Ownership' (2013) 103 *American Economic Review* 277.

and act as a market-based mechanism to internalise governance externalities among the commonly held firms.[91] In addition, common investors may have a knowledge-sharing role that enables them to transfer knowhow from one firm to benefit another.[92] As such, common institutional investors, even passive ones, are found to help facilitate the diffusion of information about new technologies between commonly held firms, leading to innovation.[93]

Similar beneficial effects are for the most part evidenced when start-ups share a common VC investor. Common VC ownership reduces duplication of R&D costs (which can help solve a market failure in patent races, for example), it leads venture capitalists to shut down lagging product development projects, withhold funding from lagging start-ups and redirect those start-ups' innovation. All this leads to improved innovation efficiency.[94] Besides, common venture capitalists and VC directors serving on other start-up boards are shown to facilitate and spur start-up growth for a number of reasons.[95] Commonly held start-ups benefit through raising more capital through more investment rounds, or through the sharing of valuable information and the efficient allocation of opportunities among start-ups thanks to accumulated expertise.[96] In addition, they are less likely to fail, and exit more successfully through an IPO or acquisition by another commonly held start-up.[97]

As a result, the procompetitive effects of common ownership, especially in fintech markets and in VC-financed start-ups that are innovation-driven and potentially subject to significant benefits from VC advising, should be taken into account by competition agencies and weighed against any anticompetitive effects.[98]

B. Common Ownership Weights

In this section, we provide an empirical estimation of the likely impact of common ownership in fintech markets in light of its observed levels in different countries and product markets. First, we explain the theory and assumptions underlying the estimation process and present the formula for the calculation of the common owners' weights or lambdas.[99] Next, we provide empirical evidence

[91] J He, J Huang and S Zhao, 'Internalizing Governance Externalities: The Role of Institutional Cross-Ownership' (2019) 134 *Journal of Financial Economics* 400.

[92] K Gao et al, 'The Power of Sharing: Evidence from Institutional Investor Cross-Ownership and Corporate Innovation' (2019) 63 *International Review of Economics & Finance* 284.

[93] L Kostovetsky and A Manconi, 'Common Institutional Ownership and Diffusion of Innovation' (2020) Working Paper, available at: papers.ssrn.com/abstract=2896372.

[94] X Li, T Liu and LA Taylor, 'Common Ownership and Innovation Efficiency' (2021) Jacobs Levy Equity Management Center for Quantitative Financial Research Paper.

[95] Eldar, Grennan and Waldock (n 8); Eldar and Grennan (n 86).

[96] Eldar, Grennan and Waldock (n 8).

[97] ibid.

[98] Schmalz, 'Recent Studies on Common Ownership' (n 8) 22.

[99] See above (n 43).

on country-level common ownership lambdas in the largest fintech markets, both overall and broken down by narrower product market segments.

Starting with the estimation process employed, we estimate investors' ownership share in a given company based on our company-funding round-investors dataset described in section II.A. Our main measure of an investor's ownership share is a weighted average of their investment shares across all financing rounds:

$$Ownership\ Share_{i,j} = \sum_{n=1}^{N} w_{j,n} \frac{Investment_{i,j,n}}{Total\ Investment_{j,n}}$$

Here, $Ownership\ Share_{i,j}$ is the estimated ownership percentage of investor i in company j; $Investment_{i,j,n}$ is the amount that investor i contributed in round n raised by company j; $Total\ Investment_{i,j,n}$ is the total capital company j raised in round n from all participating investors; N is the total number of rounds raised by company j. Weights $w_{j,n}$ are the company's average equity percentage sold in round n, adjusted for its dilution in future rounds due to issuing of new shares when new rounds of financing are raised.

Estimation of ownership shares in fintech companies is not straightforward because the companies in our sample were privately owned and thus not obliged to disclose all details of their financing process. This prompted us to make several assumptions in the estimation of the ownership shares.[100] In our data, the exact amount of capital contributed by a specific investor in each round, $Investment_{i,j,n}$, was not always known. Databases on VC financing often report information on the total size of a financing round, $Total\ Investment_{j,n}$, but not on how much each investor contributed to that round. Therefore, our estimations were based on the assumption that *all investors contributed equal dollar amounts within the same investment round (Assumption 1)*. Second, our data did not allow us to observe how much of its equity the company sold in each round. Therefore, we approximated the equity shares sold in each round, $w_{j,n}$, based on VC industry benchmarks: we assumed that *the company issued and sold 10 per cent of its equity in a pre-seed round, 25 per cent in the seed and in the Series A rounds, 20 per cent in Series B and C, and 15 per cent in each of the remaining rounds (Assumption 2)*. In this, we accounted for the fact

[100] We pursue this empirical approach because of limitations in the financing and ownership data we have access to: eg, we are not able to observe (i) whether governance of private firms is tailored ad hoc based on shareholder agreements that provide for special governance structures or atypical allocation of control rights; or (ii) whether investors indicate that they are active or passive shareholders, in order to factor in those parameters in our empirical analysis regarding the level of influence common shareholders may possess vis-a-vis other corporate actors. While there are techniques in the economic literature to override these data limitations (eg, by using proxies), these would be imperfect and largely based on additional assumptions rather than observation. With our approach, by contrast, we aim to systematically approximate the level of activism by reference to ownership share, which we estimate using two different methods described in this section. Besides, our methodology employing lower and upper bounds (and in-between control scenarios) for the 'lambda' calculations aims to capture the potential range of effects of common ownership, given the data limitations we are faced with within the universe of private companies, including start-ups.

that each following investment round dilutes previous investors' ownership. In practice, equity shares sold in each round may vary depending on the required investment amount, bargaining power of participating investors and implied company valuation. However, our conclusions are not sensitive to decreasing or increasing all or some of the used approximate equity shares by several percentage points as the estimated measures of common ownership concentration change only marginally as a result of such modifications. This is because the impact of the actual shares on the lambda calculation is less significant than there being a common owner or not. We further assumed that *all unsold equity belonged to the founder, who did not have significant holdings in other fintech firms (Assumption 3)*. To check the sensitivity of our results to using different methods of ownership estimation, we also measured the *Ownership Share* as a percentage of an investor's dollar investment in the firm relative to the total capital raised by the firm. This method may underestimate the importance of early investors and overestimate the ownership share of late investors since the latter usually contribute substantially larger amounts. Nevertheless, even when this method of estimating ownership shares was used, the results did not change significantly (not tabulated).

The formula used to calculate the weight that firm j puts on the profits of firm k due to common ownership, the lambda, is as follows:

$$\lambda_{jk} = \frac{\sum_{i\in I}\gamma_{ij}\beta_{ik}}{\sum_{i\in I}\gamma_{ij}\beta_{ij}},$$

where γ_{ij} is the control share of shareholder i in firm j, β_{ij} is the ownership share of shareholder i in firm j, and I denotes the set of shareholders in firm j. This formula applies whenever the objective function of the firm is to maximise a weighted average of shareholder profits, with the control shares γ_{ij} as weights. This objective function was used by O'Brien and Salop (2000) and can be microfounded as the equilibrium outcome of a model of shareholder voting as shown in Azar (2012).[101] Firm j's objective is then to maximise:

$$\sum_{i\in I}\gamma_{ij}\sum_{k=1}^{J}\beta_{ik}\pi_k.$$

As shown in Azar (2012),[102] this is equivalent to maximising:

$$\pi_j + \sum_{k\neq j}\lambda_{jk}\pi_k,$$

where λ_{jk} has the formula above.

[101] O'Brien and Salop (n 27); J Azar, 'A New Look at Oligopoly: Implicit Collusion Through Portfolio Diversification' (PhD dissertation, Princeton University 2012).

[102] Azar, 'A New Look at Oligopoly' (n 101) ch 7.

Based on this formula for the estimation of firm-level lambdas, we estimated average lambdas at the country level, as a simple average and as a weighted average, where we used each fintech company's sales estimate provided by Crunchbase as weights. Table 5 shows the estimated country-level common ownership lambdas in the largest fintech markets. Only countries with at least 30 fintech firms with available ownership data are included in the table.

Table 5 shows lambda estimates for two scenarios: (i) a baseline scenario using the assumptions described above ('lower-limit estimates') where a single founder holds the remaining equity of the company and possibly its sole control (when the company's equity not sold to investors exceeds 50 per cent); and (ii) an alternative scenario outlined below that is used as a robustness check for comparison ('upper-limit estimates') where external investors jointly have full control of the company (on a proportionate basis to their shares). In our baseline lambda estimations, we assumed that the founder controls the remaining equity not sold to the investors. In our sample, a fintech company was estimated to sell 33 per cent of equity, on average, to external investors (older companies with more financing rounds sell more and younger companies with fewer financing rounds sell less). Thus, the company's founder was assumed to control the remaining 67 per cent, on average. Note that company founders were assumed not to have holdings in other fintech companies as we could not observe their actual shareholdings in other private firms. Considering these assumptions, lambdas estimated with this method can be interpreted as a likely lower bound of the actual lambdas. Therefore, to make sure we do not underestimate the actual effects of common ownership in fintech markets, we proceeded to estimate an upper bound for the countries' lambdas. We assumed that equity not issued to investors recorded in the database was dispersed and none of the unrecorded owners (eg, founders and employees that typically hold shares in the start-up) had significant control. Hence, we assumed that the investors held all the control over the company, proportionally to their estimated ownership shares. This assumption allowed us to estimate a likely upper limit for lambdas. When comparing the resulting upper against the lower limits for lambdas, one may conclude that in both cases the observed common ownership overlaps may produce some effects, although the likely effects are relatively larger in the alternative, upper-limit, scenario compared to the baseline, lower-limit, scenario.

Nevertheless, the estimated lambdas under either of these scenarios are still significantly smaller than those found in public markets. This is in large part due to the fact that in public markets, there is a set of large shareholders (including the Big Three and others) that owns large blocks of shares in essentially all firms. When the same shareholder owns shares in a given number N of firms, the number of common ownership connections between the firms that this creates is N(N − 1), counting firm pairs in the two possible orders. For example, suppose a shareholder owns – for simplicity – 100 per cent of 10 firms out of a set of 500 firms in total. The lambdas for the pairs between those 10 firms are all equal to one. However, there are only 10 × 9 = 90 firm pairs with lambdas equal to one, out of a total of 500 × 499 = 249,500 firm pairs. The lambdas for the remaining 249,410 firm pairs are all equal to zero. Thus, even though there are 90 common ownership connections between the firms, the large proportion of zero lambdas implies that the average lambda is approximately zero. Compare this to a scenario in which a shareholder owns all 500 firms, creating 249,500 common ownership connections instead of 90, and yielding an average lambda of one. The latter situation approximates the common ownership pattern among large publicly traded firms (except with a common ownership connection intensity as measured by the lambda of about 0.7 instead of 1), while the former situation approximates the pattern we observe among privately held firms.

We also considered a scenario in which there is not only one, but several founders (all founders of a fintech company listed in the Crunchbase database), holding equal proportions of the equity not sold to external investors. This scenario assumed the existence of multiple founders sharing the remaining equity of the company (and possibly its control if their cumulative shareholdings exceed 50 per cent of the company's equity) in addition to several external, and potentially common, investors. Under this assumption, we obtained lambda estimates that were slightly higher than in the baseline lower-limit scenario, but significantly lower than in the upper-limit scenario. We have not separately tabulated these results, but they served as an intermediate scenario of ownership and control allocation that fit the suggested range of estimated lambdas, lower and upper limits, shown below.[103]

[103] The literature further suggests that 'control sharing' between founders and investors, albeit ad hoc, may be common in start-ups and VC backed private firms. Yet, shareholder agreements that provide for special control sharing arrangements need not be disclosed by private companies. Such arrangements are typically designed to favour minority shareholders, for instance by designating them representation on the company's board directly by contract rather than based on voting power depending on the level of their shareholding. Against this backdrop, our intermediate control scenarios could be enriched to account for such 'control sharing' arrangements where control is shared between the founders and the different external (common and non-common) investors of the company. On the above and for the definition of 'control sharing', see Rauterberg (n 36) 1144. In this shared control scenario, we expect that the lambdas estimations could surpass our upper-limit estimates only if control is not proportionate but asymmetric in favour of common investors vis-a-vis founders and other non-common shareholders. For other 'control sharing' cases (eg, disproportionate control not by common investors), the transition from 'founder' to 'shared with investors' control is not expected to generate lambdas above the upper limit of our results. In future work, one could also collect data on corporate board members to investigate and systematically analyse the ad hoc control dynamics in private companies by alternative means and compare empirical results obtained on 'lambda' estimations with those presented here using our methodology.

Table 5 Lambdas by country

		Lower-limit estimates		Upper-limit estimates	
Country	N companies	Simple average	Weighted by revenue	Simple average	Weighted by revenue
Europe					
UK	765	0.0007	0.0008	0.0089	0.0055
Germany	194	0.0014	0.0025	0.0103	0.0067
France	136	0.0015	0.0022	0.0114	0.0087
Spain	112	0.0010	0.0012	0.0164	0.0219
Switzerland	90	0.0003	0.0002	0.0050	0.0042
Sweden	63	0.0032	0.0039	0.0199	0.0113
Italy	53	0.0014	0.0012	0.0198	0.0149
The Netherlands	52	0.0022	0.0009	0.0155	0.0039
Ireland	46	0.0125	0.0172	0.1477	0.0815
Estonia	40	0.0008	0.0004	0.0473	0.0103
Denmark	31	0.0089	0.0234	0.0819	0.0842
Americas					
US	2,375	0.0005	0.0015	0.0054	0.0045
Canada	215	0.0005	0.0010	0.0102	0.0096
Brazil	191	0.0016	0.0035	0.0179	0.0216
Mexico	108	0.0025	0.0048	0.0305	0.0231
Colombia	48	0.0009	0.0002	0.0123	0.0007
Chile	38	0.0040	0.0021	0.0504	0.0162
Argentina	37	0.0018	0.0014	0.0206	0.0108
Asia					
China	400	0.0005	0.0009	0.0043	0.0035
India	380	0.0009	0.0055	0.0081	0.0102
Singapore	209	0.0006	0.0010	0.0067	0.0093
Indonesia	69	0.0038	0.0029	0.0333	0.0149
Japan	50	0.0061	0.0122	0.0305	0.0243
South Korea	42	0.0032	0.0127	0.0160	0.0224
Australia	119	0.0009	0.0005	0.0071	0.0152
Middle East					
Israel	92	0.0012	0.0010	0.0201	0.0072
United Arab Emirates	52	0.0006	0.0008	0.0100	0.0214
Turkey	35	0.0015	0.0013	0.0217	0.0112

(continued)

Table 5 *(Continued)*

		Lower-limit estimates		Upper-limit estimates	
Country	N companies	Simple average	Weighted by revenue	Simple average	Weighted by revenue
Africa					
South Africa	56	0.0006	0.0004	0.0049	0.0020
Nigeria	53	0.0014	0.0010	0.0286	0.0139
Kenya	34	0.0004	0.0013	0.0086	0.0075

As can be seen in Table 5, the highest lambdas under our baseline scenario are observed in the countries with the highest levels of combined shareholdings by top investors as reported in section II (eg Ireland, Denmark, South Korea). That is, the markets that have the highest top-10 investors' combined investment share and that are typically smaller in size in terms of the number of fintech firms in our sample. However, when measured against the benchmark common ownership weights in publicly traded firms estimated at the level of 0.72 in 2017, these country-level lambdas are generally relatively small.[104] This suggests that the average effect of common ownership in private markets across countries is rather limited or negligible by comparison to the effect in public markets.

Comparison of the different lambdas' estimations shown in Table 5 reveals that the magnitude of lambdas in the scenario representing the upper limit of the lambda estimates is found to be from two to about 10 times higher than in the baseline scenario. Nonetheless, the lambdas are still low compared with average lambdas observed in public markets. The highest weighted average lambda estimates, at 0.08, are again in Ireland and Denmark. Meanwhile, even under this scenario, the United Kingdom has a lambda of 0.006, the US 0.005 and Sweden 0.011. Therefore, we can safely conclude that even if we assume that fintech companies' founders do not hold control, which is instead proportionally distributed among investors, most of the analysed markets have low common ownership lambdas. We also benchmark our fintech lambda estimates with lambdas calculated for private companies in the biotechnology market in the US.[105] We estimate an upper-limit, simple average biotech lambda using the same method as described above and obtain the estimate of 0.01. Compared with this value, fintech lambdas are lower (0.0054 for the same type of lambda), suggesting that the likely impact of common ownership is lower compared with a similarly innovative market such as biotech.

[104] Azar and Vives, 'General Equilibrium Oligopoly and Ownership Structure' (n 10).

[105] Because our data from Crunchbase is limited to fintech companies and their financing, the estimate of benchmark lambda for the biotechnology market is based on another popular VC and PE investments database, Refinitiv.

Table 6 shows the estimated country-level common ownership lambdas by specific fintech market segment in the selected countries under the baseline scenario. These lambdas are weighted averages, with the weights being company sales. Lambdas are estimated only for product markets with at least 10 fintech companies.

Table 6 Lambdas by product market and country – lower-limit estimates

Country	Overall country lambda	Product market				
		Loans	Payments	Asset management	Insurance	Blockchain
Europe						
UK	0.0008	0.0013	0.0014	0.0002	0.0020	0.0004
Germany	0.0025	0.0029	0.0037	0.0006	0.0011	0.0008
France	0.0022	0.0053	0.0033	0.0015	0.0041	0.0004
Spain	0.0012	0.0012	0.0009	0.0016	0.0025	0.0001
Switzerland	0.0002	0.0001	0.0001	0.0001	–	0.0001
Sweden	0.0039	0.0067	0.0059	0.0073	–	–
Italy	0.0012	0.0007	0.0013	0.0046	0.0001	–
The Netherlands	0.0009	0.0003	0.0007	–	–	–
Ireland	0.0172	0.0388	0.0328	–	–	–
Estonia	0.0004	0.0008	0.0005	–	–	0.0005
Denmark	0.0234	–	0.0116	–	–	–
Americas						
US	0.0015	0.0009	0.0016	0.0023	0.0009	0.0028
Canada	0.0010	0.0019	0.0014	0.0003	0.0001	0.0003
Brazil	0.0035	0.0095	0.0101	0.0102	0.0013	0.0002
Mexico	0.0048	0.0077	0.0078	0.0049	0.0002	–
Colombia	0.0002	0.0000	0.0002	–	–	–
Chile	0.0021	–	0.0026	0.0030	–	–
Argentina	0.0014	0.0013	0.0000	–	–	–
Asia						
China	0.0009	0.0018	0.0016	0.0021	0.0013	0.0002
India	0.0055	0.0064	0.0030	0.0028	0.0004	0.0012
Singapore	0.0010	0.0028	0.0007	0.0044	0.0013	0.0006
Indonesia	0.0029	0.0016	0.0024	0.0015	–	–

(continued)

Table 6 *(Continued)*

Country	Overall country lambda	Product market				
		Loans	Payments	Asset management	Insurance	Blockchain
Japan	0.0122	0.0110	0.0136	0.0151	–	0.0041
South Korea	0.0127	0.0837	0.0476	0.0025	–	0.0211
Australia	0.0005	0.0006	0.0015	0.0023	–	0.0020
Middle East						
Israel	0.0010	0.0019	0.0013	0.0005	0.0119	0.0003
United Arab Emirates	0.0008	0.0006	0.0008	0.0019	–	–
Turkey	0.0013	0.0038	0.0019	–	–	–
Africa						
South Africa	0.0004	0.0000	0.0003	–	0.0001	–
Nigeria	0.0010	0.0007	0.0013	–	–	–
Kenya	0.0013	0.0003	0.0002	–	–	–

Table 6 confirms the findings and conclusions drawn from Table 5. Here too, when fintech markets are looked at more narrowly by specific product market segment, the estimated lambdas are generally small in absolute terms. A notable exception where higher lambdas, relatively speaking, are observed in specific fintech markets are in loans and payments in Ireland and South Korea, for example. Still, when compared with similar common ownership weights in public firms, the numbers are very small. Thus, also at the narrower product market level, the estimated likely effects of common ownership in fintech start-ups and private firms are rather small.

Table 7 follows the same structure as Table 6 but shows upper-limit estimates instead of lower-limit estimates. This again shows that the assumption of a lack of control by company founders results in significantly higher estimates than in the baseline scenario. However, the majority of country-product markets illustrated in Table 7 still have low common ownership lambdas. As previously, the exceptions are Ireland, Denmark and South Korea, which have higher common ownership lambdas in the loans and payments markets. Further, somewhat higher common ownership lambdas can also be observed in the following markets: (i) in the asset management fintech markets in Spain, Sweden, Italy and Japan; (ii) in the insurtech market in Israel; and (iii) in the blockchain market in South Korea. Overall, the common ownership lambdas tend to be higher in product markets with fewer fintech firms.

Table 7 Lambdas by product market and country – upper-limit estimates

Country	Overall country lambda	Product market				
		Loans	Payments	Asset management	Insurance	Blockchain
Europe						
UK	0.0055	0.0088	0.0098	0.0026	0.0092	0.0044
Germany	0.0067	0.0069	0.0079	0.0026	0.0093	0.0124
France	0.0087	0.0131	0.0135	0.0133	0.0227	0.0035
Spain	0.0219	0.0257	0.0097	0.0643	0.0114	0.0004
Switzerland	0.0042	0.0006	0.0027	0.0011	–	0.0005
Sweden	0.0113	0.0152	0.0120	0.0629	–	–
Italy	0.0149	0.0033	0.0102	0.0453	0.0012	–
The Netherlands	0.0039	0.0022	0.0036	–	–	–
Ireland	0.0815	0.1220	0.0946	–	–	–
Estonia	0.0103	0.0240	0.0348	–	–	0.0045
Denmark	0.0842	–	0.0532	–	–	–
Americas						
US	0.0045	0.0039	0.0046	0.0046	0.0047	0.0058
Canada	0.0096	0.0110	0.0149	0.0041	0.0005	0.0097
Brazil	0.0216	0.0211	0.0196	0.0378	0.0095	0.0064
Mexico	0.0231	0.0270	0.0304	0.0377	0.0029	0.1002
Colombia	0.0007	0.0001	0.0006	–	–	–
Chile	0.0162	–	0.0213	0.0298	–	–
Argentina	0.0108	0.0052	0.0002	–	–	–
Asia						
China	0.0035	0.0065	0.0056	0.0051	0.0060	0.0006
India	0.0102	0.0116	0.0074	0.0085	0.0020	0.0077
Singapore	0.0093	0.0206	0.0054	0.0135	0.0057	0.0143
Indonesia	0.0149	0.0088	0.0118	0.0108	–	–
Japan	0.0243	0.0206	0.0252	0.0514	–	0.0187
South Korea	0.0224	0.1201	0.0705	0.0044	–	0.0419
Australia	0.0152	0.0029	0.0057	0.0179	–	0.0906
Middle East						
Israel	0.0072	0.0110	0.0095	0.0051	0.0613	0.0079
United Arab Emirates	0.0214	0.0022	0.0057	0.0226	–	–
Turkey	0.0112	0.0393	0.0112	–	–	–
Africa						
South Africa	0.0020	0.0002	0.0011	–	0.0005	–
Nigeria	0.0139	0.0082	0.0150	–	–	–
Kenya	0.0075	0.0035	0.0020	–	–	–

C. Mergers and Acquisitions and Cross-Ownership of Fintech by Common Owners

In this section, we present data on merger and acquisition (M&A) activity among common investors in fintech markets. More specifically, we provide empirical evidence on full acquisitions of fintech companies as well as minority investments in multiple rival fintech companies by the same common investor(s). Our data also illustrate in which of those full or minority acquisitions the target was a direct competitor of the common investor prior to the acquisition. The likely motivations for such acquisitions and the implications as well as the interplay of common ownership and cross-ownership are briefly discussed.

Table 8 shows the top 20 acquirers of fintech firms globally. The table shows the acquirer's name, the number of fully acquired fintech companies, the number of those fully acquired fintech companies that operated in a similar product market as the acquirer, the number of fintech companies in which the acquirer had minority ownership, and the number of those fintech companies in which the acquirer had minority ownership that operated in a similar product market as the acquirer.

Table 8 Top acquirers of fintech companies – full M&A and minority investments in fintech

Company name	Full acquisitions	Of which are competitors	Minority stake acquisitions	Of which are competitors
PayPal	7	6	35	18
Coinbase	6	6	69	63
SoFi	5	5	2	2
Visa	5	5	41	37
JP Morgan	5	4	49	29
Goldman Sachs	4	4	76	54
Nasdaq	4	2	1	0
Zip	4	4	3	3
Stripe	4	4	13	12
PayU	4	3	6	5
Mastercard	4	4	53	43
Kraken	4	4	4	4
Q2ebanking	4	4	0	0
Intercontinental Exchange	3	1	2	0
Envestnet	3	1	1	1

(continued)

Table 8 *(Continued)*

Company name	Full acquisitions	Of which are competitors	Minority stake acquisitions	Of which are competitors
FTX Exchange	3	3	4	2
FIS	3	3	14	11
Nubank	3	3	0	0
Klarna	2	2	2	1
American Express	2	2	42	29

As can be seen, such acquisitions by common investors are not uncommon. Minority investment transactions are significantly more common than full acquisitions of fintech companies. Also, the great majority of the observed either full or minority acquisitions by common investors are transactions in which the acquirer is a competitor with the target (ie, there is cross-ownership). This may more plausibly be expected for instance in the case of corporate VC investors. As an example, PayPal pursued seven full acquisitions of fintech start-ups, in six of which it was considered a competitor of the target. Visa pursued five full acquisitions, in all of which it was considered to compete in the same product market as the target. On the other hand, PayPal completed 35 minority stake acquisitions, in 18 of which it was a competitor to the target. Visa undertook 41 minority stake acquisitions, in 37 of which it was a competitor to the target.

Table 9 includes only those of the top global acquirers of fintech firms from Table 8 that engage in full acquisitions while already having minority ownership in and being a competitor of the target. The table shows the acquirer's name, the number of fully acquired fintech companies in which the acquirer had minority ownership prior to the acquisition, and the number of those fully acquired fintech companies in which the acquirer had a pre-existing minority stake *and* which operated in a similar product market as the acquirer (cross-ownership). Companies listed in Table 8 that engage in no such acquisitions have been dropped from Table 9.

Table 9 Top acquirers of fintech companies – full M&A *given* prior minority investments in fintech and cross-ownership

Company name	Full acquisitions in which acquirer had minority ownership	Of which are competitors
PayPal	1	1
Visa	3	3
Zip	2	2
Stripe	1	1
American Express	1	1

These transactions seem to take place notably less often. Thus, their effect when they do occur is unlikely to be highly egregious. That said, given the rarity and relative obscurity surrounding their occurrence, these transactions may be hard to track and scrutinise. This in turn suggests that they should be more closely monitored. In addition to the motivations behind common ownership transactions outlined in section III.A above (ie, market power or efficiencies), full mergers taking place against the backdrop of common or cross-ownership may be driven by further anticompetitive or procompetitive motives. For instance, the presence of cross-ownership or common ownership may justify seemingly value-reducing mergers for the acquiring firm, because they may nonetheless be rational and efficient from the perspective of the acquirer's diversified common shareholders.[106] The latter may have parallel ownership stakes in the target and non-merging rival firms, whose gains from the acquisition may outweigh any losses incurred by the acquirer.[107] In addition, in a Cournot industry with asymmetric firms, where for instance nine competing firms are equally efficient and commonly owned while the tenth firm is separately owned and either more or less efficient than the others, a merger between the separately owned firm and the firms under common ownership 'may be driven by some efficiency benefits relating to the "shifting" of industry output towards more efficient firms'.[108] In other words, it may be motivated by 'rationalisation of production' efficiencies ('killer' merger) or by a motive to scale down or close their own less efficient operations ('suicidal' merger), depending on whether the separately owned firm is less or more efficient.[109]

Furthermore, acquisitions of start-ups by incumbent rivals may be driven by a 'killer acquisition' motive. That is, a dominant firm may acquire innovative targets to pre-empt future competition from nascent or potential competitors and protect its market power.[110] Similarly, start-up acquisitions may be justified as 'reverse killer acquisitions' in that an incumbent firm buys an innovative firm with the aim to discontinue its own related innovation efforts or projects.[111] On the other hand, acquisitions of high-tech start-up firms may be 'acqui-hires' or 'talent acquisitions', to get access to top human capital.[112] They may also

[106] Azar and Tzanaki (n 9) 243, 250–51, 254.

[107] G Matvos and M Ostrovsky, 'Cross-Ownership, Returns, and Voting in Mergers' (2008) 89 *Journal of Financial Economics* 391; M Antón et al, 'Beyond the Target: M&A Decisions and Rival Ownership' (2022) 144 *Journal of Financial Economics* 44; *cf* J Harford, D Jenter and K Li, 'Institutional Cross-Holdings and their Effect on Acquisition Decisions' (2011) 99 *Journal of Financial Economics* 27. Although Harford et al suggest that any stake in the target may not necessarily suffice to compensate the acquirer's shareholders for losses on the acquirer side, as Matvos and Ostrovsky purport, Antón et al show that parallel stakes in non-merging rivals may more than offset any losses of the acquirer and as a result may well rationalise such transactions from the perspective of the diversified common shareholders.

[108] Azar and Tzanaki (n 9) 254.

[109] ibid.

[110] C Cunningham, F Ederer and S Ma, 'Killer Acquisitions' (2021) 129 *Journal of Political Economy* 649.

[111] Cristina Caffarra, Gregory Crawford and Tommaso Valletti, '"How Tech Rolls": Potential Competition and "Reverse" Killer Acquisitions' (*VoxEU Blog*, 11 May 2020).

[112] JF Coyle and GD Polsky, 'Acqui-Hiring' (2013) 63 *Duke Law Journal* 281.

be a means for established companies to nurture start-up growth and competition for innovative product development with the aim to eventually acquire the best of them (ie, the winner of the innovation race), essentially outsourcing early R&D activity rather than pursuing it organically.[113] This may be a way for experienced firms to partner with and mentor start-ups to facilitate new market entry, manage 'disruptive' innovation and help them navigate complex regulatory processes.[114] Furthermore, information synergies or industry and investor expertise may explain the interest of common investors and potential rivals in full or partial acquisitions of fintech.[115]

From the data at hand, it is difficult to conclude what the precise motivations behind such transactions are or what their effects may be. The fact that they occasionally occur and may have potential unintended or under-appreciated consequences for the companies involved, whose interests may not fully align with those of their minority or common investors, warrants caution and close scrutiny on the part of antitrust agencies. For instance, while start-ups may be funded by incumbents that seek to control the process of competition or innovation, with the aim to expand or kill it, it is unclear if this is bad for competition. This is a possibility if, for example, an established company like Visa can identify ex ante who may be a potential rival – yet it is hard to draw any firm conclusions from this alone, absent a concrete context.

Thus far, our analysis has concentrated on privately held fintech firms as they represent the overwhelming majority of the market in number. Our data includes almost 6,800 privately held fintech companies, of which only 340 firms went public via an IPO. To enrich and supplement the analysis, we compared common ownership in private and public markets. Therefore, we supplemented our first analysis by estimating common ownership lambdas among 77 public fintech companies in the US, the largest fintech market by fintech IPOs. Here, we included only companies that went public after 2000, are still active and have ownership data in the Capital IQ database.

Table 10 shows two examples of the top five owners in publicly listed fintech companies from our sample. This table illustrates the diversity of the largest shareholders of publicly listed fintech companies by their type. Panel A shows the ownership structure of Robinhood Markets, Inc, which went public in July 2021 and had a market capitalisation of nearly $8 billion as of September 2022. We can see that its top five owners consist of two founders of the company, two VC funds (Index Ventures SA and DST Global), and an angel investor fund (Emergent Fidelity Technologies Ltd). In contrast, PayPal, shown in Panel B,

[113] MJ Higgins and D Rodriguez, 'The Outsourcing of R&D through Acquisitions in the Pharmaceutical Industry' (2006) 80 *Journal of Financial Economics* 351.

[114] L Enriques and W-G Ringe, 'Bank–Fintech Partnerships, Outsourcing Arrangements and the Case for a Mentorship Regime' (2020) 15 *Capital Markets Law Journal* 374.

[115] D Benson and RH Ziedonis, 'Corporate Venture Capital as a Window on New Technologies: Implications for the Performance of Corporate Investors When Acquiring Startups' (2009) 20 *Organization Science* 329.

is owned by large asset management firms. The company went public in 2015 and has a market capitalisation of around $100 billion.

Motivated by these examples, we further analyse whether these differences in the composition of top shareholders by type vary depending on when the company went public and its size in terms of market capitalisation. We compare fintech companies with IPO dates before and after 2019, with each of these periods including approximately 50 per cent of companies in the sample. We observe that companies that had an IPO since 2019 are significantly more likely to have company founders among top shareholders. For instance, 42 per cent (32 per cent) of companies with IPO after 2019 have founders among their top five (three) shareholders, while 18 per cent (13 per cent) of companies with IPO before 2019 do so. Also, 42 per cent (16 per cent) of companies with IPO after 2019 have Big Three asset managers among their five (three) largest shareholders, while 51 per cent (44 per cent) of companies with IPO before 2019 have them among the top five (three) owners. In addition, we can observe that the composition of shareholders changes with the growth of companies' market capitalisation. Thirty-four per cent (24 per cent) of smaller companies and 24 per cent (18 per cent) of larger companies respectively have founders among top five (three) shareholders. Moreover, 32 per cent (18 per cent) of smaller and 63 per cent (42 per cent) of larger companies have Big Three asset management firms among their five (three) largest owners.

From this comparison, we can observe that the presence of large asset management firms among top owners is less prevalent in recently publicly listed and smaller firms. However, for fintech companies with a longer history of being public and companies with a larger market capitalisation, the presence of large asset management companies among top shareholders is more likely. This may be due to the increased probability that the company is included in a market index and a larger weight of the company in common market indices when its market capitalisation is higher. This analysis allows us to highlight the differences in shareholder structure between newly listed and mature public fintech companies and illustrates the evolution of common ownership structure during the fintech company's lifecycle.

Table 10 Top shareholders in a newly listed and a mature public fintech company

Panel A: Robinhood Markets, Inc (IPO year 2021)	
Shareholder	**% Ownership**
Bhatt, Baiju Prafulkumar (Co-Founder, Chief Creative Officer & Director)	8.83
Index Ventures SA	8.68
DST Global	6.60
Emergent Fidelity Technologies Ltd	6.39
Tenev, Vladimir (Co-Founder, President, CEO & Chairman of the Board)	6.02

(continued)

Table 10 *(Continued)*

Panel B: PayPal Holdings, Inc (IPO year 2015 (first time in 2002))	
Shareholder	**% Ownership**
The Vanguard Group, Inc	8.20
BlackRock, Inc	6.59
State Street Global Advisors, Inc	3.81
Comprehensive Financial Management LLC	2.75
Geode Capital Management, LLC	1.75

Table 11 shows the largest common investors in public fintech companies. If we look across all shareholders of publicly listed fintech companies in our sample that have ownership in at least 10 companies, Vanguard is the top owner in terms of average ownership share (5.36 per cent). Blackrock is in third place and State Street Global Advisors in ninth (with 3.94 per cent and 1.37 per cent average ownership shares, respectively). Here, we observe ownership patterns similar to those found in other public markets, with large asset management firms being among the largest common owners of publicly listed firms. A comparison can thus be made between private and public fintech markets based on these findings and our previous analysis. While private fintech markets do not appear to exhibit extensive common ownership, such ownership is nearly as prevalent among publicly listed fintech companies as among mature public companies in other industries that have been analysed in the literature.

Table 11 Largest common owners in public fintech companies

Shareholder name	Number of fintech companies with minority ownership	Average ownership share %
Vanguard	54	5.36
Temasek Holdings (Private) Limited	10	4.33
Blackrock	63	3.94
Capital Research and Management Company	16	3.52
Massachusetts Financial Services Company	14	2.23
T Rowe Price Group, Inc. (NasdaqGS:TROW)	40	1.97
Wellington Management Group LLP	27	1.76
Fred Alger Management, LLC	12	1.50
State Street Global Advisors, Inc	55	1.37
Dimensional Fund Advisors LP	32	0.96

Finally, we contrast the estimated lambdas in the private and public fintech markets in the US. The estimate of the common ownership lambda for US public fintech companies, weighted by the companies' market capitalisation, varies between 0.23 and 0.34. The lower-limit estimate is based on the sample of all 77 firms about which we obtained information from Capital IQ. The upper bound is estimated by including only the 48 sampled companies that publicly disclosed at least 70 per cent of their ownership structure. Under both scenarios, the lambda estimates for US public fintech companies were significantly higher than the ones we observed for private fintech markets, even those with the highest common ownership lambdas estimates, such as Ireland or Denmark. These findings suggest that public markets have a significantly higher number of common owners among a large number of companies.

IV. IMPLICATIONS FOR COMPETITION LAW ENFORCEMENT

What implications do the above findings and discussion have for competition law enforcement? The theoretical and empirical analysis offers several insights. Most notably, common ownership in fintech companies presents distinct issues and concerns during the different stages of the lifecycles of such firms, ie, at the initial start-up stage, when they are still private, versus later when they succeed and go public.

First, the degree of common ownership found among fintech start-ups and private firms is rather low. Also, the estimated impact of common ownership in private fintech markets seems limited. Thus, the empirical account portrayed here suggests there is little cause for concern regarding common shareholdings in private firms and markets. This conclusion is supported by further theoretical reasoning. On the one hand, unlike public markets where the largest asset management firms (Big Three) may automatically have minority ownership in the same index of publicly listed companies, which renders common shareholdings within a given industry extensive and systematic, the documented overlapping companies in which top investors have minority ownership in private fintech markets appear limited. Furthermore, it is no surprise that estimated lambdas for common ownership in private fintech markets are low as a matter of theory: lambdas estimations are a quadratic function of the number of connections between commonly owned firms, which by definition are exponentially higher in public markets with index funds as the number and proportion of firm pair connections are higher.

In addition, the governance structure of private companies is often ad hoc and contractually tailored in contrast to publicly listed firms, in which control rights are ordinarily allocated by operation of law ('one share-one vote' default rule) and large asset managers do not seek or participate in special control sharing arrangements (eg, board seats).[116] Moreover, the complexity of the capital

[116] Rauterberg (n 36) 1144. This is also because asset management firms investing in publicly listed companies are subject to more restrictive and demanding regulation.

and governance structure of start-ups in particular may upset the control dynamics between investors and founders and weaken monitoring oversight within such firms.[117] This means that even though there might be overlapping investors with common shareholdings in rival fintech start-ups, these investors may not always have an interest in contracting for or exercising strong control rights over their commonly held firms. Thus, founders may be able to retain control longer while their start-ups remain private, for instance due to financing received by alternative VC investors (eg, corporate VC)[118] or due to the adoption of special governance structures such as dual class shares.[119] Such arrangements, putting insiders focused on specific firm value and performance in charge of directing the firms rather than managers that attend to portfolio-minded common diversified shareholders, may thus mitigate any procompetitive or anticompetitive effects of common ownership.[120] On the flip side, when common investors of fintech start-ups and private companies do have and exercise control (eg, especially VC investors), the control mechanism ('active' and concentrated) for them to produce competition effects and its basis (contractual rather than based on the 'residual claim' status of shareholders/principals mandated by corporate law) may be more easily observable and thus more easily enforceable by antitrust agencies within established frameworks.[121]

By contrast, common ownership in public fintech firms and markets seems more extensive and potentially more worrisome. Once fintech firms mature and successfully go public, common ownership takes on different qualities and characteristics that require tailored assessment. Public firm governance allows for more transparency and accountability as such firms are subject to tighter regulation.[122] Common investors, even 'passive' institutional investors with diffuse diversified shareholdings in rivals, may under certain conditions (eg, size and distribution of other shareholders) be able to implement their anticompetitive incentives.[123] This can occur regardless of the existence of managerial agency costs in large public corporations or legal constraints such as corporate law fiduciary duties which cannot be violated in cases where non-diversified shareholders also come to gain from the anticompetitive outcomes that common ownership produces.[124] Most importantly, however, the common ownership patterns observed in public fintech firms resemble, both empirically and analytically, those found in other

[117] Pollman (n 37); A Alon-Beck, 'Alternative Venture Capital: The New Unicorn Investors' (2020) Case Legal Studies Research Paper No 2020-26.

[118] Alon-Beck (n 117).

[119] V Battocletti, L Enriques and A Romano, 'Dual Class Shares in the Age of Common Ownership' (2022) European Corporate Governance Institute Law Working Paper No 628.

[120] ibid; Tzanaki, 'Varieties and Mechanisms of Common Ownership' (n 6).

[121] See above (nn 37–39) and surrounding text; Tzanaki, 'Varieties and Mechanisms of Common Ownership' (n 6).

[122] Alon-Beck (n 117).

[123] Tzanaki, 'Varieties and Mechanisms of Common Ownership' (n 6).

[124] ibid.

public markets (eg, airlines, banks) in that the largest fintech firms – once they succeed and go public – are incorporated into common ownership networks (eg, of index fund portfolios). In these instances, as suggested elsewhere, competition policy and enforcement need to intelligently develop to effectively address the novel 'diffuse' common shareholding phenomenon.[125]

Furthermore, antitrust risks from common ownership in fintech markets arise not only when fintech firms become public (eg, after a successful IPO), but also when they are acquired through M&A. Both full acquisitions and minority investments in fintech need to be monitored by antitrust enforcers since they can result in common ownership and/or cross-ownership. These investments bring about an additional layer of competition risks and strategic concerns that may be underestimated if the M&A regulatory assessment completely abstracts from and disregards the surrounding context where pre-existing common shareholding or cross-shareholding is observed.[126]

All in all, the level of common ownership in fintech markets varies and its effects are mixed. While the phenomenon is likely more limited and ad hoc in fintech start-ups and any harm potential is likely small and isolated in such cases, competition concerns may become more real and significant in public firms or in smaller product or national markets where common ownership networks appear denser. Overall, these results underline the importance of careful, case-specific analysis of common ownership among fintech firms using the proper analytical frame and empirical context as outlined in this chapter. Here, the types of firms, investors and markets as well as the quality of available data (on financing, ownership, governance and M&A deal structures) are critical parameters for a well-informed assessment of common ownership cases by antitrust agencies. Such a case-by-case, empirically informed approach would naturally add complexity to competition analysis, but without it, competition policy risks being not only obsolete but seriously misguided. This is an important lesson for competition policymakers not merely in cases relating to common ownership in the narrow sense, but also as regards M&A transactions more broadly and thus merger control enforcement.[127]

V. CONCLUSION

Is common ownership in fintech markets of any magnitude and significance? This chapter answers these questions by reference to newly accumulated empirical data and theoretical analysis, arriving at interesting and novel conclusions. First, the observed ownership and governance structures among fintech start-ups

[125] ibid.
[126] See section III.C above.
[127] Azar and Tzanaki (n 9).

and private firms suggest that common ownership is likely to raise little cause for concern. The largest fintech investors globally and by country have limited overlaps in such firms and common shareholdings are not as prevalent as in public markets. Moreover, common VC investors in start-ups are often seen to have a beneficial role for innovation, knowledge diffusion and overall welfare.

However, the picture changes substantially with fintech firms going public and becoming more mature. The ownership composition of these firms is different: while VC and private equity investors dominate private fintech firms, large asset management funds are often the largest owners in publicly listed fintech companies. Governance and control are more standardised and a function of voting power by operation of corporate law rather than contract. Most importantly, the extent and likely impact of common ownership in public fintech firms is likely significant because of the systematic presence of (quasi) index funds and widely overlapping investors in public markets. In this sense, common ownership patterns observed in public fintech firms resemble those found in other public markets (eg, airlines and banks), which may raise concerns for competition policymakers. In addition, strategic motives for fintech start-up acquisitions by common investors with several rival firms in their portfolio or by acquirers who are also a competitor of the target (cross-ownership) may add to the competition concerns and deserve more attention.

Competition law enforcement needs to take stock of this evidence and account for the differences in the types of firms, investors and markets where common shareholdings are present. Further, the distinct implications of common shareholding for both competition and innovation need to be considered in dynamic industries such as fintech. Overall, case-by-case and empirically driven analysis seems a more promising and balanced approach to address the competition implications of common ownership in fintech markets.

5

The Potential Competitive Effects of CBDC on Deposits, Payments and Bank Business Models

YOUMING LIU, EDONA RESHIDI, FRANCISCO RIVADENEYRA AND ANDREW USHER

I. INTRODUCTION

MONEY AND PAYMENTS are being disrupted by the digitisation of the economy. New digital assets emerge almost daily and new participants (some organised as firms but frequently as decentralised networks) are entering the process of money creation and intermediation. In this context, central banks are analysing and preparing their policy responses. Perhaps the most important and consequential response would be the potential issuance of a central bank digital currency (CBDC).

A CBDC is likely to have direct competitive effects on several large and important markets, including the market for deposits and the market for means of payment. Understanding these effects is crucial for the policy debates in central banks and government. While competitive effects extend beyond the considerations that central banks could take as motivations to issue (as they rarely have a mandate for overall competition policy), central banks need to understand the potential competitive consequences on these markets as they ponder the trade-offs in the issuance of CBDC. Moreover, in most jurisdictions the CBDC issuance decision will ultimately rest with the government, which, in contrast to central banks, might consider competition as part of their policy motivation. For example, in the United States, the Federal Reserve issues currency, while the Federal Trade Commission is tasked with enforcing antitrust law and achieving competition.

This chapter surveys the nascent literature on CBDC from the perspective of its potential competitive effects. Given the early stages of CBDC development, most of the academic work so far has focused on how different design features influence the potential effects of CBDC using theoretical models or stylised empirical approaches. First, we summarise the main insights of these papers.

This chapter also, however, aims to organise the general lessons of the literature on competition and provide a list of open questions from the perspective of further potential competitive effects of CBDC.

So far, the findings from the literature suggests that the effects of CBDC on commercial bank deposits and lending are not likely to be too large and will be manageable using a variety of policy choices, including the design features of the CBDC product.[1] In this area, most models highlight the importance of the market power that commercial banks hold in the market for deposits, which constrains the supply. Therefore, the reasonable initial intuition that CBDC would disintermediate deposits can be reversed by the fact that CBDC would improve the terms offered by banks on deposits, expanding demand.

Regarding the market for means of payments, the focus of the literature is on the effects of CBDC on established card payment platforms. The effects will be intricate given the network effects of platforms and the complex web of relationships between the parties involved in the card schemes. Our own analysis suggests that CBDC could improve competition in the market for payments and that the optimal pricing of CBDC is likely to consider the existing benefits that established platforms provide to their current users.

Finally, the effects on bank and payment intermediaries' business models are still being analysed by the literature and require further investigation. These effects will depend on how banks and current payment intermediaries get involved in the distribution of CBDC balances and provision of services in the ecosystem.

We divide this chapter by the relevant markets of interest. First, we discuss the effects of CBDC on commercial bank deposits. Then we discuss the market for means of payments and in particular the potential effects on established payment platforms. Finally, we discuss prospective wider effects that have received less attention from research but that will be as important to analyse, in particular the competitive effects of CBDC on firm entry, on bank business models and on new markets.

II. CBDC AND DEPOSITS

CBDC would perform several uses for households. In this section we discuss the impact on the store of value market, with a particular focus on competition with traditional bank deposits. Households lend to banks for safekeeping, usage for payments and for a rate of return. Central banks would likely offer a product that can be both a safe stable store of value and have usage for some payments. They may even pay interest. This section will highlight some of the research on

[1] See, eg, J Li, 'Predicting the Demand for Central Bank Digital Currency: A Structural Analysis with Survey Data' (2021) Working Paper 2021-65, available at: www.bankofcanada.ca/2021/12/staff-working-paper-2021-65/.

the theory of disintermediation of bank lending by CBDC, then some of the nascent empirical work on CBDC adoption, and finally anticipate the effect on competition of CBDC issuance with differing characteristics.

It is common in the industrial organisation literature to assume households value the characteristics and services of the products they consume rather than the products themselves. What characteristics then matter for the household's allocation of store of value when considering a CBDC? First, remuneration, or the direct payments to the holders of CBDC balances, has been discussed extensively in the theory literature. However, paying interest on balances may be unattractive to the central bank as it presents several challenges because of its potential effects on deposits and for the implementation of offline payments. Second, cash, holding deposits, or CBDC allows the household to make payments to retailers online and offline, as well as to peers. A more thorough discussion of the effects on the payments market succeeds this section, but the household derives value in holding balances that can be used for payments. Other characteristics, for which a full discussion is beyond the scope of this chapter, include use in budgeting, privacy from public and private agents, and other services bundled with an account.[2]

A. Market Definition

With the household demand for a CBDC formalised, we turn to defining the relevant market for considering a potential CBDC. Households can hold many products in their portfolio including mutual funds, stocks and bonds. At present, these products are very difficult to use for payments, we therefore exclude them from the relevant market. Next is cash, which in almost all countries is a direct liability of the central bank.[3] For example, an anonymous CBDC that did not pay interest that also credibly protected the privacy of the user up to a certain legal limit would be quite close to cash. An alternative example would be a CBDC that paid interest, required full know-your-customer compliance, and was accessed through the banking system. Such a CBDC would be closer to a bank deposit. For this section, we will restrict ourselves in defining the market as cash and bank deposits that can be easily used in payments.

B. CBDC and Disintermediation of the Banking Sector

The literature on CBDC as a competitor to bank deposits principally began with a discussion of the disintermediation of bank deposits, ie, the substitution

[2] For more information on the definitions and potential effects on the demand for a new CBDC, see ibid.

[3] Privately issued cash like instruments such as pre-paid cards would also be in the relevant market, but we refrain from discussing them.

away from bank deposits to CBDC. This could have the effect of reducing the overall lending in the economy, giving central banks some reason for caution. This comes from the simple accounting identity that loans equal deposits plus equity, and that without an extra source of funding, banks must reduce their lending by the amount of deposits they lose. Keister and Sanches consider the introduction of a CBDC to an economy with perfectly competitive banks (ie, banks without any market power). With competitive banks they show that a CBDC will result in disintermediation. However, they argue that one should weigh the potential efficiency gains in payments from a CBDC against the costs of disintermediation.[4]

Andolfatto adds market power in lending as well as deposit to the discussion, implying a disconnect between the lending rate and the deposit rate.[5] Further banks have access to funding outside the deposit market, namely through the central bank's lending facilities. If the interest rate on CBDC were to induce an increase in the deposit rate, the amount of lending could in fact *increase*. Chiu et al also consider a model with bank market power, except they use a model of monopolistic competition that is more likely to be empirically valid.[6] Indeed, they calibrate the model to US data and find that CBDC could raise bank lending and overall output. These models have, however, taken the demand for consumers as a theoretical object.

We now turn to the new and growing empirical literature on CBDC. Li began considering the choice of consumers to allocate their liquid assets.[7] With household level data she models the introduction of CBDC using the consumers' valuation of its attributes. These include the consumer value of interest income, the ease of use in budgeting, privacy and the bundling of bank services. Inherent in the question is the difficulty of predicting the demand for a product that does not yet exist. With this in mind, Li finds a large range of potential outcomes depending on the design as well as unknown tastes for the product by households.[8]

Whited et al estimate consumer choice from branch level data, then take the demand to a model of banking with richer features than previous papers.[9] In their model, the banks are able to replace a fraction of their deposits with wholesale funding. They predict significant disintermediation especially if the

[4] T Keister and D Sanches, 'Should Central Banks Issue Digital Currency?' (2019) Federal Reserve Bank of Philadelphia Working Paper No 21-37, available at: www.philadelphiafed.org/the-economy/banking-and-financial-markets/should-central-banks-issue-digital-currency-2021.

[5] D Andolfatto, 'Assessing the Impact of Central Bank Digital Currency on Private Banks' (2021) 131 *Economic Journal* 525.

[6] J Chiu et al, 'Bank Market Power and Central Bank Digital Currency: Theory and Quantitative Assessment' (2019) SSRN, available at: ssrn.com/abstract=3331135.

[7] See Li (n 1).

[8] ibid.

[9] T Whited et al, 'Will Central Bank Digital Currency Disintermediate Banks?' (2022) SSRN, available at: ssrn.com/abstract=4112644.

CBDC were to pay interest. Additionally, as wholesale funding is more interest rate sensitive than deposits, the introduction of a CBDC will likely make banks more fragile.

The account fees that consumers pay for their accounts have not been fully studied in the context of the issuance of CBDC. Gibney et al report the nature of the fees and penalties for retail deposit accounts. Some accounts come with monthly account fees, charges for withdraws or transfers and overdraft penalties.[10] A CBDC with attributes similar to a bank account would compete along these margins, especially if the CBDC lacked such fees. Banks would be able to respond to the attributes of a new competitor, potentially causing them to reduce some of their fees to retain consumers. A full account of the welfare and broader implications of this effect is yet to be done. We discuss some of these effects in section IV.

C. CBDC and Stability Considerations

Without an interoperable digital option for households to withdraw their deposits from a bank, the risk of bank runs could be limited in an increasingly digital economy. A CBDC would likely decrease the frictions of converting bank money to public money, as the current option is the physical withdraw of cash or the run to another form of private money, namely another bank. Some, such as Kumhof and Noone, have argued this would have a deleterious effect on stability.[11]

A different argument claims that as CBDC balances would be outside the banking system, at least a portion of the retail payments system would be cushioned from bank runs. This would allow consumers to continue making and receiving payments even during financial stress. Much earlier, Tobin argued that the separation between the functions of deposit and lending would contribute to the effective monitoring of banks' lending through depositors.[12]

Additionally, many papers have discussed the advantages of a CBDC over a bank regulator.[13] The information from a sudden inflow to CBDC would allow the central bank to identify and respond to a run with other policies. A limit on inflow to CBDC or change in the remuneration of CBDC could serve as a tool to stifle such a run directly. Ahnert et al adds a CBDC to the global games literature on bank runs and finds that a CBDC could cause the banks to endogenously

[10] C Gibney et al, 'Banking Fees in Canada: Patterns and Trends', Financial Consumer Agency of Canada (2014).

[11] M Kumhof and C Noone, 'Central Bank Digital Currencies – Design Principles for Financial Stability' (2021) 71 *Economic Analysis and Policy* 553.

[12] T Tobin, 'Financial Innovation and Deregulation in Perspective' (1985) 3 *Bank of Japan Monetary and Economic Studies* 19.

[13] See Keister and Sanches (n 4); S Priazhkina, 'Bank Runs and Central Bank Digital Currency' (2022) Working Paper on file with authors.

change their deposit rates to prevent runs, which might on net reduce the run probability.[14] There are several design choices that could affect the ability of consumers to run from banks to CBDC. For example, a limit on the amount of withdraws could forestall runs. However, this would come at the expense of usage and confidence in CBDC.

III. CBDC AND PAYMENTS

If issued, CBDC may not only serve as a store of value but also as a means of payment. In this section, we discuss the effects that a potential CBDC may have on the market for payments. More specifically, we will focus on how CBDC might affect the competition between non-bank payments service providers (PSPs), such as payment card networks and other fintechs that are entering the payments market.

First, we describe the payment industry together with its main issues and regulatory interventions. Next, we provide an overview of research in the area of platform competition, focusing specifically on payment platforms. We focus on the economic literature that studies the linkage between competition and efficiency in two-sided markets. We show that the literature has found mixed results towards competitive efficiency in two-sided markets, and that procompetitive policies alone might not be sufficient to improve market efficiency. Finally, we discuss the introduction of CBDC as a payment platform and describe the intuition behind recent research and policy work that focuses on the effects of CBDC in the payments landscape.

A. Background and Issues in the Payments Market

The payment industry is characterised by three main features. First, it is two-sided, meaning that there is interdependence between two types of end-users, consumers and merchants.[15] Specifically, consumers choosing a payment method are often concerned about the number of merchants who accept that method of payment. And similarly, merchants' decisions on whether to accept a payment method also depends on the number of consumers choosing that payment method. Examples of common payment methods include cash, debit and credit cards. The existence of this network effect adds complexity to the analysis of competitive efficiency in the payments market, and the effects of a CBDC.

[14] T Ahnert et al, 'Central Bank Digital Currency and Financial Fragility' (2022) Working Paper, available at: www.econ.queensu.ca/sites/econ.queensu.ca/files/CBDCFF.pdf.

[15] See, eg, JC Rochet and J Tirole, 'Two-Sided Markets: A Progress Report' (2006) 37 *Rand Journal of Economics* 645; M Armstrong, 'Competition in Two-Sided Markets' (2006) 37 *Rand Journal of Economics* 668.

Additionally, while there are many new entrants, the industry is relatively concentrated with a few main payment networks, including Visa, MasterCard, Discover and American Express, dominating the market. Further, all of these networks still depend on commercial banks for payment processing and clearing. In addition, some of the networks do not interact with end-users directly but depend on commercial banks for issuing and acquiring services as well. In the so-called 'open system', networks depend on issuing banks for issuing payment cards to consumers and on acquiring banks for merchant-related services that enable merchants to accept payment cards. In these systems, the networks set the interchange fee, which is paid by the acquiring bank to the issuing bank every time a transaction is made.[16]

The payment card industry has been under scrutiny for decades. Regulators and policymakers have noted that consumers are highly subsidised by the card networks, which leads to them using their cards excessively. Merchants and their banks, on the other hand, face high fees that are then passed on to consumers in the form of increased prices. Moreover, these payment networks impose restrictive, and potentially regressive rules, on the merchant side. For instance, quite often merchants must comply with no surcharge rules that forbid them from charging higher prices to consumers based on the means of payment used.[17] This implies that cards that are more expensive for merchants to accept, such as credit cards, will be cross-subsidised by cheaper means of payments such as debit and cash. As high-income consumers are the ones most likely to hold and use cards with higher reward levels that are more expensive for merchants to accept, the cross-subsidies between the payment methods are regressive transfers from low-income consumers to high-income consumers.[18]

Competition authorities and regulators in many jurisdictions, including the United States, Canada, the European Union and Australia, have taken legal action with the aim of improving some of these issues in the payments industry.[19] The most common regulatory interventions, motivated by merchants' complaints, have been in relation to interchange fees. Although following similar objectives of lowering interchange fees, jurisdictions followed different legal and theoretical approaches. Some of the interventions were initiated and executed based on

[16] See M Rysman and J Wright, 'The Economics of Payment Cards' (2014) 13 *Review of Network Economics* 303 for an overview of payment platforms.

[17] See, eg, F Hayashi, 'Discounts and Surcharges: Implications for Consumer Payment Choice' (2012) Federal Reserve Bank of Kansas City Payment System Research Briefing, available at: www.kansascityfed.org/documents/693/briefings-psr-briefingjune2012.pdf.

[18] See, eg, M Felt et al, 'Distributional Effects of Payment Card Pricing and Merchant Cost Pass-through in Canada and the United States' (2021) Bank of Canada Staff Working Paper No 2021-8, available at: www.bankofcanada.ca/wp-content/uploads/2021/02/swp2021-8.pdf.

[19] For a recent summary of regulatory interventions and investigations in different jurisdictions, see F Hayashi and J Maniff, 'Public Authority Involvement in Payment Card Markets: Various Countries, August 2020 Update' (2020) Federal Reserve Bank of Kansas, available at: www.kansascityfed.org/documents/6660/PublicAuthorityInvolvementPaymentCardMarkets_VariousCountries_August2020Update.pdf.

partial analysis while ignoring the two-sided nature of the industry. As a result, the impact of many interventions has sometimes backfired and been accompanied by many unintended effects. Most commonly, they have caused harm to consumers by inverting the traditional business model from a 'merchant-pays' to 'consumer-pays'. Such interventions usually result in reduced revenues for issuing banks, which then react by either increasing existing fees to consumers, such as higher bank account fees, fewer free checking accounts and lower consumer rewards or by introducing new fees to consumers.[20]

For instance, the Reserve Bank of Australia (RBA) aimed to lower interchange fees as it believed that credit card usage was excessively high. However, evidence from Australia shows no substantial changes in card transactions following the intervention in reducing interchange fees.[21] Furthermore, the no-surcharge rule was deemed anticompetitive in Australia. One result, however, was excessive surcharging by merchants to card users, which the RBA subsequently regulated. Another example is the Durbin Amendment in the United States that focused on debit card transactions exclusively by capping only debit interchange fees.[22] The aim of this intervention was to lower consumers' and merchants' costs. However, the Amendment ended up benefiting only some large merchants and it harmed consumers as merchants did not pass through any of their fee savings to them.[23]

B. Profit-Maximising Payment Platforms

Although the payments market is currently concentrated, with only a few dominating platforms, there are several smaller players and potential entrants that bring competition into the market. The objective of this section is to use the economic literature to answer one main question: can competition in the payments market lead to market efficiency (ie, maximising total welfare)? The key concern behind this question is whether platforms would fully internalise the network externality (an increase in value to other users when a user joins the platform): in essence, how a user's utility or a merchant's profit depends on the composition of a network's users.

[20] See, eg, C Howard et al, 'The Effect of Regulatory Intervention in Two Sided Markets: An Assessment of Interchange-Fee Capping in Australia' (2005) 4 *Review of Network Economics* 350.

[21] See especially, R Hayes, 'Is Price Regulation of Payment Card Associations Effective? Evidence from a Dramatic Policy Experiment' (2010) SSRN, available at: papers.ssrn.com/sol3/papers.cfm?abstract_id=1546869.

[22] For details, see Press Release, 'Federal Reserve issues a final rule establishing standards for debit card interchange fees and prohibiting network exclusivity arrangements and routing restrictions' Board of Governors of the Federal Reserve (29 June 2011), available at: www.federalreserve.gov/newsevents/pressreleases/bcreg20110629a.htm.

[23] See, eg, B Hubbard, 'The Durbin Amendment, Two-Sided Markets, and Wealth Transfers: An Examination of Unintended Consequences Three Years Later' (2013) SSRN, available at: papers.ssrn.com/sol3/papers.cfm?abstract_id=2285105.

We start with the most optimistic answer to the question. Jain and Townsend show that competition among platforms forces them to internalise the aforementioned externality, and consequently, leads to Pareto efficiency.[24] To prove this, they consider a general equilibrium model with an intermediary that creates an infinite number of potential platforms. Each platform specifies the number of merchants and consumers that it anticipates accommodating.[25] The intuition behind the result that the competitive equilibrium is efficient is simple. Assuming the intermediary can create platforms with all possible composition of buyers and sellers, they will expand the commodity space to incorporate the network externality in a manner suggested by Arrow.[26] The user prices for joining platforms, which each user takes as given, fully internalise the users' marginal utility gains from altering the size of the platform.

However, Jain and Townsend rely on the crucial assumption that the market is perfectly competitive, which might not be a reasonable assumption in the payments market.[27] They also study the case under which the intermediary is a monopoly. As expected, in the monopoly equilibrium the intermediary will use its market power to charge higher prices, leading to an inefficiency.

A potentially more realistic model on the payments market considers an oligopolistic economy where each platform has market power and sets prices to maximise its own profit. Armstrong considers such a market with two platforms, which sell horizontally differentiated consumption goods delivering different intrinsic values as well as two-sided network benefits to consumers.[28] Armstrong characterises the equilibrium in which both platforms charge a flat price.[29] A key insight from Armstrong's analysis is that the network effects make the market more competitive compared with a market without network effects. This is because the network effect will generate a negative feedback loop. For example, when a platform raises its price on the consumer side, consumers will leave that platform and join the rival platform, which further drives merchants of that platform to leave and join the rival platform even though the merchant side prices have not changed.

Based on the insight from Armstrong, network effects are procompetitive – a larger network effect will lead to a more competitive market – raising the question of whether it will lead to a more efficient market. The answer is: not always. The reason is twofold. First, even with a considerably large network effect, prices in the oligopolistic equilibrium are still distorted by the market power.

[24] A Jain and R Townsend, 'The Economics of Platforms in a Walrasian Framework' (2021) 71 *Economic Theory* 877.

[25] ibid.

[26] KJ Arrow, 'The Organization of Economic Activity: Issues Pertinent to the Choice of Market Versus Nonmarket Allocation' (1969) 1 *Analysis and Evaluation of Public Expenditure: The PPB System* 59.

[27] See Jain and Townsend (n 24).

[28] Armstrong (n 15).

[29] ibid.

Second, in order to focus on market-sharing equilibria,[30] Armstrong assumes that network effects are small compared with the degree of differentiation between the two platforms, and that the differentiation affects the platforms' market power in a positive way. This means that the more differentiated these two platforms are, the more market power they have to set higher prices.[31] Therefore, while the network effect is procompetitive and drives platforms to set lower prices, the greater differentiation between platforms will distort prices in the opposite direction. On the other hand, if platforms are allowed to have a large network effect without restrictions, competition between platforms will have the tendency towards a monopolistic market. In this case each consumer and merchant in the market chooses to join only one platform, which leaves the other platform with no incentive to stay in the market, and market power still distorts prices.

Surprisingly, it is possible that the procompetitive tendency of the network effect can be reversed if a pricing formula other than flat pricing is used. This is mentioned in Armstrong in the discussion of two-part tariffs and further studied by White and Weyl by focusing on a special case of this type of tariff.[32] Armstrong extends its model to accommodate more flexible pricing, a two-part tariff, under which users pay a fixed fee together with a marginal price for each user on the other side who joins the platform.[33] The equilibrium analysis shows that marginal prices enable platforms to ease the competition so that they can charge higher prices as the network benefits become larger.

White and Weyl study a special case in which users pay a marginal price exactly equal to the network benefit they receive from each user participating on the other side.[34] They then propose a solution concept, Insulated Equilibrium, based on the idea that users from each side facing this special two-part tariff will have a dominant choice of platform participation. In their model, each user's decision on which platform to join is independent of the participation decisions on the merchant's side. Following the solution concept, platforms in a duopoly commit to using this sophisticated pricing strategy and, consequently, they are able to shut down the negative feedback loop mentioned in Armstrong and reduce the competitive effects of network benefits.

While the theories mentioned above apply generally to any two-sided market, there is also a growing literature studying this topic in the context of payments market.[35] Many papers in this literature have focused on the high interchange fees. Guthrie and Wright are among the first in the literature to study whether

[30] A market-sharing equilibrium means platforms share the market. The opposite is the tipping equilibrium, in which one platform dominates the market.

[31] See Armstrong (n 15).

[32] EG Weyl and A White 'Insulated Platform Competition' (2016) SSRN, available at: papers.ssrn.com/sol3/papers.cfm?abstract_id=1694317.

[33] See Armstrong (n 15).

[34] See Weyl and White (n 32).

[35] See Rysman and Wright (n 16) for a review of this literature.

competition between payment platforms can lower interchange fees.[36] However, their analysis shows that the results are case dependent and that, in some cases, increased competition might even lead to a higher interchange fee: in a more competitive environment, payment platforms may pay more rewards to consumers while increasing the merchant fees. Chakravorti and Roson follow a different modelling approach and find that competition in the payments market unambiguously reduces equilibrium prices.[37] However, they also admit that competition may not always lead to welfare improvements because it might lead to more distortions in the interchange fees. For example, credit card companies may pay more cash-back benefits to consumers while increasing the merchant fees.

C. CBDC as a Public Payment Platform

There are abundant examples across many markets where public and private products coexist. Those examples include, more specifically, goods provided in platform-like set-ups like schools and hospitals. Yet, if issued, a CBDC would be a government-run product competing directly with existing payment platforms. While cash competes as a means of payment, it does not have the ability to cross-subsidise the way electronic payments do and cannot be used online. In this way, a CBDC would open a new competition front between public and private means of payments. In this section, we focus on discussing various potential competitive effects of CBDC on the payments industry.

i. CBDC and Payments at the Point of Sale (PoS)

In this use case, the ecosystem of firms includes the card networks (which establish the connections between consumers' and merchants' banks), the commercial banks (which issue the deposits used to transfer value between the parties and coordinate with the networks to issue the payment cards to depositors), and merchant acquirers (who provide payment services to merchants, like terminals). There are a multitude of prices and fees that could be affected by the introduction of a CBDC. But perhaps one of the most important price channels through which CBDC could affect the established payment platforms is via its effect on the interchange fee charged today by debit and credit card networks. A CBDC could enter the market as a competing platform by setting its own fees and rules. The incumbent card networks might respond by lowering their fees or modifying

[36] G Guthrie and J Wright, 'Competing Payment Schemes' (2007) 55 *Journal of Industrial Economics* 37.

[37] S Chakravorti and R Roson, 'Platform Competition in Two-Sided Markets: The Case of Payment Networks' (2006) 5 *Review of Network Economics* 118. Different from Guthrie and Wright, where it is assumed that platforms are non-profit and provide identical network effects, Chakravorti and Roson focus on profit-maximising platforms and allow them to offer different network benefits to different consumers.

the terms they set on the members of the ecosystem (such as 'honour all cards' and 'no-surcharge' rules). However, the incumbents might further distort their fee structures – giving more rewards to consumers and elevating merchant fees – in response to the entry of a CBDC platform. The equilibrium outcomes are likely to be complex, in particular because the two-sidedness of the market will play a prominent role.

ii. CBDC in Online Markets

The next frontier of competition issues will likely arise in online payments. At present, no outside or public money is offered to consumers for online transactions. Therefore, further to helping moderate interchange fees for PoS transactions, a CBDC as an online means of payment could provide end-users with an alternative to credit cards and other emerging methods of payment. According to Usher et al, CBDC for online transactions could provide the same safety and affordability that cash has offered in the offline world.[38] It is crucial to point out that while CBDC has the potential to be procompetitive in these markets, the actual impact will greatly depend on the response of the existing incumbent payment platforms. If CBDC entry were to trigger a wave of mergers and acquisitions and result in a more concentrated payments industry, then the effects might be weaker. More research is needed to understand which effect has the potential to dominate if such a scenario unfolds.

iii. CBDC as a Benevolent Payment Platform

If the CBDC payment system were to operate in the same way as the current private payment platforms, ie, focusing on maximising profits, it would exert a similar competitive effect as any other private platform and the same results as reviewed in the previous section would hold. CBDC, however, might operate as a benevolent payment platform aiming to maximise welfare instead of profits. Most of the literature so far has explored the effects of competition between profit-maximising platforms. In contrast, Liu et al focus on the payments aspect of CBDC by introducing CBDC as a benevolent payment platform that maximises total surplus instead of profits in an oligopolistic market competing with private payment platforms.[39] They find that the competitive equilibrium with a benevolent payment platform leads to higher social welfare than the equilibrium with profit-maximising platforms only. In addition, the CBDC platform faces a trade-off between attracting users to the CBDC platform and accommodating some users' preferences for using the private payment

[38] A Usher et al, 'A Positive Case for a CBDC' (2021) Bank of Canada Staff Discussion Paper 2021-11, available at: www.bankofcanada.ca/2021/07/staff-discussion-paper-2021-11/.

[39] Y Liu et al, 'CBDC and Payment Platform Competition' (2022) Working Paper on file with authors.

platform (due to heterogeneity in consumer taste). For that reason, a CBDC payment platform should not only consider undercutting the private platform but adjust its price to the level that users might still choose to use the private platform. This suggests that setting the optimal prices of using the CBDC payment platform may not be as straightforward as setting the fee consistent with a cost recovery objective, as is done in other payments systems provided by central banks. This finding also implies that while cash is an obvious alternative payment option, it might not necessarily be welfare improving because the price to pay with cash is zero to both sides, therefore precluding the cross-subsidies allowed by electronic payments.

iv. CBDC and Layers of Intermediation

One of the main features of the non-bank payment service provider (PSP) industry, as previously mentioned, is that it depends on commercial banks to act as intermediaries for completing the settlement part of their payment business. More layers of intermediation usually translate to higher mark-ups for end consumers, as financial participants in each layer need to be compensated for their services and may exert market power. Halaburda et al explore this double marginalisation problem in the card payments market.[40] One way in which CBDC could improve competition in payments is if it were to reduce the layers of intermediation. Andolfatto notes that one clear advantage for CBDC, compared with other PSPs, is that it will have access to wholesale payment rails.[41] The actual procompetitive potential of CBDC will depend on the design choices that central banks will make especially with regard to their CBDC's distribution model. In policy circles, a distinction has grown between CBDCs issued directly to end-users, named a 'unilateral' or 'single-tier' system, and an 'intermediated' or 'two-tier' system where banks and other intermediaries would deal with the end-users.[42] Bossu et al discuss this distinction and list the functions the public or private sector would have to divide in the two-tier case.[43] While a one-tier distribution model is still being considered, most central banks are discussing the implementation of a two-tier or intermediated approach for CBDC. This implies that central banks might still depend on other financial institutions (FIs) to provide end-user services. Potential intermediaries include existing commercial banks or other regulated FIs and fintech companies as well as public entities.

[40] H Halaburda et al, 'Interchange Fee, Market Structure and Excessive Intermediation in the Payments Market' (2022) Working Paper on file with authors.

[41] D Andolfatto, 'On the Necessity and Desirability of a CBDC' (2021) *Mimeo*, available at: gceps.princeton.edu/wp-content/uploads/2021/11/21oct_Andolfatto-paper_CBDC4US.pdf.

[42] China's CBDC pilot is a two-tiered system where the banks offer consumers access to CBDC wallets.

[43] W Bossu et al, 'Behind the Scenes of Central Bank Digital Currency' (2022) IMF FinTech Notes No 2022/004, available at: www.imf.org/en/Publications/fintech-notes/Issues/2022/02/07/Behind-the-Scenes-of-Central-Bank-Digital-Currency-512174.

Nonetheless, CBDC may still have the potential to exert a competitive role in the industry if it entails fewer layers of intermediation, or more efficient intermediation. CBDC might allow access for more efficient intermediaries across the distribution chain compared with other PSPs or in comparison to the current intermediated distribution models that most central banks employ for cash.

v. CBDC versus Other Interventions

Another aspect to consider is how CBDC issuance would differ in impact and interplay from traditional regulatory or antitrust interventions. First, a CBDC would be an alternative payment platform for customers and merchants and not simply a cap or restriction on existing platforms' fees. This could potentially help bring down the fees charged by the established networks as end-users would be granted with an additional payment option. This is crucial, especially if regulation or CBDC entry leads to market consolidation by incumbent payment platforms. In this way at least, the end-users that adopt the CBDC platform could benefit directly. Second, CBDC could be a powerful tool in restricting the scope of some of the unintended effects that have risen from other regulatory interventions. For instance, if caps are put on interchange fees, issuing banks can simply find alternative ways to increase their lost revenues by increasing or introducing other fees. If only private platforms are competing in the market, then doing so would be simple as all platforms have the same incentives. If, however, there were a public platform in the market that did not have such incentives then it might be more difficult for private platforms to do so without losing consumers. Therefore, CBDC could work in concert with regulation to achieve more efficient policy outcomes.

vi. Potential Limitations to CBDC's Potential Competitive Effects

CBDC will not offer rewards and benefits in the way that credit card networks offer their consumers. This might make it difficult for CBDC to attract users or exert competitive pressure especially in the credit card market. Finally, CBDC could also face the same entry barriers as private entrants in the payments market. Existing network effects, where consumers value the methods of payments that are widely accepted by merchants and vice versa, as well as privacy concerns from the public, might limit the adoption and competitive effects of CBDC.

IV. CBDC AND THE BUSINESS MODEL OF BANKS

The competitive effects in the markets discussed earlier will interact with each other. Perhaps the most evident channel of interaction will be through the effects on the business model of banks as they are both issuers of deposits, issuers of cards and participants in the electronic card schemes. In this section, we discuss some of the potential competitive effects on the business models of banks.

The question of effects on business models of banks goes beyond the effects on lending from a substitution away from deposits towards CBDC (discussed in section II). Bank deposits offer services beyond store of value and payments; further, deposits are only a part of a suite of services that banks provide to their customers. The substitution towards CBDC might also affect the product bundle that traditional banks offer. CBDC might also affect banks through its effects on the complementarity between deposits, payments, lending, investments and data. For example, the adoption of CBDC as a means of payment could affect the economies of scope between payments data and consumer and business credit, which has been documented empirically quite extensively.[44]

While the literature on CBDC has not yet explored this channel, some recent work is exploring the effects of fintech competition on banks which provides some guidance as to the potential effects of CBDC. For example, Parlour et al study the impact of fintech competition in payment services when a bank uses payment data to learn about consumers' credit quality.[45] They find that competition from fintech payment providers disrupts the information spillover. In their model, a signal about a consumer's credit quality can be extracted from payment transactions. In this way, a bank has less precise information of a loan applicant's credit quality if the applicant has made payments via a fintech rather than through the lending bank. They show that if the assumption of less precise information is relaxed, bank lending would increase, however the effect on consumer welfare would be ambiguous. If CBDC competes with banks for payments, its informational disruption effects for banks could be similar.

At the outset, the direction and overall magnitude of these effects is unclear because banks could maintain customer relationships (or even offer new services related to the CBDC product) if they become involved in the CBDC ecosystem. For example, banks could be providers of the electronic wallet services that allow customers to hold CBDC balances. In this case, the customer relationship could be largely unaffected even if the balance that a customer uses for payments is no longer issued by the commercial bank. If the complementarity between different bank products and services is determined mostly by the customer holding a relationship instead of the amount of balances she holds, then we could expect the effect of CBDC on banks to be limited via this channel. Theoretical and empirical work will be required to understand and quantify these effects.

V. CONCLUSION

This chapter surveys the emerging literature on CBDC and discusses the potential competitive effects on three areas: the market for deposits; the market for

[44] See, eg, L Mester et al, 'Transactions Accounts and Loan Monitoring' (2007) 20 *Review of Financial Studies* 529.

[45] C Parlour et al, 'When FinTech Competes for Payment Flows' (2020) SSRN, available at: papers.ssrn.com/sol3/papers.cfm?abstract_id=3544981.

means of payments; and on the business models of the established intermediaries in these two markets. The literature so far suggests that the effects on commercial bank deposits and lending are likely to be manageable while the overall effects on payment intermediaries and bank business models still require further investigation.

Looking ahead, however, CBDC is likely to have competitive effects beyond those we considered here. One such effect could be enabling the entry of new types of intermediaries to the payment ecosystem, in particular firms that are not deposit-taking institutions. These new types of firms would not compete directly with banks in issuing deposits but in offering associated financial services. This has the potential to increase the competition for customer relationships.

One last aspect that will be relevant to consider in future research is how the competitive effects discussed might vary as cash demand and usage wanes in the future. Recent literature has highlighted the role that cash has in limiting market power in payments, therefore it will be important to explore if the competitive effects of CBDC discussed above would substantively change in the absence of cash.

Part II

Data, Sustainability and Competition Law in Fintech

6

Data-Related Abuses: An Application to Fintech

NICOLO ZINGALES

I. INTRODUCTION

WITH THE ADVANCEMENT of the so-called 'data economy',[1] facilitated by an increasingly connected environment, the collection and use of data has become a key competitive factor. The exponential growth of this paradigm in the form of a 'data deluge' was recognised more than a decade ago by the *Economist*,[2] and several legislative and policy initiatives sprung up over the last decade to facilitate this phenomenon.[3] Various sectors have been significantly disrupted by increasing data availability and mobility, and the financial sector is one of those. Technology and consumer data are leveraged by so-called 'fintechs' (providers of technology-enabled innovation in financial services) to enter into a space traditionally occupied by banks and other financial institutions. Indeed, the ability of fintech providers to offer value to consumers without undertaking full-scale entry into the bundle of product and services traditionally offered by financial institutions enables those providers not only to disintermediate those institutions,[4] but also to accumulate data points on their

[1] 'A data economy is a global digital ecosystem in which data is gathered, organised, and exchanged by a network of vendors for the purpose of deriving value from the accumulated information'. See European Commission, 'Communication from the Commission to the European Parliament, the Council, the European Economic and Social Committee and the Committee of the Regions 'Building a European Data Economy' (COM(2017)9 final).

[2] 'The Data Deluge' *Economist* (25 February 2010).

[3] In the EU, a range of initiatives has been taken as part of the European Data Strategy: European Commission, 'European Data Strategy' (2020), available at: commission.europa.eu/strategy-and-policy/priorities-2019-2024/europe-fit-digital-age/european-data-strategy_en. To learn more about alternative approaches, see eg, EA Feigenbaum and MR Nelson (eds), *Data Governance, Asian Alternatives: How India and Korea Are Creating New Models and Policies* (Carnegie Endowment, 2022); African Union, 'AU Data Policy Framework' (2022), available at: au.int/en/documents/20220728/au-data-policy-framework.

[4] Iris H-Y Chiu and Despoina Mantzari, 'Regulating Fintech and BigTech: Reconciling the Objectives of Financial Regulation and Promoting Competition', ch 10 in this volume.

customers' finances and preferences across a range of unbundled products and services, which can, in turn, be used to make more targeted offers and ultimately outcompete incumbents. The entry of fintech into discrete lines of business has also taken advantage of a lighter regulatory burden, compared with traditional financial institutions: these players are merely subject to activity-based or 'bespoke' regulation,[5] and not to the supplementary prudential requirements applicable to 'systemically important financial institutions'.[6]

Unsurprisingly, these dynamics have favoured the entry of so-called 'big techs' into payments, money management, insurance and lending, in particular thanks to the advantages of what the Bank for International Settlements (BIS) calls data-network activities loop, or 'DNA': Data analytics, Network externalities and interwoven Activities,[7] allowing big techs to easily scale up taking advantage of their low-cost structure, their resources and capabilities in big data collection and analysis, and the strong direct and indirect network effects. On the one hand, it is clear that these dynamics can result in services that are both more competitive – bringing to consumers more variety and more informed knowledge about the rates and conditions of competing financial services – and more innovative – leveraging the interlinkages between different product lines and the greater precision afforded by big data analysis and prediction. On the other hand, this scenario can also give rise to anticompetitive concerns of two types: a more traditional type, whereby traditional financial institutions erect unjustifiable barriers to the development of fintech services; and a more recent concern, where fintech providers take advantage of their pivotal role in the process of disintermediation and reintermediation of transactions by granting themselves a competitive advantage, or otherwise imposing unfair conditions to their customers. With that in mind, competition law can play an important role in ensuring that the fintech revolution produces virtuous dynamics, paying heed to regulatory concerns while preventing those who offer financial services to implement sectorial regulation in a way that leads to the exclusion of actual and potential competitors.

This chapter focuses on one area of enforcement, unilateral conduct (in particular, through the lens of 'abuse of dominance' standards developed in the European Union (EU)), to provide an illustration of some of the key challenges and particularities of the application of antitrust to the data economy in the financial sector. The structure of the chapter is as follows: in section II, we outline some notable past and pending cases that involved the exercise of power in relation to data in fintech markets in Brazil, highlighting a certain uneasiness by the competition authority when analysing those practices. In section III, we sketch the main challenges raised by the data economy to the

[5] ibid.

[6] A Carstens, S Claessens, F Restoy and HS Shin, 'Regulating Big Techs in Finance' (2021) 45 *BIS Bulletin*.

[7] BIS Annual Economic Report, Chapter III, 'Big Tech in Finance: Opportunities and Risks' (2019).

application of traditional abuse doctrines, with specific reference to five different categories of conduct. We then try in section IV to fill in the gap left by some of these theories, reviewing the way in which data can confer market power and identifying a few different factors that can be used to make this assessment more predictable and consistent. Finally, section V draws the lessons that may be learned from this exercise, outlining principles that enforcers could follow when dealing with data-related abuses, and applying them to the four cases discussed in section II. Ultimately, we argue that enforcers need be less like foxes, and more like hedgehogs. In other words, they need to break free of categorical strictures and focus on what really matters: the (mis)use of economic power that emanates from the collection and use of personal data. As we illustrate, existing legal tests are often inapt to fully capture the risks of anticompetitive effects stemming from this form of economic power.

II. DATA-RELATED ABUSES IN FINTECH MARKETS: A VIEW FROM BRAZIL

Brazil offers four different cases involving allegations of data-related abuses in fintech markets. To clarify, 'data-related' abuses, we refer here to conduct through which an undertaking uses its economic power to increase data processing (which comprises both data collection and data use) and harms consumers as a result. However, none of these cases has resulted in an infringement decision by the competition authority (Conselho Administrativo de Defesa Economica, or CADE), thus leaving substantial uncertainty as to how this conduct is to be analysed. What is more, in no case has the competition authority articulated a clear theory of harm, or principles upon which one can build foundations for future case analysis. Nevertheless, a number of relevant arguments were made during the proceedings. In this section, we provide an overview of the main facts and arguments behind each of these cases.

A. *Guiabolso*[8]

The first allegation of data-related abuse of dominance in a fintech market concerned the conduct of one of Brazil's largest banks, Bradesco, which had the effect of hindering the use by its customers of a third-party application for financial management, called 'Guiabolso'. Interestingly, the case originated from a lawsuit brought in 2016 by Bradesco against Guiabolso,[9] revealing a relatively

[8] Eleventh Civil Chamber of São Paulo, Digital Proceeding no 1027396-67.2016.8.26.0100, *Bradesco. Guiabolso Finanças e Correspondente Bancário e Serviços Ltda.*

[9] The lawsuit, which was ultimately withdrawn, involved a request for *interim measures* denied by presiding judge Eduardo Palma Pellegrinelli, of the XI Civil Chamber in São Paulo on 23 March 2016. See Danielle Brant, 'Bradesco Trava Disputa Contra Aplicativo Que Coleta Dados de Clientes' *Folha de São Paulo* (28 November 2016).

low level of preparedness and receptiveness towards the entry of non-financial players into financial markets during the early phase of development of the legal framework for fintechs in Brazil.[10] In the lawsuit, Bradesco requested an injunction ordering Guiabolso to stop the collection of its customers' financial data on multiple grounds:

- Security risk, due to the fact that Bradesco would not know how to differentiate its customers' sharing of financial data with Guiabolso from fraudulent attacks, and that an expert report identified security flaws in Guiabolso's process.
- Increase in Bradesco's administration costs.
- Breach of bank secrecy and breach of contract between the customer and the bank, due to the fact that the sharing occurred via screen-scraping (ie, by transferring to Guiabolso the customer's login details) in the absence of specific authorisation received by Bradesco (either from the customer or from Guiabolso).
- Lack of transparency in the service delivered, as customers are not alerted that login details may be used for unauthorised operations.
- Unfair competition, due to a violation of copyright regarding databases.

The requests made by Bradesco had a boomerang effect: they triggered the attention of the Secretariat of Promotion of Productivity and Competition Advocacy (SEPRAC), a department within the Ministry of Industry responsible for competition advocacy and for the promotion and analysis of measures that increase the productivity of the Brazilian economy. SEPRAC intervened in the case as amicus curiae to request the dismissal of Bradesco's pleas, and formally prompted CADE to open an investigation into Bradesco's conduct.[11] SEPRAC's assessment of the case was that Bradesco had engaged in sham litigation, in the sense of making baseless claims with the aim to restrict competition, which SEPRAC proceeded to demonstrate on each of Bradesco's pleas: for instance, it rebutted Bradesco's claim of bank secrecy and intellectual property noting that the relevant legislation[12] made clear that the customer is the owner of its own financial data, who is free to share it upon express consent, and that copyright

[10] In 2018, three Resolutions adopted by the Central Bank (Resolutions 4656, 4657 and 4707) established a range of prudential requirements applicable to non-financial institutions, thereby effectively creating a more trustworthy environment for the operation of fintech players in financial services. See Banco Central do Brasil, Resolution CMN No 4.656 of 26 April 2018, available at: www.bcb.gov.br/estabilidadefinanceira/exibenormativo?tipo=Resolu%C3%A7%C3%A3o&numero=4656; Resolution CMN No. 4.657 of 26 April 2018, available at: www.bcb.gov.br/estabilidadefinanceira/exibenormativo?tipo=Resolu%C3%A7%C3%A3o&numero=4657; and Resolution CMN No. 4.707 of 19 December 2018, available at: www.bcb.gov.br/estabilidadefinanceira/exibenormativo?tipo=Resolu%C3%A7%C3%A3o&numero=4707.

[11] Advisory Opinion SEI No 1/2018/GABIN/SEPRAC-MF, Proceeding SEI no 10099.100151/2018-14 (2 July 2018).

[12] Art 1 of Complementary Law No 105 of 10 January 2001 (Congresso Nacional).

cannot be used to protect facts. Yet its most consequential observation concerned the measure taken by Bradesco to protect its customers from an alleged security risk involved in granting Guiabolso access to customer data, which it considered not necessary and proportionate to avert the risk of fraudulent transactions: when the bank's internet banking user interface pushed the option to login to the Guiabolso app, it requested a randomly generated number (token) which could not have been previously provided to Guiabolso by its customers, thereby imposing an extra step that could hinder the use and widespread adoption of the app. This was different from the measure adopted by other leading banks with Guiabolso and other third-party providers, which only required two-factor authentication prior to the performance of financial transactions; and it went even beyond the security measures adopted by Bradesco for financial transactions in its own app – where no random number generation was required.

Following SEPRAC's lead, in September 2018 CADE opened an investigation. In its preliminary analysis, its General Superintendent (SG) concluded that Bradesco's conduct of requiring an additional token to access certain areas of the customers' internet banking hindered market growth not only for Guiabolso and other fintechs, but also for new potential entrants.[13] In addition to endorsing SEPRAC's dismissal of the security and bank secrecy arguments made by Bradesco, it empirically documented the detrimental effect of this practice on the use of Guiabolso's services. Perhaps the hardest and most interesting part of the decision, however, concerns the market power assessment: after all, a conduct can only be deemed abusive when carried out by a dominant undertaking. Here, this conclusion was difficult to reach in the SG's preliminary analysis because, although Bradesco met the market share threshold determined in the law to infer the existence of dominance (25 per cent) in the national market for current accounts, it did not with regard to deposits, which would be equally relevant sources of information for Guiabolso. The SG then affirmed that such conclusion could nevertheless be reached by noting that the market was characterised by high barriers, such as the need to meet rigid regulatory requirements, make massive investments in marketing and technology, create an ample distribution network and obtain economies of scale and scope – all of which can have even more pernicious effects on the ability of competitors (such as Guiabolso) to enjoy cross-side externalities. It noted that the same conclusion could be reached following the position taken by the Dutch competition authority in a report on fintechs in payment systems,[14] where it was argued that banks enjoy a dominant position in the market for information about the payment accounts of its customers. The SG's analysis also appeared to follow the Dutch Report with

[13] Technical Note No 17/2019/CGAA2/SGA1/SG/CADE, Administrative Investigation n 08700.004201/2018-38 of 2 December 2018.

[14] Netherlands Authority for Consumers & Markets (ACM), 'Fintechs in the Payment System – The Risk of Foreclosure' (2017), available at: www.acm.nl/sites/default/files/documents/2018-02/acm-study-fintechs-in-the-payment-market-the-risk-of-foreclosure.pdf.

regard to the nature of the conduct in question, pointing out that the requirements for abuse would be satisfied where a dominant company has an incentive to engage in a particular conduct to foreclose the target as an actual or potential competitor in a secondary market where a bank operates.

The case was settled in October 2020 with the adoption of a term of conduct cessation (TCC, broadly equivalent to a commitment decision) where Bradesco committed to: (i) develop connection interfaces that enable Guiabolso to request and obtain consent from its users that are Bradesco's customers, and to access via previously established encrypted communication to Bradesco's system in a way that allows collection of all data from users that have provided consent; (ii) submit a report within 30 days containing the technical documentation made available for interconnection, the interactions occurred with Bradesco for testing purposes, and the documentation that demonstrates the effectiveness of the consent interface; (iii) the deposit of $23,878,716.72 into the collective defence fund; and (iv) the withdrawal of the action initiated by Bradesco and still pending in court.

B. *WhatsApp*[15]

A rather atypical case of data-related abuse involved WhatsApp's update of its privacy policy in 2021, which required users to accept a broader range of uses of their personal data, including the transfer of metadata (including registration data, data of interaction with third parties, IP address and mobile information) to WhatsApp's mother company Facebook (now Meta) for advertising purposes. The case is atypical in our sample for two reasons: first, because CADE participated in a joint action with the data protection authority, the consumer protection authority and the federal prosecution service that resulted in a Joint Recommendation to WhatsApp outlining the authorities' concerns, while failing short of opening an investigation. Second, because the relationship of this case to fintech is somewhat hidden: indeed, the main reason provided by WhatsApp to its customers as a justification for the update was to enable some of its new features, including the ability to chat with businesses and thus potentially make purchases on the chat. Considering that important new line of commerce being created, it is not illogical to expect that one of the goals behind the expansion of functionalities was for WhatsApp/Meta to become a payment intermediary for all these transactions, which would have provided valuable data points in addition to the wealth of metadata already available, and the ability

[15] Joint Recommendation of CADE, SENACON, MPF and ANPD to WhatsApp (7 May 2021), available at: www.gov.br/anpd/pt-br/assuntos/noticias/inclusao-de-arquivos-para-link-nas-noticias/recomendacao_whatsapp_-_assinada.pdf.

to re-use those for advertising purposes on Facebook. As a matter of fact, in June 2020 WhatsApp launched WhatsApp Pay, a new functionality allowing transfers of money via Facebook Pay, an electronic payment system available for Visa and Mastercard credit card holders. However, merely a week after the announcement both CADE and the Brazilian central bank issued an order to the effect of requiring the immediate suspension of the service. The order was directed, respectively, at WhatsApp and the settling institution Cielo as an *interim measure* to prevent foreclosure in the market for transaction settling as a result of failed notification of the agreement to CADE's merger control;[16] and to the credit card companies with the aim to preserve an adequate competitive environment, which ensures the functioning of an interoperable, rapid, secure, transparent, open and affordable payment system.[17] This gave some time for the central bank to impose some additional conditions on the operation of WhatsApp Pay, requiring it not to be used for transactions between individuals and businesses, although that possibility remains under analysis by the bank.[18] In the meantime, competition concerns associated with the agreement between WhatsApp and Cielo were dismissed by CADE by upholding an appeal against the *interim measure*, mainly due to the demonstration that the agreement did not involve an express exclusivity, nor would WhatsApp Pay be restricted to any particular providers.[19] As a result, no restrictions were imposed by CADE in relation to the operation of WhatsApp Pay.

Considering these prior conditions, WhatsApp's privacy policy update can be cast in a different light: the authorisation of WhatsApp for transfers between individuals and the prospect of it becoming a fully functional payment service in the future, makes the sharing of data between WhatsApp and Facebook more concerning from a competitive standpoint. CADE did voice concerns in the Joint Recommendation, but these were stated more in general and aspirational terms, rather than taking issue with specific aspects of the conduct in question.[20] In particular, CADE repeated the need for timely and effective action in order to prevent abuses in digital markets and promote their sustainable architectural development, also considering CADE's informational asymmetry about their structural resiliency and the potential competitive effect of the new policy. It also recognised that mechanisms of technological innovation and commercial

[16] Conselho Administrativo de Defesa Econômica, Proceeding n 08700.002871/2020-34, Technical Note No 6/2020/SG, 23 June 2020.

[17] See Vanessa Koetz and Bianca Kremer, 'WhatsApp Pay: A Próxima Fronteira Para Ampliação do Monopólio de Dados' (*Coding Rights*, May 2022), available at: codingrights.org/docs/ZapPay_monopolio_dados.pdf.

[18] Banco Central do Brasil, 'BC Autoriza Dois Arranjos e Uma Instituição de Pagamentos Relacionados ao WhatsApp' (30 March 2021), available at: www.bcb.gov.br/detalhenoticia/17359/nota.

[19] Proceeding n 08700.002871/2020-34, Technical Note No 7/2020/SG-TRIAGEM C/SGA1/SG/CADE, 30 June 2020.

[20] Joint Recommendation (n 15).

policy can be used to eliminate competition, particularly to the extent that such innovations are not necessary to produce efficiency and consumer benefits. It highlighted in particular a concern relating to the complete removal of choice for users about the sharing of data, which can amount to the unjustified disruption of a business relationship, and about the abusive nature of breaking the continuity of an essential communication service as a result of a refusal to accept the condition to share personal data with Facebook and third parties. A further relevant point expressed by the authorities related to a lack of transparency over the type of data processed and the purpose for which they will be processed after the update, which, combined with those expressed above, made evident the appropriateness of this joint action with CADE. As a result, the authorities recommended that WhatsApp should postpone the entry into force of the new policy until it responded satisfactorily to the demands of the authorities, and to refrain from restricting the availability of its services to those users who had not accepted the updated policy.

Once again, it is worth highlighting that no particular theory of harm was articulated in CADE's statements, except for a veiled reference to pressing the acceptance of the new privacy policy as a condition for continuing to receive an essential communication service. This can be contrasted with the actions brought by the competition authorities in Argentina and India, which reached somewhat different conclusions. The Commission Nacional de la Competencia, in particular, found that the practice amounted to exploitation because of the unreasonable and excessive collection of information from users, the lack of real options to limit the sharing of information outside the platform, and the conditioning of the use of the service to the acceptance of these terms.[21] It also found the practice exclusionary, due to the fact that it confers a competitive advantage that can hardly be replicated in terms of processing, crossing and consolidating information from users of all Facebook platforms. Similarly, the Indian Competition Commission found an exclusionary abuse due to lack of transparency on the sharing of data with Facebook Companies, and lack of specific and voluntary user consent (leveraging).[22] These examples illustrate that, while data-driven conduct may raise challenges for enforcers, it also presents them with opportunities to be creative in charting new paths to protect competition, planting the seeds for a modernised framework of competition analysis. The opposite reaction – refraining from going where the authority has not gone before – should be avoided as far as possible, as it creates uncertainty and makes the case law out of step with reality.

[21] Secretary of Commerce, Resolution 492/2021, adopting judgement EX–2021-42558303-APN-DGD#MDP, C 1767 – WHATSAPP INC S/ INFRACCION LEY N° 27.442 by Comisión Nacional de Defensa de la Competencia.

[22] Competition Commission of India, Suo Moto Case No 01 of 2021, n Re: Updated Terms of Service and Privacy Policy for WhatsApp Users.

C. *iFood*[23]

A third candidate of data-related abuse dealing with financial technology concerns conduct by the leading online food delivery platform in Brazil, iFood, and its conduct relating to the market for food voucher programmes. Food voucher programmes are employee benefit programmes, where employers provide their (typically low-income) employees with vouchers for the purchase of food from a network of partnering restaurants pursuant to the national Worker Alimentation Program (PAT). The big advantage for employers is that these benefits are associated with strong tax incentives, therefore representing a cost-effective way to increase the attractiveness of working conditions. To redeem a voucher, employees must make purchases from one of the partnering restaurants, which in turn requires the latter to set up an account with a provider of vouchers. iFood is one of such providers, and enjoys the advantage of running this business above its widely popular online food delivery network: it is able to tap on the existing contracts with partner restaurants for food delivery services without needing to sign up those restaurants with payment accrediting institutions, and thus with very little or no investment compared with competing food voucher providers. Upon this backdrop, on 28 April 2022 CADE opened an investigation in response to a complaint submitted by the Brazilian Association of Worker Benefits, on the basis of three different allegations:

i. Illegitimate use of data obtained in the online delivery platform, including its customers' socio-economic profile, their preferences, the frequency of their orders, the median expenditure, the financial institutions associated with them, as well as similar data about restaurants, such as the customer profile, their turnover and the percentage of voucher meals in their orders. These data would allow iFood to make offers and rebates to customers that are deemed crucial in order to gain market share over competing voucher providers: for instance, by offering discounts, cashback and other advantages to company directors with the aim to make them persuade their employer to switch over to iFood benefits, or offering extra benefits for employees in order to incentivise their exercise of their right to portability of voucher meals from other voucher providers, which the PAT has explicitly conferred since 2021.
ii. Cross-subsidies from the online food delivery market, in the form of rebates, cashback and discounts, extended payment deadlines designed to match the fees that employers must pay as a sanction to another voucher provider in case of migration to iFood, and subsidised financing of customers in case of topping up of voucher programmes for an extended period.

[23] Conselho Administrativo de Defesa Econômica, Proceeding n 08700.001797/2022-09, *Associação Brasileira das Empresas de Benefícios ao Trabalhador – ABBT v iFood.com Agência de Restaurantes Online SA*.

iii. Self-preferencing of iFood's own voucher programme in its online food delivery platform, by creating obstacles to restaurants' registration of competing voucher providers (while iFood's voucher programme is automatically enrolled) and to consumers' use of the food vouchers from other voucher providers.

On 11 October 2022, the SG closed the investigation on the grounds that it did not find sufficient evidence that the iFood platform is a gatekeeper, nor that the company engages in discrimination or cross-subsidisation. In particular, the SG noted that 90 per cent of the income derived to iFood from food vouchers is made up by offline purchases, suggesting that the platform has limited relevance in this market, and that its aggressive pricing is part of a promotional strategy as a new entrant to stimulate the adoption of online payment methods. It also dismissed the concerns associated with possible discrimination as technical difficulties that all operators in the market are facing (particularly since interoperability has been legislatively mandated),[24] and which have triggered consumer complaints not only against iFood, but also other food delivery platforms. Importantly for our purposes, the SG also concluded that it does not seem to be illicit in this specific case to use the platform's own data, nor that such data could not be obtained through research or acquisition of data from market intelligence companies. Even more forcefully, the SG argued that such use of data may be necessary to survive on the market, and that its legality is more of a legislative matter (under data protection law) than a competition law issue. Once again, then, no particular theory of harm was formulated by CADE with regard to the competitive use of data, signalling a certain degree of tolerance for practices that are at the intersection of competition and data privacy.

D. *Apple*[25]

The fourth case of data-related abuse in fintech markets refers to a very recent investigation of Apple's rules for iOS. The investigation was opened by CADE in January 2023 in response to a complaint against Apple lodged by Mercado Livre, a leading Latin American e-commerce marketplace, for restrictions imposed on Mercado Livre's ability to sell certain digital content (such as streaming subscriptions) on the iOS platform. In particular, Apple has in place rules that oblige its third-party app providers to make such sales through Apple's own payment system (Apple Pay), which is provided for a fee (varying from 15 to 30 per cent) by way of compensation for the service as well as for the intermediation ('general app store ecosystem infrastructure') in the distribution of apps

[24] Presidência da República, Decree No 10.854 of 10 November 2022.
[25] Proceeding n 08700.009531/2022-04, *Ebazar.com.br.Ltda and Mercado Pago Instituição de Pagamento Ltda v Apple Inc e Apple Computer Brasil Ltda.*

and digital content. In conjunction with the mandatory use of Apple's payment system, Apple imposes some ancillary restrictions for the use of Apple Pay's API, which include the prohibition to inform customers of the possibility to make purchases outside the app ('anti-steering rule').

According to Mercado Livre, this constitutes an abuse of Apple's dominant position in the market for distribution of iOS apps, as it prevents the rise of alternative distributors of digital goods and products within iOS and hinders the growth of developers of digital goods and services, thereby hurting consumers. In particular, it is alleged that Apple's conduct can be categorised as abusive under four different theories: (i) raising rival costs, since other distributors of digital content compete with Apple in the provision of digital content, as is the case for streaming; (ii) arbitrary discrimination, on grounds that only certain types of digital content sales are subject to the restriction, and that the security and anti-fraud concerns invoked to justify the exclusive use of Apple Pay are not sufficiently substantiated; (iii) disintermediation, whereby Apple gets to collect valuable transactional data for purchases of digital content, which can offer a competitive advantage for the development of apps; and (iv) tying of App Store services with the service of in-app payment for digital content, which are economically, functionally and technologically separate.

In its preliminary assessment that led to the opening of the investigation, the SG expressed some difficulty in defining with precision the relevant product market, having considered both the complainant's focus on the iOS app distribution market and Apple's argument that it never permitted alternative distribution channels (sideloading) of apps on iOS. It nevertheless decided to go ahead with the investigation on grounds that such precise definition was not necessary at this preliminary stage. Since this is a very recent development, we do not yet have a position from the authority about the application of the aforementioned theories of harm.

III. DATA-RELATED ABUSES: MAPPING CHALLENGES TO TRADITIONAL ANTITRUST ANALYSIS

In this section, we review the challenges involved in the application of traditional categories of abuses to data-driven environment. To do that, five different categories of conduct are presented, drawing from the facts of the cases outlined above, and using the work of the Organisation for Economic Co-operation and Development (OECD) and EU competition law case law as an inspiration for dealing with such cases.[26] The main question in the following exercise is to appreciate how these categories fare with respect to cases involving data, which

[26] While the juxtaposition of Brazilian cases to international case law and reports may seem unorthodox, the use of foreign judgments is not uncommon in Brazilian jurisprudence, which often uses such foreign sources to justify a particular position.

is a resource with its own peculiarities: specifically, it has value which can be traded in consideration for goods and services; it is an infrastructural resource,[27] meaning that it is non-rivalrous, instrumental as an input for the production of goods and services (although the relationship of input to output is not always clear or linear); and of general purpose. The latter characteristic is also linked to its nature of an inchoate resource, necessitating some cleaning, refinement and organisation to be used as a structured source of knowledge.[28] Finally, data can be individualising, meaning that it can directly or indirectly relate to an individual, and thereby enable personalised offering.

A. Discrimination

Discrimination is a versatile category of conduct, which can be applied (and has been applied) both to pricing and non-pricing. Thus, in principle, the concept does not present particular problems when it comes to its application to a zero-price context where data is used as currency. Rather, what may be tricky is to distinguish the different forms of discrimination, which have been traditionally developed with reference to pricing conduct. Famously, the OECD developed an analytical framework to assess two types of price discrimination:[29] on the one hand, where a company with significant market power set prices that maximise profits, called 'exploitative' discrimination; and on the other, where the difference in prices causes a distortion in competition among downstream input purchasers and this damages the competitive process, called 'distortionary' discrimination.

Both types of discrimination require that a different price is charged for two products that are both similar in nature, and with similar marginal costs. While similarity and supply-side considerations remain unchanged in the context of non-monetary pricing, what could be challenging is to determine how data extraction should be accounted for as part of the comparison: should the baseline for comparison be a service which processes the same type and amount of data? One that does not process more data than necessary for the provision of a particular service? Or perhaps just one which, even though collecting data for other service or ecosystem activities, respects the applicable data protection rules and principles? In other words, should data collection or data protection matter as a relevant parameter in the comparison?

[27] B Frischmannn, *Infrastructure: The Social Value of Shared Resources* (Oxford University Press, 2012), cited in T Thombal, *Imposing Data Sharing Among Private Actors: A Tale of Evolving Balances* (Wolters Kluwer, 2022) 53.

[28] R Kitchin, *The Data Revolution: Big Data, Open Data, Data Infrastructures and their Consequences* (Sage, 2014) 6.

[29] Organisation for Economic Co-operation and Development (OECD), 'Price Discrimination Background Note by the Secretariat' (2016) DAF/COMP(2016)15, 29–30.

In terms of conduct analysis, the OECD recommends examining the effects of exploitative discrimination first of all under a static analysis; then, to assess whether they are transitory, and ultimately determine if they are driven by welfare-enhancing dynamic effects (eg, innovation, or investment in fixed costs) or by the need to engage in socially wasteful activities (eg, rent seeking or practices that facilitate discrimination).[30] Here again, it must be recognised that this calculation is already daunting in the context of pricing analysis, and its complexity is likely to rise when considering the ecosystem dynamics around data collection and re-use. What is more, the difficulty of making a prima facie case of discrimination without the assistance of a reliable metric such as pricing may act as a disincentive for competition authorities to bring exploitative non-price discrimination cases, which is likely to further reinforce the enforcement reluctance already present in many jurisdictions.

By contrast, practice that is likely to remain highly relevant is distortionary price discrimination. In this case, the OECD suggests that the second step of analysis involves the assessment of whether the practice has caused distortion downstream, which depends on the degree of market power and on the relevant counterfactual, and finally, the actual effects of the practice on price, quality and innovation, or in the absence of those, its impact on market structure.[31] There is little doubt that this test could apply to discrimination among a dominant company's customers on parameters other than pricing. What is challenging, however, is how to operationalise the test of 'competitive advantage' in a non-pricing context. Recent case law from the Court of Justice recognises that what counts is whether the practice affects 'costs, profits or any other relevant interest of one or more of those partners'[32] and that proof of actual quantifiable deterioration in the competitive situation is not required: mere *capability* to unfairly distort competition between trade partners would suffice.[33] While this means that a mere possibility (not even a likelihood) that the differential treatment has a distortionary impact would be actionable, the judgment clarifies that such conclusion can only be reached on the basis of an evaluation of all relevant circumstances,[34] which include an assessment of market power, bargaining power and of the relative incidence of discrimination to the incentive structure of the discriminated undertaking, as well as the overall strategy of the dominant firm. Considering that, if discrimination occurs through content personalisation, an additional challenge involves taking into account how prevalent it is, and

[30] ibid, 16.

[31] ibid, 22.

[32] Case C-525/16 *MEO – Serviços de Comunicações e Multimédia SA v Autoridade da Concorrência* ECLI:EU:C:2018:270, para 37.

[33] ibid, para 28.

[34] Including, for the particular case of a vertical undertaking discriminating against its competitors downstream, the undertaking's dominant position, the negotiating power as regards the tariffs, the conditions and arrangements for charging those tariffs, their duration and their amount, and the possible existence of a strategy aiming to exclude from the downstream market one of its trade partners which is at least as efficient as its competitors. ibid, para 31.

whether the overall strategy of the firm reveals an anticompetitive intent – for this would require a deep enquiry into the algorithmic practices of the dominant firm. A further and related complication is that the EU case law imposes the need for a firm to suffer from a disadvantage compared with a competitor within the same relevant market.[35] This requirement may make it difficult to appreciate discrimination pertaining to data access that affects the ability of a company to leverage such data to enter a secondary market in which the two firms are not currently competing.

B. Exclusive Dealing and Rebates

Exclusive dealing is a broad category used to bring together two different practices: exclusive purchasing and loyalty rebates. Exclusive purchasing arrangements oblige a customer, either contractually or de facto, to obtain all or most of their requirements for a particular product from a given supplier. By contrast, loyalty rebates are those where a seller offers a better price conditional on the buyer demonstrating their loyalty, measured in terms of a share of that buyer's purchases. The range of criteria relevant to the assessment of these practices are summarised by the European Commission's Guidance Paper.[36] There, the EU Commission declares exclusive purchasing an enforcement priority where the dominant undertaking is an unavoidable trading partner, for instance because its brand is a 'must stock item' preferred by many final consumers, or because of capacity constraints on the other suppliers.[37] By contrast, if competitors can compete on equal terms for each individual customer's entire demand, exclusive purchasing obligations are unlikely to hamper effective competition.[38] When applying this standard to data-related abuses, one complication may be that the exclusive 'purchasing' is paid with data, implying that the seller acquires exclusive data control. However, this is without prejudice to the exercise of data protection rights, which in certain situations can be used to request a copy of the data and transfer it to a competitor,[39] thus potentially undermining that

[35] Case C-132/19 P *Groupe Canal + v Commission* ECLI:EU:C:2020:1007, para 46.

[36] European Commission, 'Communication from the Commission – Guidance on the Commission's Enforcement Priorities in applying Article 82 of the EC Treaty to abusive exclusionary conduct by dominant undertakings' [2009] OJ C 45/7.

[37] ibid, para 35.

[38] ie, unless the switching of supplier by customers is rendered difficult due to the duration of the exclusive purchase obligation.

[39] See Regulation (EU) 2016/679 of the European Parliament and of the Council of 27 April 2016 on the protection of natural persons with regard to the processing of personal data and on the free movement of such data, and repealing Directive 95/46/EC (General Data Protection Regulation) [2016] OJ L119/1, Art 20.1: 'The data subject shall have the right to receive the personal data concerning him or her, which he or she has provided to a controller, in a structured, commonly used and machine-readable format *and have the right to transmit those data to another controller without hindrance* from the controller to which the personal data have been provided (emphasis added).

exclusivity. Furthermore, the fact that data is traded does not detract from its role as an input for the development of product and services, which may raise legitimate concerns of foreclosure not only in the purchasing market, but also in the downstream product markets that are directly affected by that transaction. At the same time, due to the general purpose and inchoate nature of data, it may be difficult to identify exactly which pipelines are affected and how.

The Guidance Paper's focus on competition for the entire demand of each customer in exclusive purchasing indicates a desire to protect the ability of competitors to attain economies of scale that are necessary to effectively compete in the market, a benchmark that is also used to evaluate the legality of rebates. Specifically, the benchmark in that case is the price that a competitor would have to offer in order to gain customers (compensating them for the missed rebate) in the 'contestable' share of the market – in other words, the units that are not already captive to the dominant firm.[40] The contestable share is one of the key elements that must be considered, according to the Guidance Paper, including factors such as 'the position of the dominant undertaking', 'the conditions on the relevant market', 'the position of the dominant undertaking's competitors', 'the position of customers or input suppliers', 'the extent of the allegedly abusive conduct', 'possible evidence of actual foreclosure', and 'direct evidence of any exclusionary strategy'.[41] However, the weight that should be given to these other elements once it is proven that a loyalty-inducing effect exists remains a contentious point, as shown in the *Intel* saga,[42] which resulted in a quashing of the General Court's judgment (upholding the Commission's infringement decision) by the Court of Justice on grounds that these arguments had not been duly considered.[43] This more holistic assessment of the practice gives more leeway to consider the strategic targeting of customers that is likely to increase in a data-driven environment, and which, if proven, could be admitted as direct evidence of exclusionary strategy. Furthermore, the *Intel* ruling confirmed an earlier ruling in *Post Danmark II* that the as-efficient competitor test is only one tool among others for the purposes of assessing whether there is an abuse of a dominant position in the context of a rebate scheme,[44] thus arguably eliminating what could have proven a formidable challenge in the context of data-driven markets: determining the viability of a data-subsidised rebate for an as-efficient competitor is likely to be complex, particularly in a market riddled with personalisation and with lean businesses that are ready to adapt to constantly changing demand. On the other hand, if data constitutes the product being sold, the challenge is how to determine the costs of this production, considering it is often a byproduct of other activities. A further challenge lies

[40] European Commission, 'Enforcement Priorities' (n 36) para 44.
[41] ibid, para 20.
[42] Case C-413/14 P *Intel Corp v European Commission* ECLI:EU:C:2017:632.
[43] ibid, paras 139–40.
[44] ibid, para 6.

in determining what would constitute strategic targeting and, in particular, to what extent a rebate could be deemed unlawful when practised to a selected group of customers (such as those profiles that are considered more likely to buy from competitors). In fact, in this case one cannot rely on the leveraging theory that explains foreclosure in loyalty-inducing rebates (whereby the rebater leverages the incontestable share of the market over the contestable share): this is because, in reaction to these selective rebates, rivals could simply opt to make more sales to the remaining customers.[45] Therefore, it appears that a different test or theory of harm needs to be articulated with regard to data-driven rebates targeting. This is without prejudice, however, to the possibility of identifying leveraging effects both in purchasing and in downstream markets where data can be used, as in the case of exclusive dealing.

C. Unfair Terms

Excessive pricing is often brought as an example of exploitative conduct which may be caught under Article 102(a) of the Treaty on the Functioning of the European Union (TFEU). However, the scope of this letter goes well beyond that, including the imposition of unfair terms and conditions. In fact, several early cases of the European Commission and the Court of Justice have interpreted the text to condemn dominant firms that take advantage of their superior bargaining position to impose conditions that are not necessary and proportionate for the achievement of the legitimate objectives of a contract, thereby resulting in a significant limitation of freedom of a trading party.[46] Specific manifestations of such conduct in the past included long-term contracts with automatic renewal,[47] opacity and discretion on the granting of benefits to the other party,[48] the deprivation of one's effective property right over purchased equipment by requiring permission for transfer of ownership, prohibiting any modifications, and requiring exclusive repair and maintenance from the seller.[49] The potential relevance of these concepts in the data economy is intuitive, where the collection and use

[45] N Petit, 'Intel, Leveraging Rebates and the Goals of Article 102 TFEU' (2015) 11 *European Competition Journal* 26, 37.

[46] See, eg, Case 127/73 *Belgische Radio en Televisie v SV SABAM and NV Fonior* [1974] ECR 313; Case 311/84 *Centre Belge d'Etudes de Marche-Telemarketing (CBEM) v SA Compagnie Luxembourgeoise de Telediffusion (CLT) and Information Publicite Benelux (IPB)* [1985] ECR 3261; Case 395/87 *Ministere public v Jean-Louis Tournier* [1989] ECR 2521; Commission Decision, *Der Grune Punkt* (Case COMP D3/34493) 2001/463/EC [2001] OJ L166/1; Commission Decision, *GEMA Statutes* (Case IV/29.971) 82/204/EEC [1982] OJ L94/12. For an overview of relevant cases until 2008, see P Akman, 'The Role of Exploitation in Abuse under Article 82 EC' (2009) 11 *Cambridge Yearbook of European Legal Studies* 165.

[47] Case 247/86 *Alsatel v SA Novasam* [1988] ECR 5987, para 10.

[48] Case T-203/01 *Manufacture Française des Pneumatiques Michelin v EC Commission* [2003] ECR II- 4071, para 141 (in particular, in the granting of rebates).

[49] Case T-83/91 *Tetra Pak International SA v EC Commission* [1994] ECR II-755, para 140.

of certain data occurs under circumstances of opacity, and where such collection and use were not configured to be necessary and proportionate to achieve the contract objective. In addition to transparency, therefore, a key issue to be examined is whether the granting of an entitlement over data constituted an essential part of the meeting of minds by contracting parties, or merely an ancillary and dispensable obligation. Notably, the latter would imply that any data entitlement would have to be justified under a proportionality test, although commentators have pointed out that this test may be more akin to a standard of manifest disproportionality (meaning that the restriction is allowed unless manifestly disproportionate)[50] rather than absolute necessity for the contract (as was ruled in the early case law).[51]

When it comes to excessive pricing, the EU courts rely on the two-pronged test developed in *United Brands*,[52] determining: (1) whether the difference between the costs incurred and the price charged is excessive, in a sense that it bears no reasonable relation to the economic value of the product; and (2) whether a price has been imposed which is either unfair in itself or when compared with competing products. Clearly, there are difficulties in the application of this test, which are even more pronounced in a data-related context. With respect to the first part: how does personalisation impact the assessment? Does the disutility perceived by some consumers from certain data collection detract from the overall/median economic value of the product?

With respect to the second prong, the fundamental question is what could be considered as a competing product. Benchmarking with reference to comparable markets is an exercise typically conducted to show not only excessiveness and unfairness, but also that the price difference is both significant and persistent.[53] Once that is determined to be the case, the burden shifts onto the undertaking in question to prove that the lamented differential pricing was justified.[54] However, for a benchmark to be valid it would need to reflect a competitive market for a comparable product, where conditions of competition are reasonably similar. This raises the question of whether a service that is offered through a business model that does not rely on data collection, for instance *freemium*, could provide a valid benchmark.

[50] W Sauter and J Rutgers, 'Promoting Fair Private Governance in the Platform Economy: EU Competition and Contract Law Applied to Standard Terms' (2021) 23 *Cambridge Yearbook of European Legal Studies* 343, 352.

[51] Case 125/78 *Gesellschaft für musikalische Aufführungs- und mechanische Vervielfältigungsrechte, v Commission of the European Communities* [1979] ECR I-03173, para 36.

[52] Case 27/76 *United Brands Company and United Brands Continentaal BV v Commission of the European Communities* [1978] ECR 207, para 252.

[53] Case C-177/16 *Autortiesību un komunicēšanās konsultāciju aģentūra v Latvijas Autoru apvienība v Konkurences padome* ECLI:EU:C:2017:689, para 55.

[54] A Turina and N Zingales, 'Economic Analysis and Evaluation of "Fair Prices" – Can Antitrust and International Taxation Learn from Each Other?' (2009) CLPE Research Paper, SSRN, available at: ssrn.com/abstract=1516486; P Akman and L Garrod, 'When Are Excessive Prices Unfair?' (2011) 7 *Journal of Competition Law & Economics* 403.

D. Tying

Tying conduct refers to making the conclusion of contracts subject to acceptance by the other parties of supplementary obligations which, by their nature or according to commercial usage, have no connection with the subject of such contracts. For our purposes, it is important to note that the same effect may be achieved through contractual obligations as well as on purely technological grounds: for instance, preventing interoperability with rivals' products may be a very effective strategy to reach the end goal of forcing customers to source their supplies of complementary products from the same provider, without any mention of supplementary obligations in contractual relations. The concern with this practice when undertaken by a dominant firm is that it may hinder the ability of competitors to sell their products in a secondary ('tied') product market, as well as potentially reduce the contestability of the primary ('tying') market. This way, a firm leverages its dominant position into a second market ('offensive leveraging') or uses its position in a second market to reinforce its dominance ('defensive leveraging').

Following a similar evolutionary path as the case law in the United States (US),[55] the analysis of tying in the EU has shifted from a formalistic, quasi per se approach, in *Hilti*,[56] *British Sugar*,[57] *Alsatel*[58] and *Tetra Pak II*[59] to a structured rule of reason approach in *Microsoft*.[60] Suffice to note that prior to *Microsoft*, all that was required was showing that a dominant firm had 'reserved to itself' access to a neighbouring market and that trade between Member States had been affected. With *Microsoft*, the case law aligned with the prevalent economic thinking, introducing the requirement of foreclosure effects and breaking down its test into a number of discrete requirements: (i) the tying and the tied products are two separate products; (ii) the undertaking concerned is dominant in the market for the tying product; (iii) the undertaking concerned does not give customers a choice to obtain the tying product without the tied product; (iv) the practice in question forecloses competition; and (v) the tying is not objectively justified and/or generates efficiencies.[61]

When applying these criteria to the context of the data economy, a couple of elements are likely to give more work to the interpreter: first, if the secondary obligation concerns an entitlement to data associated with the use of the product, that entitlement will need to be evaluated considering the baseline of rights and obligations that data protection and other data-related laws establish. These laws may require a valid consent by the data subject or data holder, the

[55] This shift has also occurred in the US case law beginning from the Supreme Court's decision in *Jefferson Parish Hospital Dist No 2 et al v Hyde*, 466 US 2 (1984).

[56] Case C-53/92 P *Hilti AG v Commission of the European Communities* [1994] ECR I-00667.

[57] Case No IV/30.178 *Napier Brown v British Sugar* [1998] OJ L284/41.

[58] Case 247/86 *Alsatel v SA Novasam* (n 47).

[59] Commission Decision, *Tetra Pak II* (Case IV/31043)' [1992] OJ L72/1.

[60] Commission Decision, *Microsoft* (Case COMP/C-3/37.792) [2007] OJ L32/23.

[61] ibid, rec 794.

requirements of which would not be satisfied by a bundling of consent for multiple activities, what has been called 'privacy policy tying'.[62] Second, even where the arrangement is based on a valid consent by the data subject or data holder, one may not be certain that the additional entitlement does indeed constitute a separate product, if it is required as an input on another side of a multi-sided market (eg, advertising). Third, even where the leveraging occurs, it is difficult to establish when such leveraging effectively causes harm to competition, due to the complex and non-homogeneous relationship between data and effects. This is even more difficult to calculate when the tying depends on a targeted intervention in an individual's decision-making process to nudge them to acquire a second product on the basis of their own revealed preferences, as it is debatable whether the undertaking has given the individual an effective choice.

E. Refusal to Deal

Refusal to deal is typically considered as the type of conduct against which antitrust enforcers should exercise the highest level of self-restraint, given the clear tension of mandated access with the right of an undertaking to decide whether and with whom it wishes to establish a commercial relationship. The case law has defined a narrow set of circumstances where access can be mandated under this doctrine (also known as the 'essential facility doctrine'), namely where the undertaking is vertically integrated and enjoy dominance upstream, and its refusal towards an undertaking operating in the downstream market meets the following conditions.

1. It relates to an input that is indispensable to compete effectively on the downstream market.
2. It is likely to eliminate effective competition in the downstream market.
3. It is likely to lead to consumer harm.[63]

Now, let us posit that the input that is subject to the access request is data. In what way does this change the equation? First, it may be difficult to establish which data specifically ought to be shared: aside from the types of activities to which data relates, a crucial question concerns whether disclosure should be mandated for raw data, structured data, acquired data and/or even inferred data.

Second, in a similar way to some of the other conducts above, we have a challenge of data as an inchoate resource: the access seeker may not be currently active in the downstream market. It may even be argued that the need to identify a specific new product or technical development ex ante is misplaced, as it runs counter to the way innovation works in the context of the data-driven economy.[64]

[62] D Condorelli and J Padilla, 'Data-Driven Envelopment with Privacy-Policy Tying' (2020), available at: dx.doi.org/10.2139/ssrn.3600725.

[63] European Commission, 'Enforcement Priorities' (n 36) para 81.

[64] V Mayer-Schönberger and Y Padova, 'Regime Change? Enabling Big Data through Europe's New Data Protection Regulation' (2016) 17 *Science and Technology Law Review* 315.

Finally, one can argue that a concrete problem of measurement of consumer harm exists to the extent that the refusal prevents the emergence of a more privacy-friendly solution, as under the existing test this would not be (literally speaking) a technical development, nor a policy objective that competition authorities can legitimately pursue as such. Only a more expansive understanding of the goals of this provision, or a recognition of the relevance of privacy as a product quality dimension, would permit addressing a range of concerns relating to data privacy.

Table 1 Data-related challenges to traditional abuse analysis

↓CONDUCT → DATA CHARACTERISTIC	Tradeability	Complex instrumentality	Generality and inchoateness	Individualization
• **Exploitative discrimination:** • **Exclusionary discrimination**	Baseline for comparison ×	Ecosystem dynamics Establishing 'competitive advantage'	× Absence of presence in relevant market	Detecting prevalence and anticompetitive intent
Exclusive purchase	Tension between exclusivity and data protection rights	Establishing foreclosure	Foreclosure in which market?	Application of leveraging theory
Loyalty rebates	When data is a product, determining the costs of data production	Establishing foreclosure	Identifying anticompetitive strategy	Application of leveraging theory
Unfair terms • **Excessive pricing**	Baseline for unfairness Baseline for comparison, and role of consumer disutility	Proportionality of obligations ×	Transparency on future uses ×	× Measuring privacy preferences
Tying	Baseline for supplementary obligation	No separate product in ecosystem Establishing consumer harm	No separate product yet	Establishing coercion in targeted nudging
Refusal to deal	Scope of data to be shared	Privacy as a technical development	No dowstream activity for access seeker	×

IV. DATA AS A SOURCE OF MARKET POWER: CRITERIA FOR A MORE FOCUSED ASSESSMENT

Abuse of dominance refers to the improper use of market power, in a way that impairs competition in the market and ultimately harms consumers. Therefore, a preliminary question for our analysis is to understand if that power has anything to do with the fact that an undertaking has superior access to data, compared to its competitors, and can use this to foreclose competition. This relates to the use of data for at least two different purposes: first, as an input for *building* new products and services, including by training algorithms and second, as an asset that can be exploited to *offer* targeted products and services.

The first type of application is one that has given rise to substantial discussion both in the academic literature and in legal practice. Arguably, the most authoritative guidance on this matter has been provided by a Joint Study of the Bundeskartellamt and the French Autorité de la Concurrence entitled 'Competition Law and Data',[65] which, although starting from the well-known distinction between volunteered, observed and inferred data,[66] ends up attributing more relevance to two macro-categories, namely first-party and third-party data. While first-party data refers to datasets created by the same firm, third-party data involves a transfer from other data collectors, which typically implies that their beneficiaries obtain larger and more diverse datasets, with lower fixed costs and higher variable costs than those who merely rely on first-party data.[67] In practice, this may be a false dichotomy, as it is common for businesses to combine first-party and third-party data to enrich their datasets – something that is even encouraged now by the European Data Strategy with the creation of data spaces.[68] Nevertheless, even with widespread availability of third-party data, it might be difficult for new entrants to match the quality of first-party data sitting in the hands of established players. To determine whether this actually gives rise to a situation of market power in data collection,[69] we must take into account a number of concurring factors, as discussed in the rest of this section.

For example, Graef suggests that data-driven market power is more likely to exist in online platforms where: (i) data is a significant input into the service delivered; (ii) it is unviable for competitors to self-collect data to build a

[65] Bundeskartellamt and Autorité de la Concurrence, 'Competition Law and Data' (2016), available at: www.bundeskartellamt.de/SharedDocs/Publikation/DE/Berichte/Big%20Data%20Papier.pdf?__blob=publicationFile&v=2.

[66] OECD, 'Data-Driven Innovation: Big Data for Growth and Well-Being Paris' (2015), available at: dx.doi.org/10.1787/9789264229358-en.

[67] Bundeskartellamt and Autorité de la Concurrence (n 65) para 12.

[68] European Commission, 'Communication from the Commission to the European Parliament, the Council, the European Economic and Social Committee and the Committee of the Regions: A European Strategy for Data (2020), available at: eur-lex.europa.eu/legal-content/EN/TXT/?uri=CELEX%3A52020DC0066.

[69] Gregory Crawford, Johnny Ryan and Cristina Caffarra, 'Antitrust Orthodoxy Blind to Real Data Harms' (*Voxeu Blog/Review*, 22 April 2021), available at: cepr.org/voxeu/blogs-and-reviews/antitrust-orthodoxy-blind-real-data-harms.

competing dataset.[70] From a practical standpoint, each of these factors comes with its own challenges. The first factor is perhaps the most challenging: first and foremost, because it is focused on the importance of the input into a specific market, which is insufficient to capture the dynamics of competition between ecosystems of interconnected products and services.[71] Second, it is not clear how one would determine what data exactly ought to be collected in order to obtain equivalent knowledge, as data are not homogeneous, and it is therefore difficult to answer this question in advance.[72] It may also be necessary to consider the existence of entry barriers at other levels of the data value chain, such as data storage and analysis,[73] as the existence of market power at those levels may hinder the ability of the undertaking in question to make meaningful use of such data.

With respect to (ii), one needs to take into account the fact that multi-homing may not be sufficient to counterbalance the competitive advantage derived from access to any particular range of data, if competitors do not have access to sufficient volumes allowing them to build a comparable dataset.

Despite identifying relevant indicative elements, the academic literature has failed to articulate a test that helps determine the relative significance of data for competition which, as acknowledged by the Franco-German Report,[74] is highly context-specific. One way for this determination to be made more predictable is by referring to the four relevant 'big data' characteristics, all to be considered from a competitive standpoint (does it provide a competitive advantage?): the variety of data composing the dataset; the speed at which the data is collected (velocity); the size of the data set (volume); and the economic significance (value). This path was followed by the European Commission in *Apple/Shazam*,[75] where one of the concerns relating to Apple's acquisition of Shazam was that the latter's customer data could confer Apple an advantage over competitors, allowing it to improve existing functionalities or to make personalised offers on its digital music streaming app. Based on its investigation, the Commission concluded that Shazam's data were not more comprehensive than other datasets available in the market[76] and was significantly lower in volume.[77] Furthermore, they were generated at a lower speed and with lower per user engagement,[78] and had never been considered as a strategic asset by the merging parties.[79] This last element is particularly crucial, and arguably the most difficult to grasp in the absence of objective parameters: the perception of merging parties may not

[70] I Graef, EU *Competition Law, Data Protection and Online Platforms: Data as Essential Facility* (Wolters Kluwer, 2016) 256.

[71] MG Jacobides and I Lianos, 'Ecosystems and Competition Law in Theory and Practice' (2021) 30 *Industrial and Corporate Change* 1199.

[72] G Colangelo and M Maggiolino, 'Big Data as Misleading Facilities' (2017) 13 *European Competition Journal* 249.

[73] DL Rubinfeld and M Gal, 'Access Barriers to Big Data' (2017) 59 *Arizona Law Review* 339.

[74] Bundeskartellamt and Autorité de la Concurrence (n 65).

[75] Commission Decision, *Apple/Shazam* (Case M.8788)' [2018] OJ C 417/4.

[76] ibid, paras 318–19.

[77] ibid, para 323.

[78] ibid, para 332.

[79] ibid, para 324.

be the most accurate reflection of the true competitive value and may have been prefabricated in anticipation of an investigation.

Another useful approach towards the assessment of data-related market power has been put forward by the Report on 'Big Data and Competition' delivered to the Dutch Ministry of Economic Affairs.[80] The Report identifies five relevant criteria. One, relating to the availability of an alternative (not data-driven) business model, is negatively correlated with market power. By contrast, the four remaining criteria bear a positive correlation: the exclusive availability of such data for one company; their ability to generate learning effects that can be used to improve a product or service; their use as 'glue' to bring together different types of users; and the firm in question's availability of assets that are complementary to the data. Note, however, that these elements do not encompass the use of data as an input for the creation of new products and services, which give the firm in question an ability to protect its market power by way of defensive leveraging. Therefore, in that sense it seems relevant to understand the scope of a company's datasets both in relation to its linkability to others, and in terms of how many different domains (which potentially represent new areas of expansion) a single dataset can provide information about.[81] This leads us to identify the additional criterion of 'leveragability', which is therefore added to the list of competitive factors drawn in the Report. Admittedly, these are just indicative criteria, but they do help by providing more focus and precision for competition analysis.

Table 2 Factors to identify risks of use of data for competition

	Factor	Effect on market power
1	**Exclusivity** – Is the data exclusively available to one company or can other companies obtain access as well?	+
2	**Learning effects** – Does the use of data contribute to learning effects that can be used to improve the product or service?	+
3	**Orchestration of interaction on a network** – Is data used to bring together various types of users on a platform?	+
4	**Complementary assets** – Are there any assets that can be considered complementary to the data? Are they exclusive or are substitutes available?	+
5	**Leveragability** – Can this data be used across different markets to facilitate the provision of new products or services?	+
6	**Competing business models** – Are there any companies that use a different business model but compete with the company considered?	–

Author's adaptation from van Til et al (2017).

[80] H van Til, N van Gorp and K Price, 'Big Data and Competition', Report for the Dutch Ministry of Economic Affairs (2017), available at: zoek.officielebekendmakingen.nl/blg-813928.pdf.

[81] I Lianos and B Carballa-Smichowski, 'A Coat of Many Colours – New Concepts and Metrics of Economic Power in Competition Law and Economics' (2022) 18 *Journal of Competition Law & Economics* 795.

The second type of manifestation of data power, as mentioned above, relates to the ability to use personal data of individuals to make targeted offers. This is another contentious area, especially due to the possible interaction of competition with data protection law, which imposes limits on how personal data can be used as an input in those offers, and consumer protection law, which imposes limits relating to their transparency. The key question here is whether and to what extent competition law should take into account the existence of a violation of those other laws. On the one hand, supporters of limited antitrust intervention argue that competition authorities should not replicate or replace the job of data protection and consumer protection authorities, arguing that data privacy and consumer protection considerations are not within the purview of antitrust.[82] Under this view, competition authorities should refrain from assessing those violations so as to respect the institutional division of competences, in particular because different regimes protect against different kinds of harm.[83] On the other hand, it is argued that an infringement of those two laws can be used to strengthen one's market position, and therefore could be cognisable under competition law. This is considered appropriate because all these areas share the goal of promoting consumer welfare;[84] and specifically for data privacy, because it is a fundamental right that as such must be recognised, protected and promoted by other regulators.[85] An intermediate position is also possible, holding that data protection violations should be considered only to the extent that data protection is a relevant dimension of competition in that market, for instance from the perspective of product quality.[86] Regardless of the view taken, this intersection points to the need for cross-institutional collaboration, which has been initiated in a number of jurisdictions between competition, consumer protection and data protection authorities: examples are the Digital Clearinghouse initiative in the EU[87] and the Digital Regulation Cooperation Forum in the United Kingdom.[88]

[82] JC Cooper, 'Privacy and Antitrust: Underpants Gnomes, the First Amendment, and Subjectivity' (2013) 20 *George Mason Law Review* 1129, 1146; MK Ohlhausen and AP Okuliar, 'Competition, Consumer Protection, and the Right [Approach] to Privacy' (2015) 80 *Antitrust Law Journal* 121, 138–43.

[83] ibid.

[84] A Albors-Llorens, 'Competition and Consumer Law in the European Union: Evolution and Convergence' (2014) 33 *Yearbook of European Law* 163; SY Esayas, 'Competition in (Data) Privacy: "Zero"-Price Markets, Market Power, and the Role of Competition Law' (2018) 8 *International Data Privacy Law* 181.

[85] Graef (n 70); F Costa-Cabral and O Lynskey, 'Family Ties: The Intersection Between Data Protection and Competition in EU Law' (2017) 54 *Common Market Law Review* 11; N Zingales, 'Data Protection Considerations in EU Competition Law: Funnel or Straightjacket for Innovation?' in P Nihoul and P van Cleynenbreugel (eds), *The Roles of Innovation in Competition Analysis* (Edward Elgar, 2018).

[86] E Douglas, 'The New Antitrust/Data Privacy Law Interface' (2021) 647 *Yale Law Journal Forum* 1.

[87] See 'Digital Clearing House', available at: www.digitalclearinghouse.org.

[88] Competition & Markets Authority (CMA), Information Commissioner's Office (ICO) and Ofcom, 'Digital Regulation Cooperation Forum', available at: www.ofcom.org.uk/__data/assets/pdf_file/0021/192243/drcf-launch-document.pdf.

At the same time, this is not a silver bullet to understand all competitive concerns arising from the use of personal data: there may be situations in which, despite complying with data protection and consumer protection laws, the processing of vast amounts of personal data raises competitive concerns due to a state of social dependence of individuals. We can define social dependence as an antagonist to 'consumer sovereignty', a state in which consumers have the power 'to define their own wants and the opportunity to satisfy those wants at prices not greatly in excess of the costs borne by the providers of the relevant goods and services'.[89] One of the reasons for the disconnection between consumer preferences and the price mechanism may be that the seller or an intermediary that facilitates transactions possesses vast data points revealing an individual's behaviour and preferences, to a level that can hardly be matched by entrants, and enables it to engage in exclusionary or exploitative conduct. This can happen even in the absence of a wealth of individual-level data, simply because strategic data points can be used to infer additional data through probabilistic reasoning.[90] In these situations, competitive harm may arise if certain market players derive an objective advantage from the loss of agency that individuals may suffer, despite the theoretical possibility for such individuals to avail themselves of the safeguards provided by consumer and data protection legislation, such as, most notably, transparency and the exercise of data subjects rights. Accordingly, it may be necessary to take into account other aspects of domination over individuals alongside market power, so as to ensure fairness and contestability, in a similar vein as media plurality considerations are relevant in the context of media mergers.[91] However, competition authorities currently lack metrics, methodologies and tools to determine when data concentration should be deemed problematic for creating a risk of undue influence over individuals.

V. ADJUSTING THE LENSES FOR DATA-RELATED ABUSES

The framework described in section IV does not solve the many questions raised in section III relating to the application of traditional forms of abuse to data-related markets. However, it contributes by bringing additional focus into the competitive analysis. In this section, we summarise the insights drawing attention to the areas of enquiry that are likely to gain more relevance in the future and apply those concepts to the fintech cases mentioned in section II.

[89] N Averitt and R Lande, 'Consumer Sovereignty: A Unified Theory of Antitrust and Consumer Protection Law' (1997) 65 *Antitrust Law Journal* 713.

[90] O Lynskey, 'Grappling With "Data Power": Normative Nudges from Data Protection and Privacy' (2019) 20 *Theoretical Inquiries in Law* 189.

[91] ibid.

A. Market Definition and Market Power

A first fundamental challenge that affects antitrust analysis in data-driven markets relates to market definition and market power. Where data are not traded in the market, authorities typically have looked at it merely as an input for downstream use, which may lead them to ignore markets which are not yet developed around an identified product or service. This raises a legitimate concern of monopolisation for markets that are quickly developing in response to a technological or regulatory innovation, and for which market boundaries are blurred. One reaction to that is simply to protect all possible markets that depend on access to certain data with a presumption of dominance of the data holder, which may be reasonable in specific contexts. For instance, we know that the innovation of open banking led the Dutch Report on fintech competition to the conclusion that banks enjoy a dominant position in the market for information about the payment accounts of their customers.[92] By this, the Dutch Report meant, presumably, any market which depends on the availability of information about customers' payment accounts. A similar argument can be made for other markets that offer clear downstream use-cases for data collected as part of a primary activity, as is the case for connected cars. Not coincidentally,[93] the expert report delivered in 2019 to the European Commission for competition policy in the digital age warned about the lack of contestability that follows from exclusive control to such data, and a report of 2018 to the German Federal Ministry for Economic Affairs and Energy affirmed that a denial of access to data in energy markets can constitute an unreasonable exclusionary conduct even if markets for such data do not yet exist.[94] The big question is, of course, when that would be the case. In the absence of clearly delineated ex ante rules or presumptions, how are parties to predict if a refusal to grant access to data in a not-yet-existent market is anticompetitive? Some inspiration can be found in the framework available in many jurisdictions to deal with situations of economic dependence on the part of undertakings, including Austria, Belgium, China, France, Germany, Italy, Japan, Korea, the Slovak Republic, South Africa, Switzerland and Taiwan. This concept requires a different analysis from that of market power. Although it similarly focuses on the ability of an undertaking to switch to alternative providers, its enquiry includes both an objective element as to the sufficiency of the alternatives and a subjective element about

[92] ACM, 'Fintechs in the Payment System' (n 14).

[93] '[A] number of experts and industry participants argue that exclusive control over machine usage data then leads to the foreclosure of secondary markets and may significantly reduce the contestability of a machine producer's position on the primary market, due to a data-driven lock-in of machine users'. J Crémer, Y-A de Montjoye and H Schweitzer, 'Competition Policy for the Digital Era: Final Report' (2019) 88.

[94] H Schweitzer, J Haucap, W Kerber and R Welker, 'Modernising the Law on Abuse of Market Power: Report for the Federal Ministry for Economic Affairs and Energy (Germany)' (2018) 6.

the reasonableness of the efforts that would be required for the switching.[95] The case law has established a range of factors that are relevant to establish the existence of economic dependence, such as the existence of alternative distribution or production paths, the importance of a product for the retailer, brand strength, and the existence of aggregated buyer power.[96] To these factors, we should add a data-related element that was recently introduced in Germany by the Tenth Amendment to its Competition Law, establishing in § 20, 1a that 'dependence may also arise from the fact that an undertaking is dependent on access to data controlled by another undertaking for its own activities'.

Another way to recognise prospective data-related advantages would be to use the concept of research and development (R&D) or so-called 'innovation' markets developed by Gilbert and Sunshine,[97] and subsequently adopted in the US Guidelines on Intellectual Property,[98] which refer to a market for the R&D directed at particularly new or improved goods or processes and the close substitutes for that research and development.[99] However, this approach can only be taken when the relevant R&D assets can be associated with specialised assets or characteristics of specific firms,[100] which makes it inapt to capture data-driven innovation: the availability of big data and data analytics reverses the direction of discovery, using data to formulate hypotheses rather than to prove existing hypotheses.[101] This means that R&D is now more closely informed by the observation of the daily activity of consumers and, where applicable, of business partners. Innovation and R&D are therefore relevant not just to the next model or version of something a customer might buy, but also to how the customer might use it next.[102]

A third approach is to consider consumer data as a special asset which positions the data collector in competition for a range of markets, together with other significant data collectors.[103] Under this solution, antitrust analysis would focus on the impact on competition between ecosystems, rather than within narrowly defined markets. As aptly put in a recent market study by the Dutch competition authority on mobile app stores: 'the battle fought by online

[95] Thombal (n 27). See also L Féteira, *The Interplay Between European and National Competition Law After Regulation 1/2003: 'United (Should) We Stand?'* (Wolters Kluwer, 2016) 150.

[96] See I Lianos and C Lombardi, 'Superior Bargaining Power and the Global Food Value Chain: The Wuthering Heights of Holistic Competition Law?' (2016) CLES Research Paper Series, available at: ssrn.com/abstract=2773455.

[97] R Gilbert and S Sunshine, 'Incorporating Dynamic Efficiency Concerns in Merger Analysis: The Use of Innovation Markets' (1995) 63 *Antitrust Law Journal* 569.

[98] US Department of Justice and Federal Trade Commission, 'Antitrust Guidelines for the Licensing of Intellectual Property § 3.2.3' (1995).

[99] ibid.

[100] ibid.

[101] Mayer-Schönberger and Padova (n 64).

[102] HA Shelanski, 'Information, Innovation, and Competition Policy for the Internet' (2013) 161 *University of Pennsylvania Law Review* 1663.

[103] Graef (n 70).

platform-ecosystems is not about dominating markets, but it is about becoming the default gateway to the internet and content for a critical mass of users that can be monetised in various ways'.[104] Due to this particular dynamic, ecosystem markets must be based on a clear understanding of their users' trends of demand and biases, together with that of the technological and organisational affordances (including data) that are necessary for competition in these markets. Furthermore, particular attention should be placed on quality (rather than price) as the attribute that drives competition.[105]

Whatever the approach, it is important to formulate a compelling theory of how and why the leveraging of data occurs. This brings to bear the relevance of the second type of manifestation of power described in section IV which, as discussed, presents challenges both in terms of measurement and coordination that will need to be resolved. As far as the first manifestation of power is concerned, instead, the data significance criteria listed in Table 1 can provide a useful metric. Specifically, an additional source of market power could be found in data whenever the six-pronged test shown in Table 1 suggests, on balance, that the competitive risks from data enclosure are significant. The test could even be used to resolve the hesitation in establishing dominance by banks on the market for fintech services, as in the *Guiabolso* case,[106] where all factors in the text weigh in favour of a finding of market power: (1) prior to the establishment of open banking, the data is exclusively held by the banks; (2) it allows banks to improve their offer to customers, including (5) offering new products and services downstream; (3) it allows them to bring together various different stakeholders offering their services being accredited within the bank ecosystem; (4) there may be complementary assets that are relevant, for example in terms of specialised staff working on financial products and recommendation algorithms that are based on extremely detailed data records, but these may also become more widely available in the market after the rolling out of all the phases of open banking. Finally (6) there is no business model available to offer the bundle of services that banks offer today other than by obtaining the bank customer's account information. Interestingly, this shows that dominance in downstream markets was clear before the implementation of open banking, while less so afterwards – as the regulatory framework specifically mandated the sharing of certain data to increase openness and contestability of these secondary markets.

The case of Apple, where the legitimacy of an iOS-focused app distribution market was contested, had less to do with market definition for the downstream use of data than with control of the ecosystem that Apple has built. The fact that Apple does not allow third parties to distribute apps on its iOS, or that only

[104] ACM, 'Market Study into Mobile App Stores' (2019) 5.

[105] F Jenny, 'Competition Law and Digital Ecosystems: Learning to Walk Before We Run' (2021) 30 *Industrial and Corporate Change* 1143.

[106] Eleventh Civil Chamber of São Paulo (n 8).

20 per cent of consumers use iOS-running phones, cannot bar antitrust analysis from viewing the aftermarket as a relevant market. Indeed, the US Supreme Court in *Kodak* did consider that a firm with about 20 per cent in the primary market (for high-volume copies) can be deemed to have monopoly power in its wholly controlled aftermarkets.[107] The justifications for refusing to view this as a system market, where consumers decide at the outset which ecosystem they join on the basis of the characteristics of the primary as well as the secondary products that the ecosystem orchestrator provides, can largely mimic those offered by the Supreme Court in holding that consumers are unable to inform themselves of the total life-cycle pricing of the durable equipment they acquire (in this case, iPhones) and suffer from significant lock-in effects due to the costs of that equipment. Furthermore, consumers might not be able to appreciate the effects of the data collection tax imposed by Apple on app developers through the mandatory use of its own payment system, which adds to the lifecycle costs of being part of the Apple ecosystem and thus may result in higher prices for third-party products.

B. Abuse

i. Refusal to Deal

The first abuse that is relevant to consider for the purpose of addressing the issues raised by the cases presented in section II is refusal to deal. Indeed, in the context between *Bradesco* and *Guiabolso*, it was appropriate to consider whether hindering the process of granting access to customer data could be considered as a constructive refusal to deal. Hindering access to data manifested itself in two different ways: first, by requiring an additional two-factor authentication; second, and more generally, by initiating a legal action aimed to stop Guiabolso's data collection.

One might also recall that SEPRAC claimed that Bradesco's lawsuit constituted vexatious or 'sham' litigation. Arguably, this conclusion could not be reached under EU competition law: its case law requires proof that the lawsuit is objectively baseless, in the sense that the undertaking could not reasonably consider itself to be legitimately asserting its rights,[108] and that it forms part of a plan to eliminate competition. The first requirement, in particular, appears difficult to satisfy, as Bradesco could legitimately believe that security and transparency requirements are a prerequisite for it to allow third parties to access customer information under the conditions established in its contracts. Since at the time of the proceeding there was no obligation for banks to provide interconnection, the claim of violation of the rules established in the contract with

[107] *Eastman Kodak Co v Image Technical Servs, Inc*, 504 US 451 (1992).
[108] Commission Decision, *ITT Promedia NV /Belgacom* (Case IV/35.268) [1996] para 73.

customers could not be seen as pretextual. In the same vein, one should consider the legitimacy of Bradesco's arguments as a possible defence to refusal to deal. Indeed, CADE examined the security standards that applied to transactions made within the Bradesco app, as well as those applied by competing banks, ultimately rejecting those arguments on grounds of proportionality.

There are some open questions, as we discussed in section III, concerning the application of refusal to deal in these scenarios: first and foremost, it might be impossible to identify a downstream market where the dominant firm operates and competition is effectively eliminated without access to the required input. In this case, CADE followed the Dutch Report arguing that Bradesco was dominant in the market for customer account information, which has the implication that banks are present in virtually every conceivable market that depends on the use of such information. As was pointed out above, dominance may no longer exist after the introduction of open banking, but this does not detract from the leveragability of data into secondary markets. Therefore, as others have noted,[109] a sensible interpretation of the refusal to deal test appears to require a relaxation of the requirement of presence in a downstream market, in order to prevent the erection of barriers to the emergence of new competitive forces that can challenge the position of banks in various kinds of financial services.

A further issue pertains to the types of data that should be disclosed, and under what conditions. It is questionable, for instance, whether the customer account information ought to involve added-value data developed by the bank through probabilistic inferences, most obviously the customer's spending and credit profile. In this case, one could argue that the balancing of the benefits of disclosure with the incentives to innovate should result in the exclusion of this type of data from the scope of the obligation: these data have been produced as a result of skill and effort, rather than being merely a by-product of the account holding service provided by the bank. By contrast, all provided and observed data should be included, with the additional requirement that such data be disclosed in a format that allows meaningful reuse by the access seeker, in this case the fintech. For this reason, CADE rightly demanded Bradesco in the commitment decision to develop a dedicated interface designed to ensure that customers can effectively give consent (without two-factor authentication required) for the transfer of their account information to Bradesco. What the commitment failed to address, and could have been useful to specify, is the format of the transferred data. For instance, merely transferring raw data seems unlikely to be a suitable solution, because it could be argued to be generating another hindrance to meaningful data access, as would a transfer in a very uncommon processing format. It is important that such data be structured, ie, sub-divided into categories, and formatted, in the sense of saved in a particular type of protocol that permits meaningful reuse.

[109] See, for instance, Graef (n 70); Thombal (n 27) 242.

ii. Unfair Terms and Conditions

The second abuse that is relevant to mention is the imposition of unfair terms and conditions. The imposition of terms lacking transparency over the counterparty's conduct may fall into this category's scope provided they have a distorted effect on consumers' decisions.[110] An example would be the uniformed consent of users who accepted WhatsApp's new privacy policy. The hurdle here is to understand whether this data collection formed part of the essential purpose of the agreement between WhatsApp and its user, the object of which is the provision of services of instant messaging in exchange for licences to intellectual property associated with those services[111] and to re-use the information that the user uploads, submits, stores, sends or receives for purposes relating to those services.[112] Indeed, these terms are deliberately broad enough to encompass a series of purposes, potentially also legitimising the transfer of data to Meta for advertising purposes. However, the interpreter cannot limit itself to the plain meaning of the text, and must understand the object of the meeting of minds between parties. In particular, it must ascertain whether users would in fact enter into such a contract if they were truly aware of the nature, extent and scope of personal data obtained by Meta and whether any additional data processing could be considered proportionate to the objective of the contract. The latter can be doubted because contextual advertising would likely generate sufficient revenues to fund WhatsApp's operation. Furthermore, the view that Meta cannot rely on 'necessity for the performance of the contract' as a legal basis for behavioural advertising has been recently confirmed by the European Data Protection Board.[113]

A parallel argument about unfair terms could be made by considering data as the currency or means of exchange against which instant messaging services are provided, thus opening the door for the assessment of the potential excessiveness of the price imposed in personal data terms. This is indeed the position taken by the Argentinian competition authority in its legal action to stop WhatsApp from rolling out the new privacy policy in the country.[114] It is also the core argument of the plaintiffs in a class action that is pending at the UK's Competition Appeal

[110] See, to that effect, Competition Commission of India (n 22).

[111] WhatsApp's Terms of Service (updated 4 January 2021), available at: www.whatsapp.com/legal/terms-of-service/?lang=en. 'We own all copyrights, trademarks, domains, logos, trade dress, trade secrets, patents, and other intellectual property rights associated with our Services'.

[112] ibid. 'In order to operate and provide our Services, you grant WhatsApp a worldwide, non-exclusive, royalty-free, sublicensable, and transferable license to use, reproduce, distribute, create derivative works of, display, and perform the information (including the content) that you upload, submit, store, send, or receive on or through our Services. The rights you grant in this license are for the limited purpose of operating and providing our Services'.

[113] European Data Protection Board, 'Binding Decision 3/2022 on the dispute submitted by the Irish SA on Meta Platforms Ireland Limited and its Facebook Service (Art 65 General Data Protection Regulation)' (2022), available at: edpb.europa.eu/our-work-tools/our-documents/binding-decision-board-art-65/binding-decision-32022-dispute-submitted_en.

[114] Secretary of Commerce (n 21).

Tribunal against Meta, considering that the incremental cost to Meta of offering Personal Social Network and/or Social Media Services to each additional user is very low, while the revenues generated by Meta's advertising activities by virtue of the personal data are very high, and Meta's excess profits are substantially above the competitive level.[115] That is a difficult calculation to make, as it depends on the utility that consumers derive both from the service and (comparatively) from the withholding of personal data from Facebook. An undertaking that has invested to create a long-term infrastructure should not be prevented from profiting from it, even after it has recouped its initial investment, especially to the extent that the investment was made under risky conditions. However, the words 'reasonably related to economic value' in the case law suggest the existence of an upper limit to the reward that the undertaking can legitimately request, also taking into account non-cost factors, such as the demand for the product or service.[116] If non-cost factors also include consumer characteristics which give rise to personalisation, this calculation runs into the problem of measurement of heterogeneous consumer preferences and sensitivity: studies have demonstrated that revealed privacy preferences are idiosyncratic, subjective, context-dependent, subject to change over time,[117] inextricably related to risk aversion[118] and widely different from stated preferences.[119] Therefore, empirical research in this area is needed, both on an ad hoc basis to identify the preferences of the relevant consumers, and more generally, to provide tools that can assist with these assessments. For example, frameworks that identify different levels of privacy protection and distinct categories of consumers based on their privacy and data protection attitudes and individuals' willingness to pay for not disclosing certain data in certain contexts. This would facilitate the comparison between services that are paid monetarily and those which rely on the collection of personal data and advertising.

iii. Rebates

The third relevant conduct to be discussed is rebates, which seems important to understand the potential anticompetitive conduct relating to data use in the *iFood* case. While the European Commission's Guidance Paper in its discussion on rebates helpfully points to the benchmark of the price that would need to be paid by an as-efficient competitor to gain customers from the dominant

[115] *Dr Liza Lovdahl Gormsen v Meta Platforms* (2022) Case No 1433/7/7/22, Notice of an Application to Commence Collective Proceedings Under Section 47b of the Competition Act 1998.

[116] See, to that effect, Commission Decision, *Scandlines Sverige v Port of Helsingborg* (Case AT 36568) [2006] 4 CMLR 23.

[117] A Acquisti, C Taylor and L Wagman, 'The Economics of Privacy' (2016) 554 *Journal of Economic Literature* 442.

[118] A Frik and A Gaudeul, 'A Measure of the Implicit Value of Privacy Under Risk' (2020) 37 *Journal of Consumer Marketing* 457.

[119] A Acquisti, L Brandimarte and G Loewenstein, 'Privacy and Human Behavior in the Age of Information' (2015) 347 *Science* 509.

firm, this is only an indicative element, with the Paper mentioning a few other factors. As discussed in section III, there are difficulties in the application of the leveraging theory to selective rebates, due to the theoretical ability of competitors to make up for these lost customers by channelling their sales and rebates to other customers. However, this critique relies on the assumption that competitors have perfect information over the rebates that are granted, which is unlikely in data-driven rebates, simply because they would have a harder time figuring out the profile of the dominant firm's rebate targets (not having access to the firm's datasets).

Even if the leveraging theory applies, it remains challenging to compute whether, in a particular case, a rebate results in a rate that makes it impossible for competitors to gain a contestable share. To do that, one needs to average out the rate charged to a multitude of different customers, and also to consider that the pricing structure may be a manifestation of a legitimate price discrimination strategy. Therefore, for practical reasons we suggest that an authority should slightly change the test to reflect these elements: the difficulty of detection of rebates; the challenge of calculating the average; and the potential procompetitive explanation of an uneven pricing scheme. The proposed test would go as follows. First, if it is established that one or more rebates have been granted that would require below-cost selling (in terms of average avoidable costs, or AAC) for an as-efficient competitor to match them, then the conduct is presumed to be abusive. However, if the dominant firm produces evidence of a procompetitive justification, for example, incentivising the retention of a particular type of buyer due to supply-chain disruption issues, then the presumption is defeated and all circumstances have to be considered. To facilitate that assessment, it is useful to consider another element mentioned by the Guidance Paper, which refers to 'direct evidence of exclusionary strategy'.[120] This element gives relevance to both subjective and objective intent, which can be used to corroborate a non-conclusive finding of illegality.[121] On that basis, one could formulate a second presumption, similar to the one applicable in the context of predation (but focused on the costs of the dominant firm's competitors), where pricing between average avoidable costs and average total costs (ATC) is deemed anticompetitive if it constitutes part of a plan to eliminate competition. By replicating the same bifurcated structure applicable to predation (presumption for <AAC selling + presumption for >AAC<ATC in the presence of exclusionary strategy), this test would help bridge the consistency gap between the assessment of rebates and predatory conduct, which is particularly confusing when it comes to selective price-cutting.

In the context of the *iFood* case, then, this approach would require the authority to examine whether the prices charged by iFood were below the average variable costs of an as-efficient competitor, and, in the negative, whether

[120] European Commission, 'Enforcement Priorities' (n 36).

[121] N Zingales, 'Antitrust Intent in an Age of Algorithmic Nudging' (2019) 7 *Journal of Antitrust Enforcement* 386.

they were below average total costs and whether a plan to eliminate competition could be gleaned from the company's strategy, including especially who were the selected targets for the rebates. Only where the authority cannot reach its conclusions based on these two presumptions, would the analysis require an in-depth look at the effects of the practice. In that context, the authority should also consider the fact that vouchers programmes increase the volume of data collection on the iFood delivery platform, which in turns fuels its downstream restaurant business (so-called 'dark kitchens'), and thus may enable the exercise of market power at a different level of the value chain – despite having a small market share in the voucher programme market.

iv. Tying

The fourth abuse is tying. This discussion is relevant to understand two conducts: the one investigated in the *Apple* case, in particular the mandatory condition imposed on apps on the App Store to use Apple Pay for in-app sales of digital content; and the one in the context of WhatsApp's privacy policy update – in particular, the imposition of data sharing with Meta in addition to the acceptance of other data uses necessary for the performance of the contract. In the first case increased data processing is one of the objectives of the defendant's conduct, whereas in the other, it is the object, ie, the tied product. In the former scenario, the difficulty concerns the separability of the two products in question. This depends on the decision-maker's willingness to view the entire Apple ecosystem as a market with multiple interconnected segments, each offering an opportunity for the collection of data or to generate other efficiencies that benefit certain products and services of the ecosystem, including advertising. However, this argument must be supported by convincing evidence by the dominant firm that any restriction of competition is necessary and proportionate to achieve the claimed efficiencies, which is a tall order – especially since it can be impossible to determine with precision what will be the effect from the collection or use of certain data.

In the latter scenario, additional challenges apply, as pointed out in section III. First, to determine whether the additional entitlement to data processing constitutes a separate product, a competition authority will have to examine the extent to which such data entitlement could be legitimately grounded on the applicable data protection legislation,[122] which requires cooperation with

[122] For instance, a firm may argue that intra-group sharing is already permissible under a legitimate interest test (Art 6(f) of the General Data Protection Regulation), and therefore agreement to the privacy policy was not meant to signify consent, but merely to give more transparency to a lawful use of personal data. This argument could not be accepted in this case, however, both because of the significant risks of harm caused to individuals whose data is used for targeted advertising and because some of the shared data may actually be special categories of data of more sensitive nature (such as race, sexual, religious or philosophical beliefs, sexual preferences, political opinions, or trade union membership), which cannot be processed under Art 6(f).

the competent authority. Second, even if the data entitlement is not justified by data protection legislation, the separate nature of the product can be challenged by the interdependent relationship between the two. For instance, agreeing to the privacy policy relating to advertising services is necessary for a social media user to be able to benefit from social media services. However, this reasoning cannot justify the provision involving a transfer of data between WhatsApp and Meta, as WhatsApp users receive no apparent benefit from this, nor is behavioural advertising necessary to run the entire ecosystem. Third, and most crucial for our purposes, is the difficulty in establishing harm to competition based on the tying due to the complex relationship between data and effects. While a precise answer to this can only be given bearing in mind the specifics of the case, much like in the Apple investigation, a helpful framework in this regard is the data significance framework discussed in section IV. Indeed, considering that WhatsApp metadata would only be available to the Meta Group, that such data generates learning effects and enables the recipient to bring together different types of users, that its use is associated with powerful algorithms, and that it can be used across different markets to facilitate the provision of new products or services, the mere fact that alternative models exist to provide advertising services without relying on metadata of instant messaging does not seem sufficient to rebut the weight in favour of data significance.

v. Discrimination

The fifth type of abuse is anticompetitive discrimination. This is relevant to the *iFood* and the *Apple* cases. The former is a relatively simpler scenario, where the conduct is data-related only in the sense that it creates higher customer adoption and therefore higher volumes of data regarding beneficiaries of meal vouchers. The authority considered the claim of limited interoperability for competing voucher providers on the iFood platform, but dismissed it as it was a technical problem in the whole industry that would be addressed by new legislation. Should the issue persist, the authority could reopen the case and consider whether this type of discrimination (also called self-preferencing) creates a distortionary effect not only in the meal voucher market, but also in the online delivery market and the restaurant market, due to the feedback effects generated by data of meal voucher consumers. It may even give an advantage to iFood in markets that do not yet exist, such as markets for complementary items designed for specific profiles of meal voucher consumers (eg, sushi lovers, pizza lovers, etc).

Regarding the Apple case, it may be recalled that it concerns the fact that Apple prohibits in-app purchases for the sale of digital content, combined with the fact that it charges a transaction fee to its competitors in the provision of digital content. While this restriction is not directly relating to data, it is instrumental, together with the payment restriction, to achieving a strategy of 'disintermediation'.[123] Apple gets to collect valuable transactional data for purchases of digital content, which can give it a competitive advantage in developing apps.

To examine the discrimination claim, it is important to understand the monetisation policy of the App Store, according to which the fee is charged to all sellers of digital content sold and consumed on the app, but not to sellers of physical products and services, nor to digital content that is monetised exclusively through advertising.[124] The complainant's contention is that this distinction is arbitrary in distinguishing between physical and digital goods. The rationale for the distinction appears to be that Apple cannot verify the completion of the transaction, whereas in digital content sales Apple is party to the transaction, dealing with the payment and other financial services. At the same time, those financial services are offered by competitors at rates (15–30 per cent) that are significantly higher than those of competing payment processors. Not surprisingly, Apple attributes the costs to a bundle of services, including app review, app development tools and marketing services.[125] However, those are services offered by all applications, in the same way for apps selling digital and physical content. This implies that the only additional work that Apple must do in a case of digital content is precisely that associated with the handling of the payment, which it has decided to impose through its own processor. This justification clearly cannot be accepted, for it is circular. Therefore, in the absence of additional explanations by Apple, this conduct amounts to dissimilar treatment of equivalent transactions prohibited by Article 102 TFEU, provided that a distortionary effect on the downstream market can be demonstrated and that

[123] MG Jacobides, 'What Drives and Defines Digital Platform Power? A Framework, With an Illustration of App Dynamics in the Apple Ecosystem' (2021) White Paper, available at: events.concurrences.com/IMG/pdf/jacobides_platform_dominance.pdf.

[124] ibid. 'i. All developers who choose to distribute an app on the App Store must pay an annual fee of USD 99.00. ii. If a developer offers their software for free on the App Store or adopts a business model that relies solely on advertising or selling physical goods and services, then they do not pay Apple any commission. Developers of approximately 84% of the apps currently available on the App Store do not pay Apple any commission, a percentage that applies evenly worldwide. iii. If a developer charges for downloading an app from the App Store or selling digital content through an app, they will pay Apple a 15% commission (30% if they make more than $1 million a year). This also applies to subscriptions to digital content sold through the app, for which the fee is 30% in the first year even for developers earning more than USD 1 million per year, and 15% for others. iv. If a developer is paid for selling digital content outside the app, there is no obligation to pay any commission. Content acquired by users on an external platform can still be accessed through an iOS-compatible app'.

[125] 'Apple's commission is not a payment processing fee: it reflects the value of the App Store as a channel for the distribution of developers' apps and the cost of many services – including app review, app development tools and marketing services – that make the App Store a safe and trusted marketplace for customers and a great business opportunity for developers'. See Kyle Andeer, 'Letter to Subcommittee on Antitrust, Commercial and Administrative Law of the Committee on the Judiciary' (2020) 2, available at: docs.house.gov/meetings/JU/JU05/20200117/110386/HHRG-116-JU05-20200117- SD004.pdf. Cited in D Geradin and D Katsifis, 'The Antitrust Case Against the Apple App Store (Revisited)' (2020) TILEC Discussion Paper 77, available at: ssrn.com/abstract=3744192.

this has impacted price, quality and innovation, or market structure. This is not the appropriate context for an evaluation of effects, which require an assessment of all the evidence. However, the fact that the distortion has had some distortionary impact downstream is clear from the second discrimination claim, which is concerned with the charging of transaction fees to competitors that Apple does not have to pay for its own downstream products, such as Apple TV and Apple Music. Furthermore, one can argue that a distortion is taking place in the market for app development, where Apple can leverage the information it collects through payments into specific secondary markets. One could try to apply the test of data significance, but the results in this scenario are more ambiguous here than in previous examples. The information is certainly exclusive and leverageable and produces learning effects, but it does not benefit from complementary assets, and an alternative business model can certainly be conceived. Leveragability is significant because of the variety of domains which the data refer to. However, these data cannot serve to bring together a network of players (at least, in the absence of a legitimate legal basis to transfer these data to third parties for their own re-purposing).

The imposition of the transaction fee and the mandatory use of the payment app should be viewed holistically, as part of a continuous infringement, similar to the way in which the European Commission viewed the various restrictions imposed by Google in the *Android* case.[126] In that light, one interesting consideration from a data perspective is whether the imposition of Apple's payment system in apps selling digital content is necessary to bring those apps in line with Apple's own standards of security and trustworthiness, and thus preserve the image of security, privacy and user experience which are critical to the success of Apple's products.[127] In other words, the transactions with digital and physical content providers are treated differently because Apple makes them different, and the question is thus whether the values of security, privacy and user experience cannot be preserved through other payment methods. While we make no claim to know the data privacy and security standards of different payment providers, an interesting question concerns the baseline for assessing the equivalence of two (payment) alternatives in relation to privacy and security standards. Should it not include an equivalence of the type and amount of data these services process, as those tend to increase the related risks? In the same vein, the purposes for which these data can be used could arguably play a relevant consideration. Would not the fact that some of the processed data may be used as an input into other ecosystem products and services diminish Apple's proffered privacy standards compared with those offered by non-integrated payment

[126] Commission Decision, *Google Android* (Case AT.40099) [2018] para 1340.

[127] Conselho Administrativo de Defesa da Concorrência, Preparatory Proceeding nº 08700.009531/2022-04, 'Technical Note No 4/2023/CGAA11/SGA1/SG/CADE' 8, *Ebazar.com.br. Ltda and Mercado Pago Instituição de Pagamento Ltda.*

systems? These questions illustrate the difficulty of measuring privacy standards, as they often involve trade-offs between different components.[128] While legislation such as the General Data Protection Regulation and case law provide guidance by giving a few benchmarks for these measurements, ultimately there will be innumerable scenarios in which the decision will depend on the empirical assessment of consumer privacy preferences. Furthermore, these preferences may have to be traded off with other values, such as security.

VI. CONCLUSION

In this chapter, we used four cases examined by CADE involving financial technology and allegations of anticompetitive data processing to map some of the main challenges for antitrust in dealing with data-related abuses. In doing so, we observed that the allegations of data-related abuses in fintech markets can be divided into two patterns: refusal to grant access to data by traditional financial institutions; or abuse of a fiduciary relationship by fintech providers – which in turn can materialise into both an exclusionary and an exploitative conduct. In accordance with this and the four aforementioned cases, some the key categories of abuses in these markets were presented, outlining the challenges faced in a data-related context to apply the traditional legal tests for unfair terms and conditions, discrimination, tying, exclusive dealing and rebates, refusal to deal. We then defined a structured test for the assessment of one type of market power emanating from data and used it to address some of those challenges. In particular, we submitted that the use of a six-pronged test for data significance allows the interpreter to better answer the important questions about market power and competitive advantage. This test was used, for instance, to establish market power and dominance, tying and anticompetitive discrimination. At the same time, it was recognised that a second manifestation of market power deriving from personal data (targeting ability) raises further challenges that are not captured by this test and require cooperation with consumer and data protection authorities. Nevertheless, targets and targeting criteria constitute important elements of enquiry for the purpose of identifying the strategy of the dominant firm which, it was argued, could serve to establish a prima facie case of abuse in the context of targeted rebates. This would allow dealing more consistently with rebates, a key anticompetitive practice by which fintechs may leverage their low-fixed costs to capture market share, and the success of which can be substantially boosted by strategic use of customer data. The cases discussed above have also shown the importance of understanding the role of ecosystems of interconnected products and services, where fintech can use data

[128] M Veale, R Binns and J Ausloos, 'When Data Protection by Design and Data Subject Rights Clash' (2018) 8 *International Data Privacy Law* 105.

as a flywheel that increases the power of the ecosystem orchestrator in related markets.

All in all, the foregoing analysis sought to demonstrate that the main legal tests used to assess the legality of the conducts examined in this chapter are fundamentally challenged when applied in a data-related environment. However, it is argued that an appropriate reaction by competition authorities facing those challenges is not to walk away alleging a failure to meet one of the elements of the existing tests. Rather, it is to adjust these tests (as suggested for refusal to deal, discrimination and rebates) or seek alternative routes (for instance, choosing general unfairness jurisdiction for overbroad collection of personal data instead of pursuing a case of 'excessive' data collection) considering the peculiarities of these markets. Given the relatively few data-related cases and the early stage of research on the interactions between data and competition, these tests are likely to be refined over time, along with the creation of new metrics for measurement of data privacy in competition analysis. If so, let us all play our part to get the ball moving.

7

Vertical Agreements in Fintech Markets

LUCY M.R. CHAMBERS*

I. INTRODUCTION: THE CALM BEFORE THE STORM?

THE CONSIDERATION OF vertical agreements in the context of financial institutions is certainly not new, nor does it require a novel approach or recognition of new issues.[1] Nonetheless, the rapid advancement of fintech brings about new questions of when vertical agreements, which could otherwise be seen as anticompetitive, could, in fact, be procompetitive.[2]

Before addressing specific questions relating to the application of the legal and economic treatment of vertical agreements to fintech, it is important to define what we mean by these concepts. The concept of fintech, the commonly used contraction for referring to financial technologies, is multifaceted and is the evolving intersection of financial services and technology. It involves multiple players including large, established financial institutions such as banks, technology companies such as Apple and Google, companies providing infrastructure or technology to facilitate transactions involving existing payment services, and banking players such as Visa, disruptors including start-ups focused on innovative technologies or processes such as Stripe (mobile payments), or challenger banks like Starling, or new technology providers focusing on applications such as blockchain in the finance space, including through cryptocurrency. For the purposes of this chapter, fintech will be used most frequently to refer to technologies in the context of banking and finance as well as blockchain and cryptocurrency.

It is also important to outline what is meant by 'vertical agreements'. In competition law, a vertical restraint is some type of limitation on the action of one or more parties at different levels or stages within the production or distribution

* The views expressed in this chapter are the personal views of the author and do not necessarily represent the views of Slaughter and May. All errors are the author's own.

[1] See, eg, Case C-382/12 P *MasterCard and Others v Commission* [2014] ECLI:EU:C:2014:2201.

[2] See further LMR Chambers, 'Mind the Gap: The Consideration of Financial Technologies and Blockchain in the Reform of the Vertical Agreements Block Exemption Regulation' (2019) 18 *Competition Law Journal* 116.

chain. An example of such vertical restraints would be exclusive dealing obligations between an upstream provider of services and a downstream purchaser. A vertical agreement is a contract (formal or informal) containing such restraints. Vertical agreements often can produce welfare-enhancing efficiencies, for example through the reduction of free-riding or double marginalisation.[3] However, vertical agreements can also be used to prevent or restrict competition through the reduction of horizontal competition, for example by foreclosing other downstream competitors, or facilitating collusion between market participants.

This chapter will explore vertical agreements in the context of fintech in three sections. The first section will focus on potential competition issues arising from vertical agreements in the context of fintech. The second section will address the question of whether the typical analysis of vertical agreements in the context of fintech means potential efficiency benefits are being missed, with specific reference to platform economics. Finally, the third section will consider the consequences of the previous analysis for the ongoing considerations of vertical agreements, paying particular attention to the European Commission's (the Commission) revised Vertical Agreements Block Exemption Regulation (VBER) and Guidance, which came into force on 1 June 2022, the United Kingdom (UK) Competition and Markets Authority (CMA) replacement for the VBER in the form of the UK Vertical Agreements Block Exemption Order (the UK Order), which also came into force on 1 June 2022 and is substantively similar to the revised VBER but with some notable differences, and the treatment of vertical agreements in the United States including the controversial 2020 Vertical Merger Guidelines.

Overall, it will be demonstrated that vertical agreements in the context of fintech can have both positive and negative consequences, depending on the fintech markets in question. In payment solutions technologies, vertical agreements can have positive consequences in promoting entry and solving free-riding concerns while also providing a solution which is more flexible than front-end and back-end integration. The approach to hardcore restrictions in the revised VBER does not impede these positive consequences from being realised. By contrast, however, vertical agreements can also create potentially novel issues including exclusion, bundling and entrenched market power when used in the context of blockchain. Given the novel nature of such technologies, the revised VBER (and the UK Order) does not address such issues specifically. However, the current competition law framework can presently address any such novel issues that may arise in the blockchain space. Nonetheless, there remain additional

[3] See, eg, P Ray, 'Vertical Restraints – An Economic Perspective' (2012) *Mimeo*, available at: www.fne.gob.cl/wp-content/uploads/2012/10/Vertical-restraints.pdf; Massimo Motta and Stephen Hansen, 'The Logic of Vertical Restraints, Revisited' (2012) Workshop ANR & DFG Market Power in Vertically Related Industry, available at: www.tse-fr.eu/conferences/2012-workshop-anr-dfg-market-power-vertically-related-industry; DP O'Brien, 'The Economics of Vertical Restraints in Digital Markets' (2020) *Global Antitrust Institute Report on the Digital Economy* 9.

steps that can be taken to ensure that vertical agreements do not prevent the necessary innovation and flexibility in fintech that is required in order to allow the digital economy to benefit from fintech to the fullest extent possible.

II. THE GATHERING CLOUDS: COMPETITION CONCERNS ARISING FROM VERTICAL AGREEMENTS IN FINTECH

Given the broad landscape that is fintech, including multiple types of users, operators and services, it is necessary to segregate the potential competition challenges into categories, based upon the market and the nature of the financial technology in question.

A. Vertical Agreements in the Retail Payment Market with Fintech Applications

The retail payment landscape is characterised by a diversity of payment instruments and activities at the various stages of the payment process.[4] A payment technology provider needs to compete at all stages of the payment process in order to provide a service to consumers. However, as the process is made up of multiple stages, the provider need not own all the necessary facilities to provide the service, assuming it can access the necessary facilities from other providers. Taking into account all the stages of the payment chain, providers of retail payment services are usually classified as (i) front-end providers; (ii) back-end providers; (iii) operators of retail payment infrastructure; and (iv) end-to-end providers.[5]

Front-end providers include technologies such as Apple Pay, and offer front-end services including pre-transaction and authorisation services. They usually rely on the back-end services and infrastructure provided by others, such as large financial institutions, and as a result can be seen as downstream firms. End-to-end providers, by contrast, can be seen as vertically integrated, and include banks, credit card companies and other fintech companies such as PayPal. These providers can afford both the front-end and back-end services and have their own infrastructure. Often, front-end providers are more innovative, smaller entrants into the market for retail payment services and hence fintechs play a particularly important role at the front end of the payment market.

[4] Typically seen as five stages: (i) pre-transaction; (ii) authorisation; (iii) clearing; (iv) settlement; and (v) post-transaction. See Committee on Payments and Market Infrastructures, 'Non-Banks in Retail Payments' (Bank for International Settlement) (2014) 5, available at: www.bis.org/cpmi/publ/d118.htm.

[5] ibid, 1.

For the purposes of vertical agreements, the relationship between end-to-end providers and front-end providers is most relevant. The recent approach taken by the Commission to vertical agreements in the context of minimum pricing and financial services[6] demonstrates that such vertical agreements, under the current (and revised) VBER rules, are likely to be interpreted as a back-end or end-to-end provider (such as an incumbent financial institution) leveraging its market power to the downstream front-end services, potentially implementing minimum pricing requirements, and therefore foreclosing potential competitors or softening competition from the front-end entrant.

The possibility of foreclosure of front-end fintech providers in the context of the payment market has been considered by several competition authorities, including the Netherlands Authority for Consumers and Markets (ACM) and the French Authorité de la Concurrence (Authorité), as well as the European Parliament.

In its 2017 report, the ACM outlined the foreclosure risk where a fintech firm is providing a front-end product (such as a payment app) which relies on certain (upstream) inputs from a back-end provider (such as a bank), for example customer account information.[7] There are certain 'essential conditions' for foreclosure of fintechs providing front-end services.[8] First, the bank (or upstream provider) has a dominant position in the upstream market with the crucial input that the front-end provider requires. Second, the fintech firm could compete with the bank (now or in the future). This could occur either through the fintech firm competing with the bank directly in the downstream market (eg, through payment initiation services or providing account information services or financial management software for bank customers), or through the fintech firm evolving into a competitor to the bank in the upstream market. The latter could occur as access to the upstream information (such as customer account information) could give downstream fintech firms an opportunity to offer payment accounts to the customers whose information it is using to provide downstream services. Third, there must be a genuine incentive for foreclosure, so the bank must consider that the potential competitive threat of the fintech provider is sufficiently important to foreclose market access.

Although the revised Directive on Payment Services[9] means that providers other than a customer's bank will have access to information about customer payment accounts if the customer authorises it, it is still conceivable that a dominant bank could deny or restrict access to the relevant information resulting in

[6] See above (n 1), contrasted with the (albeit controversial) US approach in *Ohio et al v American Express Co* (2018) 585 U.S. ___, 138 S Ct 2274 (Slip Opinion) 2, where the rule of reason approach was applied and issues in the two-sided market such as free-riding were taken into account.

[7] Autoriteit Consument & Markt, Report, 'Fintechs in the Payment System: The Risk of Foreclosure' (2017) 25–29, available at: www.acm.nl/sites/default/files/documents/2018-02/acm-study-fintechs-in-the-payment-market-the-risk-of-foreclosure.pdf.

[8] ibid, 29–31.

[9] Commission Directive (EU) 2015/2366 Payment Services (PSD 2) [2015] OJ L337/35.

foreclosure of fintech firms from access to the downstream market or higher barriers to entry if access is made more difficult.[10] It can be the case that such conditions arise particularly due to the increase in technologies for mobile banking and payments because mobile technologies create a direct method of access to banking customers and in turn such technologies create advantages to offer other services to the customers, thereby potentially incentivising switching. The creation of such barriers to accessing customer information occurred in Poland and the Netherlands, where lenders created barriers to fintech firms seeking access to customer account information even in circumstances when users had given their consent. This conduct resulted in Commission raids to investigate suspected potential anticompetitive practices.[11]

A similar issue was also raised by the European Parliament in its 2018 fintech report, which highlights interoperability between fintech providers and established finance providers as a challenge to competition, particularly where data is at issue.[12] Data can be a competitive advantage and, particularly in finance, it can be difficult to replicate or substitute because data typically contains individual customer information combined with specific analytics relating to the customer's use of the service.[13] Furthermore, including in the finance context, the self-reinforcing effects of data are particularly important – data becomes valuable due to the information that it provides which can be used to deliver products or services generating additional value.[14] The more data that can be collected, the greater the value that can be generated, thus creating competitive advantage and higher barriers to entry.

The potential risks around the collection and use of data, particularly relating to payments, is also recognised by the Authorité in its 2021 report on new technologies applied to payment activities.[15] However, interestingly, the

[10] This can occur, in particular, because of the 'economies of scope' across the digital economy which favour the development of digital ecosystems giving (dominant) incumbents a strong competitive advantage which makes it difficult for new entrants. See Y-A de Montjoye, H Schweitzer and Js Crémer, 'Competition Policy for the Digital Era' (Report for the European Commission) (2019) 3. In particular, obligations for data access and interoperability were flagged as important in the context of vertical integration and the rise of 'powerful ecosystems' (ibid, 9, 125), although imposing access to data to prevent foreclosure or other anti-competitive effects does need to be balanced against the need to ensure sufficient investment incentives to collect and process data (ibid, 76).

[11] Mehreen Khan and James Shotter, 'EU raids Polish and Dutch Banking Groups over Fintech Access' *Financial Times* (8 October 2017), available at: www.ft.com/content/a8a208e8-ac3d-11e7-aab9-abaa44b1e130. Although such conduct took place before PSD2, it is conceivable that such conduct could happen again given the prevalence of large banking groups in Europe and globally.

[12] A Fraile Carmona et al, 'Competition issues in the Area of Financial Technology (FinTech)' (European Parliament Report) (2018) 51 (hereafter European Parliament Report).

[13] I Vandenborre, S Levi and C Jessens, 'Banking and Big Data: Fintech and Access to Data' (2019) 4 *Concurrences* 22; A Hagiu and J Wright, 'When Data Creates Competitive Advantage' (2020) 98 *Harvard Business Review* 94.

[14] See the economic discussion of the self-reinforcing effects of data in P Belleflamme and M Peitz, *The Economics of Platforms: Concepts and Strategy* (Cambridge University Press, 2021) 70.

[15] Authorité de la Concurrence, 'Opinion 21-A-05 on the Sector of New Technologies Applied to Payment Activities' (April 2021) 115, available at: www.autoritedelaconcurrence.fr/sites/default/files/attachments/2021-06/21-a-05_en.pdf (hereafter Authorité Report).

Authorité also discussed the potential anticompetitive effects that could result from fintech firms having access to excessive customer and payment data, resulting in competitive advantages for the fintech firm, potential entrenchment of dominance (particularly where fintech services are being offered by BigTech firms), and higher barriers to entry for other fintech providers.[16] This illustrates the fact that data and access to it, including via vertical agreements, can cause competition issues cutting both ways – it can cause issues of both foreclosure (where there is upstream dominance and/or incentive to foreclose) and issues of entrenchment at the downstream level, particularly where the fintech provider is already a significant technology player (whether in fintech or elsewhere) and can leverage the data into other areas.

Anticompetitive conduct can also arise in the context of vertical agreements in the payment market where fintech firms are providing a platform between upstream retailers/sellers and downstream end-customers (rather than providing a substitute for a part of the downstream system, or adding a new technology at the downstream level, as is the case with payment applications). In particular, exclusivity arrangements between the platform provider and the upstream or downstream service provider are likely to be interpreted as leading to foreclosure concerns.[17] Such concerns were explored by the CMA in its Auction Services antitrust investigation, scrutinising providers of online platform technology to link downstream bidders with auction houses due to, among other issues, vertical restraints imposed on auction houses including exclusivity provisions.[18] The CMA's investigation and foreclosure allegations relating to, among other practices, ATG Media's practice of obtaining exclusive deals with auction houses so they did not use other providers of online bidding services, resulted in commitments being given by ATG Media.[19] As will be outlined below, fintech firms acting as platforms in this manner, in particular where the fintech provider is also providing an upstream or downstream service itself, are particularly affected by the provisions in the revised VBER.

B. Vertical Agreements in Blockchain Technology

Blockchain, a common iteration of distributed ledger technology, is a technology that facilitates transactions in a secure and decentralised manner, without

[16] ibid, 116.

[17] See, eg, Commission, 'Revised Guidelines on Vertical Restraints' (10 May 2022).

[18] CMA Auction Services: 'Anti-competitive Practices Investigation Final Decision' (29 June 2017), available at: assets.publishing.service.gov.uk/media/5954be5c40f0b60a44000092/auction-services-commitments-decision.pdf.

[19] CMA Auction Services, 'Anti-competitive Practices Investigation – Final Commitments' (29 June 2017), available at: assets.publishing.service.gov.uk/media/5954be6ee5274a0a69000085/statement-of-commitments.pdf.

the need for an intermediary.[20] Its main components are an open and distributed ledger recording all transactions or assets that are part of its domain, an encryption protecting this ledger from being altered and permanently storing the information once it is in the blockchain, and distributed storage of all data through the sharing of drive and network capacity on computers and in data centres.[21] Blockchain transactions can be seen by all users because of the distributed architecture of the system, and no single participant controls the information as no one ultimately is in charge of a public blockchain, and no one can unilaterally alter it. When using a blockchain, all the users agree to a set of procedures, known as a protocol, which governs the blockchain.

Blockchain has the potential to apply in multiple different areas of the digital economy, beyond things such as Bitcoin and other cryptocurrencies, and differs from 'traditional' platforms.[22] This means that it is important to consider the impact of blockchain when assessing competition policy in the digital age, and also when considering the impact of vertical agreements.[23]

Importantly for the analysis of vertical agreements, there are two different forms of blockchain: public and private.[24] A public blockchain is a blockchain that anyone can read, and on which anyone can propose a new transaction. On a public blockchain new transactions are secured by 'proof of work', or by solving the mathematical problem necessary to prove transactions are valid and create a new block on the chain.[25] By contrast, a private blockchain is a blockchain that restricts permissions to certain participants. For example, in a private blockchain the protocol can be established either by a single entity, or by a consortium of participants. Where a consortium of participants is involved, verifying a transaction usually requires the participation of more than a majority of participants. Other restrictions may also be imposed, for example, pre-selection of nodes which control the consensus.

Maintaining strategic advantage is vitally important in a fast-moving area of the digital economy, and blockchain is no exception, particularly private blockchains. This is where the importance of vertical agreements comes in. There are two principal uses of vertical agreements in the broader blockchain context, and

[20] See, eg, T Schrepel, *Blockchain + Antitrust: The Decentralization Formula* (Edward Elgar, 2020) 2.

[21] Commission Joint Research Centre Report, 'Blockchain Now and Tomorrow: Assessing Multi-dimensional Impacts of Distributed Ledger Technologies' (2019) 13 (hereafter JRC Report).

[22] 'Traditional' platforms in the sense of markets in which users enjoy benefits that depend on the decisions of other users but there is also a firm, operating the platform where interaction takes place, which takes decisions that determine (to a greater or lesser extent) the amount of those benefits and who will obtain the benefits. See Belleflamme and Peitz (n 14) 1.

[23] For a more complete discussion of the potential antitrust issues arising from blockchain, see further, T Schrepel, 'Is Blockchain the Death of Antitrust Law?' (2019) 3 *Georgetown Law Technology Review* 281; Schrepel, *Blockchain + Antitrust* (n 20).

[24] JRC Report (n 21) 14.

[25] For a full description, see A Narayanan et al, *Bitcoin and Cryptocurrency Technologies: A Comprehensive Introduction* (Princeton University Press, 2016).

further implications of the use of vertical agreements specifically in the context of cryptocurrency (a specific application for blockchain).

Considering blockchain generally: first, exclusive dealing agreements linking private blockchains with specific off-blockchain applications through agreements imposed at the point of entry to the blockchain could present significant vertical foreclosure concerns (both input and customer foreclosure).[26] Such an agreement would impose an obligation on the downstream application to only use the private blockchain, and no other applications or platforms, for its transactions. For example, a private blockchain is created and hosts a social network allowing job adverts to be posted; the private blockchain operator can impose an exclusive dealing condition in its blockchain protocol to ensure only certain users can read information on the blockchain, new transactions cannot be proposed on the blockchain, or competitors could be refused access altogether from the outset.[27] Therefore, where access to the blockchain is necessary to compete (ie, post job adverts, in the example) exclusive dealing can have significant impacts when used in the context of private blockchains: by imposing an exclusive dealing vertical restraint at the point of entry of the blockchain (eg, through the user agreement), other competitors in the same market can be excluded from the start. This goes further than traditional exclusive dealing either in relation to platforms or physical products as typically, in those instances, access is not necessary to compete.

Second, blockchain firms could seek to maintain a strategic competitive advantage, beyond the initial period of hype about the technology, through vertical agreements linking blockchain with complementary spheres or markets where the firm maintains strategic advantage, and thus leverage market power.[28] Such vertical agreements may have some positive economic benefits for the blockchain firms (and complementary service providers),[29] however they could also have a substantial anticompetitive impact, particularly in markets in the blockchain space as they exhibit significant network effects.[30] An example

[26] Obviously, the idea of being able to prevent access is at the core of a private blockchain, however this does not mean that foreclosure (or refusal to deal) is conduct that should be overlooked (Schrepel, *Blockchain + Antitrust* (n 20) 195).

[27] Schrepel, 'Is Blockchain the Death of Antitrust Law?' (n 23) 317.

[28] See I Lianos, 'Blockchain Competition – Gaining Competitive Advantage in the Digital Economy: Competition Law Implications' in P Hacker et al, *Regulating Blockchain: Political and Legal Challenges* (Oxford University Press, 2019).

[29] One of the basic economic trade-offs for parties is being between enabling transactions and controlling them. For the parties to a transaction, vertical agreements can be used to control transactions, which can be helpful to prevent commitment problems as between service providers in the blockchain market because the control rights for the transaction are kept as between the parties to the vertical agreement rather than permitting the residual control rights to go to the customers (Belleflamme and Peitz (n 14) 110). However, such control over transactions through vertical agreements can lead to the anticompetitive effects as outlined here even if there are benefits in solving commitment problems for the parties to the transactions. See further below in section III.

[30] There are also separate, but very important, questions whether the nature of blockchain markets will lead to collusive behaviour, particularly as a result of increasing network effects (European Parliament Report (n 12) 65–66; Schrepel, *Blockchain + Antitrust* (n 20) 145 et seq).

provided by the Organisation for Economic Co-operation and Development (OECD) is of 'firms that sell the specialized hardware that is required for mining tokens, which might find themselves with market power over inputs required by blockchain users which may seek to leverage their market power in (specialized) mining hardware into downstream markets'.[31] Indeed, such issues may arise as a result of private blockchains that are being created and operated by firms that have significant market power in other, related, markets. For example, Liquid is a blockchain-based[32] settlement network for traders and exchanges of cryptocurrencies such as Bitcoin (the largest public cryptocurrency). Liquid enables 'faster, more confidential Bitcoin transaction and the issuance of cryptoassets' such as securities.[33] Liquid, however, is operated by large financial services entities which benefit from its use.[34] Although within the Liquid ecosystem, consensus is needed between the entities that operate it, it is possible that the financial services entities could leverage their positions on Liquid to be the dominant exchange or financial institution providing innovative services involving Bitcoin.

Such potential anticompetitive conduct presents significant issues for the analysis of market power within vertical agreements, particularly as the traditional 'upstream' and 'downstream' analysis cannot always be applied for the reason that more frequently in the blockchain context the market power being leveraged is across complementary markets or is on the blockchain itself, from the initial network to the application running on the blockchain network itself.[35] Moreover, considerations of blockchain arrangements in general are likely to require a fundamental reconsideration of market power. There are multiple possible ways of analysing the leveraging of market power in the context of blockchain and how dominance can be analysed.[36] The most viable analysis for doing this is by analysing market power based on the types of applications running on the blockchain, which allows market power to be assessed in comparison to other digital and non-digital products and services.[37]

Cryptocurrency is a specific application of blockchain technology and similar issues with vertical agreements can arise in the specific context of cryptocurrency too. Before considering this, however, it is important to outline the nature of competition in the context of cryptocurrency. Competition in the context of cryptocurrency has been characterised previously as divided into competition

[31] Organisation for Economic Co-operation and Development (OECD), 'Blockchain Technology and Competition Policy' (Issues Paper by the Secretariat, 2018) (hereafter OECD Report).

[32] Technically, Liquid is a sidechain of Bitcoin, rather than a blockchain in itself. A sidechain is a mechanism that allows tokens from one blockchain to be used securely in an independent blockchain which runs in parallel and uses a different set of rules, performance requirements, and security mechanisms.

[33] Blockstream Liquid: blockstream.com/liquid/.

[34] Blockstream Technical Overview: docs.blockstream.com/liquid/technical_overview.html.

[35] Chambers (n 2).

[36] Schrepel, 'Is Blockchain the Death of Antitrust Law?' (n 23) 302.

[37] ibid, 304.

between different cryptocurrencies and competition between exchanges for currencies.[38] Taking into account the whole blockchain ecosystem, this can be widened and translated into two different markets: an inter-cryptocurrency market (where two different cryptocurrencies compete with one another); and an intra-cryptocurrency market (where different service providers (eg, miners, exchanges) compete).[39] Vertical agreements are relevant for both markets, and could have potentially anticompetitive effects in both.

In inter-cryptocurrency markets, several previous studies have highlighted that one of the significant aspects of the market is the presence of network effects due to cryptocurrencies resembling platforms (the more people and institutions using a particular cryptocurrency, the more users will want to use it).[40] Based on traditional analysis, network effects can create high barriers to entry and give incumbent cryptocurrencies significant market power.[41] However, there have been some recent studies suggesting that network effects in cryptocurrency markets specifically do not serve to concentrate the market and, indeed, there may be reverse network effects and a high degree of price sensitivity, both of which serve to diminish market power.[42] Nonetheless, as cryptocurrencies and the market mature it is possible that network effects will become more prevalent and it is important to bear in mind the consequences of network effects for vertical agreements. As a result of network effects, vertical agreements can have anticompetitive effects in this market because particular cryptocurrencies can use vertical agreements to exclude other currencies from the market, for example using vertical agreements to ensure that downstream retailers only use one particular cryptocurrency for its transactions.[43]

Intra-cryptocurrency markets are made up of multiple service providers including exchange providers, banks, miners and electronic wallet providers (which allow users to store the keys for their cryptocurrency transactions securely). When considering intra-cryptocurrency markets, vertical agreements may be used in at least two forms, leading to potentially anticompetitive effects in the market.[44]

First, as banks are now moving into the space of running exchanges and providing wallet services to customers, vertical agreements between banks and

[38] H Halaburda and N Gandal, 'Competition in the Cryptocurrency Market' (Bank of Canada Report, 2014) iii.

[39] European Parliament Report (n 12) 65–66.

[40] P Østbye, 'The Adequacy of Competition Policy for Cryptocurrency Markets' (2017) *SSRN Electronic Journal* 16, available at: doi.org/10.2139/ssrn.3025732.

[41] B Fung and H Halaburda, 'Central Bank Digital Currencies: A Framework for Assessing Why and How' (Bank of Canada Staff Discussion Paper, 2010) 6.

[42] K Stylianou et al, 'Cryptocurrency Competition and Market Concentration in the Presence of Network Effects' (2021) 6 *Ledger* 81.

[43] Here it can be seen that exclusivity has similar problems in the context of blockchain and cryptocurrency vertical agreements as it does in the context of the retail payments market (see also, Schrepel, *Blockchain + Antitrust* (n 20) 199).

[44] European Parliament Report (n 12) 66–67.

third-party cryptocurrency providers (in addition to other abuses of dominance, including tying and bundling) could be used in a similar way in the payment services markets by banks to foreclose access by cryptocurrencies not provided by the bank (typically those using the public blockchain) so that users are forced to use bank-owned cryptocurrencies (operating on the bank's private blockchain).[45] This occurred in a recent case in which a Brazilian National Association of Cryptocurrencies and Blockchain asked the national competition authority, in June 2018, to investigate Banco do Brasil's (along with several other banks including Santander and Inter) refusal to allow cryptocurrency and blockchain brokerage operators access to banking services.

Another practice in the context of the intra-cryptocurrency market could consist in a vertical agreement between a cryptocurrency and a provider of wallet or mining services, therefore tying or bundling the uses of a dominant cryptocurrency to the use of a specific digital exchange or wallet, or combining a wallet with an exchange.[46] This would not normally be an issue on a public blockchain as such practices would have to be implemented from the blockchain's creation. Such strategies could lead to a reduction in the number of users, as the value to users of joining the platform at the outset is very high given the incentive that the value of a token or currency on a particular blockchain could rise, meaning that the use of a vertical agreement in this way could be unprofitable. However, the use of vertical restraints in this way could present issues if private blockchains required an account on another platform (eg, a certain wallet provider) to connect to its blockchain or obtain cryptocurrency tokens. Indeed, a majority of wallets provide an integrated currency exchange feature currently.[47] Such strategies are unlikely to reduce the number of users on a private blockchain as the network effects do not manifest themselves in the same way as on a public blockchain, thus making tying practices through vertical agreements even more likely.[48]

[45] 'Brazil Antitrust Watchdog Probes Banks in Cryptocurrency Trade' *Reuters* (18 September 2018), available at: www.reuters.com/article/us-brazil-antitrust-cryptocurrency-idUSKCN1LY31G. Initially the investigation was closed by CADE in December 2018, but the tribunal asked for the investigation to be reopened in 2020. At the time of writing, the case is ongoing. For further analysis of the case, and its potential weaknesses given the nascent nature of the blockchain and cryptocurrency markets, see N de Lima Figueiredo, 'Banks v Cryptocurrency Exchanges: CADE's Investigation and the Search for a Villain' (2021) 9 *Journal of Antitrust Enforcement* 388.

[46] Østbye (n 40) 26; Lianos (n 28) 76; Schrepel, 'Is Blockchain the Death of Antitrust Law?' (n 23) 312.

[47] G Hileman and M Rauchs, 'Global Cryptocurrency Benchmarking Study' (Cambridge Centre for Alternative Finance, 2017) 47.

[48] European Parliament Report (n 12) 68 which outlines the negative effects of vertical integration in the intra-cryptocurrency market – a more extreme version of the anticompetitive effects as a result of vertical agreements – which can arise as a result of the same incentive to foreclose as with vertical agreements but the anticompetitive effects can be increased by the use of cross-subsidisation between activities (eg, between mining and exchange activities in vertically integrated players). See also Østbye (n 40) 26.

III. CLOUDS WITH SILVER LININGS? POTENTIAL EFFICIENCIES FROM THE PERSPECTIVE OF PLATFORM ECONOMICS

As a result of the retail payment services market being two-sided, and therefore benefiting from network effects and cross-platform externalities,[49] it is particularly important to ensure that new entrants that can provide potentially novel and innovative retail payment services have as few barriers to entry as possible. This is where vertical agreements can play an important role.

There are numerous examples of vertical agreements between banks and payment services providers and fintech companies which are welfare enhancing for all parties involved, including the ultimate consumer or business. This is particularly because banks can take advantage of the innovation that fintech can provide, and fintech firms, particularly new entrants, can benefit from the reputation and distribution channels, customer base and expertise of banks.[50] In its 2021 report the Authorité provides some important illustrations of this in the French market.[51] One of these examples concerns eZyness (a subsidiary of La Banque Postale) and the French company TagPay, an API developer, that have recently joined forces. The press release announcing the deal stated that 'the partnership with French FinTech TagPay coupled with La Banque Postale's expertise will enable eZyness to deploy a state of-the-art payment services offering with comprehensive APIs'.[52] Similarly, in its 2020 report, the OECD draws attention to how TransferWise, a retail foreign exchange platform offering an alternative to high bank transaction fees, has recently begun operating with banks such as N26 in Germany, Starling in the United Kingdom and LHV in Estonia in order to expand its customer base.[53] Such partnerships can be achieved through the use of agreements involving vertical restraints such as exclusivity, so that the fintech firm can benefit from exclusive access to the particular technology or customer base and thereby expand.

Usually, front-end providers face barriers to entry due to the requirement to have back-end services in order to provide a full service to consumers. It has been demonstrated that, where vertical agreements for the provision of back-end services on the basis of a vertical restraint such as exclusivity or minimum prices between (often incumbent) end-to-end providers and a new front-end provider

[49] Committee on Payments and Settlement Systems, 'Innovations in Retail Payments' (Bank for International Settlement, 2012) 17.

[50] OECD, 'Digital Disruption in Banking and Its Impact on Competition' (2020) 23.

[51] Authorité Report (n 15) 70–71. Further examples can be found in Table 6 of the same report (71).

[52] Press Release eZyness, 'L'établissement de paiement et de monnaie électronique de La Banque Postale, choisit TagPay pour moderniser son offre de services bancaires' (*La Banque Postale*, 17 January 2019), available at: www.labanquepostale.fr/content/dam/groupe/journalistes/communiques/2019/CP-eZyness-TagPay.pdf (author's translation).

[53] OECD Report (n 31) 23.

are possible, then overall market welfare is enhanced.[54] This is often because the end-to-end provider can collect fees for providing the back-end services from the front-end entrant, so competitive pressure is weakened. The end-to-end provider therefore is less pressured to lower the pre-transaction fee charged to merchants so more merchants will adopt the entrant's platform, thereby increasing overall welfare as a result of allowing new entry and additional options to be presented to merchants and consumers.[55] Furthermore, banks and other incumbents will permit such welfare-enhancing vertical agreements to be entered into and facilitate the entry of fintechs because any impact on revenues that may affect the banks will be compensated for by an increase in customers due to additional technologies being offered.[56] It may also promote increased innovation on the part of banks, which in turn fuels innovation in fintech firms, ultimately increasing overall welfare.[57]

The benefits of such vertical agreements, and how such benefits could serve as efficiency defences, can be demonstrated more clearly by considering the impact of vertical agreements from the perspective of platform economics. Although not directly applicable in the context of vertical agreements, there are useful analogies from the analysis employed in platform economics. One of the areas of scholarship in platform economics analyses why establishing a platform is a good idea or whether an alternative model of organisation would provide more economic benefits.[58] The opposition that is identified in economic terms is between *enabling* a transaction or *controlling* a transaction: ie, between allowing independent entities to provide goods or services to customers over a platform, or employing professionals to provide the services or produce the goods for customers in a vertically integrated model. There are, of course, options along this spectrum, but considering the opposite extremes enables the relevant economic trade-offs to be understood. Contemplating the choice between the platform model of organisation and the vertical integration model involves a fundamental trade-off between motivation and adaption on the one hand, and coordination on the other.[59] Motivation refers to the ability to induce

[54] J Jun and E Yeo, 'Entry of FinTech Firms and Competition in the Retail Payments Market' (2016) 45 *Asia-Pacific Journal of Financial Studies* 159.

[55] ibid, 162.

[56] OECD Report (n 31) 23.

[57] Authorité Report (n 15) 74–75 demonstrating that banking groups are investing in research and development to help integrate innovations into their service offering following fintech firms offering similar services, and outlining that certain fintechs believe that banking innovations have contributed to the emergence of further fintechs in the French market.

[58] Belleflamme and Petiz (n 14) 108.

[59] A Hagiu and J Wright, 'Marketplace or Reseller?' (2015) 16 *Management Science* 184, 188. See also A Hagiu and J Wright, 'Multi-sided Platforms' (2015) 43 *International Journal of Industrial Organisation* 162; A Hagiu and J Wright, 'Controlling vs Enabling' (2019) 65 *Management Science* 577.

effort that improves the customer experience; adaption concerns the capacity to adjust decisions to the private information that service providers or sellers may have; and coordination relates to the internalisation of potential spillovers or externalities. In general, the enabling model (a platform structure) fares better in terms of motivation and adaption, whereas the controlling model (a vertically integrated structure) fares better in terms of coordination.[60] In models which incorporate these elements, it is shown that the enabling mode (ie, the platform structure) is preferred in situations where the magnitude of the spillover parameter is sufficiently small relative to moral hazard and private information.[61] Furthermore, the two organisational models also differ in terms of costs, development and quality of services offered. The enabling model offers the ability to exploit network effects and frequently be more flexible than integrated firms in terms of adaption to the needs of consumers and the potential for expansion into adjacent markets.[62]

Applying the analysis in platform economics to fintech, there is a clear difference between end-to-end providers (which are akin to the vertically integrated model) and fintech providers operating through vertical agreements, such as in the payments space (which is akin to the platform model). Operating through vertical agreements enables the parties to the agreement, such as a bank and a front-end fintech provider, to take advantage of the economic benefits of the enabling model of facilitating transactions, allowing greater flexibility to adapt and inducing innovation and improvement to the service provided to the customer. It is therefore the case that fintech firms operating through the use of vertical agreements can experience significant efficiencies by using this model as compared with integrating vertically.

Consequently, such vertical agreements in the context of retail payment services may benefit from an efficiency analysis, particularly where subjected to a case-by-case analysis under Article 101(1) of the Treaty on the Functioning of the European Union (TFEU) if the vertical agreement does not fall within the terms of the VBER. It is possible that such arguments could be made under Article 101(3) TFEU on the basis of efficiency gains, promotion of entry and solving potential free-riding and commitment problems. In addition, preventing the use of vertical agreements in the fintech context could thwart the opportunity to realise such efficiencies. In the next section, it will be considered whether the revised VBER could move towards thwarting such efforts.

[60] Belleflamme and Petiz (n 14) 111. There are tools that can be used to alleviate the drawbacks from a particular model, eg, platforms can charge a positive use fee if spill-overs are negative so that harmful activities can be minimised.

[61] Such as the model employed in Hagiu and Wright, 'Multi-sided Platforms' (n 59).

[62] Belleflamme and Petiz (n 14) 112–13.

IV. OR GATHERING STORM CLOUDS? THE REVISED VBER AND UK ORDER ATTITUDE TO PLATFORMS AND VERTICAL AGREEMENT FORECLOSURE

The Commission's final revised VBER and Guidelines came into force on 1 June 2022.[63]

The Commission's re-evaluation of the VBER sought to ensure that the VBER was fit for purpose given the developments in technology and the digital economy. The Commission has specifically drawn attention to areas including e-commerce and the increasing importance of platforms. However, in light of the discussion in the foregoing sections it is unclear whether issues relating to the development of fintech are addressed adequately in the revised VBER. Indeed, the previous sections have highlighted where the use of vertical agreements in fintech and blockchain-related markets could pose novel issues; however, the revised VBER either does not adequately address these or the amendments to the VBER could actually prevent procompetitive benefits being realised. The new provisions in the revised VBER relating to 'online intermediation services' could prevent procompetitive benefits of vertical agreements in fintech, specifically in the retail payments context. In contrast, in the context of blockchain technologies, it has been demonstrated that vertical agreements could impose exclusivity and cause anticompetitive foreclosure, but it will be shown that it is not clear that this is adequately addressed in the revised VBER. This section will address each of these potential issues with the revised VBER.

A. The Revised VBER and the Potential for Procompetitive Benefits of Vertical Agreements in the Fintech Retail Payments Context

The VBER creates a presumption of legality for certain vertical agreements, depending on the market shares of the supplier and buyer and whether or not the vertical agreements contain restrictions of competition by object. This is known as the VBER 'safe harbour'. The revised VBER seeks to alter the scope of the VBER safe harbour and clarify the role of online platforms (or providers of online intermediation services) within the revised VBER. Specifically, the revised VBER clarifies that online platforms are suppliers for the purposes of the revised VBER.[64]

In addition to this, as specified in the revised VBER Guidelines,

> both the provision of online intermediation services and the goods or services subject to the transactions it facilitates are considered contract goods or services for the purpose of applying the VBER to the agreement on the basis of which online

[63] Commission Regulation (EU) 2022/720 on the application of Article 101(3) of the Treaty on the Functioning of the European Union to categories of vertical agreements and concerted practices [2022] OJ L134/4.

[64] ibid, Art 1(d).

intermediation services are provided and the agreement on the basis of which the intermediated goods or services are supplied.[65]

This suite of amendments is designed to ensure that any online platforms are not able to circumvent the application of the VBER by arguing that they are agents or solely intermediaries who only provide platform services (where no vertical agreements may apply) and are unrelated to the transactions they facilitate. The Commission cites strong network effects and related features of the online economy as being the reasons for extending the meaning of 'supplier' to providers of online intermediation services.[66]

This revised definition could apply in the context of fintech, particularly if fintech providers that operate as platforms are considered (eg, those facilitating forex transfers, retail payments platforms, or payment management services), as companies that allow other financial institutions to provide services to users with a view to facilitating transactions between those parties. As a result, fintech firms falling under the definition of 'online intermediation services' providers would then also be considered as 'suppliers' of the 'contract services' that they are facilitating upstream or downstream. This would mean that any vertical agreements between the fintech firm and the upstream or downstream players would be within scope of the VBER. Although this is helpful in ensuring that vertical agreements which could potentially cause anticompetitive effects of the type discussed in section II.A are adequately assessed, there is the potential that the classification of fintech firms involved in platform services as online intermediation services providers could undermine any efficiencies defence based on platform economics, as outlined in section III.

The efficiency analysis of vertical agreements in the context of fintech providers in payment services depends on an analysis of the economic model of the transactions involved. If, as is the case under the revised VBER definition, online intermediation services providers are considered to also provide the services at the upstream or downstream level for the purposes of analysing the vertical agreements involved, this changes the analysis of the economic incentives surrounding the transactions involved. When online intermediation services providers such as fintech firms are considered to also provide the contract goods at the upstream or downstream level, this is more akin to *controlling* the transactions rather than simply *enabling* them, as the analysis of the vertical agreements implies a greater degree of influence over the transactions and a greater ability to internalise the externalities that may be caused by such upstream or downstream supply.

Indeed, such analysis in the revised VBER may undermine more general considerations of platform efficiencies, which will particularly affect fintech providers. As discussed above, the revisions in the VBER are designed to target 'platforms', which avoid the application of the VBER in relation to up

[65] Commission, 'Revised Guidelines on Vertical Restraints' (n 17) para 58.
[66] ibid, para 44.

or downstream supply by arguing that they are agents or solely intermediaries who only provide platform services (where no vertical agreements may apply), and are unrelated to the transactions they facilitate. Such arguments are most typically seen in relation to e-commerce 'platforms' and big tech companies.[67] However, such arguments are not correctly levied at platforms, when properly defined.[68] The concerns that the revised VBER is seeking to address are more correctly raised in relation to aggregators (such as e-commerce marketplaces, or big tech companies such as Airbnb), which seek to offer only the most relevant downstream options (reducing choice through the information presented), rather than platforms, which are (largely) open from the upstream side, and on the downstream side offer a wide choice to meet the needs of users. In the case of aggregators, competition concerns arise if the practices (such as anticompetitive vertical agreements) result in a reduction in overall consumer choice (ie, compared with available alternatives).[69] Fintech providers, such as those examined in the context of retail payments, are 'platforms' in the correctly defined sense because they do not present a reduction in downstream choice through filtering of information.

Therefore, applying a broad definition of 'online intermediation services' (which encompasses both platforms and aggregators, and therefore captures certain fintech firms) to the concept of supplier fails to take account of the nuances and insights we gain from platform economics when analysing transactions. As a result, an important path for the analysis of vertical agreements in the context of fintech in the retail payments space may be diminished or removed entirely. Although it would be possible to make arguments relating to potential efficiencies in submissions around the effect of vertical agreements, or in defending potential foreclosure allegations under the existing law or the revised VBER, such a sweeping effect of the revised VBER should be considered carefully when analysing future vertical agreements in the fintech space and counter-arguments such as those from platform economics advanced in order to ensure that the economic and consumer benefits of procompetitive vertical agreements in the retail payments space are not lost.

B. The Revised VBER and the Potentially Anticompetitive Impact of Vertical Agreements in the Context of Blockchain Technologies

The potential use of blockchain technology in the fintech context has been an important part of the EU policy agenda in previous years and has been the

[67] Commission, 'Vertical Block Exemption Regulation Staff Working Document' (September 2020) 32.

[68] T Schrepel, 'Platforms or Aggregators: Implications for Digital Antitrust Law' (2021) 12 *Journal of European Competition Law & Practice* 1.

[69] ibid, 2.

subject of several cross-sectorial initiatives as a result of the Commission seeing blockchain as an important technology for the future.[70] Indeed, the Commission FinTech Action Plan, published in March 2018, highlighted blockchain as one of the new technologies that is changing the finance industry and how consumers access services.[71] The Action Plan, however, emphasises that blockchain is still a developing technology and therefore the emphasis should be on appropriate safeguards without stifling innovation.[72]

However, it does not appear that such appropriate safeguards have been taken into consideration in the revised VBER. As outlined in section II.B, vertical agreements have the potential to be used anticompetitively in the context of blockchain applications: exclusive dealing agreements linking private blockchains with specific off-blockchain applications through agreements imposed at the point of entry to the blockchain could present significant vertical foreclosure concerns, and blockchain firms could seek to maintain a strategic competitive advantage through vertical agreements linking blockchain with complementary spheres or markets where the firm maintains strategic advantage, and thus leverage market power. The revisions to the VBER do not go towards restricting vertical agreements which would otherwise fall within the VBER (eg, due to market share or duration of non-compete) but, due to the nature of the blockchain markets, could be anticompetitive and therefore should require an analysis under Article 101 TFEU. Furthermore, as outlined in section II.B, the operation of blockchain poses challenges for the analysis of market power. As a result, the possible leveraging of market power in a vertical agreement context may not be captured by the typical market share or upstream/downstream analysis in the revised VBER.

Nonetheless, given that blockchain technologies are continually developing, and the possibility of foreclosure effects is also likely to similarly develop as the market around blockchain increases, vertical agreements in the blockchain context can be subjected to analysis under the VBER (which already captures the impact of potential exclusivity arrangements and non-compete clauses) and Article 101 TFEU. Indeed, the concept of a dominant supplier leveraging its practices to downstream markets is not a novel issue and similar analysis can be applied in the context of blockchain until the market develops further and a further revision of VBER or related case law allows for a more nuanced application of existing law to the issues arising relating to foreclosure and market power in the context of blockchain.[73]

[70] JRC Report (n 21) 39–50.

[71] European Commission, 'FinTech Action Plan: For a More Competitive and Innovative European Financial Sector' (2018).

[72] ibid, 10.

[73] Similar analysis of exclusionary abuses under existing law has been proposed, with analogies made to ongoing cases concerning digital platforms whose business models rely heavily on user data (eg, Commission opening of proceedings of 4 June 2021 in Facebook leveraging (Case AT.40684)), see M Davilla, 'Unravelling the Complexity of Blockchain and EU Competition Law' (2022) 1 *Journal of European Competition Law & Practice* 1.

C. The Impact of the UK Order

In November 2021, the UK Competition and Markets Authority published its final recommendation for the UK Order, a UK Vertical Agreements Block Exemption Order setting out how UK competition law applies to vertical agreements from June 2022 when the VBER expires. The draft UK Order was published and put out for consultation in February 2022, with the UK's draft guidance on the UK Order being published in March 2022. Following the consultation, the Competition Act 1998 (Vertical Agreements Block Exemption) Order 2022 was made on 4 May 2022 and came into force on the expiry of the VBER on 1 June 2022. The final VABEO Guidelines were published on 12 July 2022.

Overall, the revised VBER and the UK Order (and their accompanying guidelines) are substantively the same. There are a small number of important differences between the UK Order and both the existing VBER and the revised VBER. Most notably the UK Order allows for a continued exemption for dual distribution, however it is tighter, as compared with the revised VBER, in its treatment of wide retail price parity provisions. However, importantly none of those amendments addresses the issues outlined above in relation to the treatment of vertical agreements in the retail payment fintech space – the UK Order takes the same approach as the retained VBER to the definition of online intermediation services and treats providers of those services as suppliers without consideration of the impact of such analysis on potential efficiencies relating to platforms that fintechs could benefit from.[74]

V. FORECAST: CONSEQUENCES FOR ONGOING CONSIDERATIONS OF VERTICAL AGREEMENTS

The previous sections have outlined the potential anticompetitive effects, but also the potential competitive benefits of vertical restraints in the form of vertical agreements in certain areas of fintech. However, it has also been outlined that the revised VBER and the UK Order may either undermine potential efficiencies or not adequately address potential issues in fintech relating to retail payment solutions and blockchain respectively. Although fintech is continually developing, and the existing law may be able to capture potential issues and submissions on efficiencies can be made, it should be considered whether there are lessons to be learned from other jurisdictions (namely the United States) and how the law could be revised going forward in order to ensure that procompetitive benefits of fintech are not lost and potential anticompetitive effects in blockchain do not slip through the net.

[74] The Competition Act 1998 (Vertical Agreements Block Exemption) Order 2022, s 2 and VABEO Guidelines para 6.32 et seq. See also, CMA 'Recommendation on Vertical Agreements Block Exemption Regulation' (October 2021) paras 7.9 and 7.10.

A. Revising the Definition of Online Intermediation Services

As outlined above in section IV.A, the broad definition of 'online intermediation services' as suppliers in both the revised VBER and the UK Order applies to both platforms and aggregators, when properly defined. As the definition captures certain fintechs, it fails to allow for the analysis and potential efficiencies in platform economics when analysing transactions.

In order to address this, the integration of 'online intermediation services' into the definition of supplier and the analysis of vertical agreements and vertical restraints more broadly needs to be amended in order to take into account the distinction between 'platforms' and 'aggregators'.[75] Fintechs, such as those examined in the context of retail payments, are 'platforms' in the correctly defined sense because they are not presenting a reduction in downstream choice through filtering of information. Therefore, there has to be more scope for such fintech applications to make arguments around efficiencies in vertical restraints without being stymied by the existing narrow definitions.

B. Considering Developments Across the Pond

Improving the analysis of the competitive benefits of vertical restraints in certain areas of fintech could also benefit from considering the recent treatment of efficiencies in vertical relationships in the United States.

Vertical agreements in the United States are analysed under three statutes: the Sherman Act 1890 (sections 1–3, covering restraints of trade and firms with market power engaging in conduct such as tying, bundling or exclusive dealing); the Clayton Act 1914 (also covering exclusive dealing and tying which may substantially lessen competition); and the Federal Trade Commission Act 1914 section 5(a)(1) covering unlawful unfair methods of competition. In general, an assessment of a vertical agreement under any statutes will apply a 'rule of reason' approach,[76] meaning that each case will be analysed on a case-by-case basis. This involves considering whether the anticompetitive effects of the agreement outweigh its procompetitive effects and business rationale with reference to a number of factors including the history, purpose and probable effects of the agreement.

Historically, the US approach to vertical agreements has focused on the procompetitive benefits and efficiencies of such agreements.[77] This approach has been extended into the recent and controversial 2020 Vertical Merger Guidelines. The Vertical Merger Guidelines specifically recognise that vertical mergers may

[75] Schrepel, 'Platforms or Aggregators' (n 68) 2.
[76] As outlined in *Chicago Board of Trade v United States*, 246 US 231 (1918).
[77] See, eg, *Continental Television v GTE Sylvania*, 433 US 36 (1977).

bring a range of benefits including the elimination of double marginalisation and efficiencies from streamlined production and distribution which may lead to the creation of 'innovative products in ways that would not likely be achieved through arm's length contracts'.[78]

The Vertical Merger Guidelines have now been withdrawn by the Federal Trade Commission on the basis that the guidelines take a flawed approach to procompetitive benefits in vertical mergers.[79] However, the analysis in the Vertical Merger Guidelines is helpful in drawing attention to the potential competitive benefits of vertical relationships which can be extended into the consideration of vertical restraints in the form of vertical agreements in certain areas of fintech.

C. Addressing Potential Anticompetitive Effects of Vertical Restraints in Blockchain Through the Application of a FRAND Concept

In relation to blockchain technologies, it has been outlined in section II.B and section IV.B that anticompetitive foreclosure effects could result from vertical restraints, and in particular vertical agreements between blockchain and complementary spheres or markets or linking private blockchains with specific off-blockchain applications. Although the current legal framework can capture aspects of such an analysis and amendments could be made to the revised VBER or UK Order at a later date once blockchain technology has further developed and the markets have become more established, there could be a potential solution for such potential anticompetitive effects of vertical restraints through developing case law.

Any potential foreclosure and exclusionary effects relating to blockchain technology are similar to the anticompetitive effects as a result of narrowing or refusal to access standard-essential patents (SEPs). As a licence to use SEPs is frequently essential for competing on particular markets, the holders of SEPs are often encouraged to license SEPs on fair, reasonable and non-discriminatory (FRAND) terms to avoid breaches of competition law. It is possible that the concept of FRAND licensing could be extended to blockchain technologies where access to the particular blockchain technology was considered necessary or essential.[80] This could be particularly applicable where access to private blockchains by multiple off-blockchain applications was required in order to avoid exclusionary effects – private blockchain 'gatekeepers' could be encouraged to allow access to their blockchains for SEPs on terms similar for FRAND.

[78] US Department of Justice and Federal Trade Commission, 'Vertical Merger Guidelines' (2020) 11.

[79] Federal Trade Commission statement, 'Federal Trade Commission Withdraws Vertical Merger Guidelines and Commentary' (15 September 2021).

[80] Schrepel, *Blockchain + Antitrust* (n 20) 196.

Of course, such access conditions do not eliminate the risk of foreclosure or disputes arising, and such conditions will not be necessary in all circumstances as the analogy only holds where access to a particular blockchain technology is a necessity. In other circumstances, applying the refusal to supply doctrine may be sufficient. However, considering access conditions could be a more effective step to ensuring that access to blockchains or related technologies are not restricted through the use of vertical restraints (or, indeed, other mechanisms).[81] Access conditions on FRAND terms also avoid the potential pitfalls of general, enforced standardisation in the blockchain context which could stifle innovation.[82] It should therefore be considered whether the potential foreclosure issues in blockchain relating to vertical restraints for SEPs, particularly in the form of vertical agreements, could be ameliorated by the use of access conditions similar to FRAND terms.

VI. CONCLUSION

This chapter has outlined the areas of fintech where vertical restraints, particularly in the form of vertical agreements, become relevant. The analysis has concentrated on fintech relating to retail payment solutions and blockchain.

In particular, it has been demonstrated that there are potential competition issues created by vertical agreements in the context of fintech, including potential novel issues around exclusion, bundling and market power when used in the context of blockchain technologies, many of which have not yet been fully considered in the context of vertical restraints, including in the revised VBER.

Importantly, however, this chapter has sought to draw attention to the potentially beneficial and efficiency-enhancing solutions that vertical agreements can bring in certain fintech markets, in particular by analogy to platform economics and the use of vertical agreements as transaction-enabling. It has been queried whether the revised VBER and the new UK Order might prevent such efficiencies being realised through its treatment of platforms (and therefore potentially certain fintech providers, depending on interpretation) as 'suppliers' both of online intermediation services and the contract services the platform is facilitating. This chapter has also sought to outline how such issues could be ameliorated, including by the use of regulations analogous to those we have seen in the context of intellectual property.

Overall, it is clear that vertical restraints and vertical agreements are important in the fintech space, and will likely have positive consequences for our future use of fintech (particularly in the payments sector and building on the learnings from this space), but could have negative implications if regulators do not take into account the novel issues that vertical agreements could pose particularly in the context of blockchain technologies.

[81] Davilla (n 73) 12.
[82] ibid, 11.

8

Data Sharing and Interoperability: From Open Banking to the Internet of Things (IoT)

OSCAR BORGOGNO* AND GIUSEPPE COLANGELO

I. INTRODUCTION

OVER THE LAST decade, the international landscape has witnessed the emergence of a wide array of different and heterogeneous legislative initiatives aimed at fostering competition by means of data sharing. In the span of a few years, policymakers have attempted to enhance competition and consumer engagement by means of data portability, in situ data access, free flow of data and re-use of data. At the same time, interoperability has been targeted as the key enabler for implementing such measures in an effective way. This chapter delves into the implementation experience of consumer financial data-sharing regulatory frameworks to assess how interoperability obligations can prove effective in fostering competition and innovation across the digital economy.

When it comes to policy initiatives dealing with data sharing, the European Union (EU) is unanimously recognised a front-runner in the field and it is often praised as a brilliant example of the Brussels effect (ie, the EU's unilateral power to shape global regulation).[1] However, such efforts consistently struggled to deliver on their procompetitive promises.[2]

European policymakers initially centred on enabling inter-platform competition by ensuring free flows of data through a broad array of different and heterogeneous initiatives. At first, the regulatory efforts dealing with the issue

* Any opinions expressed in this paper are personal and are not to be attributed to the Bank of Italy.

[1] A Bradford, *The Brussels Effect: How the European Union Rules the World* (Oxford University Press, 2020).

[2] O Borgogno and G Colangelo, 'Data Sharing and Interoperability: Fostering Innovation and Competition through APIs' (2019) 35 *Computer Law & Security Review* 105314.

were aimed at ensuring competition between platforms by means of data portability mechanisms. It was believed that allowing consumers to freely move their personal data from one holder to another would facilitate multi-homing and reduce data-induced lock-in problems in the digital economy.[3] While the General Data Protection Regulation (GDPR) introduced a data portability right for individuals,[4] the Regulation on the free flow of non-personal data has eased data-sharing practices for business-to-business relationships.[5] Along the same lines, the European Commission (Commission) put forward the Open Data Directive with the final aim of putting government data to good use for private players.[6] In addition, the Data Governance Act promotes the voluntary sharing of data by individuals and businesses and harmonises conditions for the use of certain public sector data.[7] Interestingly, all these measures share a strong reliance on application programming interfaces (APIs) as a key enabler of smooth data sharing. On the other hand, they are inherently different in terms of their implementation, functioning and ultimate scope.[8]

Nevertheless, the common underlying rationale of such measures proved to be misaligned with real-world market dynamics. The rapid growth of mobile ecosystems and large technology platforms within large networks of interconnected devices (Internet of Things – IoT) has demonstrated that the competitive landscape took on a different shape than that envisaged by European policymakers.[9] Digital ecosystems, grounded on widely adopted mobile operating systems, have emerged as digital infrastructures within which a huge number of consumer and business interactions take place every day. As it happens, the digital economy increasingly departed from a market for information where individuals actively transfer their digital footprint from one provider to another. Indeed, the issue of consumer data lock-in remains the main target of recent European data strategy initiatives.[10]

[3] O Lynskey, 'Aligning Data Protection Rights with Competition Law Remedies? The GDPR Right to Data Portability' (2017) 42 *European Law Review* 793.

[4] Regulation (EU) 2016/679 of the European Parliament and of the Council of 27 April 2016 on the protection of natural persons with regard to the processing of personal data and on the free movement of such data, and repealing Directive 95/46/EC [2016] OJ L119/1, Art 20.

[5] Regulation (EU) 2018/1807 of the European Parliament and of the Council of 14 November 2018 on a framework for the free flow of non-personal data in the European Union [2018] OJ L303/59.

[6] Directive (EU) 2019/1024 of the European Parliament and of the Council of 20 June 2019 on open data and the re-use of public sector information [2019] OJ L172/56.

[7] Regulation (EU) 2022/868 of the European Parliament and of the Council of 30 May 2022 on European data governance and amending Regulation (EU) 2018/1724 (Data Governance Act) [2022] OJ L152/1.

[8] Borgogno and Colangelo, 'Data Sharing and Interoperability' (n 2).

[9] European Commission, Commission Staff Working Document accompanying the 'Final Report – Sector inquiry into consumer Internet of Things' COM(2022) 10 final, 41 (recognising that Amazon, Google and Apple hold a key and well-entrenched position within and beyond the consumer IoT sector).

[10] See European Commission, 'A European strategy for data' COM(2020) 66 final, 10; and European Commission, 'Towards a common European data space' COM(2018) 232 final, 10.

As a result, new policy campaigns have gradually embraced a different approach aimed at fostering competitive dynamics eminently within and between the perimeter of platform-based ecosystems. To this aim, interoperability is shining out as the new mantra of competition policy in the digital space.[11] Indeed, a lack of interoperability among platform-providers may constitute a technical hurdle for consumer switching and multi-homing. More broadly, the current focus on interoperability reveals the commitment of policymakers to turn large digital platforms into common infrastructure, ultimately allowing third-party businesses to enjoy network effects and economies of scale, while capping monopolist rents. Interoperability requirements are also meant to avoid redundant investments for the development of rival ecosystems, thus lowering the barriers to entry and promoting greater contestability within platform-based business environments.

The concepts of interoperability and data portability have been widely used in different contexts and with heterogeneous purposes over the years. Thus, before we engage in our analysis, we consider it worthwhile to clarify the two concepts and offer different definitions.[12] First, vertical or protocol interoperability refers to the ability of different products and services to work together in a complementary fashion. When vertical interoperability (protocol interoperability) is in place in a platform-based scenario, third-party providers can offer different services capable of seamless connection with the underpinning infrastructure. A second sub-category is represented by horizontal or full protocol interoperability, which ensures that substitute services can interoperate. While protocol interoperability is limited to information disclosure and design amendments, full protocol interoperability comes with deeper levels of integration and standardisation as a broad range of services need to abide by a common overall architecture. The concept of data interoperability refers, instead, to the ability of sharing data and accessing datasets on a continuous or even real-time basis. Such form of interoperability relies usually on APIs, which are sets of protocols defining how software components communicate with one another. Finally, data portability is usually meant as the ability of having data transmitted directly from one service provider to another.

Interoperability is now emerging throughout the whole spectrum of European legislative initiatives dealing with technological innovation, promising to put an end to network effects which work only in favour of the most prominent digital ecosystem owners.[13] Notably, in its data strategy, the Commission launched the

[11] See European Commission, Commission Staff Working Document accompanying the Communication on the 'Digitising European Industry Reaping the full benefits of a Digital Single Market' SWD(2016) 110 final, 9 (targeting the lack of common standards and interoperable solutions throughout the products and services life cycles as one of the main hurdles to IoT innovation).

[12] See J Crémer, YA de Montjoye and H Schweitzer, 'Competition Policy for the Digital Era' (European Commission 2019) 58–59, available at: www.ec.europa.eu/competition/publications/reports/kd0419345enn.pdf.

[13] W Kerber and H Schweitzer, 'Interoperability in the Digital Economy' (2017) 8 *Journal of Intellectual Property, Information Technology and E-Commerce Law* 39, 52.

establishment of EU-wide common, interoperable data spaces in strategic sectors to overcome legal and technical barriers to data sharing.[14] In this context, the European Data Innovation Board, proposed by the Data Governance Act, will support the Commission in identifying the relevant standards and interoperability requirements for cross-sector data-sharing. Furthermore, as of November 2022 the Digital Markets Act (DMA) has entered into force, introducing, among its other provisions, interoperability obligations for online platforms having a gatekeeping position.[15] Further, in the proposal for an Artificial Intelligence Act, the Commission referred to the possibility of developing further measures aimed at 'lowering technical barriers hindering cross-border exchange of data for AI development, including on data access infrastructure, semantic and technical interoperability of different types of data'.[16]

By the same token, although adopting a different model, the regulatory initiative undertaken in the United Kingdom (UK) considered interoperability as a key tool for promoting competition and innovation in the digital arena.[17] Meanwhile, on the other side of the Atlantic, some bills unveiled by the House of Representatives have embarked on a similar path.[18]

With specific regard to IoT environments, the role of platform ecosystems and the significance of interoperability were underlined by the Commission in a recent sector inquiry[19] and are explicitly addressed in the proposal for a Data Act.[20] With a view to facilitating access to and use of data by consumers and businesses, the latter lays down rules to allow users of connected devices to gain access to data generated by them and to share such data with third business parties. Furthermore, the proposal acknowledges that data sharing within and between sectors requires an interoperability framework.[21] Accordingly, it supports the adoption of open interoperability specifications and standards to facilitate switching between data processing services[22] and envisages the

[14] European Commission, 'A European strategy for data'; 'Towards a common European data space' (n 10).

[15] Regulation (EU) 2022/1925 on contestable and fair markets in the digital sector and amending Directives (EU) 2019/1937 and (EU) 2020/1828 (Digital Markets Act) [2022] OJ L265/1.

[16] European Commission, 'Proposal for a Regulation laying down harmonised rules on artificial intelligence (Artificial Intelligence Act)' COM(2021) 206 final, recital 81.

[17] UK Competition and Markets Authority (CMA), 'A New Pro-competition Regime for Digital Markets. Advice of the Digital Markets Taskforce' (2020), available at: www.gov.uk/cma-cases/digital-markets-taskforce.

[18] See HR 3849, 'Augmenting Compatibility and Competition by Enabling Service Switching Act' (ACCESS Act); and S 2992, 'American Innovation and Choice Online Act' (AICOA).

[19] European Commission, 'Final Report – Sector inquiry into consumer Internet of Things' COM(2022) 19 final.

[20] European Commission, 'Proposal for a Regulation on harmonised rules on fair access to and use of data (Data Act)' COM (2022) 68 final. See also G Colangelo, 'European Proposal for a Data Act – A First Assessment' (2022) CERRE Assessment Paper.

[21] European Commission, 'Proposal for a Regulation on harmonised rules on fair access to and use of data' (n 20) 2.

[22] ibid, Art 26(2) and (3).

possibility of mandating the development of formal interoperability European standards for data re-use between sectors.[23]

With the DMA and the Data Act proposal, the Commission is implicitly extending to the broader digital economy the same paradigm already deployed for the retail payment sector with the access-to-account rule enshrined in the Second Payment Service Directive (PSD2), which can be considered an early case of an in situ data right.[24] The concept implies that users are not expected to move their data from one platform to another, but can freely determine when and under what conditions third parties can access such in situ data held by the original collector.

PSD2 forced banks to share real-time data on customers' accounts if the user has provided explicit consent and the account is accessible online. Perhaps more importantly, the PSD2 laid the ground for the Retail Banking Market Investigation Order issued in 2017 by the UK Competition and Markets Authority (CMA).[25] Interestingly, this remedy mandated incumbents to develop open standards for APIs with the final goal of ensuring interoperability between different service providers and smooth data sharing. By so doing, these measures provided the building blocks of Open Banking, meant as a secure environment that allows consumers and small businesses to share their transaction data with trusted third parties who can analyse such information to offer them new services or make payments on their behalf. In the span of a few years, Australia and other countries mirrored this initiative in order to spur competition beyond the retail financial industry.

Also the United States seems now finally ready to join the club. Indeed, President Biden recently stressed the urgency to complete the process initiated by the Department of the Treasury, which in 2018 required the Consumer Financial Protection Bureau to provide for data portability rights in financial services under section 1033 of the Dodd–Frank Act, thereby promoting the adoption of standardised formats for consumer data interoperability and re-use between different providers.[26] In a similar vein, the Canadian Minister of Finance appointed an

[23] ibid, Art 29(5) and recital 79.

[24] Directive (EU) 2015/2366 of the European Parliament and of the Council of 25 November 2015 on payment services in the internal market, amending Directives 2002/65/EC, 2009/110/EC and 2013/36/EU and Regulation (EU) No 1093/2010, and repealing Directive 2007/64/EC, [2015] OJ L337/35, Art 67. See B Martens, G Parker, G Petropoulos and M van Alstyne, 'Towards Efficient Information Sharing in Network Markets' (2021) Bruegel Working Paper No 12.

[25] CMA, 'The Retail Banking Market Investigation Order 2017' (2017), available at: www.gov.uk/government/publications/retail-banking-market-investigation-order-2017.

[26] US White House, 'Executive Order on Promoting Competition in the American Economy' (2021), available at: www.whitehouse.gov/briefing-room/presidential-actions/2021/07/09/executive-order-on-promoting-competition-in-the-american-economy/. See also US Department of the Treasury, 'A Financial System that Creates Economic Opportunities Nonbank Financials, Fintech, and Innovation' (2018) 29, 31–32, available at: www.home.treasury.gov/sites/default/files/2018-08/A-Financial-System-that-Creates-Economic-Opportunities---Nonbank-Financials-Fintech-and-Innovation.pdf.

Advisory Committee to guide the government's review into the merits of Open Banking[27] and the Canadian Competition Bureau proposed to support a flexible use of open standards for API interoperability with the ultimate goal of enabling new and innovative use cases.[28]

The global excitement generated by the Open Banking experience convinced many jurisdictions to expand data sharing to a broader range of financial services and products, thereby bringing Open Finance and Open Insurance into discussion.[29] These initiatives are part of a broader data governance strategy under which policymakers are looking to expand data access tools in all regulated markets (such as the energy and pensions markets) to help consumers benefit from their own digital footprint.[30]

Against this background, the standardisation experiences underpinning Open Banking projects provide useful lessons as to the potential and limits of extending data sharing and interoperability remedies throughout the rest of the financial sector and the digital economy. The chapter is structured as follows. Section II offers an up-to-date comparative overview of the development of Open Banking by focusing on the different approaches taken towards API standardisation in the United Kingdom, Australia and the European Union. Section III illustrates how interoperability got centre stage within the European digital strategy. Section IV explores how the Open Banking experience could serve as a blueprint for promoting interoperability in the IoT sector. Section V concludes.

II. THE CHALLENGES OF OPEN BANKING: DIVERGENT APPROACHES TO STANDARDISATION

Open Banking legislative projects deserve close attention as they constitute the most advanced testing ground for data sharing and interoperability remedies in the digital economy. In particular, such experiences demonstrate how impactful the approach taken towards standardisation could be for the proper functioning of interoperability requirements.

[27] Government of Canada, 'Consumer-Directed Finance: The Future of Financial Services' (2019), available at: www.canada.ca/en/department-finance/programs/consultations/2019/open-banking/report.html.

[28] Canadian Competition Bureau, 'Supporting a Competitive and Innovative Open Banking System in Canada' (2021) para 19, available at: www.competitionbureau.gc.ca/eic/site/cb-bc.nsf/eng/04571.html.

[29] Financial Conduct Authority, 'Open Finance – Feedback Statement' (2021), available at: www.fca.org.uk/publication/feedback/fs21-7.pdf.

[30] Department for Business, Energy and Industrial Strategy, 'Smart Data Working Group' (2021), available at: www.gov.uk/government/publications/smart-data-working-group-spring-2021-report. See also D Awrey and J Macey, 'The Promise and Perils of Open Finance' (2023) 40 *Yale Journal on Regulation* 1 arguing that the existence of more and more specialised data-enabled financial service providers would then reduce the structural reliance on a small number of large incumbents, thereby ameliorating the too-big-to-fail problem.

Standards can facilitate the creation and integration of markets, trigger positive feedback loops, and lower development costs for downstream services and products. As long as interoperability is concerned, they play a key function in enabling wide complementarities between products and services. Further, standards can also facilitate competition on the merits and market contestability. However, they might pose competitive risks if developed and harnessed with collusive or exclusionary goals in mind.

On a general note, it is important to devote proper consideration on how standards are designed and implemented. The first distinction we can draw is between formal and industry-led standardisation initiatives.[31] The former are developed by standard development organisations (SDOs) officially appointed by policymakers following a top-down paradigm.[32] They comply with procedures that are transparent and open to broad participation by market participants and stakeholder.[33] The latter are instead developed by firms which voluntarily agree to market products and services complying with specific common characteristics and procedures. Their success depends eminently on widespread market adoption by business players and consumer reaction. Once manufacturers need to implement privately led solutions which became so successful to be the only way for accessing a relevant market, such rules rise into de facto standards. While formal standardisation is driven by consensus building and social welfare concerns, industry-led standards prioritise speed, market readiness and the need for widespread adoption by the market players in order to succeed.

The second distinction involves the degree of control retained by the developer over who can make use of the standard.[34] To implement proprietary standards, which are covered by contractual or intellectual property restrictions, manufacturers need to obtain and pay for a licence. Developers may also set forth proprietary enhancements for administering access to the standard with reference to specific market niches. Conversely, open standards are freely available to any services providers and manufacturers seeking to enter the market with interoperable services and make use of data sharing.[35]

[31] Organisation for Economic Co-operation and Development (OECD), 'Data Portability, Interoperability and Digital Platform Competition' (OECD Competition Committee Discussion Paper 2021) 21–22, available at: www.oecd.org/daf/competition/data-portability-interoperability-and-digital-platform-competition-2021.pdf; OECD, 'Standard Setting: Background Note by the Secretariat' (2010), available at: www.oecd.org/daf/competition/47381304.pdf.

[32] Under EU law, formal SDOs are those recognised by Regulation (EU) No 1025/2012 on European standardisation [2012] OJ L316/12.

[33] See M Singh, 'Tracing the Evolution of Standards and Standard-Setting Organizations in the ICT Era' (2020) 24 *Marquette Intellectual Property Law Review* 217, pointing out that while SSOs have been operating in the standard-setting sector for several decades, it was not until the late 1980s that de jure standard-setting consortia emerged in the United States to expand across the world at a later stage.

[34] European Commission, Commission Staff Working Document accompanying the 'Final Report – Sector inquiry into consumer Internet of Things' (n 9) 117–18.

[35] Kerber and Schweitzer (n 13).

Against this background, the European Union, the United Kingdom and Australia opted for different approaches in promoting Open Banking.

The United Kingdom and Australia adopted forms of mandated open standardisation to accelerate the implementation of Open Banking. Based on a review into the retail banking market, the CMA acknowledged that incumbents were benefiting from excessive oligopolistic rents because of consumer stickiness and high barriers to entry.[36] Thus, it relied on its market investigation powers to tackle such structural competitive deficiencies by significantly smoothing the functioning of the access-to-account rule enshrined in the PSD2.

EU law imposed on banks and any other payment account providers a duty to share customers' transaction data with authorised third parties, but it did not go as far as imposing a common methodology for complying with obligation.[37] Given the lack of a legal framework imposing common implementation procedures, third-party providers were likely to sustain significant economic frictions to adapt to each incumbent bank data-sharing interface. In order to interoperate with different banks' infrastructures, they had no other choice than to develop software applications working with diverse providers or return to technical service providers.[38] In addition, the incumbents' incentive frameworks were clearly not aligned with the procompetitive goal of Open Banking. In fact, incumbents were reasonably driven by the objective to keep their own infrastructure as closed as possible to new disrupting rivals.[39]

To address these issues and help new entrants to calibrate their applications according to a single set of specifications, the CMA ordered the nine largest banks in Britain and Northern Ireland to develop common and open API standards, security protocols and data formats.[40] Further, it established the Open Banking Implementation Entity as a special purpose body with the goal of facilitating the negotiations between fintech third-party providers, consumer representatives and incumbent banks involving the design of common standards for financial data sharing. Moreover, it entrusted an Implementation Trustee with the task of imposing binding decisions on all nine major banks subject

[36] CMA, 'Retail Banking Market Investigation: Final Report' (2016) www.gov.uk/cma-cases/review-of-banking-for-small-and-medium-sized-businesses-smes-in-the-uk.

[37] O Borgogno and G Colangelo, 'Data, Innovation and Transatlantic Competition in Finance: The Case of the Access to Account Rule' (2020) 31 *European Business Law Review* 4.

[38] Recent competition inquiries outlined the risk that API standard fragmentation could translate into higher barriers to entry for new entrants: see Autorité de la Concurrence, 'Opinion on the Sector of New Technologies Applied to Payment Activities' (2021) para 384, available at: www.autoritedelaconcurrence.fr/en/opinion/sector-new-technologies-applied-payment-activities; Hellenic Competition Commission, 'Interim Report on the Sector Inquiry into Financial Technologies' (2021) para 49, available at: www.epant.gr/en/enimerosi/sector-inquiry-into-fintech.html.

[39] Portuguese Competition Authority, 'Sector Inquiry on FinTech' (2021), available at: www.concorrencia.pt/en/articles/adcs-sector-inquiry-fintech-74-companies-operating-portugal-consider-there-are-barriers#:~:text=The%20findings%20of%20the%20sector,a%20closed%20ecosystem%20as%20barriers.

[40] CMA, 'The Retail Banking Market Investigation Order 2017' (n 25).

to the order in case negotiations failed.[41] As a result, the CMA made full use of mandated standardisation to deliver vertical interoperability between data-enabled providers and the digital infrastructure of incumbent banks.

The increasing pace of financial technology innovation raised worldwide attention among policymakers to the Open Banking project enacted by the United Kingdom[42] and convinced British authorities to promote its model well beyond the banking industry. As early as 2019, the Financial Conduct Authority and the government declared their intention to take stock of Open Banking extending consumer financial data access to the whole spectrum of financial services (so-called Open Finance business environments).[43] The project fits into the broader Smart Data strategy enacted by the UK government to extend consumer data sharing across several regulated markets in order to foster consumers' bargaining power vis-a-vis service providers through data-enabled innovation.[44]

Along the same lines, the Australian government envisaged an economy-wide consumer data-sharing framework (the Consumer Data Right), which allows individuals to share their data between any kinds of service providers within each industry.[45] The banking sector was targeted as the first sector for its implementation. Accordingly, the Australian Competition and Consumer Commission mandated the four major banks to develop a single set of API standards for data sharing and sharing product reference information with accredited data recipients.[46]

The common standard approach allowed the United Kingdom and Australia to gain a leading position in the global race towards the implementation of financial data sharing. Mandated standardisation plays a crucial role in fastening the systemic adoption of Open Banking as it prevents incumbent players from hijacking the pro-competition impact of the of the access-to-account regime. As demonstrated by the UK experience, publicly driven standardisation

[41] CMA, 'Agreed Timetable and Project Plan' (2022), available at: www.gov.uk/cma-cases/review-of-banking-for-small-and-medium-sized-businesses-smes-in-the-uk.

[42] See A Land and B Roberts, 'Open Banking, the UK Experience' (2021) 1 *CPI Antitrust Chronicle* 8, listing the following states: Australia, New Zealand, Hong Kong, Singapore, Malaysia, Vietnam, the Philippines, Indonesia, Japan, Korea, Taiwan, China, India, Pakistan, the Gulf States (Bahrain, Kuwait, the United Arab Emirates, Saudi Arabia, Qatar, Oman), Egypt, Israel, Nigeria, Rwanda, Kenya, South Africa, Brazil, Colombia, Chile, Mexico, Dominican Republic, United States and Canada.

[43] Financial Conduct Authority (n 29).

[44] UK Department for Business, Energy and Industrial Strategy, 'Smart Data Working Group' (2021), available at: www.assets.publishing.service.gov.uk/government/uploads/system/uploads/attachment_data/file/993365/smart-data-working-group-report-2021.pdf.

[45] Treasury Laws Amendment (Consumer Data Right) Act 2019 (Cth) (CDR Act). See RP Buckley, N Jevglevskaja and S Farrell, 'Australia's Data-Sharing Regime: Six Lessons for Europe' (2022) 33 *King's Law Journal* 61.

[46] Australian Competition and Consumer Commission, 'Competition and Consumer (Consumer Data Right) Rules 2020' (2020), available at: www.accc.gov.au/media-release/consumer-data-right-rules-made-by-accc.

is also likely to be followed by service providers which are under no obligation to comply with data-sharing rights. Rather than developing their own interfaces, market players prefer to adopt the (free) API standards designed under the Open Banking framework. As of August 2021, there were 119 firms with live-to-market Open Banking-enabled products and services while Open Banking ecosystems gathered around three million users in Great Britain and Northern Ireland.[47]

On the flipside, the data-sharing project envisaged by British and Australian policymakers comes with hot-boiling issues involving the institutional framework. In particular, it is of the utmost importance to ensure that both incumbents and new entrants are subject to trusted and consistent oversight over time. The importance of enforcement and policing against surreptitious forms of non-compliance was recently highlighted by Barclays and Lloyds's breaches of the CMA Open Banking Remedy in relation to open APIs for data access.[48] Moreover, as the implementation of the CMA orders is soon to be completed, there is a need to conceive a workable future governance and enforcement of data sharing and interoperability requirements.

In response to the consultation launched by the government,[49] the leading industry body for financial services (UK Finance) proposed to let the nine largest banks free to withdraw from membership (and funding duties) after only three years. This spurred a great deal of discussion with market players and stakeholders.[50] According to several fintech firms, the proposal at stake would easily turn into an unfair leverage to manipulate the new supervisor's activity, especially when it comes to oversight of interoperability requirements and standardisation initiatives.[51] From its part, to ensure an holistic approach towards the different areas intersected by the consumer data right (data protection, technical standardisation and competition issues), the Australian legislator appointed the Secretary of Treasury as the central policy agency in charge of rule-making and sectoral assessment responsibilities.[52]

[47] Open Banking Implementation Entity, 'Open Banking Impact Report' (2021), available at: www.openbanking.foleon.com/live-publications/the-open-banking-impact-report-october-2021-ug/home/.

[48] CMA, 'Lloyds Banking Group's Breaches of The Retail Banking Market Investigation Order 2017 in Relation to Open APIs under the Open Banking Remedy' (2022), available at: www.assets.publishing.service.gov.uk/government/uploads/system/uploads/attachment_data/file/1061956/LBG_Article_12_draft_public_letter__public_version_.pdf; CMA, 'Barclays Bank's breaches of The Retail Banking Market Investigation Order 2017 in relation to Open APIs under the Open Banking Remedy' (2022), available at: www.gov.uk/government/publications/cma-letter-to-barclays-about-13-breaches-of-the-retail-banking-order.

[49] CMA, 'The Future Oversight of the CMA's Open Banking Remedies' (2021), available at: www.gov.uk/government/consultations/future-oversight-of-the-cmas-open-banking-remedies/the-future-oversight-of-the-cmas-open-banking-remedies.

[50] UK Finance, 'Open Banking Futures: Blueprint and Transition Plan' (2021), available at: www.ukfinance.org.uk/system/files/Open-Banking-Phase-II-report-FINAL.pdf.

[51] Nicholas Megaw, 'Watchdog Criticised over Plans to Combat Dominance of Big Banks' *Financial Times* (7 June 2021), available at: www.ft.com/content/c7cba98a-b8fe-415b-9cc9-bfd765b4f7d5.

[52] Treasury Laws Amendment (2020 Measures No 6) Act 2020 (Cth) sch 2 ('Amendments of the Consumer Data Right').

As already mentioned, in contrast to the United Kingdom and Australia, the European Union did not go as far as mandating API standardisation. Banks were let free to develop their own data-sharing interfaces and voluntarily join privately led standardisation initiatives across the Internal Market. The underpinning rationale for such a policy choice was hinged on the concern that a common API standard could jeopardise innovation and dynamic competition between standards.

However, given the broad variety of standardisation initiatives implemented across the European Union, the Commission acknowledged that the lack of APIs interoperability could increase transaction costs and complexities for newcomers.[53] Notably, fintech providers face the risk of duplicative investments for complying with certification processes and heterogeneous interfaces, ultimately leading to scarce reusability of technical solutions and major hurdles for product innovation. Thus, the European Digital Finance and the Retail Payments Strategies launched in 2020 explicitly committed to establish an Open Finance framework by the end of 2024 as well as to overhaul the PSD2 framework.

III. THE RISE OF INTEROPERABILITY ACROSS EUROPEAN LEGISLATION

Over the last years the Commission has taken stock of the data-access mechanisms enshrined in the PSD2 and implemented an ambitious legislative strategy centred on interoperability obligations. Thus, a wave of regulatory initiatives was put forward to address the economic power enjoyed by large platform-based digital ecosystems.

Notably, significant interoperability provisions are included in the DMA, which represents the cornerstone of the Union's legislative strategy for the digital economy.[54] Under this piece of legislation, app store providers shall ensure full interoperability with third-party apps and stores.[55] Further vertical interoperability requirements are introduced for hardware and software features accessed or controlled via an operating system or a virtual assistant (eg, near-field-communication technology elements and authentication mechanisms),

[53] European Commission, 'Communication on a digital finance strategy for the EU' COM (2020) 591 final, 14; European Commission, 'Communication on a on a retail payments strategy for the EU' COM (2020) 592 final, 15. As to the concerns arising from PSD2-enabled Open Banking, see European Supervisory Authorities, 'Joint response to the European Commission's February 2021 Call for Advice on digital finance and related issues' (2022) paras 50–51, available at: www.eba.europa.eu/sites/default/documents/files/document_library/Publications/Reports/2022/1026595/ESA%202022%2001%20ESA%20Final%20Report%20on%20Digital%20Finance.pdf. As to consumer data access with regard to insurance services (so-called Open Insurance) within the EU, see EIOPA, 'Open Insurance: Accessing and Sharing Insurance-related Data' (2021), available at: www.eiopa.europa.eu/document-library/consultation/open-insurance-accessing-and-sharing-insurance-related-data_en.

[54] Digital Markets Act (n 15).

[55] ibid, Art 6(4).

and for complementary and supporting services (eg, payment services).[56] This is meant to avoid gatekeepers exploiting their dual role as orchestrator of operating systems or device manufacturers to undermine third-party service and hardware providers. Moreover, the final version of the DMA has accepted the European Parliament's amendment aimed at also introducing horizontal interoperability obligations on gatekeepers that provide number-independent interpersonal communications services (ie, instant messaging services).[57]

An additional step towards mandated interoperability in the digital economy was taken by the Commission with the Data Act proposal.[58] The rationale of this new piece of legislation is to refrain manufacturers of data-collecting devices from enjoying de facto exclusive control over personal and non-personal information generated by connected smart devices (eg, smartphones, wearable devices, automated personal assistants).[59] With this goal in mind, the Data Act envisages an access-by-default requirement under which products and services should be designed 'in such a manner that data generated by their use are, by default, easily, securely and, where relevant and appropriate, directly accessible to the user'.[60]

The Data Act is clearly inspired by the access-to-account regime enshrined in the PSD2. Indeed, the proposal places on data holders an obligation to share the data generated by the use of connected products or related services with third parties upon user request.[61] Further, by echoing the asymmetric treatment imposed by the PSD2 over banks, firms designated as gatekeepers under the DMA are not eligible to receive data, either directly or indirectly.[62] In the eyes of the Commission, it would have been disproportionate to include them as beneficiaries in light of the 'unrivalled ability of these companies to acquire data'.[63] Under the same logic, micro or small enterprises are not required to comply data-sharing obligations.[64] Having said that, the Commission made sure to preserve incentives to innovate by prohibiting data receivers from developing rival products that compete with the one from which the accessed data originate.[65]

[56] ibid, Art 6(7).

[57] ibid, 7. The obligation is limited to the basic functionalities of these services (ie, initially only one-to-one text messaging, including images/video/other types of files; two years later, text messaging within a group; four years later, voice/video calls between two individuals, and a group and an individual) and only to the extent that the level of security (including end-to-end encryption) ensured by the gatekeeper to its own end users is preserved.

[58] European Commission, 'Proposal for a Regulation on harmonised rules on fair access to and use of data (Data Act)' (n 20).

[59] ibid, 67.

[60] ibid, Art 3(1) and Art 5(1).

[61] ibid, Art 2(2) and recital 14.

[62] ibid, Art 5(2).

[63] ibid, recital 36.

[64] ibid, Art 7(1).

[65] ibid, Art 6(2)(e).

German and British jurisdictions decided to push interoperability as well. Alongside the adoption of codes of conduct for platforms with strategic market status, the United Kingdom has planned a wide range of procompetitive interventions, including third-party access to data, interoperability and common standards.[66] In particular, interoperability is considered a key tool for significantly improving opportunities for competition and innovation in relation to the activities of strategic market status firms.[67]

As part of the Payment Services Supervisory Act, Germany has instead introduced interoperability obligations on providers that enable the offer of payment services or the operation of electronic money business by means of technical infrastructure services (named as 'system undertaking').[68] The initiative is aimed at opening up access to the near-field-communication (NFC) technology of smartphones, which is particularly relevant to the payment system as it facilitates tap-and-go contactless payments between smartphones or smartwatches and payment terminals without the need for consumers to carry a physical card. Indeed, the provision is commonly known as 'Lex Apple Pay' since it is mostly meant to affect the iPhone maker's business model based on a walled garden ecosystem by mandating system undertakings to leave their NFC interface open for third-party payment service providers.

However, since the 'appropriate fee' for accessing the technical infrastructure under this law was similar to the fee charged for using Apple Pay, traditional banks and other payment service providers preferred relying on Apple in-house products rather than developing their own apps with direct access to the NFC antenna of smart devices. To make the interoperability requirement more effective, the law was amended in 2021 by the Bundestag and, upon payment of the mere actual costs, system undertakings are now obliged to grant a standardised technical interface to smartphones and other end devices.[69] Further, the amendments require that interoperability is implemented in a way which ensures functional equality across hardware components and authentication methods (eg, fingerprint sensors, facial recognition and iris scanners), thereby also enabling payment services offered via internet-based devices (like in-car payments) as well as IoT devices (such as smart refrigerators and voice assistants).

IV. INTEROPERABILITY AND STANDARDISATION IN IOT ECOSYSTEMS

In light of these legislative strategies hinged on data access and interoperability to overcome the current situation of de facto control over data generated by users, it is worth assessing which precautions are needed to avoid unintended

[66] CMA, 'A New Pro-Competition Regime for Digital Markets' (n 17).
[67] ibid, 'Appendix D: The SMS regime: pro-competitive interventions', para 34.
[68] Zahlungsdiensteaufsichtsgesetz (ZAG) 2020, s 58a.
[69] Bundesgesetzblatt Jahrgang 2021 Teil I Nr 37, 2083.

consequences in terms of competitive dynamics. Indeed, interoperability is context dependent, hence it is of the utmost importance to tailor it according to the dynamics and features of the industry sector at hand.

First of all, open access and interoperability significantly constrain product design as well as the business model of business providers. This is even more true when it comes to multisided markets.[70] As their market value depends on the quality of the offer provided by the third-party business players hosted by the platform, there is a symbiotic relationship between them and the orchestrator. According to the key characteristics of their business model, IoT platforms match individual users with device manufacturers, app developers, service providers, advertisers and so on. It should not come as a surprise that the economic attractiveness of the whole platform relies on the overall quality of the services offered by ancillary operators acting within the ecosystem.[71] Thus, platform orchestrators need to react promptly to eliminate moral hazard and exploitative behaviours by third-party users which could undermine user trust.[72] Governance mechanisms and private regulation (legal, technical and behavioural) serve exactly the purpose of preserving the integrity of the whole ecosystem.[73]

For instance, when it comes to the app stores, it is commonly understood that governance mechanisms are key to incentivise value-creation activities from the side of app developers (such as development of innovative complements and knowledge sharing).[74] Conversely, allowing large numbers of software producers to enter the platform would generate crowding-out effects, ultimately jeopardising third-party incentives for developing new apps.[75] Hence, an artificial restraint on governance power could lead to a decline in product innovation and a consequent loss of value for the technology platform at stake.[76]

In light of the delicate nature of platform business models, there is a risk that broad-brushed interoperability requirements would force platform ecosystems

[70] KJ Boudreau and A Hagiu, 'Platforms Rules: Multi-Sided Platforms as Regulators' in A Gawer (ed), *Platforms, Markets and Innovation* (Edward Elgar Publishing, 2009).

[71] DS Evans and R Schmalensee, *Matchmakers: The New Economics of Multisided Platforms* (Harvard Business School, 2016); A Hagiu and J Wright, 'Multi-Sided Platforms' (2015) 43 *International Journal of Industrial Organization* 162; JC Rochet and J Tirole, 'Platform Competition in Two-Sided Markets' (2003) 1 *Journal of the European Economic Association* 990; J-C Rochet and J Tirole, 'Two-Sided Markets: A Progress Report' (2006) 37 *Rand Journal of Economics* 645.

[72] D Evans, 'Governing Bad Behavior by Users of Multi-sided Platforms' (2012) 27 *Berkeley Technology Law Journal* 1201.

[73] A Hagiu and J Wright, 'Controlling vs Enabling' (2019) 65 *Management Science* 577.

[74] See Y Zhang, J Li and TW Tong, 'Platform Governance Matters: How Platform Gatekeeping Affects Knowledge Sharing Among Complementors' (2022) 43 *Strategic Management Journal* 599; and KJ Boudreau, 'Open Platform Strategies and Innovation: Granting Access vs. Devolving Control' (2010) 56 *Management Science* 1849.

[75] KJ Boudreau, 'Let a Thousand Flowers Bloom? An Early Look at Large Numbers of Software App Developers and Patterns of Innovation' (2012) 23 *Organization Science* 1409.

[76] O Borgogno and G Colangelo, 'Platform and Device Neutrality Regime: The New Competition Rulebook for App Stores?' (2021) 67 *Antitrust Bulletin* 451, 492.

to be sub-optimally open to external players. In turn, whenever the activities pursued by such new entrants is not entirely compatible with the platform business model or governance safeguards, ecosystem profitability and customer experience would be jeopardised. Moreover, the complexities brought about by the interaction of different business players within IoT environments are likely to exacerbate this problem. In addition, regulators are not necessarily best placed to dictate and engage in the detailed planning of ecosystem governance.[77] This is why broad regulatory remedies mandating open access and interoperability obligations could undermine the business model of key ecosystem orchestrators, with huge drawbacks for consumer welfare.

Horizontal interoperability requirements operating across different platform-based ecosystems come with an additional layer of complexity. Indeed, these obligations would force platforms to offer complete substitute products and services, ultimately preventing differentiation between ecosystems for the sake of achieving an artificial level playing field contestability. Further, from a competition policy perspective, horizontal interoperability risks being a double-edged sword. By artificially lowering barriers to entry and impeding product differentiation, such a strong remedy would facilitate dominant players to become even bigger by leveraging economies of scale and scope.[78] Finally, horizontal interoperability in the field of digital ecosystems brings significant technical challenges in terms of data minimisation, data security and content moderation.

In sum, while horizontal interoperability hinged on open standards has proven to work well in the field of electronic communications networks, it is far from clear whether it can be just as successful in IoT environments. For instance, mandating standardised interoperability in order to allow smooth entry by third-party providers implies redesigning an entire ecosystem.

Interoperability needs standardisation to be effective and avoid technology fragmentation. Different service providers can benefit from data access and interoperability requirements as long as the technical protocols and interfaces are well designed and widely adopted by both incumbents and new entrants. Standards serve exactly this purpose by providing a set of technical rules and characteristics which allow devices not only to connect and integrate, but also to ensure the security and quality of user switching. Moreover, from the perspective of competition policy, open and transparent standards reduce the likelihood of self-preferencing tactics by incumbents through technology fragmentation.

However, the most recent European legislative initiatives dealing with data access and interoperability are echoing the same fuzzy approach which

[77] Boudreau and Hagiu (n 70).

[78] D Awrey and J Macey, 'Open Access, Interoperability, and DTCC's Unexpected Path to Monopoly' University of Chicago Coase-Sandor Institute for Law & Economics Research Paper (2021) 934, available at: papers.ssrn.com/sol3/papers.cfm?abstract_id=3885194, investigating the evolution of US securities clearinghouses and depositories markets to argue that poorly designed open access and interoperability requirements can help dominant firms to obtain and entrench their monopoly power rather than enhancing competition.

significantly slowed down the adoption of Open Banking in the European Union compared with the United Kingdom. Notably, the forthcoming DMA and Data Act do not take a clear stance towards standardisation. While recognising, in principle, the importance of interconnection for competition data-driven environments, there is no clear indication as to how standards should be developed and implemented in order to ensure workable interoperability across digital markets. In particular, the DMA states that 'where appropriate and necessary', the Commission may mandate European standardisation bodies to develop appropriate standards.[79] With regard to number-independent interpersonal communications service, gatekeepers are obliged to provide the necessary technical interfaces or similar solutions that facilitate interoperability, upon request and free of charge.[80] In a similar vein, the Data Act proposal sets aside the possibility of imposing the adoption of technical standards or common interfaces.[81] Only in the case of a specific need to 'encourage parties in the market to develop relevant open interoperability specifications' between data processing services, could the Commission delegate the development of European harmonised standards.[82]

Formal standardisation bodies have tried to facilitate interoperability for IoT applications by opening several work streams both at EU and at international level. However, they struggle to deliver on their promises as they are constrained by lengthy consensus decision-making among all the stakeholders involved. This translates in compromise solutions lacking a clear concrete business case, and are thus obsolescence-prone.[83]

Given the difficulties of achieving consensus through formal standardisation initiatives, industry-led projects have surfaced over recent years. They include not-for-profit organisations, industry alliances and temporary consortia with heterogeneous institutional origins, logics and goals. Unlike formal standardisation initiatives, these projects are orchestrated by the largest technology platforms. This usually increases the adoption rate of standardised solutions, but raises concerns on how fairness and conflicts of interests are tackled throughout the negotiation.[84] In particular, it is true that discussions among market players in the context of standard setting can facilitate collusion and ultimately hinder competition. This is why such initiatives need to be carried out in accordance

[79] Digital Markets Act (n 15) Art 48.

[80] ibid, Art 7.

[81] European Commission, 'Proposal for a Regulation on harmonised rules on fair access to and use of data (Data Act)' (n 20) Art 28.

[82] ibid, recital 76.

[83] European Commission, 'Study to support an Impact Assessment on enhancing the use of data in Europe' (2019) 39, available at: digital-strategy.ec.europa.eu/en/library/impact-assessment-report-and-support-studies-accompanying-proposal-data-act.

[84] European Commission, Commission Staff Working Document accompanying the 'Final Report – Sector inquiry into consumer Internet of Things' (n 9) 117.

with antitrust law, for instance by ensuring unrestricted access, transparency and fair access conditions.[85]

So far, industry-led standardisation has proved to be the most convenient route when it comes to delivering interoperability as it hinges on unfettered market processes and does not require lengthy negotiations to build wide consensus. As a result, there is high heterogeneity when it comes to the IoT standardisation environment.[86] While formal standards prevail only at the level of basic connectivity technologies (eg, WiFi and Bluetooth), de facto standards have taken centre stage in the field of wearable devices, user interfaces and operating systems.[87]

One of the initiatives most likely to succeed is the Connectivity Standards Alliance which drew leading firms to develop open standards for wireless device-to-device communication and agree on easy certification procedures for third-party manufacturers. In 2019, within this group, Apple, Google and Amazon established a new working group (now named Matter) to launch a new, royalty-free connectivity standard enabling compatibility between a large range of smart home devices. Moreover, since July 2014 the Thread Group alliance has been operating to provide network protocols to connect and control products for home automation. Finally, in 2019 both Amazon and the Linux Foundation launched initiatives (the Voice Interoperability Initiative and the Open Voice Network respectively) to facilitate multi-homing and interconnection between voice-assistants.

The main risk stemming from such a heterogeneous framework is posed by legal uncertainty and technology fragmentation. Similarly to the delays and inconsistencies witnessed in the European Union with reference to the Open Banking implementation, the high number of industry-led standards may generate economic frictions undermining broader market adoption and, eventually, frustrating interoperability remedies.[88] At the same time, the lack of common standards exacerbates manufacturers and software developers' compliance costs for meeting interoperability technical requirements.

Against this background, Open Banking could serve as a reference for delivering a workable interoperability tailored around the features of major digital ecosystems in the IoT universe. In line with the approach adopted in the United Kingdom and Australia with reference to Open Banking and Open Finance,

[85] With reference to EU law, see European Commission, 'Guidelines on the applicability of Article 101 of the Treaty on the Functioning of the European Union to horizontal co-operation agreements (Communication)' [2011] OJ C 11/1. For an overview on the matter, see O Kanevskaia, *The Law and Practice of Global ICT Standardization* (Cambridge University Press, 2023).

[86] European Commission (n 19) 6.

[87] European Commission, Commission Staff Working Document accompanying the 'Final Report – Sector inquiry into consumer Internet of Things' (n 9) 71.

[88] European Commission, Commission Staff Working Document accompanying the 'Final Report – Sector inquiry into consumer Internet of Things' (n 9) 101.

providers of the largest technology platforms should be required to engage in open and transparent standardisation processes together with other market players. Arguably, this proposal should be understood as a proper regulatory intervention rather than a competition law remedy in order to be as comprehensive as possible in tackling the market structure problems of data sharing. Under the oversight of a public-appointed supervisor, market players would define common certification procedures, APIs and open standards capable of delivering smooth third-party data access and interoperability within each platform-based ecosystem. Notably, such a regulatory measure would require some form of continuous oversight of the industry in order to ensure effective implementation of interoperability requirements and to avoid moral hazard conducts or exploitation of the ecosystem from the side of third-party business players.

In the event of no deal or a failure to reach a compromise between the different stakeholders, the competent supervisory body would have the power to impose a middle-ground solution on all parties. By adopting an ecosystem-based approach to standardisation, such option would foster dynamic innovation and ecosystem diversification as platform operators would not be bound to level their offer between themselves. Moreover, interoperability could work smoothly in a vertical fashion thereby facilitating ecosystem entry by newcomers and lowering the risk of technological self-preferencing.

However, as the standards would be tailored to the specific features of each ecosystem, unlike Open Banking, this proposal would not lead to a one-size-fits-all solution. Indeed, because the IoT encompasses a wide range of heterogeneous products and services interconnected within diverse digital ecosystems, it would not be appropriate to impose a single set of interoperability standards on the whole sector.

This solution yields several benefits by lowering the technical costs of mandated interoperability while at the same time preserving inter-platform competition and product differentiation across the IoT economy. Indeed, for ecosystem orchestrators the proposal would shield platform business models from disruptive regulatory interventions, so that ecosystem differentiation and incentives to innovate would be preserved. For policymakers, an ecosystem-tailored approach to standardisation is more easily administrable compared with broad-brush remedies imposing identical interfaces on all players. In turn, market entry and contestability at the downstream level of each ecosystem would be significantly eased.

V. CONCLUSION

Open Banking and the IoT are at the forefront of legislative strategies centred on data access and interoperability. An increasingly high number of financial service providers, device manufacturers and software developers from different sectors need to make sure that their products easily interconnect with the infrastructure of large data holders, be they banks or technology platforms. Because of the concerns about the power exerted by orchestrators of such ecosystems, policymakers around the world have started conceiving data access mechanisms to ensure a level playing field with third-party providers.

By taking stock of the Open Banking implementation experience, we suggest that competition-oriented reform in the IoT field should aim at delivering vertical interoperability within each ecosystem and that industry-led standardisation under the oversight of independent public bodies would represent the right solution to tackle the challenges of interoperability in the IoT world. Accordingly, digital ecosystem orchestrators would be expected to design open interoperability standards together with third-party providers and manufacturers. In this way, it is possible to circumvent the hurdles of formal standardisation processes while countering the risks of de facto standards developed under the lead of large technology platforms. This solution holds the promise of ensuring effective and workable interoperability in digital markets while safeguarding incentives to innovate.

9

Sustainable Finance and Fintech: Market Dynamics, Innovation and Competition

BEATRICE CRONA AND MARIOS C IACOVIDES*

I. INTRODUCTION

IN 2020 THE UN launched its 'decade of action' – a call for all sectors of society to mobilise to accelerate sustainable solutions to all the world's biggest challenges – ranging from poverty and gender to climate change, inequality and closing the finance gap.[1] Two years into this decade, climate change and its effects on natural environments, humans and our economies are unfolding at a rate constantly exceeding scientific predictions. The concurrent rapid loss of biodiversity,[2] which threatens to undermine many of the ecosystem services on which humans depend, further exacerbates climate change and our ability to deal with it.

The Paris Agreement, one of the most crucial international legal instruments in the common effort to tackle the climate crisis, mentions that its efforts to strengthen the global response to the threat include 'making finance flows consistent with a pathway towards low greenhouse gas emissions and climate-resilient development'.[3] Nevertheless, there is no globally agreed definition on what constitutes sustainable finance under the United Nations Framework Convention on Climate Change Conference of the Parties process (UNFCCC COP), with parties disagreeing as to the classification of certain types of financing

* The authors would like to thank Christos Vrettos for valuable input on earlier drafts of this chapter. All errors and omissions remain the authors'.

[1] For information on this initiative, see: www.un.org/sustainabledevelopment/decade-of-action/.

[2] Intergovernmental Science-Policy Platform on Biodiversity and Ecosystem Services, 'Global Assessment Report on Biodiversity and Ecosystem Services of the Intergovernmental Science-Policy Platform on Biodiversity and Ecosystem Services' (Zenodo, 2019), available at: zenodo.org/record/3831673.

[3] The Paris Agreement under the United Nations Framework Convention on Climate Change, FCCC/CP/2015/L.9/Rev.1 (12 December 2015) Art 2.1.

as sustainable finance, for instance high interest loans (as opposed to grants) for climate mitigation, and financing of gas projects.

As became apparent during the COP27 and COP15 in Egypt and Canada respectively in 2022, the issue of financing the costs associated with the measures that need to be taken to tackle the environmental and climate crises, as well as alleviating the losses caused by natural disasters associated with these crises, is thorny. The reasons for this are complex, ranging from past injustices, to colonisation, exploitation, the difference in impact caused by the industrialised North on the one hand and developing countries in the Global South on the other, as well as the different impacts climate change is having in different regions of the world, and on different groups within each region.[4]

A lot of the focus on closing the finance gap[5] has been put on the pledges of different states, organisations or regions, especially with regard to loss and damage.[6] Yet, financing does not depend solely on governmental action. Private capital will also have to play an instrumental role. This means that financing also relates to what companies can and are willing to do to contribute to tackling the crises, either on account of different governmental policies and incentives, or out of their own self-interest. Naturally, in capitalist free market economies, ensuring the transformation of company conduct is crucial for addressing the climate and environment crises. As discussed elsewhere, companies, especially large ones, are directly or indirectly disproportionately responsible for greenhouse gas emissions and environmental degradation.[7] At the same time, their power can be leveraged to precipitate rapid change for the better.[8] That change will

[4] J Hickel et al, 'Imperialist Appropriation in the World Economy: Drain from the Global South through Unequal Exchange, 1990–2015' (2022) 73 *Global Environmental Change* 102467; J Hickel et al, 'National Responsibility for Ecological Breakdown: A Fair-Shares Assessment of Resource Use, 1970–2017' (2022) 6 *Lancet Planetary Health* e342; T Abi Deivanayagam et al, 'Climate Change, Health, and Discrimination: Action towards Racial Justice' (2023) 401 *Lancet* 5. For suggestions relating to how best to address this related to the degrowth movement, see P Chiengkul, 'The Degrowth Movement: Alternative Economic Practices and Relevance to Developing Countries' (2018) 43 *Alternatives: Global, Local, Political* 81.

[5] For an overview, see D Doumbia and M Lykke Lauridsen, 'Closing the SDG Financing Gap – Trends and Data' Report of the International Finance Corporation (World Bank, October 2019), available at: openknowledge.worldbank.org/bitstream/handle/10986/32654/Closing-the-SDG-Financing-Gap-Trends-and-Data.pdf?.

[6] UNFCCC, Decision CP.27/CMA.4 on Funding Arrangements for Responding to Loss and Damage Associated with the Adverse Effects of Climate Change, Including a Focus on Addressing Loss and Damage (20 November 2022).

[7] M Iacovides and V Mauboussin, 'Sustainability Considerations in the Application of Article 102 TFEU: State of the Art and Proposals for a More Sustainable Competition Law' in J Nowag (ed), *Research Handbook on Competition Law and Sustainability* (Edward Elgar, 2023).

[8] ibid. For some leading examples, see H Österblom et al, 'Transnational Corporations as "Keystone Actors" in Marine Ecosystems' (2015) 10 *PLOS ONE* e0127533; C Folke et al, 'Transnational Corporations and the Challenge of Biosphere Stewardship' (2019) 3 *Nature Ecology & Evolution* 1396; C Folke et al, 'An Invitation for More Research on Transnational Corporations and the Biosphere' (2020) 4 *Nature Ecology & Evolution* 494; J Virdin et al, 'The Ocean 100: Transnational Corporations in the Ocean Economy' (2021) 7 *Science Advances* eabc8041; H Österblom et al, 'Scientific Mobilization of Keystone Actors for Biosphere Stewardship' (2022) 12 *Scientific Reports* 3802.

require enormous investment, for instance in new infrastructure or in research and development. Thus, it pertains to the issue of financing too.

Sustainable finance is a topic that is receiving increasing attention from practitioners, researchers and policymakers alike.[9] In this chapter, we address the intersection between sustainable finance, fintech and competition policy, an issue that has hitherto received little, if any, specific attention from the aforementioned scholarly fields or policymakers, despite being of significant relevance to companies. Our approach is to regard European Union (EU) competition policy through a socio-ecological lens,[10] allowing us to explore how competition policy could be used as a tool to facilitate sustainable finance, while addressing any anticompetitive unilateral conduct or collusion or tendencies to market concentration.

The rest of this chapter is organised as follows. In section II, we first set the scene by briefly explaining how achieving sustainability is a complex matter. We also briefly review current engagement with sustainability by the financial sector (sustainable finance) and contrast the phenomena of greenwashing versus greenwishing. This background allows us to provide a more nuanced picture of sustainable finance, something which will be relevant in later sections when we explore how fintech can contribute to achieving it, while at the same time striking a good balance vis-a-vis competition policy. In section III, we add on the dimension of fintech and explore different ways in which fintech can facilitate sustainable finance. In section IV, we explain how sustainable finance can be seen as a parameter of competition, and in section V, we explore what competition problems may arise out of the intersection between sustainable finance and fintech and how those could possibly be addressed. We conclude in section VI and offer some ideas for future research and some suggestions for the direction in which policy could move.

II. FINANCIAL SECTOR ENGAGEMENT WITH SUSTAINABILITY

A. Environmental Sustainability and Complexity: More than Emissions Reductions

Finance and sustainability have so far predominantly interacted in relation to reductions in greenhouse gas emissions. Yet global environmental sustainability is a complex matter that goes far beyond the need for rapid reductions in greenhouse gas emissions. While emissions reductions are absolutely necessary, they alone will not halt or prevent climate change, and they will not ensure adequate

[9] See, eg, the EU's policy initiatives, available at: finance.ec.europa.eu/sustainable-finance/overview-sustainable-finance_en; and the UK's Financial Conduct Authority's ESG Strategy (3 November 2021), available at: www.fca.org.uk/publications/corporate-documents/strategy-positive-change-our-esg-priorities.

[10] For an exposition of this method see MC Iacovides and C Vrettos, 'Falling through the Cracks No More? Article 102 TFEU and Sustainability: The Relation between Dominance, Environmental Degradation, and Social Injustice' (2021) 10 *Journal of Antitrust Enforcement* 32, 34–35 and 40–43.

food production, access to water or many other fundamental human necessities, such as access to green space for health and recreation. Furthermore, our planet is a system – the Earth system – that is made up of multiple interacting subsystems, or processes. When discussing global environmental change, four of these are of particular importance: land, water, atmosphere and living ecosystems. Changing land use is particularly important for how the planet functions because it affects vegetation and, through this, the storage of carbon in plants and soil, where vast amounts of organic carbon lie stored.[11] How we use our land also affects moisture recycling at local, regional and global scales,[12] which in turn create feedbacks that affect what grows where and how much carbon that vegetation can store, but also whether land can provide other vital services, like food production, timber, bioenergy etc. Finally, changes in landcover, or loss of ice or snow cover, affect global warming by changing how much radiation is reflected, thus altering the Earth's energy balance.[13]

The examples highlighted here are only a fraction of the dense network of interactions between the Earth system processes for which evidence now exists, some of which are also at risk of passing irreversible tipping points.[14] We use them here to highlight the fact that every economic sector and type of human activity will need to look for solutions to address these complex issues. Finding those solutions will depend on providing funding for research, development, adaptations and changing practices. Thus, it is worth keeping in mind throughout this chapter that achieving sustainability will involve the contribution of the financial sector in multiple different ways than simply ensuring financing for projects relating to greenhouse gas emissions.

B. Sustainable Finance: Greenwishing or Greenwashing?

So, what is the financial sector doing to contribute to our sustainable future? One of the primary frameworks through which capital investments have engaged with sustainability is what is lumped together as 'ESG' – ie, environmental, social and governance issues. This represents a wide range of issues that may have a direct or indirect impact of financial relevance to companies

[11] Intergovernmental Panel on Climate Change, 'Climate Change and Land – An IPCC Special Report on Climate Change, Desertification, Land Degradation, Sustainable Land Management, Food Security, and Greenhouse Gas Fluxes in Terrestrial Ecosystems: Summary for Policymakers' (Geneva, 2020), available at: www.ipcc.ch/site/assets/uploads/sites/4/2020/02/SPM_Updated-Jan20.pdf.

[12] PW Keys et al, 'Variability of Moisture Recycling Using a Precipitationshed Framework' (2014) 18 *Hydrology and Earth System Sciences* 3937.

[13] W Steffen et al, 'Trajectories of the Earth System in the Anthropocene' (2018) 115 *Proceedings of the National Academy of Sciences* 8252.

[14] TM Lenton et al, 'Climate Tipping Points – Too Risky to Bet Against' (2019) 575 *Nature* 592; J Rockström et al, 'Planetary Boundaries: Exploring the Safe Operating Space for Humanity' (2009) 14 *Ecology and Society* 32; W Steffen et al, 'Planetary Boundaries: Guiding Human Development on a Changing Planet' (2015) 347 *Science* 1259855.

and investors. Recently, the (in)ability of ESG to significantly move the needle towards real environmental and social sustainability has been called into question by scholars[15] and financial practitioners alike.[16] Such discussions have also articulated the problematic confusion that arises from equating ESG with environmental and social sustainability.[17] In short, the single most important reason why ESG is not synonymous with environmental and social sustainability is that it is a concept designed to assess risks *to* companies, not impacts caused *by* companies.[18] In other words, ESG is about identifying what ESG-related risks a company is exposed to and to which extent the company can manage and mitigate them. These generally include transitions risks such as reputational, regulatory and market risks, as well as physical risks to companies and their assets.[19] Using the ESG framework as a means to communicate that investments are reducing our pressure on key planetary processes is therefore treacherous and misleading.

Relying on reputational risks, for example, means that where a company is situated in a global supply chain will often end up becoming a stronger determinant of risk than the environmental externality itself. Companies with consumer-facing brands are generally more vulnerable to reputational risk, even though their environmental impact on climate and other environmental and social processes may be less severe than companies operating in other segments. In contrast, a company with significant environmental or social impact, such as one that contributes to deforestation in a tipping element like the Amazon, may not consider reputational and litigation risk to be high despite their severe negative externalities, simply because they do not have a consumer-facing brand and are operating in a weak institutional environment,[20] where the likelihood of being penalised for illegal deforestation is minimal.[21]

[15] N Buhr, Roland Gray and Markus J Milne, 'Histories, Rationales, Voluntary Standards and Future Prospects for Sustainability Reporting: CSR, GRI, IIRC and Beyond' in J Bebbington, J Unerman and B O'Dwyer (eds), *Sustainability Accounting and Accountability* (Routledge, 2014); B Crona, C Folke and V Galaz, 'The Anthropocene Reality of Financial Risk' (2021) 4 *One Earth* 618; B Crona and E Sundström, 'Sweet Spots or Dark Corners? An Environmental Sustainability View of Big Data and Artificial Intelligence in ESG' in T Rana, J Svanberg, P Öhman and A Lowe (eds) *Handbook of Big Data and Analytics in Accounting and Auditing* (Springer Nature, 2023).

[16] Economist Leader Article, 'Three Letters that Won't Save the Planet – ESG Should be Boiled Down to One Simple Measure: Emissions' *Economist* (21 July 2022), available at: www.economist.com/leaders/2022/07/21/esg-should-be-boiled-down-to-one-simple-measure-emissions; Henri Tricks, 'A Broken System Needs Urgent Repairs' *Economist* (21 July 2022), available at: www.economist.com/special-report/2022/07/21/a-broken-system-needs-urgent-repairs.

[17] Crona, Folke and Galaz (n 15); Crona and Sundström (n 15).

[18] Buhr, Gray and Milne (n 15); Crona, Folke and Galaz (n 15).

[19] See, eg, Task Force on Climate-Related Financial Disclosures 'Status Report' (October 2022), available at assets.bbhub.io/company/sites/60/2022/10/2022-TCFD-Status-Report.pdf.

[20] A well-documented example is Brazil, see C Silva Junior et al, 'The Brazilian Amazon Deforestation Rate in 2020 is the Greatest of the Decade' (2021) 5 *Nature Ecology & Evolution* 144; and RD Garrett et al, 'Forests and Sustainable Development in the Brazilian Amazon: History, Trends, and Future Prospects' (2021) 46 *Annual Review of Environment and Resources* 625.

[21] V Galaz et al, 'Finance and the Earth System – Exploring the Links between Financial Actors and Non-Linear Changes in the Climate System' (2018) 53 *Global Environmental Change* 296.

Furthermore, even ESG investment approaches that attempt to explicitly invest with environmental or social outcomes in mind generally rely only on relative measures of impact. Various forms of positive or negative screening are an example. These strategies aim to create socially responsible investment funds by including or excluding companies that perform better or worse (respectively) on a particular metric. A commonly used metric is carbon intensity, which measures the emissions per unit of a produced good or service. The problem is that humanity is currently faced with hard limits beyond which large-scale planetary dynamics, such as climate and large-scale ecosystem change and concurrent biodiversity loss, can cause significantly worsening conditions for societal prosperity.[22] These hard limits do not only relate to carbon intensity and emissions, as explained above in subsection II.A.

In conclusion, approaches to sustainable investments that rely only on ESG, and are based on financial materiality, may provide more accurate assessments of the company's financial value, but are unlikely to truly address environmental and social sustainability at scale.[23] This results in a situation where, despite the apparently sincere and rising ambitions of the financial sector to engage with the climate and sustainability challenge – 'greenwishing' – the ESG system has been structured in a way that does not allow an assessment of whether we are increasing or decreasing the resilience of the biosphere, approaching or exceeding planetary boundaries,[24] or how investments are affecting multiple other social goals, such as those found in the UN Sustainable Development Goals.[25] To put it simply and bluntly, we are flying blind, while also at risk of enabling, encouraging and promoting greenwashing.

III. SUSTAINABLE FINANCE AND FINTECH

It is against this backdrop that fintech, which is developing at breakneck speed, is making strides into sustainability. In this section, we explore what fintech is and its relationship to sustainable finance.

Fintech has been defined in greater detail in other contributions to this volume.[26] For the purposes of our chapter, we adopt a rather loose working definition that understands fintech as the phenomenon of applying to the financial and banking sector new technologies and new tools made possible

[22] Steffen et al, 'Planetary Boundaries' (n 14).

[23] This may also be attributable to institutional investors and sovereign borrowers lacking incentives, making the ESG contractual bargain very difficult to negotiate and implement: F Lupo-Pasini, 'Sustainable Finance and Sovereign Debt: The Illusion to Govern by Contract' (2022) 25 *Journal of International Economic Law* 680.

[24] Rockström et al (n 14); Steffen et al, 'Planetary Boundaries' (n 14).

[25] United Nations Resolution Adopted by the General Assembly 'Transforming our World: the 2030 Agenda for Sustainable Development' A/RES/70/1 (United Nations, 25 September 2015).

[26] See, eg, Claire Ingram Bogusz and Jonas Valbjørn Andersen, 'The Boundaries of Fintech: Data-Driven Classification and Domain Delimitation', ch 1, section II in this volume.

by digitalisation. In other words, fintech is a term used to describe firms using new(er) technology to compete with traditional financial methods in the delivery of financial services. A typical example that will be known to most readers are neobanks, also known as virtual banks or digital banks.

The application of new technologies to well-established, and at times rather mature, markets like banking, loans, mortgages, payments, financial services, investment, trade in shares, commodities, securities and the like, has been disruptive and invigorating, creating new market dynamics and decoupling value chains.[27] An area with a lot of potential for innovation is where fintech meets sustainability. As attention is increasingly put on sustainability aspects of fintech, the definition of what can be considered fintech appears to have expanded too, to also include various tech-oriented solutions for reducing the environmental footprint of financial services, as we will see in this section. Systematic academic analysis of the sustainability contribution of fintech is largely absent. Therefore, we offer a rudimentary attempt at delineating some broad means and mechanisms by which fintech attempts to support sustainability, noting that it is neither systematic, nor all-encompassing.

In our view, the contribution of fintech to sustainability can be discussed in terms of three broad categories, namely: (i) reducing or removing so called 'scope 1' sustainability impacts of financial services; (ii) enabling or steering money towards consumption and investment in goods or services with less, or no, sustainability impact; and (iii) enabling or facilitating companies' compliance with emerging environmental regulations and reporting requirements through increased supply chain transparency. In what follows, we elaborate further on these broad categories.

When it comes to the first category, the most well-established form of fintech, the neobanks, eliminate the need for physical locations, thus reducing the use of office space, heating, electricity, commuting, transports and other typical office resources, such as paper. All this contributes to reducing the environmental impact of the sector as a whole. Moreover, mobile payment providers such as Apple Pay, Google Wallet, PayPal and Venmo have similar positive effects to neobanks on scope 1 sustainability impacts. Their alternative payment methods reduce the need for both paper bills[28] and the plastic that goes into the staggering six billion plastic payment cards distributed each year.[29]

[27] See, eg, Iris H-Y Chiu and Despoina Mantzari 'Regulating Fintech and BigTech: Reconciling the Objectives of Financial Regulation and Promoting Competition', ch 10 in this volume.

[28] On the impact of cash and cards on the environment, see De Nederlandsche Bank, 'Life Cycle Assessment of Cash Payments' DNB Working Paper 610 (9 October 2018), available at: www.dnb.nl/en/news/dnb-publications/dnb-working-papers-series/dnb-working-papers/Workingpapers2018/dnb379444.jsp.

[29] See, eg, EnViro30, 'Mastercard has Sustainable Alternatives to 6 Billion Non-Recyclable and Virgin Plastic Payment Cards' (24 July 2020), available at: www.enviro30.com/post/mastercard-has-sustainable-alternatives-to-6-billion-non-recyclable-and-virgin-plastic-payment-cards.

That said, data storage and processing is a major consumer of power[30] and could contribute towards a substantial footprint, something which is less often discussed in this context. Of course, every sector nowadays relies on data storage and processing, thus this is not a unique issue for banking and financial services. Be that as it may, certain aspects of fintech, for instance its reliance of cryptocurrencies, blockchains or other technologies necessary for payments and security, does require a very high amount of energy for processing and storage, in particular because of the need to cool servers.[31] That energy does not, and cannot, always come from renewable electricity. Thus, several digital banks are using carbon offsetting, primarily via tree planting, to attempt to reduce their net footprint.[32] While talk of sustainability and net-zero ambitions indicate that the topic is becoming material to these new actors, offsetting is fraught with many problems. Carbon offsetting by planting trees is not a robust long-term strategy for reducing climate change if there are significant risks of large-scale forest fires in the wake of a warming climate.[33] Tree planting can also have negative effects on biodiversity when non-native trees and low tree diversity are used,[34] and poses significant competition to other types of land use, with sometimes detrimental effects on food production and food security for local populations. Additionally, there is a high risk that offsetting does not genuinely reduce carbon emissions. For instance, a recent investigation into Verra – the world's leading carbon standard for the voluntary offsets market – by newspapers the *Guardian* and *Die Zeit*, and the non-profit investigative journalism organisation, SourceMaterial, found that more than a staggering 90 per cent of their rainforest offset credits, which are the most commonly used by companies, are likely to be 'phantom credits' and do not represent genuine carbon reductions.[35] In sum, neobanks and mobile payment providers can help reduce the 'scope 1' impacts of financial services, but their sustainability contributions could hardly be called transformational in this regard.

[30] E Masanet et al, 'Recalibrating Global Data Center Energy-Use Estimates' (2020) 367 *Science* 984.

[31] H Mullan, M Braithwaite and R Cheetham-West, 'Potential Competition Concerns as the Banking and Finance Industry Responds to Climate Change' in S Holmes, D Middelschulte and M Snoep (eds), *Competition Law, Climate Change & Environmental Sustainability* (Concurrences, 2021) 266.

[32] See, eg, the examples available at: topmobilebanks.com/blog/sustainability-in-fintech/.

[33] G Badgley et al, 'California's Forest Carbon Offsets Buffer Pool is Severely Undercapitalized' (2022) 5 *Frontiers in Forests and Global Change* 930426.

[34] SE Andres et al, 'Defining Biodiverse Reforestation: Why it Matters for Climate Change Mitigation and Biodiversity' (2023) 5 *Plants, People, Planet* 27.

[35] For reporting on this story, see Patrick Greenfield, 'Revealed: More than 90% of Rainforest Carbon Offsets by Biggest Certifier are Worthless, Analysis Shows – Investigation into Verra Carbon Standard finds Most are "Phantom Credits" and may worsen Global Heating' *Guardian* (18 January 2023), available at: www.theguardian.com/environment/2023/jan/18/revealed-forest-carbon-offsets-biggest-provider-worthless-verra-aoe. It should be noted that Verra disputes these findings.

Fintech solutions that can assist other companies, but also (importantly) consumers and more broadly citizens in making better consumption and investment choices (our second category) are more promising. Such fintech-enabled assistance can be achieved either through the use of analytics to enhance transparency and traceability of invested funds, or by improving understanding of systemic risks to economies, businesses and communities through the use of satellite data and artificial intelligence that can collect information on everything from traffic patterns and greenhouse gas emissions to food production and deforestation.

The potential for aiding and guiding *consumer* action is particularly important from a sustainability perspective. Informed and discerning consumers can gain, through fintech, the power to make or break the fortunes of firms based on parameters of sustainability. This has the potential to steer companies' market conduct, as well as investment. Moreover, citizens can be enabled, through fintech, to come together through crowdfunding, to finance bottom-up genuine sustainability projects that may face difficulties in accessing other forms of financing, for instance because they may not be profitable enough in the eyes of systemic investors or because they want to operate on a non-profit basis.

Two examples can be explored further to show how this works, namely Klarna and Genervest.[36] Each represents one of these potentially important consumer and citizen-facing sustainability-oriented fintech models. Klarna, a neobank established in Sweden with a global reach, includes, in the consumer app that it has developed, the carbon footprint of purchases made with its virtual card. The app does so by computing data regarding the products purchased and adding the emissions caused by the products' delivery. The information provided is, of course, only indicative, as it calculates emissions based on average emissions per merchant category and the value of the purchase based on the entire product lifecycle. The app also includes an 'emissions overview' section, where the consumer can get more insights into their emissions, including emissions per month to track trends and a highlighted section on 'high emission purchases' for the previous half year. Fun facts comparing a consumer's emissions to easily identifiable goods (eg, emissions for your trip to New York were about the same as those of 9,424 cinnamon rolls) add to the section's appeal and consumers' engagement with the information, whereas at the end of the section there is a dedicated part named 'act on your emissions', with a link for donating to various carbon removal and emission reduction projects supported by the neobank.[37]

Genervest is an initiative of Greenpeace Greece that provides, through its energy cooperative established in Croatia, a peer-to-peer investment platform which showcases energy communities and cooperatives around the world and

[36] For more examples, see, eg: www.fca.org.uk/firms/innovation/green-fintech-challenge.

[37] For more information on Klarna's emissions tracking, see: www.klarna.com/us/klarna-app/emissions-tracker/.

allows investors, big and small, to grow their money while supporting renewable energy projects. Essentially, the platform guarantees a reasonable return for the investment akin to a savings account with a fixed interest rate that compares favourably with what savings accounts in traditional banks offer. According to Genervest, investors earn more from their savings and it costs the people behind renewable energy projects less to borrow the money because there is no bank involved in the middle.[38] So far, Genervest has successfully fully funded energy communities in Greece which will create solar panel projects with large capacities that will be providing CO_2 emissions savings of hundreds of tons per year, as well as partially funded the Kaboni Electrification Program, the first ever energy community in Burundi. The projects provided investors with interest between 6 and 8 per cent, well above average interest rates available in savings accounts in banks in the Global North. At the time of authoring this chapter, Genervest was in the process of providing peer-to-peer funding to another four projects.[39]

Much less explored to date, but interesting from a sustainability perspective, are fintech businesses that can help companies comply with emerging environmental regulations and reporting requirements (such as the standards developed by the International Sustainability Standards Board (ISSB)[40] or the Corporate Sustainability Reporting Directive that is part of recent EU regulation)[41] by increasing supply chain transparency. Simultaneously, this gives consumers the information needed to select and support businesses that prioritise carbon accountability and other environmental reporting. Thus, it relates strongly to the second category presented above. Supply chain transparency is a necessity to uphold accountability in any supply chain, but to make sure that businesses who promise consumers reduced waste and increased cost-effectiveness in fact deliver on their ambitions, such transparency is essential in 'green' supply chains. Fintech could, thus, contribute to increasing consumers' awareness of their social or environmental consumption footprint, while also improving accountability, enforcement and the possibility for penalising non-compliance with regulations.

Sustainability reporting is a new reality for many companies, where the European Union now leads the way through the implementation of the recently adopted Directive on Corporate Sustainability Reporting. The Directive introduces more detailed reporting requirements and a requirement to report according to mandatory EU sustainability reporting standards.[42] It requires large companies

[38] For more information on Genervest, see: genervest.org.

[39] Information on the projects is available on Genervest's website, available at: members.genervest.org/en/open-opportunities.

[40] For information on the ISSB, see: www.ifrs.org/groups/international-sustainability-standards-board/issb-frequently-asked-questions/.

[41] Directive (EU) 2022/2464 of the European Parliament and of the Council of 14 December 2022 amending Regulation (EU) No 537/2014, Directive 2004/109/EC, Directive 2006/43/EC and Directive 2013/34/EU, as regards corporate sustainability reporting [2022] OJ L322/15.

[42] ibid.

and listed companies to publish regular reports on the social and environmental risks they face and on how their activities impact people and the environment. Its standards add to a growing body of reporting initiatives undertaken by companies on a voluntary basis. The majority of their disclosure recommendations focus on targets, existing corporate policies and progress indicators, which are certainly relevant. However, because such progress indicators often obscure the underlying data and represent relative measures – such as carbon intensity and progression against set targets – they preclude an analysis of actual aggregate impact, and often also do not make possible a reliable comparison between companies.[43]

Many more fruitful opportunities for understanding and monitoring corporate impact would open up if data regarding some core company activities and their environmental impact were to be reported. This would allow science to use such data in state-of-the-art models, but it would also open up a space where analytical services would be needed to convert company reported data into impact assessments of corporate revenue streams or aggregate impact of investment portfolios. This is not dissimilar from the role ESG rating institutes have played to date. Yet these rating providers have recently come under heavy critique since their proprietary models and 'black-box' analytics do not allow for external scrutiny or sustainability verification.[44] With its inherent use of big data, artificial intelligence and real-time information, fintech is a potentially perfect role model to develop sophisticated analytical platforms for impact assessment of corporate activity. Thus, there are feasible models for technology and analytics to overcome these issues and help companies remain profitable, while also promoting competition.

IV. SUSTAINABLE FINANCE AND FINTECH AS A PARAMETER OF COMPETITION

In the section above, we explored the ways in which fintech can support sustainable finance. While it is not a given, fintech's intermingling with sustainable finance has the possibility to disrupt markets and change market dynamics as well as operate as a catalyst for innovation. Thus, sustainable finance, charged with the potential offered by fintech, can be seen as a significant parameter of competition in financial markets. In this section, we elaborate further on sustainable finance and fintech's relation to competition.

First, sustainable finance is being used today as a new and additional way for companies to compete. As one would expect, the same is true for fintech. This

[43] E Wassénius, B Crona and S Quahe, 'Essential Environmental Impact Variables for Improved Sustainability Reporting' (forthcoming, on file with the authors).

[44] See *Economist*, 'Three Letters that Won't Save the Planet' (n 16); Tricks (n 16); and Crona, Folke and Galaz (n 15).

is the case irrespective of whether the technology relates to the business model of the company as such (eg, neobanks) or if it is used to support sustainability initiatives, claims and reporting of other companies. Sustainability, supported by fintech, can therefore be seen as a qualitative parameter of competition as consumers or customers take it into account as one of the qualities that adds value to the good or service that is being purchased.[45] For instance, a consumer who is weighing up which bank to open a savings account with may make their choice, partially or wholly, on the fact that a bank may offer a fintech-enabled app that helps them track the carbon footprint of their purchases, or that the bank has made certain pledges, supported by fintech-enabled reporting, as to how they will invest the money saved into their savings accounts. Alternatively, a producer may choose suppliers based on their fintech-enabled environmental or social impact reporting. In turn, such producers may highlight the sustainability credentials of their company and those of their suppliers, subcontractors etc to differentiate their offering to customers or consumers from that of their competitors and, thus, increase profit margins or enhance their brand image and the loyalty of customers or consumers.[46]

As with all quality aspects, whether sustainability as a qualitative parameter of competition will actually matter or not, and hence whether it will be profitable and adopted long-term and industry-wise, and if it will outweigh negative effects on competition, will depend on whether there is willingness to pay on the part of customers and consumers.[47] Naturally, willingness to pay increases with increased transparency and accountability, as customers and consumers can be reassured that what they are paying for will indeed make a positive impact. Fintech significantly facilitates that, as explained above, in section III. As

[45] R Inderst and S Thomas, 'Sustainability Agreements in the European Commission's Draft Horizontal Guidelines' (2022) 13 *Journal of European Competition Law & Practice* 571.

[46] V Colaert, 'The Changing Nature of Financial Regulation: Sustainable Finance as a New EU Policy Objective' (2022) 59 *Common Market Law Review* 1669, 1687.

[47] See Annex to the Communication from the Commission, 'Approval of the content of a draft for a Communication from the Commission, Guidelines on the applicability of Article 101 TFEU to horizontal co-operation agreements' COM(2022) 1159, final (Brussels, 1 March 2022) ('Draft Guidelines on horizontal co-operation agreements') s 9, points 597–600. The Commission notes that certain sustainability benefits, which it terms as 'collective benefits' may not depend on willingness to pay, see s 9.4.3.3. See also the economic analysis jointly commissioned by the Greek and Dutch competition authorities, R Inderst, E Sartzetakis and A Xepapadeas, 'Technical Report on Sustainability and Competition' (January 2021), available at www.epant.gr/enimerosi/ygiis-antagonismos-viosimi-anaptyksi/item/download/2164_01da38f02a026af57e2ac10ba5b4f73e.html; S Thomas and R Inderst, 'Reflective Willingness to Pay: Preferences for Sustainable Consumption in a Consumer Welfare Analysis' (2021) LawFin Working Paper No 14, available at: dx.doi.org/10.2139/ssrn.3755806. For an application where lack of willingness to pay meant an exception of the agreement from competition rules could not be granted, see Dutch ACM, 'ACM's analysis of the sustainability arrangements concerning the "Chicken of Tomorrow" case' (2015), available at: acm.nl/en/publications/publication/13789/ACMs-analysis-of-the-sustainability-arrangements-concerning-the-Chicken-ofTomorrow.

sustainability disclosures become better due to the use of fintech, one can therefore expect the significance of this as a parameter of competition to increase.[48]

A second way in which the combination of sustainability and fintech can become a parameter of competition becomes clear as we reason around the relationship between increased adoption of fintech and the spurring of sustainability-related innovations, not only in the financial and banking sector, but also in every other industry. In this regard, the European Commission acknowledges the adoption of fintech as something that can make the financial sector more innovative.[49] Part of that may well be related to sustainability, even though this is not specifically mentioned. The combination of the two, ie, sustainability and fintech, can certainly spur innovation, as seen for instance in the initiatives supported by the UK's Financial Conduct Authority (FCA) as part of its Innovation Hub. These range from access to green energy, facilitation in reaching net-zero, reporting, carbon-offsetting, reporting savings, and sustainable transport.[50] From a sustainability perspective, such innovations would ideally truly benefit the environment, biodiversity, reduce inequality, etc, rather than represent mere greenwashing or greenwishing endeavours such as those we discussed above in section II.

Third, fintech can help bring down barriers to entry for green initiatives, especially innovative or small-scale ones, although, as we will discuss in section V, this may not happen if BigTech manages to capture the market. As large-scale initiatives are often undertaken by incumbents that already possess the means and expertise to finance their endeavours, fintech can prove to be crucial for the entry and expansion of newcomers.[51] A clear example of this is the use of fintech to microfinance, through crowdfunding, energy communities that can offer an alternative to bigger energy providers. Genervest, highlighted above in section III, is a good example of this. From a competition policy perspective, any new entry or facilitation of expansion will have the positive result of disrupting market dynamics, challenging the market position of incumbents and controlling or reducing their market power. This ought to ensure that incumbents are not able to behave anticompetitively, either unilaterally or in coordination with other large market participants, and should ultimately have a disciplining effect on prices, ensure continued innovation and increase consumer welfare.

[48] Climate Financial Risk Forum, 'Climate Financial Risk Forum Guide 2020: Disclosures Chapter' (June 2020), available at: www.fca.org.uk/publication/corporate/climate-financial-risk-forum-guide-2020-disclosures-chapter.pdf, 5.

[49] See European Commission, 'FinTech Action Plan: For a More Competitive and Innovative European Financial Sector' COM(2018) 109 final (Brussels, 8 March 2018) 11 et seq.

[50] See the latest innovations supported by the Financial Conducts Authority, available at: www.fca.org.uk/firms/innovation/green-fintech-challenge.

[51] This positive effect of fintech is identified by the Hellenic Competition Commission in 'Final Report of the Sector Enquiry in Fintech' (December 2022) 6, available at: www.epant.gr/files/2022/fintech/FINTECH_Final_Report_EL.pdf (in Greek).

Fourth, fintech can help create tools that bring sustainable products and services directly to consumers, thus removing instances of double marginalisation and intermediary costs. For instance, a consumer who would wish to invest their savings responsibly might have been required, in the absence of sustainability initiatives backed by fintech, to do so through a traditional bank. That bank would have charged fees on the savings or investments. Instead, the consumer may use a fintech-enabled platform to directly save or invest in this manner and avoid such costs. The same is true for businesses. By borrowing money through a fintech-enabled platform that is specifically created to fund sustainability initiatives, an entrepreneur or collective entity such as an energy community or cooperatively owned producer or service provider, may avoid having to pay costs to more traditional banking institutions. This is positive both from a competition and from a sustainability perspective, as it avoids a transfer of wealth from undertakings that truly have sustainability at the core of their business model and from sustainability-minded consumers to undertakings that do not. Moreover, in instances where abuse of market power would be likely, deadweight loss to society is avoided, and productive assets are put where they are intended to serve the purposes of sustainability.

Overall, we see great potential in the pairing of fintech with sustainability to reduce barriers to entry and expansion, disrupt markets and empower both consumers and producers or service providers with a true interest in sustainability, while leading to increased competition and innovation not only in financial markets, but also in every other market where sustainability matters.

V. COMPETITION LAW ISSUES AND SOLUTIONS

Even *without* the explicit involvement of fintech, corporate strategies to address sustainability are likely to intersect with competition law as they affect market dynamics and impact innovation and several parameters of competition.[52] In previous sections we presented a first attempt at exploring specifically how the combination of fintech and sustainability may affect market dynamics and competition in general. The question we address in this section is what impact the combination of fintech with sustainability will have on the relationship between sustainability and competition law, by considering five competition law issues that are likely to arise because of the reorientation of markets towards sustainability and trying to explore specifically how bringing fintech into the picture may exacerbate or alleviate those issues.

First, a commonly identified issue with efforts to green corporate operations is that there are costs associated with moving first when customers or consumers

[52] For one of the most complete coverages of sustainability considerations in competition law see S Holmes, D Middelschulte and M Snoep (eds), *Competition Law, Climate Change & Environmental Sustainability* (Concurrences, 2021).

are not yet willing to pay for the increased costs of a more sustainable product or service.[53] This is typically an argument put forward by the industry when arguing for the inclusion of sustainability considerations in the analysis undertaken for the application of Article 101(3) of the Treaty on the Functioning of the European Union (TFEU) to exempt otherwise anticompetitive agreements between competitors.[54] To a certain extent, this has been accepted by the Commission, as indicated by the dedicated chapter on sustainability agreements in the new Draft Guidelines on Horizontal Agreements.[55] It has also been accepted by several national competition authorities, most notably the Dutch,[56] Greek,[57] Austrian,[58] Belgian,[59] French[60] and United Kingdom[61] authorities, as well as having been debated within the context of the European Competition Network,[62] the Organisation for Economic Co-operation and Development (OECD)[63] and the International Competition Network (ICN).[64] The Hellenic

[53] For an overview, see H Zhang and M Song, 'Do First-Movers in Marketing Sustainable Products Enjoy Sustainable Advantages? A Seven-Country Comparative Study' (2020) 12 *Sustainability* 450.

[54] See, eg, Catherine Baksi, 'The Cost of Green Collaboration' *Times* (28 January 2021) 53; and Kate Beioley and Camilla Hodgson, 'UK Competition Watchdog to Ease Rules on Climate Change Action' *Financial Times* (25 January 2023), available at: www.thetimes.co.uk/article/competition-law-is-an-obstacle-to-green-innovation-hdk25c89z.

[55] Draft Guidelines on horizontal co-operation agreements (n 47) s 9.

[56] Dutch ACM, Draft Guidelines on 'Sustainability Agreements' (9 July 2020), available at: www.acm.nl/en/publications/draft-guidelines-sustainability-agreements.

[57] Hellenic Competition Commission, Staff Working Document 'Competition Law and Sustainability' (2021), available at: www.epant.gr/en/enimerosi/competition-law-sustainability.html. See also Inderst, Sartzetakis and Xepapadeas (n 47).

[58] The Austrian Cartel and Competition Law Amendment Act 2021, available at: www.parlament.gv.at/PAKT/VHG/XXVII/ME/ME_00114/index.shtml#, clarifies that consumers are considered to be allowed a fair share of an efficiency claimed as a defence by undertakings that enter into anticompetitive agreements, if the efficiency contributes to an ecologically sustainable or climate-neutral economy.

[59] Belgian Competition Authority, 'Key Policy Priorities for 2021' (Brussels, 10 March 2021), available at: www.abc-bma.be/fr/propos-de-nous/publications/note-de-politique-de-priorites-2021.

[60] French Competition Authority, Press Release 'Eight French Regulators Publish a Working Paper on their Role and Tools in the Face of Climate Change' (Paris, 5 May 2020), available at: www.autoritedelaconcurrence.fr/en/press-release/eight-french-regulators-publish-working-paper-their-role-and-tools-face-climate.

[61] Competition and Markets Authority, 'Draft Guidance on the application of the Chapter I prohibition in the Competition Act 1998 to horizontal agreements' (January 2023), available at: assets.publishing.service.gov.uk/government/uploads/system/uploads/attachment_data/file/1131039/HBER_Draft_guidance.pdf, part 11 and paras 1.12-1.13.

[62] At the end of 2020, the ECN Working Group on Horizontals and Abuse launched the project 'Sustainability and antitrust', headed by the Dutch and Greek NCAs, with the participation of France, Finland, Hungary, Germany, Luxembourg and Ireland.

[63] Organisation for Economic Co-operation and Development (OECD), 'Sustainability and Competition' OECD Competition Committee Discussion Paper (Paris, 2020), available at: www.oecd.org/daf/competition/sustainability-and-competition-2020.pdf.

[64] Hungarian Competition Authority, 'Sustainable Development and Competition Law – Survey Report' (Special Project for the 2021 ICN Annual Conference, 30 September 2021), available at: www.gvh.hu/en/gvh/Conference/icn-2021-annual-conference/special-project-for-the-2021-icn-annual-conference-sustainable-development-and-competition-law.

Competition Commission has also created the possibility for undertakings to collaborate on sustainability initiatives within the parameters of a sandbox,[65] modelled on the sandboxes that have become so common in financial markets, acknowledging that competition law may sometimes need to take a step back to enable undertakings to experiment with solutions that may contribute to sustainability.

In those situations where collaboration – at the expense of competition – is deemed necessary to achieve a sustainability goal, fintech may in fact come to the rescue of competition. As discussed above in section III, fintech adoption may increase the transparency and reliability of ESG reporting and of sustainability-related data. This may have the effect of increasing consumers' and customers' willingness to pay for the quality of sustainability, as they can be assured that any increased prices do in fact relate to increased sustainability rather than simply enriching producers.[66] Such increased willingness to pay will also mean that costs associated with moving first with regard to sustainability in a certain market are in fact reduced, if not eliminated altogether. In turn, this ought to result in fewer situations in which collaboration between competitors will truly be indispensable to achieve the sustainability goal, thus safeguarding the competitive process. Leaving ample space for companies to compete ought to have a further positive effect on sustainability, as (under the currently predominant global system of profit-driven capitalism) companies deliver sustainability benefits better under conditions of competition rather than through cooperation.[67]

Second, an argument often put forward in the context of the sustainability and competition law debate is that it would always be better for democratically elected institutions to regulate and set standards to achieve sustainability goals rather than try to incorporate sustainability considerations in the application of competition law, or that the Commission does not have the competence to take into account such considerations in the application of EU competition law.[68] Even leaving aside for a moment the consideration that this argument

[65] J Malinauskaite and F Buğra Erdem, 'Competition Law and Sustainability in the EU: Modelling the Perspectives of National Competition Authorities' (2023) *Journal of Common Market Studies*, available at: jcms.13458, 15. More Information about this initiative is available at: sandbox.epant.gr/en/.

[66] For strategies used by producers and sellers generally to manipulate consumers' willingness to pay, see P Bordalo, N Gennaioli and A Shleifer, 'Salience and Consumer Choice' (2013) 121 *Journal of Political Economy* 803, 826–27. For some examples of such misleading green claims, see the Competition and Markets Authority's dedicated webpage on enforcement action, available at: www.gov.uk/government/collections/misleading-environmental-claims.

[67] M Pieter Schinkel and Y Spiegel, 'Can Collusion Promote Sustainable Consumption and Production?' (2017) 53 *International Journal of Industrial Organization* 371; M Pieter Schinkel and L Treuen, 'Green Antitrust: Friendly Fire in the Fight Against Climate Change' in S Holmes, D Middelschulte and M Snoep (eds), *Competition Law, Climate Change & Environmental Sustainability* (Concurrences, 2021).

[68] E Loozen, 'Strict Competition Enforcement and Welfare: A Constitutional Perspective Based on Article 101 TFEU and Sustainability' (2019) 56 *Common Market Law Review* 1265; L Peeperkorn, 'Competition Policy is Not a Stopgap!' (2021) 12 *Journal of European Competition Law & Practice* 415.

may be flawed for reasons ranging from corruption[69] to regulatory capture,[70] to exporting externalities to other jurisdictions with lower standards,[71] standard-setting may also be caught between Scylla and Charybdis. This is because too low standards will risk leading to greenwashing, as explained above in section II, whereas too high standards will risk excluding competition altogether, or in cementing or increasing the market power of the few undertakings that will be able to follow them.[72]

The increased occurrence of greenwashing would, naturally, be bad from a sustainability perspective, giving the semblance of market participants doing something to alleviate the climate and environment crisis while in fact continuing to contribute to it.[73] Moreover, it may lead to a race to the bottom, as toxic competition of the sort that has thrived in markets and between nations since the Great Acceleration,[74] and the current lessening of standards and of competition law enforcement,[75] will continue. On the other hand, the decrease in competition and increase in concentration that high standards may bring, can also be problematic. Although high standards would initially be good from a sustainability perspective, the long-term decrease in competition may stifle innovation and force market participants to adopt certain solutions that fit those standards. The risk is thus that alternative solutions that could be better from a sustainability perspective do not take root and flourish, and entry barriers remain high or are raised further,[76] thus simply maintaining a sort of 'Wall Street climate consensus'[77] that is neither good for competition nor for sustainability. Moreover, it would be problematic both for competition and for sustainability if compliance with the high standards were to be possible only for a handful of undertakings that are only able to do so not out of merit but for reasons related to exploitation of their market power or possible influence on the regulatory

[69] Iacovides and Vrettos, 'Falling through the Cracks No More?' (n 10).

[70] F Beneke, 'Competition Law and Political Influence of Large Corporations – Antitrust Analysis and the Link between Political and Economic Institutions' (2021), available at: www.ssrn.com/abstract=3831269, 7–11.

[71] MC Iacovides and C Vrettos, 'Radical for Whom? Unsustainable Business Practices as Abuses of Dominance' in S Holmes, D Middelschulte and M Snoep (eds), *Competition Law, Climate Change & Environmental Sustainability* (Concurrences, 2021).

[72] Mullan, Braithwaite and Cheetham-West (n 31).

[73] E Bengtsson and O Mossberg, 'Greenwashing och Grön Marknadsföring' *Retorikförlaget* (*Helsingborg*, 13 March 2022), available at: www.retorikforlaget.se/greenwashing-och-gron-marknadsforing/ (in Swedish).

[74] W Steffen et al, *Global Change and the Earth System: A Planet under Pressure*, 1st edn (Springer, 2004).

[75] Iacovides and Vrettos, 'Unsustainable Business Practices as Abuses of Dominance' (n 71).

[76] Nordic Competition Authorities, Report 1/2010 'Competition Policy and Green Growth: Interactions and Challenges' (October 2010) 62, available at: www.kkv.fi/uploads/sites/2/2021/12/nordic-report-2010-competition-policy-and-green-growth.pdf.

[77] Adrienne Buller, 'Doing Well by Doing Good'? Examining the Rise of Environmental, Social, Governance (ESG) Investing' (*Common Wealth*, December 2020), available at: www.common-wealth.co.uk/publications/doing-well-by-doing-good, 33.

process.[78] From a climate justice perspective, it also matters if the undertakings able to follow the standards are disproportionately from former colonial powers, thus perpetuating economic inequalities.

Fintech might again come to both sustainability's and competition's rescue in this regard. Its potential for better reporting and monitoring can ensure better compliance with the given adopted standard in a jurisdiction, while ensuring also that consumers and customers can reward undertakings that choose to go further than the minimum required by the standard. This would have the effect that a certain sustainability goal can be achieved to the same extent demanded by societies by less draconian regulation, thus enabling the calibration of regulatory standards at the level where sustainability is achieved as required democratically by citizens, while balanced in terms of their effect on competition and proportionate to the achievement of the goal.

Third, similar possible competition law hazards to those just identified with regard to regulation have also been suggested for multi-stakeholder and sectoral voluntary sustainability standards.[79] Specifically for sustainable finance, these considerations would be relevant for horizontal collective self-commitments of financial institutions, such as alignment of products and services, common methodologies for measurement or supporting each other in collecting the necessary data on emissions.[80] Despite being voluntary, the issues *will* arise under certain conditions, for instance if access to standards, certification and the like is discriminatory, selective or exclusionary, or if the standards facilitate or lead to horizontal collusion.[81] As the issues are similar, our arguments as to how fintech might be able to help strike a good balance between competition and sustainability considerations are also relevant with regard to voluntary sustainability standards. Accordingly, fintech may help alleviate or altogether avoid anticompetitive objectives or effects of voluntary standards and self-commitments, by supporting better monitoring and empowering consumers and businesses seeking access to sustainable products or sustainable finance, and by lowering barriers to entry and spurring innovation.

[78] See, eg, Office of Fair Trading, 'The Competition Impact of Environmental Product Standards' Report prepared by Frontier Economics for the Office of Fair Trading (2008).

[79] E Partiti, 'Voluntary Sustainability Standards Under EU Competition Law' in E Partiti (ed), *Regulating Transnational Sustainability Regimes* (Cambridge University Press, 2022) 117–22 and 138–42; United Nations Conference on Trade and Development, 'Better Trade for Sustainable Development: The Role of Voluntary Sustainability Standards' UNCTAD/DITC/TAB/2021/2 and Corr.1 (2021) 10.

[80] S Bredt, 'Competition Law as an Obstacle to Financing a Sustainable Economy?' in S Holmes, D Middelschulte and M Snoep (eds), *Competition Law, Climate Change & Environmental Sustainability* (Concurrences, 2021). Note, however, that Bredt considers that the horizontal self-commitments of financial institutions would not breach EU competition law.

[81] Communication from the Commission, 'Guidelines on the Applicability of Article 101 of the Treaty on the Functioning of the European Union to Horizontal Co-Operation Agreements' [2011] OJ C/11, s 7.

A fourth issue worth highlighting is that, despite many positive effects, there is, nevertheless, a downside to increased transparency in the market. As we explained in section III, ESG reporting requires the disclosure of information from undertakings. This may pose an increased threat to competition, as the more detailed the reporting and the greater the demand for data and information, either from regulators or from customers and consumers, the greater the likelihood that competitors will be able to share or exchange strategic information. This would be increasing the risk for anticompetitive concerted practices through information exchange.[82] Moreover, undertakings could have an incentive to collude in order to reduce the quality of disclosures, so as to face less competition on that particular parameter,[83] or to collude to provide misleading information as to emissions, as was the case in the *Diesel scandal* cartel.[84]

Finally, there is the possibility of fintech being used by BigTech undertakings, such as Google, Apple, Meta, Amazon and Microsoft, to make further inroads into banking and other financial services such as consumer loans, payments, credit and insurance.[85] From the outset, this would seem to be good for competition, as BigTech undertakings will bring increased competitive pressure on incumbent banks and financial actors.[86] At the same time, there are risks associated with BigTech's entry and expansion in these markets. One such risk would be in BigTech undertakings engaging in leveraging their already strong position in entire ecosystems of services (and sometimes even hardware)[87] to attract consumers to their financial services products. Although this would increase competition initially, BigTech undertakings would have the possibility to lock in consumers in these products, thereby further gaining market power that can then be used to harm competition and consumers in the long term.[88] Another risk relates to consumer data, already a matter of great concern for competition policy.[89] BigTech undertakings are already in possession of a vast amount of personal consumer data that they gain through the engagement of consumers with the array of services they offer to them online or through engagement

[82] Case C-8/08 *T-Mobile Netherlands* ECLI:EU:C:2009:343; Case C-286/13 P, *Dole Food and Dole Fresh Fruit v Commission* ECLI:EU:C:2015:184.

[83] Mullan, Braithwaite and Cheetham-West (n 31) 272.

[84] Commission Decision in Case AT.40178 – *Car Emissions* C(2021) 4955 final (Brussels, 8 June 2021).

[85] K Stylianou, 'Exclusion in Digital Markets' (2018) 24 *Michigan Technology Law Review* 181.

[86] See, FCA, 'The Potential Competition Impacts of Big Tech Entry and Expansion in Retail Financial Services' Discussion Paper DP22/5 (October 2022), available at: www.fca.org.uk/publication/discussion/dp22-5.pdf.

[87] MG Jacobides and I Lianos, 'Ecosystems and Competition Law in Theory and Practice' (2021) 30 *Industrial and Corporate Change* 1199.

[88] FCA Discussion Paper (n 86) para 7.15.

[89] Laura Alexander, 'Privacy and Antitrust at the Crossroads of Big Tech' (2021) American Antitrust Institute Report, available at: ssrn.com/abstract=4013003; M Stucke and A Grunes, 'No Mistake About It: The Important Role of Antitrust in the Era of Big Data' (April 2015) *Antitrust Source* 1.

with their devices. BigTech firms could gain even more data by entering financial services markets, which can then be combined with other data and be used in ways which harm competition and consumers.[90] Additionally, BigTech undertakings could hold such data exclusively and either refuse to share it with incumbent banks, new fintech providers or potential competitors, thus stripping them of possibilities to use fintech to enter into or expand in financial services markets, or only provide the data subject to exploitative terms and prices.[91] From a sustainability perspective, BigTech's entry and expansion in financial services markets might mean that the potential positive effects of introducing more fintech in sustainable finance may never materialise. The solution for this would be strong competition law enforcement[92] and use of new enforcement tools such as those available through the Digital Markets Act.[93]

VI. CONCLUSION

As attested by this volume, the interaction between fintech and competition law and policy is a topic that is receiving a lot of attention from industry, practitioners, policymakers and competition law enforcers. The same can be said of the interaction between competition policy and sustainability, as shown by the proliferation of research and policy initiatives on the matter.[94] Yet, the intersection between sustainable finance, fintech and competition law and policy has remained hitherto unexplored. In this chapter, we made a first attempt at exploring this intersection, to identify how market dynamics but also, eventually, competition law and policy, will be affected in the years to come by the emergence and increasing importance of fintech for sustainable finance.

The single most important conclusion that can be drawn from our research is that fintech holds a unique promise: namely to ensure that sustainable finance goes beyond greenwishing and avoids greenwashing, while at the same time increasing competition. Fintech has this potential as it can on the one hand enable better

[90] FCA, Discussion Paper (n 86) para 7.16.

[91] ibid, para 7.17.

[92] Importantly, this would require the admittance that conduct that harms sustainability can be seen as anticompetitive, as suggested by Iacovides and Vrettos, 'Unsustainable Business Practices as Abuses of Dominance' (n 71).

[93] Regulation (EU) 2022/1925 of the European Parliament and of the Council of 14 September 2022 on contestable and fair markets in the digital sector and amending Directives (EU) 2019/1937 and (EU) 2020/1828 (Digital Markets Act) [2022] OJ L265/1.

[94] See eg, above (nn 55–65) and Iacovides and Vrettos, 'Falling through the Cracks No More?' (n 10); S Holmes, 'Climate Change, Sustainability, and Competition Law' (2020) 8 *Journal of Antitrust Enforcement* 354; S Holmes and M Meagher, 'A Sustainable Future: How Can Control of Monopoly Power Play a Part?' (2022), available at: www.ssrn.com/abstract=4099796; Iacovides and Vrettos, Unsustainable Business Practices as Abuses of Dominance' (n 71); V Mauboussin, 'Environmental Defences as a Shield from Article 102 TFEU' (2022) 3 *Concurrences* 30; Iacovides and Mauboussin (n 7).

reporting, monitoring, data collection, supply chain transparency, crowdfunding and microfinancing – all of which ought to support true sustainability-related financing – and on the other hand, can increase innovation, disrupt markets, help reduce barriers to entry and expansion, and challenge incumbents' market power, thereby safeguarding and promoting healthy competition for sustainability solutions and helping avoid welfare transfers from consumers (or citizens) and customers to a small number of undertakings. Large, (politically) powerful, incumbent companies are already preventing rapid transformation through innovation by retaining market shares and buying up through killer acquisitions smaller innovative companies and by otherwise preventing market access for potential small competitors. This is in great part aided by various procurement norms and by regulations as well as by weak competition law enforcement. As we showed in this chapter, fintech can help democratise sustainable finance, but to ensure fintech's unique promise is realised, policymakers should ensure regulation is designed at an optimal level, striking a balance between high standards with regard to sustainability while not stifling competition, whereas competition law enforcers must ensure competition in sustainability solutions is safeguarded by enforcing competition rules in a manner that takes into account the impact of businesses' market conduct on parameters of sustainability such as climate change, biodiversity and social justice.

Strong enforcement of competition rules ought also to assist in avoiding the two ways in which increased presence of fintech in sustainable finance would be problematic and which we identified above, namely the increasing possibilities for collusion or information exchange and the further strengthening of BigTech companies' market power.

Overall, in our view, if a right balance is struck between regulation and competition and if the competition that remains is safeguarded by strong competition law enforcement, fintech ought to be a great tool in the democratisation of sustainable finance and will, thus, greatly assist in closing the finance gap in an equitable way.

Part III

Fintech's Institutional and Regulatory Setting

10

Regulating Fintech and BigTech: Reconciling the Objectives of Financial Regulation and Promoting Competition

IRIS H-Y CHIU AND DESPOINA MANTZARI

I. INTRODUCTION

INNOVATIONS IN TECHNOLOGY have been developing that change the way financial services are delivered. Financial assets and services, many of which are globally mobile and capable of being represented in digital form, are highly susceptible to the developments in information, communications and transmission technologies. The Financial Stability Board, a global body that monitors trends and coordinates policy in international financial regulation, defines the new industry of 'fintech' as: 'technologically enabled innovation in financial services that could result in new business models, applications, processes or products with an associated material effect on financial markets and institutions and the provision of financial services'.[1] At the same time, 'BigTech' firms, ie, large technology companies whose primary activity is platform-based digital services, are also becoming increasingly active in the provision of financial services.[2]

Fintech and BigTech offer potential to change financial services through digital transformations and delivery. In general, the value chain of banks and incumbent financial institutions includes many bundled services and activities. Fintech companies, including BigTech, could focus on one or a few of

[1] Financial Stability Board, 'Fintech' (2021), available at: www.fsb.org/work-of-the-fsb/financial-innovation-and-structural-change/fintech/, 1.

[2] D Evans and R Schmalensee, 'The Antitrust Analysis of Multi-Sided Platform Businesses' in R Blair and D Sokol (eds), *The Oxford Handbook of International Antitrust Economics* (Oxford University Press, 2014).

these activities in an unbundled way (what we call disintermediation),[3] and/or rebundle with other services, financial or non-financial, in new ways. Langley et al[4] observe that the initial hype regarding the 'disintermediation', 'decentralisation' and 'democratisation' of fintech is giving way to new forms of reconsolidation or recentralisation, in the hands of partnerships between incumbents and fintechs, or among fintechs themselves, notably, the BigTech companies such as Google or Facebook that leverage their technological superiority in other fields and foray into finance.[5] In response to both the rise of fintech and the inroads of BigTech into finance, a number of incumbent bank and non-bank financial institutions are also moving to a platform model by making greater use of big data and automation to offer third-party services, such as digital payments, credit insurance and wealth management, to their existing customers. This entails a change to the traditional business model of financial institutions, where firms seek to match different groups of clients in the market.

Fintech and BigTech pose new challenges to regulators in three ways. First, the transformation of financial services entail 'boundary' considerations for financial regulation, such as whether financial services or products could fit into existing financial regulation 'categories'. The main categories relate to banking services (which involve full intermediation by banks of financial risks); insurance products (which relate to full intermediation by insurance companies that underwrite certain future risks); and securities products and services, which relate to fundraising in public markets; and fund products which relate to the management of pooled assets over different time horizons and for different savings objectives.[6] All categories have developed regulatory tenets based on certain assumptions of compliance capacity on the part of the industry incumbents. These can be over-inclusive for new services or products led by fintechs. Second, financial regulators such as the UK Financial Conduct Authority (UK FCA), struggle with the need to promote competition enabled by disruptive innovation while ensuring a level regulatory playing field for the same function of financial intermediation.[7] But, financial regulatory regimes are hardly technologically neutral and the mantra of functional rather than entity-based regulation is more idealistic than implemented in reality. In this respect, we observe in section III

[3] For a survey of fintech applications and innovations see J Madir, 'What is Fintech?' in J Madir (ed), *Fintech: Law and Regulation* (Edward Elgar, 2019).

[4] P Langley and A Leyshon, 'The Platform Political Economy of FinTech: Reintermediation, Consolidation and Capitalisation' (2021) 26 *New Political Economy* 376.

[5] L Enriques and W-G Ringe, 'Bank–Fintech Partnerships, Outsourcing Arrangements and the Case for a Mentorship Regime' (2020) 15 *Capital Markets Law Journal* 374.

[6] See a broad overview of the categories of financial activities in J Armour et al, *Principles of Financial Regulation* (Oxford University Press, 2016) ch 2.

[7] Expert Group on Regulatory Obstacles to Financial Innovation (ROFIEG), *30 Recommendations on Regulation, Innovation and Finance* (December 2019) 67 (Recommendation 13 on 'same risks, same rules'), available at: ec.europa.eu/info/sites/default/files/business_economy_euro/banking_and_finance/documents/191113-report-expert-group-regulatory-obstacles-financial-innovation_en.pdf.

that financial regulators have increasingly carved out specialist regulatory regimes for fintech sectors, such as crowdfunding platforms and crypto-assets in the European Union (EU).

Nevertheless, the Organisation for Economic Co-operation and Development (OECD) has observed that bespoke regulation is not needed where the innovation is not disruptive enough, for example in roboadvice or online insurance distribution.[8] Further, the introduction of specialist financial regulatory regimes catering for particular types of fintech can also lead to regulatory fragmentation. Nevertheless it can be argued that such fintechs would not be subject to competitive disadvantage, since similar business models are grouped together and regulated in the same fashion. But, as will be discussed in section IV below, this bespoke approach may fail to capture the operation of fintech ecosystems, where financial services may be part of a wider business model, which can be financial or otherwise, such as that provided by BigTech companies. Implications for financial regulation and its interaction with other regulatory systems, such as data governance, competition law, privacy and consumer rights etc, would also arise. These are new and unfamiliar challenges that extend beyond the realm of financial regulation as traditionally conceived.

Owing to the limitations of the bespoke approach, we argue that two further regulatory approaches have arisen. The first is (re)consolidatory movements in regulation where new and common risks are identified, and across-the-board regulatory proposals are introduced. The second is BigTech-specific regulatory measures, which the European Union and United Kingdom (UK) are increasingly inclined towards (eg, the introduction of the EU's Digital Services Act and Digital Markets Act).[9]

Reconsolidatory regulatory measures address cross-cutting issues such as data governance, privacy, platform responsibilities, digital delivery responsibilities and codes of conduct. These can address similar modes of digital interaction or delivery in different sectors, avoiding duplication or arbitrage between the regulations that apply to different sectors. However, one question remains – whether some BigTechs in finance are special, in the sense that they have such a global footprint and vast market share that special rules and responsibilities should apply to them apart from cross-cutting rules that apply to platforms in general. The BigTechs in question, such as Meta, Google and Amazon, possess platform powers beyond many other types of platform businesses and it is queried to what extent they should be subject to distinct regulations that reflect that.

This chapter maps what we refer to as a three-pronged regulatory response to the rise of fintech firms and BigTech in finance, as discussed above. Section II

[8] Organisation for Economic Co-operation and Development (OECD), 'Digital Disruption in Banking and its Impact on Competition' (2020), available at:www.oecd.org/competition/digital-disruption-in-banking-and-its-impact-on-competition-2020.pdf.

[9] See below (n 91) 103.

discusses the new regulatory challenges posed by fintech. Section III discusses specialist or bespoke regulatory regimes that financial regulators have introduced in the European Union and United Kingdom in response to the differences observed between fintech and conventional financial services, primarily based on the need to promote innovation and competition so that disruptive movements are not snuffed out by onerous existing regulatory categories. Section IV explores the special issues posed by BigTech and considerations for BigTech-specific regulatory measures that are beyond 'normal' competition law tools. Section V discusses the reconsolidatory movements in cross-cutting rules, such as the EU's Digital Services Act and Digital Markets Act, and critically discusses their achievements and limitations. We recognise that one single integrated regulatory solution is unlikely to be either feasible or optimal at the moment, but there is likely a need to consider an institutional response in due course, which is beyond the scope of this chapter to provide in detail. A number of commentators have urged financial regulators to move towards new, radically disrupted and holistic regulatory models,[10] where financial regulation is integrated with regulatory issues such as digital identity infrastructures, global finance and trade policy implications, while punctuated with competition vigilance throughout, monitoring the power concentration risks in new business models and developments.[11] In section VI, where we provide concluding remarks, we sketch out some thoughts in relation to the existential implications for regulatory agencies and the need to reconfigure their capacities in light of new regulatory needs. The need for interdisciplinary openness and technological competence on the part of public bodies will be imminent, to match the radical recombinations and innovations introduced by fintech and beyond.

II. NEW REGULATORY CHALLENGES POSED BY FINTECH

Fintech is understood here to mean a technologically enabled configuration of a financial product or means of delivery of financial services; hence, fintech is not necessarily a new species of financial activity in the eyes of financial regulators. In other words, it is not assumed that fintech-specific financial regulation is either necessary or warranted. Indeed, many financial regulators and policymakers conceive of financial regulation as ideally based on economic function, so that financial products or services that serve the same economic function should be regulated in the same manner. The UK FCA adopts the 'functional regulation'[12]

[10] DW Arner, DA Zetzsche, RP Buckley and JN Barberis, 'FinTech and RegTech: Enabling Innovation While Preserving Financial Stability' (2017) 18 *Georgetown Journal of International Affairs* 47; ST Omarova, 'Dealing with Disruption: Emerging Approaches to Fintech Regulation' (2020) 61 *Washington University Journal of Law & Policy* 25.

[11] T Smith and D Geradin, 'Maintaining a Level Playing Field when Big Tech Disrupts the Financial Services Sector' (2022) 18 *European Competition Journal* 129.

[12] *FSA v Anderson* [2010] EWHC 599, see chapter on the granting of regulatory licences based on the economic function of services offered.

approach inherited from its predecessor the Financial Services Authority, so that its licensing regime is based on specific financial activities[13] and not on the entity of the financial institution concerned. Further, European policymakers' doctrine of 'same risks, same rules'[14] reflects the same policy preference. In this manner, it is arguable that fintech should be regulated according to its essential economic functions and the involvement of technology is a matter of *modus* but not of substance. The underlying regulatory regime applicable to the economic function being served, such as lending, investment intermediation, brokerage etc, should just be extended. This would be the essence of technologically neutral financial regulation,[15] whose regulatory objectives and classifications attain a timeless and normative quality. On the face of it, such application of financial regulation to fintech would also raise no competition implications, especially adverse ones, as the same economic functions in finance are subject to the same rules in a level playing field.

However, the basis for technologically neutral financial regulation, ie, timeless and fully comprehensive regulatory objectives expressed in perfect classifications of financial products and services according to economic function, is arguably flawed.[16] Therefore, financial regulation is essentially not capable of being fully technologically neutral, and in this manner, technological changes to product configuration or delivery of services do matter in relation to the optimality of existing regulation being applied to such products or services. Over the years of its evolution, financial regulation has mapped onto certain business models developed by financial institutions. In brief, two models of financial intermediation are adopted by different entities in financial markets, these entities also having combined and bundled certain products and services over time to attain sectoral recognition for their differences.

First, deposit-taking banks or financial institutions that provide capital guarantee promises perform a full intermediation financial model whereby investors are promised capital safety and sometimes a small guaranteed return on capital. The institutions that make such promises take on the full risks of intermediation of investors' capital, but also keep the full rewards of returns.[17] These institutions often also become social utilities for the safeguarding of money and

[13] Financial Services and Markets Act 2000, s 19, and Schedule 2.

[14] See above (n 7).

[15] eg, ESMA Keynote Speech by Steven Maijoor, 'Cryptoassets: Time to Deliver' (26 February 2019), available at: www.esma.europa.eu/document/keynote-steven-maijoor-crypto-assets-time-deliver. See critically R Brownsword, 'Regulatory Fitness: Fintech, Funny Money, and Smart Contracts' (2019) 20 *European Business Organisations Law Review* 5.

[16] See the discussion on various forms of 'shadow banking' where similar risks are being managed but policymakers ultimately conclude that existing rules, such as banking regulation are inappropriate for products such as money market funds despite very similar financial promises made and risks transformed, in IH-Y Chiu, 'Transcending Regulatory Fragmentation and the Construction of an Economy-Society Discourse: Implications for Regulatory Policy Derived from a Functional Approach to Understanding Shadow Banking' (2016) 42 *Journal of Corporation* Law 327.

[17] *Foley v Hill* [1848] 2 HLC 28.

assets and have a vast social footprint.[18] This allows them to engage with diversified and bundled lines of financial businesses, thus extending their economic, risk and social footprint more widely. Such institutions attract regulatory policy aimed at securing their prudential management in order to avoid failure and damaging public confidence.

Second, financial institutions including those that call themselves 'banks' may engage in a partial intermediation financial model whereby investors are served in terms of expert allocations of their capital, but intermediaries do not promise capital safety and returns may be variable.[19] In this model, intermediaries are not bound by strict capital safety promises but would have to account for the results made on investments. Partial intermediation is often reflected in capital markets activities and investment fund management. Financial regulatory policy for partial intermediation business models focuses on client protection and rights, and prudential concerns may be aimed at qualities such as governance and liquidity rather than the prevention of institutional failure.[20]

The brief account above explains why financial regulators have ultimately developed regulatory regimes that cater for the different implications of full and partial intermediation models and their different combinations by different entities. Full intermediation models are undertaken largely by banking entities and despite the mantra of functional regulation, 'bank regulation' has very much become a recognised regime of financial regulation, ensuring that the full range of entity risks are captured by regulators. For example, in the United Kingdom, the Prudential Regulation Authority (PRA) oversees banks and large insurers due to their full intermediation business models and risk. Other financial institutions are overseen by the FCA whose objectives differ from the PRA's by being more focused on protecting users and well-functioning markets.[21] Despite the mantra of functional regulation, financial regulation is very much dependent on the dominant business models adopted by financial institutions, so that sectoral supervision along the lines of banking, securities services, collective investing, insurance providers, brokerage services, etc have been developed. Firms that engage in their dominant business models often combine financial services in particular manners. In sum, financial regulation and supervision, albeit designed to an extent for specific economic functions, reflects categories

[18] Such as 'too big to fail' banks, discussed in Financial Stability Board, Global Systemically Important Financial Institutions (G-SIFIs), available at: www.fsb.org/work-of-the-fsb/market-and-institutional-resilience/post-2008-financial-crisis-reforms/ending-too-big-to-fail/global-systemically-important-financial-institutions-g-sifis/.

[19] See above (n 6).

[20] The dominant paradigm for financial regulation in capital markets and investment fund management is disclosure-based governance of customer relations and conduct duties where other principal-agent issues are involved, MB Fox, 'Rethinking Disclosure Liability in the Modern Era' (1997) 75 *Washington University Law Quarterly* 903; AM Pacces, 'Financial Intermediation in the Securities Markets Law and Economics of the Conduct of Business Regulation' (2000) 20 *International Review of Law and Economics* 479.

[21] ss 1B–1E, Financial Services and Markets Act 2000 amended in 2012.

of economic functions or activities as adopted by financial services business models observed in the industry. Hence, regulation is often carried out in an entity-based approach, recognising that certain firms would carry out certain dominant activities under an umbrella entity label. Entity-based financial regulation is even more pronounced in the United States (US) as regulatory agencies have been instituted based on established financial services business lines.[22]

The reality of entity-based financial regulation may not be appropriate for fintech firms as the extension of similar regulatory regimes is often over-inclusive and likely to impose more regulatory cost than warranted.[23] This results in an adverse competitive impact for certain fintech firms. The group of fintechs likely to be most adversely affected are challenger or start-up firms that do not have an established anchor (or parent company) in the financial sector and are not part of the BigTech corporate groups.

Challenger fintech firms frequently disintermediate the bundled economic functions carried out by established incumbent financial institutions, by specialising in particular services in a novel and more efficient manner.[24] For example, a challenger firm may focus on disintermediating the payment interface business so that payments can be initiated online, on mobile apps, on peer-to-peer networks, etc, innovating away from established manners of payment interfaces that rely on carrying certain card instruments or having to go through account-holding banks.[25] In this manner, although challenger payment services firms are carrying out a similar economic function as a bank, it would be over-inclusive to impose on them the corpus of bank regulation. This explains why e-money institutions became specifically regulated under more precise and proportional regulatory treatment by the European Union[26] and payment services firms are now treated distinctly under the Second Payment Services Directive of 2015 (PSD2).[27] In the United Kingdom, regulators and policymakers explicitly encourage the creation of challenger banks in order to address the oligopolistic hold by a few high street banks.[28] Even such challenger banks arguably do not deserve to have the same entity-based bank regulation applied to them as their digital only interfaces and limited range of retail services may require specific regulatory thinking about

[22] HE Jackson, 'The Nature of the Fintech Firm' (2020) 61 *Washington University Journal of Law & Policy* 9.

[23] OECD (n 8).

[24] Similar to the process of disruption described in J Bower and C Christensen, 'Disruptive Technologies: Catching the Wave' (1995) 73 *Harvard Business Review* 43, where disruption starts at a 'low' or not spectacular end of the market then mobilised to capture attention at greater scale.

[25] See IH-Y Chiu, 'A New Era in Fintech Payment Innovations? A Perspective from the Institutions and Regulation of Payment Systems' (2017) 9 *Law, Innovation and Technology* 190.

[26] Directive 2009/110/EC on the taking up, pursuit and prudential supervision of the business of electronic money institutions [2009] OJ L267/7.

[27] Directive (EU) 2015/2366 on payment services in the internal market [2015] OJ L337/35.

[28] Bank of England, 'New Bank Start-up Unit' (2022), a facility dedicated to overseeing the induction of potential challenger banks, available at: www.bankofengland.co.uk/prudential-regulation/new-bank-start-up-unit.

their prudential risks.[29] Changes in customer interaction may also trigger different policy thinking about customer protection aspects.[30] Further, in relation to capital markets activities, the regulatory regime catering for securities offerings has tended to assume that large, mature companies go to market and investor protection is designed in comprehensive and costly terms.[31] Such a regulatory regime has always been criticised to be inappropriate for smaller, less mature companies now intermediated by new technologically enabled platforms.[32]

The perception of over-inclusiveness in financial regulation that would apply to fintech firms that innovate upon similar services is arguably a key reason that shapes fintech innovation in ways that evade established regulatory boundaries. In one sense, many challenger-type fintech firms (and also BigTech firms to an extent) are able to come to market or achieve early mover success by exploiting regulatory arbitrage. Commentators have reported that although the success of some fintech firms operating in regulatory grey areas is attributed to regulatory arbitrage, they also seemed to have reached into markets where access and inclusion were previously challenging.[33] It seems that fintech firms enjoy some competitive benefits, regardless of regulatory arbitrage, a point we flesh out more in section III.

In our view, financial regulators like the UK FCA seem to covertly appreciate the potential over-inclusiveness of existing regulatory regimes if applied to fintech.[34] This may explain why the UK FCA waited to regulate online crowdfunding platforms which were in operation a few years ahead of regulation. For example, the peer-to-peer lending platform Zopa has been in operation in the United Kingdom before any specific regulation of online loan or equity crowdfunding came into being.[35] The UK FCA did not strictly extend regulation over Zopa in respect to the intermediation of lending activities, or treat such

[29] Bank of England, 'A Strong and Simple Prudential Framework for Non-Systemic Banks and Building Societies' Discussion Paper, 2021, available at: www.bankofengland.co.uk/prudential-regulation/publication/2021/april/strong-and-simple-framework-banks.

[30] eg, digital fraud on consumers requires specific regulatory responses such as the authorised push payment fraud issue for online and digital banking and payment services, see Siddharth Venkataramakrishnan, 'Regulator to Force UK Banks to Offer Scam Victims Compensation' *Financial Times* (10 May 2022), available at: www.ft.com/content/aabeea7a-324c-4850-a91d-fc41aa6d8802.

[31] SM Solaiman, 'Revisiting Securities Regulation in the Aftermath of the Global Financial Crisis: Disclosure – Panacea or Pandora's Box?' (2013) 14 *Journal of World Investment & Trade* 646; E Howell, 'An Analysis of the Prospectus Regime: The EU Reforms and the "Brexit" Factor' (2018) 15 *European Company and Financial Law Review* 69.

[32] See section III below on online equity crowdfunding.

[33] H Bollaert, F Lopez-de-Silanes and A Schwienbacher, 'Fintech and Access to Finance' (2021) 68 *Journal of Corporate Finance* 101941; G Buchak, G Matvos, T Piskorski and A Seru, 'Fintech, Regulatory Arbitrage, and the Rise of Shadow Banks' (2018) 130 *Journal of Financial Economics* 453.

[34] See below (n 35) paras 2.7–2.13 on the FCA explaining how crowdfunding platforms potentially fall within existing regimes and the benefits of rationalising them under a specialist regulatory regime.

[35] The UK's regulatory regime came into force in 2015, FCA, 'The FCA's Regulatory Approach to Crowdfunding over the Internet, and the Promotion of Non-Readily Realisable Securities by Other Media', Policy Statement PS14/4 (March 2014), available at: www.fca.org.uk/publications/policy-statements/ps14-4-fca%E2%80%99s-regulatory-approach-crowdfunding-over-internet-and.

intermediation as functionally akin to a collective investment scheme,[36] which would need to be approved and comply with regulation designed essentially for investment funds.[37] An evidence-based approach and period of consultation ultimately allowed the UK FCA to introduce bespoke regulation for online crowdfunding platforms.[38]

This is not to say that fintech products and services must give rise to tailor-made regulatory regimes, as such regimes also result in increased regulatory fragmentation[39] Regulatory fragmentation may serve the needs of more effective and fair competition among like business models but may also reflect the capture of regulators by 'glittering' innovators and their pro-competition rhetoric. Such regimes also tend to be market-building and enabling in nature. Compelling categorical neatness in regulatory classifications may minimise regulatory arbitrage among similar economic functions and risks, but may be conservative and contrived, giving rise to the oft-quoted critique of innovation stifling. For example, the US Securities Exchange Commission's uncompromising categorisation of many crypto-tokens as securities raises a number of fit-for-purpose problems[40] and has also distorted the market towards pivoting only to accredited investors.[41] We argue that trends of regulatory fragmentation are observed in both the United Kingdom and European Union, alongside emerging trends of (re)consolidation of financial regulatory regimes for common risks and problems.

III. SPECIALIST REGIMES FOR FINTECH IN FINANCIAL REGULATION

Bespoke regulation for fintech is an approach taken by financial regulators in the United Kingdom and European Union as a response to certain developments that persuade policymakers[42] of distinguishing characteristics and market impact.

[36] Financial Services and Markets Act 2000, s 235. Zopa's business model is to allocate an investor's capital across different loans, in a way undertaking management of a pool of capital on an operational basis for investors expecting a return.

[37] Such as FCA Handbook COLL in relation to non-UCITs retail investor schemes.

[38] See: www.zopa.com/.

[39] A Smoleńska, J Ganderson and A Héritier, 'The Impacts of Technological Innovation on Regulatory Structure: Fintech in Post-Crisis Europe' in A Héritier and MG Schoeller (eds), *Governing Finance in Europe: A Centralisation of Rule-Making?* (Edward Elgar, 2020).

[40] J Rohr and A Wright, 'Blockchain-based Token Sales, Initial Coin Offerings, and the Democratization of Public Capital Markets' (2019) 70 *Hastings Law Journal* 463; L Rinaudo Cohen, '"Ain't Misbehavin": An Examination of Broadway Tickets and Blockchain Tokens' (2019) 65 *Wayne Law Review* 81, distinguishing crypto-tokens from securities, but see U Rodrigues, 'Semi-Public Offerings? Pushing the Boundaries of Securities Law' (2018), available at: ssrn.com/abstract=3242205; SEC, 'Framework for Investment Contract Analysis of Digital Assets' (2019), available at: www.sec.gov/corpfin/framework-investment-contract-analysis-digital-assets.

[41] SAFT or Simple Agreement for Future Tokens, developed as a template for ICOs clarifying that sales are of tokens for future use, saftproject.com/.

[42] eg, FCA PS14/4 (2014) (n 35).

In this manner, it seems contrived to subject certain fintech innovations to existing financial regulatory regimes.[43] Regulators see the introduction of the bespoke regime as enabling in nature, legitimating and helping to build out the fintech sector, while addressing erstwhile regulatory objectives such as retail investor/customer protection.[44] This enabling role takes over from market-based governance, where the development of credible voluntary standards can be slow.[45] The protective side of regulation also provides for standards underpinning market confidence, reinforcing the enabling effect.

We introduce two brief case studies to explain the pathway to bespoke fintech regulation. First, the rise of online crowdfunding platforms in the early 2010s took place in an unregulated landscape, although commentators took the view that investment firm regulation in the European Union, such as the Markets in Financial Instruments Directive,[46] would functionally capture the investment activities conducted on these platforms.[47] Online crowdfunding platforms comprise many types,[48] where a digital platform operator would be able to bring together those who seek to provide funds and those who seek to receive funds, in multi-sided markets. The supply side of the market could be retail, institutional or even corporate providers, while the demand side could be personal or business recipients. Platforms match C2C (consumer to consumer), C2B (consumer to business), B2C (business to consumer) and B2B (business to business) funding. They can do so at various levels of intermediation or disintermediation, from providing a mere information presentation and choice service, to intelligent matching, or even fund management, such as slicing up investors' capital and allocating it to minimise portfolio risk.[49] In this respect, credit intermediation activities on online crowdfunding platforms have changed in character in terms of supply source, the nature of the demand side accessing such services, the modus of credit underwriting (in terms of differences in technologically enabled information services underpinning such underwriting), and the modus of credit intermediation, with platforms performing an array of gatekeeping, diligence

[43] Explanatory Memorandum to European Commission, 'Proposal for a Regulation of the European Parliament and of the Council on European Crowdfunding Service Providers (ECSP) for Business' (2018) para 1, available at: eur-lex.europa.eu/legal-content/EN/TXT/?uri=CELEX%3A52018PC0113.

[44] A Minto, M Voelkerling and M Wulff, 'Separating Apples From Oranges: Identifying Threats to Financial Stability Originating from Fintech' (2017) 12 *Capital Markets Law Journal* 428.

[45] eg, P2PFA, the trade association for loan-based crowdfunding platforms, has not taken off to provide robust industry standardisation.

[46] Directive 2014/65/EU of the European Parliament and of the Council of 15 May 2014 on markets in financial instruments and amending Directive 2002/92/EC and Directive 2011/61/EU [2014] OJ L173/349.

[47] G Ferranini, 'Regulating Fintech: Crowdfunding and Beyond' (2017) 2 *European Economy* 121.

[48] Donation-based, loan-based, investment or reward-based, see F de Pascalis, 'Fintech Credit Firms: Prospects and Uncertainties' in IH-Y Chiu and G Deipenbrock (eds), *Routledge Handbook of Financial Technology and the Law* (Routledge, 2021).

[49] Such as by Zopa.

and managing services.[50] The introduction of structural changes in terms of platforms' roles, as well as new user protection needs[51] have been recognised by UK and EU policymakers.

The United Kingdom introduced bespoke regulation for online crowdfunding platforms starting in 2014. The UK FCA required a minimal set of platform governance such as prudential regulation to limit risk creation on platforms, as well as investor protection through mandatory advice for retail participants on the supply side and caps on maximum amounts of investment they can make.[52] The EU's Crowdfunding Regulation was only finalised in 2020,[53] and it adopted some different approaches in terms of placing more duties on platform operators to ensure adequate standardised disclosure to supply-side investors, and harmonising platforms' duties of governance and conduct to an extent with the EU Markets in Financial Instruments Directive 2014 (MiFID) standards. The EU Regulation recognises that the platform may be the most powerful corporate player in the landscape and establishes a new form of sectoral regulation for platforms. The EU Regulation also provides for a new form of 'shared responsibility' on the part of investors on the supply side to show evidence of knowledge and competence before participating in the market. This reflects the balance achieved in a lighter form of regulation overall for crowdfunding products in order not to stifle the sector.[54] Although these regimes came about after extensive evidence gathering and consultation, the sector continues to change. Platforms may partner with incumbents, or in the case of Zopa, the online crowdlending platform, attain a full banking licence in the United Kingdom. It may be queried whether regulation is able to capture the reintermediation dynamics that are occurring as fintech firms attempt to capture the market share and revenues of incumbents. It may also be queried to what extent the sectoral distinction for fintech firms, now recognised, is used as an advantageous foothold to compete unfairly against incumbents. On the other hand, fintech firms may complain that they are prevented from competing fairly in other respects. For example, the government favours accreditation of incumbent banks, compared with the few accredited crowdlending platforms, for government-backed lending to support business recovery in the wake of the Covid-19 pandemic.[55] Borrowers

[50] Platforms' array of intermediation or gatekeeping activities, JA Ande and ZG Kavame Eroglu, 'Could New Zealand's Equity Crowdfunding Regulations Be the Model for the Developing World?' (2021) 29 *New Zealand Universities Law Review* 557.

[51] D Ahern, 'Regulatory Arbitrage in a Fintech World: Devising an Optimal EU Regulatory Response to Crowdlending' (2018) 3 *Journal of Business Law* 193.

[52] FCA Handbook COBS 4.7.10.

[53] Regulation (EU) 2020/1503 of the European Parliament and of the Council of 7 October 2020 on European crowdfunding service providers for business, and amending Regulation (EU) 2017/1129 and Directive (EU) 2019/1937 [2020] OJ L347/1.

[54] E Macchiavello, 'Disintermediation in Fund-raising: Marketplace Investing Platforms and EU Financial Regulation' in IH-Y Chiu and G Deipenbrock (eds), *Routledge Handbook of Financial Technology and Law* (Routledge, 2021).

[55] de Pascalis (n 48). On the Coronavirus Business Interruption Loan Scheme, see: www.british-business-bank.co.uk/ourpartners/coronavirus-business-interruption-loan-scheme-cbils-2/.

from regulated credit institutions and from crowdlending platforms are treated differently, exacerbating fintechs firms' disadvantage.[56] For example, the right for borrowers to take payment holidays during the pandemic lock-down applied to regulated lenders but not to borrowers on online crowdfunding platforms.[57] This resulted in each platform developing its own rules to cater for lenders' and borrowers' emergency needs. The continued unavailability of the Financial Compensation Services guarantee for customers of platforms also remains a disadvantageous policy for investors.

The second case study concerns bespoke regulation in the European Union for initial coin offerings which have exploded since 2017,[58] although the United Kingdom is still debating the matter.[59] Entrepreneurs who have an idea to develop an application for blockchain technology that facilitates peer-to-peer economic activity usually through automated code protocols called 'smart contracts',[60] can make direct offers of yet to be developed digital tokens to funders. Funders provide financial support with a view to bringing the project to life, and afterwards to enjoying the multiple features that the digital tokens provide in connection with the blockchain project. Tokens are designed to confer rights to digital goods and services and even participation and governance in the blockchain community.[61] The development of secondary markets for

[56] Responsible lending obligations for regulated lenders are not applicable to platforms or participating lenders; see also, CK Odinet, 'Predatory Fintech and the Politics of Banking' (2021) 106 *Iowa Law Review* 1739.

[57] FCA, Mortgages and coronavirus: information for consumers, available at: www.fca.org.uk/consumers/mortgages-coronavirus-consumers (updated 19 June 2020); Coronavirus: information for consumers on personal loans, credit cards, overdrafts, motor finance and other forms of credit (updated 1 July 2020), available at: www.fca.org.uk/news/press-releases/fca-confirms-further-support-consumer-credit-customers. Payment holiday rights extended from early November 2020: www.fca.org.uk/news/press-releases/fca-announces-further-proposals-support-mortgage-borrowers-impacted-coronavirus; www.fca.org.uk/news/press-releases/fca-announces-proposals-further-support-consumer-credit-borrowers-impacted-coronavirus.

[58] European Commission, 'Proposal for a Regulation of the European Parliament and of the Council on Markets in Crypto-assets, and amending Directive (EU) 2019/1937', available at: eur-lex.europa.eu/legal-content/EN/TXT/?uri=CELEX%3A52020PC0593, arts 4–14. The Council and Parliament have agreed to a final text on the Regulation, TBC.

[59] HM Treasury, 'UK Regulatory Approach to Cryptoassets and Stablecoins: Consultation and Call for Evidence' (January 2021), available at: www.gov.uk/government/consultations/uk-regulatory-approach-to-cryptoassets-and-stablecoins-consultation-and-call-for-evidence. The government's response in April 2022 indicates its wish to study further a comprehensive crypto-regulatory regime, see: www.gov.uk/government/news/government-sets-out-plan-to-make-uk-a-global-cryptoasset-technology-hub. See earlier call for a bespoke regulatory approach in *The Kalifa Review of UK Fintech* (2021), available at: www.gov.uk/government/publications/the-kalifa-review-of-uk-fintech.

[60] N Szabo, 'Smart Contracts: Building Blocks for Digital Markets' (1996), available at: www.fon.hum.uva.nl/rob/Courses/InformationInSpeech/CDROM/Literature/LOTwinterschool2006/szabo.best.vwh.net/smart_contracts_2.html. For a layman's version, see: www.coindesk.com/information/ethereum-smart-contracts-work.

[61] S Díaz-Santiago, LM Rodríguez-Henríquez and D Chakraborty, 'A Cryptographic Study of Tokenization Systems' (2016) 15 *International Journal of Information Security* 413; C Goforth, 'Securities Treatment of Tokenized Offerings under US Law' (2018) 46 *Pepperdine Law Review* 405.

pre-sold tokens, however, also means that tokens have investment value.[62] The market for such cryptotokens or cryptoassets is not insignificant, but as transactions are mostly in private cryptocurrency, this market is not financialised in a mainstream manner,[63] resulting in many regulators delineating their regulatory oversight to exclude them.[64] EU policymakers, however, see the opportunity to mobilise a potentially beneficial market that may serve small business financing in the blockchain universe and are providing a light touch regulatory regime to standardise the legitimation of cryptoasset issuances and investor protection.

The bespoke approach in the European Union is still controversial in terms of whether there is sufficient distinction between cryptoassets and securities or investment assets to warrant lighter regulatory treatment.[65] Further, commentators raise doubt that the Regulation fully captures innovations in decentralised finance (DeFi), a broad array of blockchain-enabled automated financial protocols and activities that are currently unregulated.[66] This also brings to question the aptness of bespoke treatment for cryptoassets, namely are the products of cryptoassets sufficiently distinct to warrant a bespoke sectoral approach that would be lasting, or is the blockchain technology that underlies them the truly distinguishing aspect? The latter is described to be structurally disruptive,[67] but this technology permeates many forms of business, including finance. Hence, it is queried if it is more appropriate to reconsolidate regulatory policy around the deployment of blockchain technology more broadly.[68]

The critical review of bespoke regulatory regimes is not intended to be disparaging toward the regulatory efforts made to build out new challenger market sectors. However, even when policymakers attempt to transcend the existing limits of entity-based regulatory regimes, limits in financial regulation reforms remain. Bespoke financial regulatory regimes raise issues regarding establishing (new) scope of coverage, under-inclusion or over-inclusion as business models are being developed. Further, standards for enabling markets may underserve

[62] P Maume and M Fromberger, 'Regulation of Initial Coin Offerings: Reconciling US and EU Securities Laws' (2019) 19 *Chicago Journal of International Law* 548; A Collomb, P de Fillippi and K Sok, 'Blockchain Technology and Financial Regulation: A Risk-Based Approach to the Regulation of ICOs' (2019) 10 *European Journal of Risk Regulation* 263.

[63] Argument against regulating, G Ferranini and P Giudici, 'Digital Offerings and Mandatory Disclosure: A Market-based Critique of MiCA' (2021) ECGI Working Paper, available at: ssrn.com/abstract_id=3914768.

[64] FCA, 'Guidance on Cryptoassets Policy Statement' (July 2019), available at: www.fca.org.uk/publication/policy/ps19-22.pdf.

[65] DA Zetzsche, F Annunziata, DW Arner and RP Buckley, 'The Markets in Crypto-Assets Regulation (MICA) and the EU Digital Finance Strategy' (2020), available at: papers.ssrn.com/sol3/papers.cfm?abstract_id=3725395 call for clarification in terms of crypto-asset definition.

[66] G Maia and J Vieira dos Santos, 'MiCA and DeFi' (2021), available at: ssrn.com/abstract=3875355.

[67] S Davidson, P de Fillippi and J Potts, 'Blockchain and the Economic Institutions of Capitalism' (2018) 14 *Journal of Institutional Economics* 639.

[68] IH-Y Chiu, *Regulating the Crypto-economy: Business Transformations and Financialisation* (Hart Publishing, 2021).

the needs for protection, while the characteristics of supply and demand sides are also being figured out. It is also inevitable that bespoke regimes do not stand alone and need to be comparatively considered with existing regulatory regimes in relation to where advantages and disadvantages lie for both challengers and incumbents. It is possible to conceive of bespoke regulation as transitory or experimental. For example, after regulating loan-based and equity-based online crowdfunding differently, the UK FCA has made harmonising adjustments between the two regimes. Regulators more than ever need to consider when regulatory fragmentation serves certain purposes and when such fragmentation may need to be revisited.

Next, we interrogate the rise of BigTech in finance which raises pressing issues for considering if financial regulation should reconsolidate around the risks they pose, instead of fragmenting along more specialist lines.

IV. THE ENTRY OF BIGTECH INTO FINTECH: REGULATORY ARBITRAGE, COMPETITION CONCERNS AND THE CORRESPONDING REGULATORY RESPONSES

This section first explores the challenges brought about by the advent of BigTech into fintech (section 4.A). Next, it examines the corresponding, financial regulation and BigTech-specific, regulatory responses that have recently emerged (section 4.B).

A. Challenges

We identify two main challenges. First, the risk of regulatory arbitrage. Second, the competition risks that arise from the various competitive strategies and business models adopted by BigTech in finance. Each will be examined in turn.

As already discussed above, many authorities around the globe explicitly adopt a 'same business, same risks, same rules' approach to fintech providers, including those with a platform-based business model. In other words, they apply existing licensing, regulatory reporting, deposit insurance, capital and liquidity requirements to fintech and BigTech platforms.[69] This effort to fit new models into existing regulatory schemes, so as to make sure that entities carrying out the same activity follow the same set of rules (regardless of how they carry them out) is explained by the need to avoid regulatory arbitrage.

However, the recent foray of BigTech into finance and the challenges surrounding its regulation reveal that the promotion of a level playing field between incumbents and new entrants and the promotion of, mostly, innovation-based

[69] JC Crisanto, J Ehrentraud and M Fabian, 'Big Techs in Finance: Regulatory Approaches and Policy Options' (March 2021) FSI Briefs No 12.

competition do not always go hand-in-hand.[70] Primarily because of the variety of business models characterising their operation, BigTech cannot be easily pigeonholed into existing regulatory frameworks. This creates opportunities for regulatory arbitrage. For example, differences in the regulatory treatment of banks and non-bank financial institutions may have an implication for what type of financial services BigTechs choose to provide and how to provide them. Banks and certain non-bank financial institutions are subject to microprudential requirements based on internationally agreed standards.[71] These make them subject to minimum capital obligations calculated on the basis of their consolidated balance sheets, and supervisors must review the main activities of the group as a whole. In addition, banks identified as global systemically important banks are subject to additional prudential measures to mitigate the problems which would emanate from their failure.[72] In cases where a BigTech entity operates through partnerships or joint ventures with incumbents and provides its financial services in collaboration with financial entities, it will normally not need any licence. This, however, can be problematic, since the unbundling of financial services across multiple players can render unclear who is accountable for which risk or activity and, relatedly, it may encourage risk-taking behaviour when it comes to screening and monitoring activities that could impact the financial condition of the firms involved. More concretely, with regard to financial stability, partnerships with incumbents could diffuse accountability and promote excessive risk-taking when BigTech firms provide only the customer-facing layer of the value chain while not bearing any underwritten risks themselves.

Before we turn to examine the competition risks, it is useful to first appreciate the advent of BigTech into finance and the various competitive strategies they have implemented. This is crucial for better understanding the competition concerns that call for BigTech-specific regulation. While BigTech firms do not operate primarily in financial services, they offer them as part of a much wider set of activities. BigTech firms' involvement in finance started with payments and they are now also involved in the provision of credit banking, crowdfunding, asset management and insurance. BigTech firms provide their financial services either in competition with traditional financial institutions (head-to-head competition), raising funds and lending them to consumers and firms, or in partnerships with financial institutions, with BigTech firms only providing the customer-facing layer (eg, Apple/Goldman Sachs and Amazon/JPMorgan Chase to offer credit cards). Traditional financial regulation, even in a functional manner, may not fully capture the entity-based risks posed by BigTech as

[70] F Restoy, 'Fintech Regulation: How to Achieve a Level Playing Field' (2021) FSI Occasional Paper No 17.

[71] See the Basel III regulatory framework, available at: www.bis.org/bcbs/basel3.htm#:~:text=Basel%20III%20is%20an%20internationally,and%20risk%20management%20of%20banks.

[72] See discussion in IH-Y Chiu and J Wilson, *Banking Law and Regulation* (Oxford University Press 2019) chs 8 and 9.

well as govern their tremendous power. Apart from providing financial services themselves, BigTech firms are also investing in financial institutions outside their groups. When competing with traditional financial institutions, BigTech firms can either effectively become banking intermediaries, bundle their offers, and exploit economies of scope using different activities within their platforms, or they can become a multi-sided intermediary platform. For example, as intermediaries they may offer cheap credit to customers who subscribe to their online services outbidding incumbents with a narrower product portfolio.[73] When acting as a multi-sided platform, they may benefit from network effects by bringing together lenders and borrowers (marketplace model). In the latter case, the advent of BigTech's platform-based business model in financial services can change the market structure. As Padilla explains, banks may need to join these platforms in order to reach out to borrowers and 'borrowers who have joined a marketplace that is participated by many banks or other lenders will likely benefit from increased banking competition'.[74] This is in contrast to the status quo where each borrower is de facto locked into the bank with which it has a relationship.

Where platforms collect large amounts of data for a variety of different business lines, this may lead to network effects and economies of scale and scope. Also, BigTech firms have the potential to become dominant through the advantages afforded by the so-called data analytics, network externalities and interwoven activities loop (otherwise referred to as 'data-network-activities loop' or 'DNA loop'), raising competition concerns.[75] Once a BigTech has attracted a sufficient mass of users on both sides of its platform, network externalities kick in, accelerating its growth and increasing returns to scale leading to a 'winner-takes-all' situation.[76] Every additional user creates value for all others – more buyers attract more sellers and vice versa. The more users a platform has, the more data it generates. More data, in turn, provides a better basis for data analytics which enhance existing services and attracts more users. As an example, payment services generate transaction data, network externalities facilitate the interaction among users, and this helps BigTech firms in other activities such as wealth management generating more engagement with existing users and attracting new ones.[77] Thus, network externalities are stronger on platforms

[73] J Padilla, 'Big Tech "Banks", Financial Stability and Regulation' (20 April 2020), available at: papers.ssrn.com/sol3/papers.cfm?abstract_id=3580888.

[74] ibid, 5.

[75] For instance, in the UK, Google and Facebook have already been found dominant in the online advertising market. See UK Competition and Markets Authority (2020), 'Online Platforms and Digital Advertising Market Study', 5: 'Both are now protected by such strong incumbency advantages – including network effects, economies of scale and unmatchable access to user data – that potential rivals can no longer compete on equal terms'.

[76] P Belleflamme and M Peitz, *The Economics of Platforms: Concepts and Strategy* (Cambridge University Press, 2021).

[77] For an analysis see K Croxson, J Frost, L Gambacorta and T Valletti, 'Platform-based Business Models and Financial Inclusion' (10 January 2022) BIS Working Papers No 986, available at: www.bis.org/publ/work986.pdf.

that offer a broader range of services. One would expect the source and type of data and related DNA synergies to vary across BigTech platforms, depending on their main focus and activity. For example, BigTech firms with a focus on social media have data on individual preferences as well as their network of connections. E-commerce platforms collect data from vendors, and combine financial and consumer preferences information. This data can be invaluable in credit scoring models.

While BigTech's DNA loop can lower the barriers to the provision of financial services by reducing transaction costs, they could at the same time introduce new risks if the DNA loop is left unchecked. BigTech's market power and business models raise specific issues such as customer protection as part of financial regulation, as well as general problems in terms of market power and the governance of data privacy. Significant network effects may enable BigTech firms to become gatekeepers, 'allowing them to leverage their dominant position in a given market to exert influence over its functioning'.[78] This may include control over who can enter the market, who receives what kind of data and how the market operates. Their sphere of influence in one market often extends to other adjacent markets connected to it. Furthermore, BigTech firms' large and captive user base allows them to scale up quickly in market segments that are outside their core business. Once a captive userbase has been established, potential competitors may have little scope to build rival platforms.

Dominant platforms can consolidate their position by raising entry barriers and over time become bottlenecks for a host of services. There is the potential for various anticompetitive practices. First, price discrimination, including through the use of big data. Once their dominant position in data is established, BigTech companies can divide a customer population in categories each charged a different price representing the maximum price each individual is willing to pay.[79] By extracting more of the consumer surplus by those willing to pay more, prices can also be reduced for those able to pay less. But such price discrimination may overlap with protected categories such as gender and race.[80]

Second, anticompetitive behaviour, such as creating barriers to entry and 'enveloping' competitors. Envelopment refers to entry by one platform provider into another provider's market by bundling its functionality with that of the target, to leverage shared user relationships.[81] To explain this further, when BigTech firms have accumulated large datasets about individual consumers they

[78] Crisanto et al (n 69) 4.

[79] O Bar-Grill, 'Algorithmic Price Discrimination When Demand Is a Function of Both Preferences and (Mis)Perceptions' (2019) 86 *University of Chicago Law Review* 217; M Stucke, 'Should We Be Concerned About Data-opolies?' (2018) 2 *Georgetown Law Technology Review* 275.

[80] See L Sweeney, 'Discrimination in Online Ad Delivery' (2013) 11 *Communications of the ACM* 44.

[81] T Eisenmann, G Parker and M van Alstyne. 'Platform Envelopment' (2011) 32 *Strategic Management Journal* 1270.

can combine them with payments data in order to deliver products that traditional banks cannot replicate. Banks then risk being enveloped by the platform operator who can now bundle services that cannot be replicated by traditional players, such as banks, ultimately leading to market tipping in the banking sector too.[82] In principle, financial services can also help platform operators to tip other markets. For example, if a consumer is buying a car or a refrigerator, and a platform operator offering financial services like loans or insurance knows consumer preferences and creditworthiness in real time, this may help it to tip these markets as well. A platform operator may also steer users towards its own (or its preferred partners') financial services, for instance by putting these offers at the top of a list of offers. Or it may favour its own products and try to obtain higher margins by making financial institutions' access to prospective clients via their platforms more costly.

Third, the use of sophisticated algorithms by BigTech may impede competition 'on the merits', for example a platform operator might self-preference its own goods and services over the offerings of competitors on its platform. In its recently published paper the UK Competition and Markets Authority (UK CMA) also discusses how algorithmic design in search ranking practices might achieve self-preferencing outcomes leading to foreclosure.[83]

Fourth, there exists also the risk of data privacy violations. Unlike the case of credit reporting, where the data can only be accessed by licensed entities and only upon customer consent and for authorised purposes, in the case of BigTech the data those firms capture are far more granular and touch several aspects of one's personal life, thus increasing the impact of privacy-related violations.

Differentiation strategies and multi-homing can temper platforms' winner-takes-all dynamic. For example, a platform offering banking services may distinguish itself by specialising in enhanced privacy protection. Multi-homing, ie, the possibility of users to utilise more than one platform at the time,[84] also plays a role in constraining the winner-takes-all dynamic. However, this is not easy to achieve in practice, because of behavioural biases such as default bias, or consumer inertia in switching.[85] Hence the need for regulation to promote, inter alia, interoperability, as we shall explain in the section below.

Having explored the competition risks arising from the entry of BigTech in finance, we can now turn to the regulatory responses. The remainder of this chapter surveys the regulatory approaches in competition, general and financial

[82] J Padilla and M de la Mano, 'Big Tech Banking' (2018) 14 *Journal of Competition Law & Economics* 494.

[83] CMA (2021), 'Algorithms: How They Can Reduce Competition and Harm consumers', available at: www.gov.uk/government/publications/algorithms-how-they-can-reduce-competition-and-harm-consumers/algorithms-how-they-can-reduce-competition-and-harm-consumers.

[84] JP Choi, 'Tying in Two-Sided Markets with Multi-Homing' (2010) 58 *Journal of Industrial Economics* 607.

[85] D Kahneman, *Thinking, Fast and Slow* (Allen Lane, 2011).

regulation in order to determine to what extent a holistic or joint approach is perceived by regulators to address the mixture of objectives in regulating BigTech and fintech firms' emergence in finance. We argue that the response is generally reactive and can be improved.

B. Regulatory Responses

While BigTech firms are subject to several regulations, the regulatory approach up to now is mostly activity based and does not seem to pay due attention to the unique features of their business models and the corresponding risks. Because platform-based business models differ from traditional modes of offering financial services, there is the potential for regulatory arbitrage. Finance-specific regulations and cross-industry regulations are geared towards individual legal entities within BigTech groups or the specific activities they perform and not the risks from possible spillover effects across all the activities BigTechs perform. Further, this activity-specific approach in financial regulation has already not coped well with financial supermarkets, which are financial services firms with multiple lines of businesses and scale, performing regulatory arbitrage among different types of financial services to benefit from most favourable regulatory treatment. Hence, the mixing of financial activities with other non-financial operations and activities in the BigTech context will further challenge financial regulators. This may lead to some activities and risks falling into the cracks of existing regulation and supervision. Moreover, the current policy approach falls short of allowing for recognition of the potential systemic impact of incidents in BigTech operations. There may therefore be the need to complement the activity-based approach with an entity-based approach, particularly when BigTech platforms become systemically important.[86]

Another approach to address the disruption caused by the entry of fintech and BigTech firms, adopted by many countries around the globe is to set up innovation facilitators, such as sandboxes, innovation hubs and accelerators.[87] These can help reduce uncertainty about financial regulation, such as licensing expectations, but they fail to address the issues brought about by BigTech. Other countries have adopted new licensing regimes to account for new entities and activities and/or have updated existing regulations. This has included defining new types of licences, for example for virtual banks that allow for digital-only banks with targeted regulatory requirements.[88]

[86] See Crisanto et al (n 69) 10.

[87] 'Regulatory Sandboxes and Innovation Hubs for Fintech', available at: www.europarl.europa.eu/RegData/etudes/STUD/2020/652752/IPOL_STU(2020)652752_EN.pdf.

[88] eg, China's first virtual bank, aiBank, a joint venture between China CITIC Bank and tech player Baidu offers financial solutions to underbanked younger customers.

Other approaches include enhancing competition through application programming interfaces (APIs) to enhance data portability. The most salient case comes from the relatively recent Open Banking initiative that was introduced in the United Kingdom in 2018.[89] Open Banking allows users to securely share banking data with third parties through application programming interfaces pursuant to PSD2 thus allowing competitors to offer services based on the same user data. The UK CMA requires banks to adopt and maintain a common and open API standard that permits authorised intermediaries to access information about bank services, prices and service quality. Among the many firms enrolled in Open Banking, there are several fintech firms developing innovative solutions helping consumers manage their cash flow more effectively or improve how they save.[90] However, under the General Data Protection Regulation (GDPR), BigTech platforms are obliged to facilitate data portability only where it is *technically feasible*, thus allowing them to retain economic sovereignty over their customers' data.[91] Hence, BigTech platforms benefit from a *regulatory asymmetry* when competing with established banks in Europe.

Thus, the foray of platform-based business models in finance requires more proactive, regulatory in nature policies to address the potential risk of the various anticompetitive practices discussed above. Prominent among these is data sharing, data unbundling and interoperability, all contemplated in the Digital Markets Act (DMA), a legislative proposal of the European Commission to deal with dominant digital companies (defined as 'gatekeepers') that was recently adopted by the EU Parliament.[92] Article 6(1)(h) of the DMA proposal requires gatekeepers to provide

> effective portability of data generated through the activity of a business user or end user, and shall, in particular, provide tools for end-users to facilitate the exercise of data portability, in line with Regulation EU 2016/679, including by the provision of continuous and real-time access.

Article 5(a) of the DMA limits the scope for bundling banking data with data stemming from, say, a search engine, unless there is consent. However, it is not entirely clear what is meant by 'specific choice' and 'consent' according to Recital 36. Finally, platforms are interoperable if the users of one platform are

[89] A Brener, 'EU Payment Services Regulation and International Developments' in IH-Y Chiu and G Deipenbrock (eds), *Routledge Handbook of Financial Technology and Law* (Routledge, 2021).

[90] Plum offers a savings app that links to a person's bank account, analyses their income, expenses and spending habits and helps to set aside an affordable amount for savings. It can also help people review their spending, understand where they may be overpaying on bills and engage a utility switching service.

[91] Regulation (EU) 2016/679 of the European Parliament and of the Council of 27 April 2016 on the protection of natural persons with regard to the processing of personal data and on the free movement of such data (General Data Protection Regulation) [2016] OJ L119/1, Art 20 (2).

[92] 'Proposal of the Commission of 15 December 2020 for a Regulation of the European Parliament and of the Council on contestable and fair markets in the digital sector (Digital Markets Act)' COM(2020) 842 final (hereafter DMA).

able to interact with the users of another platform. Seen this way, interoperability plays a similar role to multi-homing, in that the implications of choosing a particular platform do not prevent users from interacting with users on the other platform. For example, interoperability in payment systems can facilitate competition and lead to greater efficiency in payments. Interoperability may have to be supported by *ex ante* competition policy tools. Indeed, interoperability is one of the key proposals in the DMA. Provisions are made for gatekeepers to ensure interconnection and interoperability with competing core platform services providers: gatekeepers should grant access to technical functionalities used in the provision of ancillary services,[93] grant access to data held by the gatekeeper and provider or generated by businesses and users,[94] and in the case of search engines, grant access to search-related data.[95]

In the United Kingdom, the Digital Markets Taskforce has recommended the creation of a Digital Markets Unit (now established in shadow form) with new powers to support greater competition in digital markets.[96] The Taskforce has proposed that there should be an ex ante code of conduct for the most powerful of digital firms. In the United States, the House of Representatives Subcommittee on Antitrust, Commercial, and Administrative Law issued a list of recommendations to regulate BigTech platforms so as to reduce anticompetitive behaviour.[97] In China, the State Administration for Market Regulation in November 2020 published draft guidelines to prevent monopolistic behaviour by internet platforms,[98] which were finalised and issued by the Anti-Monopoly Commission of the State Council in February 2021.[99] Together, these measures show that a more proactive, entity-based approach to antitrust policy for platforms is being adopted globally, in many cases defining new frameworks and institutions to keep markets competitive.

V. TRENDS TOWARDS REGULATORY (RE)CONSOLIDATION AND LEVELLING THE PLAYING FIELD?

This section discusses the trends towards regulatory 'stock-taking' and 'reconsolidation' of regulatory governance in response to market and structural changes introduced by fintech and BigTech. These may apply beyond the fintech sectors

[93] DMA, 6 (1)(f).

[94] DMA, 6(1)(i).

[95] DMA, 6 (1)(j).

[96] See Digital Markets Taskforce (2020), available at: www.gov.uk/cma-cases/digital-markets-taskforce.

[97] See: judiciary.house.gov/uploadedfiles/competition_in_digital_markets.pdf?utm_campaign=4493-519.

[98] For a full Chinese version of the draft guidelines, see: www.samr.gov.cn/hd/zjdc/202011/t20201109_323234.html.

[99] For the Chinese version, see: gkml.samr.gov.cn/nsjg/fldj/202102/t20210207_325967.html.

as new technologies raise governance issues in a cross-cutting manner for many businesses, such as in relation to digitalisation, cloud computing, platformisation, use of machine learning in artificial intelligence systems and blockchain technology enabling peer-to-peer automated transactions. We see reconsolidating regulations as a means of addressing similar digital commercial risks across sectors in a consistent manner, including in finance. On the one hand, these may fill gaps in financial regulation where the nature of risks emanating from a financial activity is not merely financial in nature but relates to cross-cutting issues such as data governance and privacy. On the other hand, this trend may create a more regulatory patchwork in addition to sectoral regulation. Further, such reconsolidating regulation also needs to be mindful of a level playing field for digital services and should not be pitched at a level only targeted at BigTech. In this section, we briefly survey a number of reconsolidating regulatory proposals from the European Union.

The GDPR is often regarded as a key legislative endeavour of cross-cutting nature, ensuring common standards in business handling of personal data and data subjects' horizontal, cross-cutting rights.[100] The GDPR gives customers more control over their data compared with Open Banking regulations. To the extent that they entail the transfer of data ownership from BigTech firms to customers, both regulations can promote market contestability. At the same time, however, they limit the scope of data sharing. Open Banking regulations restrict the range of data that can be shared (financial transaction data) as well as the institutions among which such data can be shared (accredited deposit-taking institutions). Similarly, the GDPR requires a customer's active consent before a firm can use their personal data. The Platform to Business Regulation (P2B Regulation)[101] aims to promote transparency and fairness of all 'intermediation services' and search engines linking businesses and corporate websites with consumers, including on access to data. The recently agreed Data Governance Act[102] will further provide rights of data portability between businesses as well as government and business. The recently agreed DMA[103] addresses the technological innovation of platformisation, and the techniques deployed by platforms in relation to big data, bundling and cross-selling or tying of services or products, profiling and marketing, etc.

[100] ME Kaminsky, 'Binary Governance: Lessons from the GDPR's Approach to Algorithmic Accountability' (2019) 92 *Southern California Law Review* 1529.

[101] Regulation (EU) 2019/1150 of the European Parliament and of the Council of 20 June 2019 on promoting fairness and transparency for business users of online intermediation services [2019] OJ L186/57.

[102] 'Proposal for a Regulation of the European Parliament and of the Council on European data governance (Data Governance Act)' (2020), available at: eur-lex.europa.eu/legal-content/EN/TXT/?uri=CELEX%3A52020PC0767.

[103] 'Proposal for a Regulation of the European Parliament and of the Council on contestable and fair markets in the digital sector (Digital Markets Act)' (December 2020), available at: eur-lex.europa.eu/legal-content/en/TXT/?qid=1608116887159&uri=COM%3A2020%3A842%3AFIN.

That said, sectoral specific differences continue to be maintained such as in terms of financial data portability in the PSD2[104] and in the Regulation of online crowdfunding platforms.[105]

The proposed Digital Services Act[106] (DSA) provides cross-cutting rules for a range of digital services providers from web-hosting services to online platforms, reserving a definition of very large platforms upon which more regulatory obligations are imposed. The proposed Act sets out common obligations of conduct of business and standardises for platforms certain consumer protection measures such as removal of illegal content,[107] transparency of advertising,[108] instituting complaint and redress mechanisms.[109] Very large platforms are obliged to be subject to regulations on their organisational governance and controls.[110] These cross-cutting rules provide a set of consistent expectations for conduct of digital business. However, one queries if the obligations have been distilled from the strongest sectoral regulations found in EU legislation, such as in MiFID. The investor protection provisions such as complaints and redress handling and oversight of third-party suppliers are relatively strong[111] and seem to have influenced the DSA, although it is arguable that outsourcing regulations in finance are more prescriptive and detailed. In this manner, cross-cutting regulation may not be genuinely cross-cutting if it results largely in an exercise of upgrading for consistency across sectors.

The proposed Regulation for artificial intelligence (AI) systems[112] purports to set out governance expectations of systems with unacceptable, high, limited or minimal risks to persons and society, but regulatory delineations as well as governance standards and design are subject to controversy and critique.[113] When introduced, this cross-cutting legislation will affect not only fintech

[104] See O Borgogno and G Colangelo, 'Data Sharing and Interoperability Through APIs: Insights from European Regulatory Strategy' (2018), ssrn.com/abstract=3288460; 'Data, Innovation and Competition in Finance: The Case of the Access to Account Rule' (2020) 31 *European Business Law Review* 573.

[105] PSD2, s 3.

[106] 'Proposal for a Regulation of the European Parliament and of the Council on a Single Market For Digital Services (Digital Services Act) and amending Directive 2000/31/EC', available at: eur-lex.europa.eu/legal-content/en/TXT/?qid=1608117147218&uri=COM%3A2020%3A825%3AFIN (hereafter DSA).

[107] DSA, Arts 8, 13–15, 19–20.

[108] DSA, Art 24.

[109] DSA, Arts 17, 18.

[110] DSA, Arts 25–28, 32.

[111] MiFID, Art 75.

[112] 'Proposal for a Regulation of the European Parliament and of the Council Laying Down Harmonised Rules on Artificial Intelligence (Artificial Intelligence Act)' (2021), available at: eur-lex.europa.eu/legal-content/EN/TXT/?uri=CELEX%3A52021PC0206.

[113] N Smuha et al, 'A Response to the European Commission's Proposal for an Artificial Intelligence Act' (2021), available at: ssrn.com/abstract=3899991; M Veale and F Zuiderveen Borgesius, 'Demystifying the Draft EU Artificial Intelligence Act' (2021) *Computer Law Review International*, available at: doi.org/10.9785/cri-2021-220402.

businesses applying algorithmic credit scoring[114] or algorithmic compliance such as with anti-money laundering,[115] but also other sectors dealing with self-learning systems in production, marketing and other operations, such as in medical diagnostics.[116] We also observe examples of more limited forms of reconsolidating regulatory initiatives such as in the Digital Operational Resilience Act[117] (DORA) and proposed Regulation for Market Infrastructures using Distributed Ledger Technology (DLT).[118] DORA applies exclusively to financial firms although digital operational resilience is increasingly becoming pervasive for businesses that pivot towards digitalisation. DORA is also heavily based on the assumption that observed technological outsourcing is largely made to cloud computing providers dominated by BigTech,[119] hence necessitating a form of direct supervision of outsourcees by European financial regulatory agencies. Arguably, DORA may not be taking into account the rise of blockchain-based cloud computing[120] and how this may affect the market. The proposed Regulation for Market Infrastructures using DLT is highly limited to existing markets for securities and financial instruments, although DLT may be more widely used for a variety of digitalised commercial markets.

Reconsolidating regulatory endeavours in the European Union are horizontal legislative initiatives, ie, they apply across one or more business sectors. Commentators see this as positive, since common standards for certain technologies can be established, addressing common governance problems in a consistent manner.[121] This minimises opportunities for unintended regulatory arbitrage by businesses. In particular, horizontal legislative initiatives may capture BigTech companies' activities that are increasingly diversified, whereas sectoral regulation may fail to address the full extent of their governance problems or large-scale risks.[122] In relation to the EU's proposed regulation for

[114] K Langenbucher, 'Responsible A.I-based Credit Scoring – A Legal Framework' (2020) 31 *European Business Law Review* 527; N Aggarwal, 'The Norms of Algorithmic Credit Scoring' (2020), available at: papers.ssrn.com/sol3/papers.cfm?abstract_id=3569083.

[115] Accenture, *Evolving AML Journey* (2017), available at: www.accenture.com/_acnmedia/pdf-61/accenture-leveraging-machine-learning-anti-money-laundering-transaction-monitoring.pdf.

[116] EJ Topol, 'High-Performance Medicine: The Convergence of Human and Artificial Intelligence' (2019) 25 *Nature Medicine* 44.

[117] 'Proposal for a Regulation of the European Parliament and of the Council on digital operational resilience for the financial sector and amending Regulations (EC) No 1060/2009, (EU) No 648/2012, (EU) No 600/2014 and (EU) No 909/2014' (September 2020), available at: eur-lex.europa.eu/legal-content/EN/TXT/?uri=CELEX%3A52020PC0595.

[118] 'Proposal for a Regulation of the European Parliament and of the Council on a pilot regime for market infrastructures based on distributed ledger technology', available at: eur-lex.europa.eu/legal-content/EN/TXT/?uri=CELEX%3A52020PC0594.

[119] H Scott, 'The EU's Digital Operational Resilience Act: Cloud Services & Financial Companies' (2021), available at: ssrn.com/abstract=3904113.

[120] eg, Filecoin.io.

[121] Borgogno and Colangelo (n 104).

[122] A Boot, P Hoffmann, L Laeven and L Ratnovski, 'Fintech: What's Old, What's New?' (2021) 53 *Journal of Financial Stability* 100836; LP Rodríguez and P Urbiola Ortún, 'From Fintech to Bigtech: An Evolving Regulatory Response' (2020) 229 *Boletín de Estudios Económicos* 119.

AI systems, Floridi argues in favour of the nature of horizontal legislative initiatives, as they are rooted in the common values and protective rights enshrined as fundamental in the European Union and constitute an emerging 'EU digital constitution'.[123] There may also be scope for EU regulation to influence international harmonisation but, equally, such regulation may present tensions and opportunities for regulatory arbitrage for global technology companies where international regulatory fragmentation persists.[124]

However, reconsolidating regulatory endeavours is fraught with challenges. Although policymakers observe cross-cutting issues, themes and the need for common standards, the identification of issues may be incomplete and the framing of scope of application may be challenging. The scope of application can be over-inclusive and there may be cases yet again for exceptions for sectoral approaches with specific needs.[125] There may also be a risk that all-inclusive cross-cutting regulation would be high-level and based on principles which are susceptible to varied implementation. As observed in the proposed Regulation for AI systems, as well as DORA, cross-cutting legislation often imports heavy doses of meta-regulation. Meta-regulation refers to a regulatory technique whereby only broad standards or principles are spelt out in legislation, such as 'robust risk governance', while firms are left to implement the exact processes and frameworks that would achieve the set standards or principles.[126] Meta-regulation can be heavily relied upon when technical implementation details are not yet mature for standardisation and the regulator relies on firms' technical and organisational expertise for their individual implementation, subject to regulators' meta-level oversight. Such regulatory designs can effectively co-opt the private sector to work together with public regulatory goals, but can also give rise to minimalism, shirking and cosmetic compliance that are difficult to oversee by the regulator.[127]

Further, the scope of cross-cutting regulation can also be under-inclusive if based on certain assumptions of technological development. For example, in the proposed Regulation for DLT market infrastructures, EU policymakers have decided to provide standardisation for the use of DLT in the settlement

[123] L Floridi, 'The European Legislation on AI: a Brief Analysis of its Philosophical Approach' (2021), available at: ssrn.com/abstract=3873273.

[124] DW Arner, G Castellano and E Selga, 'The Transnational Data Governance Problem' (2022) *Berkeley Technology Law Journal*, forthcoming, available at: papers.ssrn.com/sol3/papers.cfm?abstract_id=3912487.

[125] eg, whether platformisation raises special issues for finance, EBA, *Report on Use of Digital Platforms* (September 2021), available at: www.eba.europa.eu/sites/default/documents/files/document_library/Publications/Reports/2021/1019865/EBA%20Digital%20platforms%20report%20-%20210921.pdf.

[126] C Parker, *The Open Corporation* (Cambridge University Press, 2000); F Akinbami, 'Is Meta-Regulation All it is Cracked Up to Be? The Case of UK Financial Regulation' (2013) 14 *Journal of Banking Regulation* 16.

[127] J Black, 'Paradoxes and Failures: "New Governance" Techniques and the Financial Crisis' (2012) 75 *Modern Law Review* 1037.

and clearing of existing markets for financial instruments, but this may turn out to be under-inclusive given the developments in DeFi and the engagement of non-conventional financial assets. The scope of this proposal might also not capture the deployment of DLT in other forms of commerce. Reconsolidation can indeed lead to new siloes.

Horizontal legislative endeavours may also have the effect of introducing new normative responsibilities, duties and obligations. These are not uncontroversial. For example, the proposed Regulation for AI systems imposes an array of compliance duties for 'providers' of systems, while 'approved representatives', 'distributors' or 'users' are subject to relatively less burden, relying on providers' primary compliance. It is questionable whether the optimal balance is achieved in such allocation of responsibility in cases where users commission bespoke systems and are intensely involved in design. It is also commented that private enforcement rights for harms are not articulated in the proposed Regulation.[128] In the DMA, although certain prescriptive standards for platforms' gatekeeper conduct are based on observed monopolistic practices, one of us has argued that there is scope to consider standardising more of the expected governance standards and users' rights in relation to platforms.[129]

Although reconsolidation poses a regulatory risk, regulators are in a continuous learning landscape in relation to introducing bespoke regulation as well as reconsolidation initiatives. This may not appeal to needs for legal certainty, but stability of law or regulation may, in fact, be inefficient, if maintained in the face of disruptive change.[130]

VI. CONCLUSION

Fintech and BigTech entrants have already made substantial inroads in some market segments and incumbent traditional financial institutions are also moving closer to a platform-based business model. The overall public policy objective is to respond to these disruptors so as to benefit from the gains while limiting the risks. But as their operations span regulatory perimeters, regimes and geographical borders, new challenges emerge both to substantive regulation and to regulatory agencies.

We propose a high-level response both when it comes to substantive regulation and to regulatory agencies. As shown in this chapter, much work is under

[128] Smuha et al (n 113).

[129] IH-Y Chiu, 'The Platform Economy and the Law of Organisations and Governance' in RM Barker and IH-Y Chiu (eds), *The Law and Governance of Decentralised Business Models* (Routledge, 2020).

[130] For the debates between keeping law coherent in spite of technological changes and instrumentally refashioning law, see R Brownsword, *Law, Technology and Society: Reimagining the Regulatory Environment* (Routledge, 2019).

way in relation to substantive regulation, in terms of: (a) specialist fintech regulation where evidence suggests they are sufficiently different and that their innovative potential should not be damaged by applying existing over-inclusive and onerous regulations; and (b) reconsolidatory regulations that attempt to minimise sectoral inconsistencies and duplication where digital services are concerned. Together, they form an evolutionary process, as this corpus need not be the end point in substantive regulation. This corpus benefits from allowing sectoral specific risks to be addressed while also recognising cross-cutting issues.

The more challenging aspect is at the level of regulatory agencies. Many regulatory agencies are sector-facing in nature, although cross-cutting agencies such as the competition or data/information authorities have been set up to deal with cross-cutting competition law and new GDPR compliance. Perhaps there needs to be more institutional thinking about the needs for sectoral regulators to absorb new risk perceptions while also cooperating with existing cross-cutting agencies. Such cooperation should also be extended internationally, given the cross-border nature of many innovations. Applying a cross-agency approach to fintech (involving relevant ministries and agencies) could help foster domestic coordination and reinforce the policy framework. Coordination across multiple arms of government and regulatory agencies (financial and non-financial) is needed in fintech, as it often generates novel complexities from new firms, products and activities that lie outside the current regulatory perimeter. However, cross-agency coordination is not straightforward in nature and can involve trade-offs between multiple policy goals. For example, consider the interplay between competition objectives and financial stability. One would expect entry of new firms into banking to foster competition and reduce the incumbent's market power, but this may come at a cost of financial stability. Furthermore, the relationship between entry and effective competition may be far from obvious when the BigTech's DNA feedback loop is taken into account. New entry may not increase market contestability and competition, when BigTech firms are able to entrench their market power through the control of key digital platforms, such as e-commerce platforms. Such coordination, between competition authorities and financial services regulators is likely to be more difficult than coordination between financial authorities. Interoperability is a prime example of the need for a joined-up approach in government to create a conducive policy environment for fintech. Interoperability stands out as a critical component in building up the backbone of the fintech ecosystem and achieving it requires coordination of several foundational infrastructures (eg, telecommunications) along with digital and financial infrastructures (such as broadband internet mobile data services, data repositories, and payment and settlement services). Further, cross-agency coordination also gives rise to questions regarding the enforcement turf, ie, who has responsibility for supervision and enforcement, and hence the committal of regulatory resources that may benefit the wider network of agencies involved. Finally, this chapter foreshadows further questions, which cannot be explored fully, such as whether new cross-cutting agencies are needed, and to what extent would there be existential threats to present regulatory agencies, whether sectoral or cross-cutting. A telling example comes from the United Kingdom, where the Penrose Report suggests a number of radical changes to the architecture and operation of UK competition and utility regulation.[131] One of the most radical proposals is that of centralising monopoly regulation under a proposed new unit in the UK CMA – a Network and Data Monopolies Unit (NDMU). In time, the Report envisages the role of sectoral regulators being entirely subsumed by the UK CMA, with regulators' residual oversight of core network monopolies being handed to the NDMU. The evolution of agencies has not caught up with the evolution of legal standards we canvass above, but is a development we look forward to.

[131] In September 2020, John Penrose MP was commissioned by the UK Chancellor of the Exchequer and the Secretary of State for Business, Energy and Industrial Strategy to write an independent report on how the UK's approach to competition and consumer issues could be improved. The report was published in February 2021; see, 'Power to the People: Independent Report on Competition Policy' available at: www.gov.uk/government/publications/power-to-the-people-independent-report-on-competition-policy.

11

Enforcing Fintech Competition: Some Reflections on Institutional Design

JENS-UWE FRANCK

I. INTRODUCTION

WITH THE ADVENT of fintech comes the expectation of fruitful disruption: the integration of financial services into the internet and mobile devices, and their combination with technologies such as artificial intelligence, cloud computing and distributed ledger technology, promise better products at lower prices. This development affects all facets of the financial industry: payment, lending and capital raising, investment and trade, as well as clearing and settlement.[1] Whether consumers – business users as well as end consumers – and investors ultimately benefit from those developments depends on various preconditions, one of which is open markets and functioning competition. This is essentially no different in fintech markets than in other markets.

Several aspects may make safeguarding competition for fintech services particularly challenging. The level of financial market regulation may be inappropriately high and thus create unjustified entry barriers for fintech firms. At the (European Union (EU) level, we can see that bespoke regulation, for example via the Crowdfunding Regulation[2] or the proposed Regulation on Markets in Crypto-assets,[3] aims at promoting competition through fintech.[4] The focus of this chapter is more specific than these legislative instruments:[5] the market

[1] E Carletti and A Smolenska, '10 Years On from the Financial Crisis: Co-operation between Competition Agencies and Regulators in the Financial Sector', OECD Note DAF/COMP/WP2(2017)8 (13 October 2017) 19.

[2] Regulation (EU) 2020/1503 of the European Parliament and of the Council of 7 October 2020 on European crowdfunding service providers for business and amending Regulation (EU) 2017/1129 and Directive (EU) 2019/1937 [2020] OJ L347/1.

[3] 'Proposal for a Regulation of the European Parliament and of the Council on Markets in Crypto-assets, and amending Directive (EU) 2019/1937' COM/2020/593 final (MiCA Proposal).

[4] See MiCA Proposal (n 3) recital 2.

[5] But see section VI on dealing with conflicting regulatory objectives.

entry of technology-enabled innovation in the financial sector may depend on access to other (competing) market operators' data and facilities or the enabling of data portability and interoperability of complementing financial services.[6] While all types of competitors – incumbent firms, start-ups and the large digital gatekeepers ('BigTech') – make use of and benefit from new technologies, their stakes in these developments differ. Start-ups bring innovative business models to the market and seek to scale them as quickly as possible, attacking established business models of incumbent players such as the traditional commercial banks. The latter, therefore, may fear for their cash cows and the preferential access to their customer base, but may also want to benefit from the rise of fintech services. Furthermore, the large digital gatekeepers operating commercial platforms or controlling the integration of new financial services in mobile devices, may strive for monetising their quasi-exclusive access to their user base. Therefore, various players in fintech markets may have specific interests in foreclosing competitors and exploiting consumers.

Competition law enforcement in these scenarios can involve complex factual issues as well as the considering and balancing of conflicting interests beyond concerns of competition and, ultimately, the drafting and monitoring of remedies that entail detailed technical instructions. Therefore, while swift intervention may seem vital to keep markets open for fintech, the enforcement of competition law may prove to be demanding, burdensome and lengthy. For these reasons, among others, it may appear appropriate to take recourse to legislation for facilitating fintech services' market access. Examples at the EU law level include the obligation imposed on account-holding institutions to provide payment initiation services and account information services with dedicated interfaces under the revised Payment Services Directive (PSD2)[7] and the access and interoperability requirements imposed on large digital gatekeepers under the Digital Markets Act (DMA), which apply not least for the benefit of payment service providers.[8]

This raises the question of the avenue most appropriate for the formation of fintech competition rules: competition enforcement, legislative rule-making, or possibly a hybrid form of rule-making such as UK-style market investigation? While we have addressed this question of adequate institutional design

[6] Certainly, this does not apply exclusively to fintech innovation. See, eg, Commission Decisions in Cases COMP/39.592, *Standard & Poor's*, C(2011) 8209 final; COMP/39.654 *Reuters Instrument Codes (RICs)*, C(2012) 9635 final; Case AT.39745 *Credit Default Swaps – Information Market* C(2016) 4583 final (ISDA); and C(2016) 4585 final (Markit), where the Commission accepted binding commitments that aimed at facilitating market entry by granting third parties access to financial data via FRAND licensing agreements, allowing for the portability of information and interoperability.

[7] See rec 93 and Arts 66, 67, 68 and 98 of Directive (EU) 2015/2366 of the European Parliament and of the Council of 25 November 2015 on payment services in the internal market, amending Directives 2002/65/EC, 2009/110/EC and 2013/36/EU and Regulation (EU) No 1093/2010, and repealing Directive 2007/64/EC [2015] OJ L337/35.

[8] See rec 43 and Art 6(7) of Regulation (EU) 2022/1925 of the European Parliament and of the Council of 14 September 2022 on contestable and fair markets in the digital sector and amending Directives (EU) 2019/1937 and (EU) 2020/1828 [2022] OJ L265/1 (Digital Markets Act or DMA).

of fintech competition rule-making elsewhere,[9] this contribution focuses on the bureaucratic side of the enforcement of procompetitive rules and standards. The two topics are, of course, interrelated: when considering passing new law, a legislature needs to take into account how effective available competition law enforcement is, which essentially depends on institutional factors. Furthermore, the legislature will have to consider how a new statutory procompetitive rule could be implemented institutionally. This chapter is thus motivated by the question of how fintech competition enforcement should be designed so that the related objectives – keeping fintech markets open and competitive – can best be achieved.

A word of caution is appropriate at the outset. Addressing normative questions of institutional design is rather intricate. One can hardly hope for universally valid answers. The significance of the constitutional framework and the political, social and economic environment in which procompetitive policy is pursued, as well as the status quo of the enforcement architecture in a particular jurisdiction, cannot be overstated. What is more, the various features, factors and criteria that will be considered in the following are interrelated. Taken together, it should be clear that normative statements of a general nature can only be made to a limited extent.

The ambitions of this chapter are therefore modest. Starting from the typical real-world choice a legislature faces in allocating powers of fintech competition enforcement, relevant trade-offs and interrelations will be identified, and factors that need to be considered and weighed in this context will be outlined and illustrated. Ideally, this will contribute to the understanding of how certain choices of institutional design may have an impact on the effectiveness of fintech competition enforcement and may be considered when legislating. For, as Hawkins and Thomas noted, '[K]knowledge of the way the agency bureaucracy develops and implements enforcement policy can be of considerable value at the lawmaking stage of regulation'.[10]

This contribution proceeds by identifying the basic options a legislature may have at its disposal when allocating competences for enforcing fintech competition (section II). Five topics of institutional design or related to it will be touched upon thereafter. Section III discusses models of enforcement style and strategies. Section IV considers the efficient use of administrative resources, whereas section V addresses the motivation of staff. Section VI is dedicated to the dealing

[9] J-U Franck, 'Competition enforcement versus regulation as market-opening tools: An application to banking and payment systems' (2023) *Journal of Antitrust Enforcement*, available at: www.researchgate.net/publication/370157333_Competition_enforcement_versus_regulation_as_market-opening_tools_an_application_to_banking_and_payment_systems.

[10] K Hawkins and JM Thomas, 'The Enforcement Process in Regulatory Bureaucracies' in K Hawkins and JM Thomas (eds), *Enforcing Regulation* (Springer Science & Business Media, 1984) 20.

with conflicting regulatory objectives and section VII focuses on legitimising elements in competition procedures. Section VIII concludes.

II. ALLOCATION OF BUREAUCRATIC ENFORCEMENT COMPETENCES: BASIC CHOICES AND MODELS

The various aspects of institutional design discussed in the following may contribute to a better understanding of bureaucratic enforcement. In doing so, they also offer starting points for considering how enforcement should be designed so that procompetitive interventions are most effective. Yet enforcement mechanisms are not designed on a clean slate. On the contrary, individual interventions in fintech markets are unlikely to prompt a legislature to invest resources to change authority structures or to make small-scale changes to the organisational structure of a particular authority. Institutional design decisions therefore often (merely) boil down to the question of which of the existing authorities should be responsible for enforcing a certain procompetitive provision.

Against this background, this section will briefly outline the main choices that are available to a legislature when allocating enforcement powers. This concerns not only the available authorities, but also their role in relation to the judiciary.

A. Options for the Allocation of Enforcement Competences: Competition Authorities and Sector Regulators

i. Competition Authorities

Competition authorities typically have the power to enforce competition laws across all industries, including those most relevant for fintech competition, namely the digital industry and the financial sector. Furthermore, it is quite common that the authority responsible for enforcing competition law also has the power to enforce other bodies of law. The most common combinations seem to be competition law with public procurement law and/or consumer protection law.[11] The latter combination appears to make sense in particular because of consumer protection law's impact on the level of market entry barriers and thus possible repercussions on competition: on the one hand, it will often be easier for incumbent players with a large user base to meet high consumer protection standards. On the other hand, consumer protection rules can lower the switching costs for consumers and, thus, their rigorous enforcement may lower barriers to entry and promote competition.

[11] WE Kovacic and DA Hyman, 'Competition Agency Design: What's on the Menu?' (2012) 8 *European Competition Journal* 527, 533.

In addition, competition authorities can also be entrusted with the enforcement of particular legislative measures that aim at facilitating market access.[12] A case in point is Article 8 of the Interchange Fee Regulation,[13] which is meant to ensure that payment card issuers have the option of co-badging and that consumers may even require their bank to co-badge a single device – which may be a card or a smartphone (wallet app) – 'with all other brands offered as compatible apps (for a wallet) or other card products offered by the bank (for a card)'.[14] Various Member States, including France, the Netherlands and Denmark,[15] assigned to their respective competition authorities the power to enforce this provision.[16] Moreover, the enforcement of the DMA by the European Commission can also be seen as an example of a competition authority enforcing procompetitive legislative intervention: as far as is known, the Directorate-General for Competition will be responsible for the case handling, while the Directorate-General for Communications Networks, Content and Technology will mostly supply the technical expertise required for monitoring compliance and enforcement of the DMA.[17]

ii. Sector Regulators

a. Financial Market Regulators

Financial markets are typically supervised by one or several authorities the core competence of which is the implementation of financial regulation. In practice, we find jurisdictions where a single authority is competent to supervise the entire financial sector. A case in point is Germany's Bundesanstalt für Finanzdienstleistungsaufsicht (BaFin) (Federal Financial Supervisory Authority). In most jurisdictions, including the United States and the United Kingdom (UK), but also at EU level,[18] we may observe a division of responsibilities among different authorities. Such a division can be based on institutional criteria (banks, dealers); functional criteria (banking, securities, insurance); or regulatory objectives (stability, market efficiency, consumer protection etc).[19]

[12] Franck, 'Competition enforcement versus regulation as market-opening tools' (n 9) sub II, subsection 'Third scenario: Enforcement of procompetitive regulation by a competition authority' 18–19.

[13] Regulation (EU) 2015/751 of the European Parliament and of the Council of 29 April 2015 on interchange fees for card-based payment transactions [2015] OJ L123/1.

[14] European Commission – Fact Sheet, Antitrust: Regulation on Interchange Fees (9 June 2016), available at: ec.europa.eu/commission/presscorner/detail/de/MEMO_16_2162.

[15] Note that in these Member States the authority competent for competition policy is also responsible for the enforcement of consumer protection laws.

[16] A list of the competent national authorities may be found on DG Comp's website, available at: ec.europa.eu/competition/sectors/financial_services/national_competent_authorities.pdf.

[17] See Euractiv of 5 July 2022, available at: www.euractiv.com/section/digital/news/commissioner-hints-at-enforcement-details-as-eu-parliament-adopts-dsa-and-dma.

[18] For an oversight see J Armour et al, *Principles of Financial Regulation* (Oxford University Press, 2016) 538–45.

[19] ibid, 534–35.

While the enhancement of competition does not typically lie at the heart of financial market regulation, in the United Kingdom, for example, the legislature has clarified that the promotion of effective competition must be considered a crucial objective of the Financial Conduct Authority (FCA). For this purpose, the FCA has even been granted responsibilities for competition enforcement, which it can exercise alongside the Competition and Markets Authority (CMA), the UK's essential competition enforcer.[20] Furthermore, authorities responsible for the supervision of the financial sector have not uncommonly also been entrusted with the enforcement of rules that are meant to enhance competition. This also applies to procompetitive regulation in support of fintech. Thus, the German BaFin is responsible for enforcing provisions designed to facilitate the market entry of payment initiation services.[21]

b. Network Regulators

In some jurisdictions, network regulators, traditionally responsible for sectors such as energy and telecommunications, have also been given powers to enforce regulation affecting digital services. In Germany, for example, the Bundesnetzagentur (Federal Network Agency) has been assigned the enforcement of the Geoblocking Regulation.[22] Consequently, it seems not far-fetched that some network regulators will also get involved in the enforcement of procompetitive rules in fintech markets.

c. Digital Industry Regulators

As far as can be seen, there is as yet no example of an independent authority established specifically to enforce rules imposed on the digital sector. This hesitancy may have various reasons. Established authorities certainly have little interest in relinquishing competences in such a prestigious and attention-grabbing field. Further, the relevant business models are so heterogeneous that it seems doubtful how such a thing as a 'digital industry' should be properly defined. Nevertheless, to designate an authority responsible for the supervision of digital gatekeepers seems a plausible option to create enforcement synergies and to ensure a coherent digital competition policy. The question would then remain whether this authority should only be competent for the enforcement of rules that address only those gatekeepers (as in the case of the DMA) or also of provisions that are otherwise enforced by specialised authorities (such as in the case of competition law or data protection law).

[20] For a brief oversight, see Carletti and Smolenska (n 1) 27–28.

[21] ss 48–52 of the German Payment Services Act (PSSA), transposing Arts 64 and 66 PSD2.

[22] Regulation (EU) 2018/302 of the European Parliament and of the Council of 28 February 2018 on addressing unjustified geo-blocking and other forms of discrimination based on customers' nationality, place of residence or place of establishment within the internal market and amending Regulations (EC) No 2006/2004 and (EU) 2017/2394 and Directive 2009/22/EC [2018] OJ L601/1.

The UK's Digital Markets Unit comes quite close to the model of a 'digital industry regulator'. While the Digital Market Unit is located within the CMA, its creation rests on the notion of a supervisor authority for the digital economy, bundling regulatory powers that go beyond the enforcement of competition law.[23]

A remarkable example of a separate authority designated for digital business models in finance is Dubai's Virtual Assets Regulatory Authority (VARA), which was established in 2022[24] 'as the competent entity in charge of regulating, supervising Virtual Assets[25] … and Virtual Asset Service Providers … conducting authorised Virtual Asset activities'.[26]

iii. Modes of Competence Allocation

Where enforcement competences are distributed among different authorities, a multitude of variants and combinations are conceivable. In any case, it is indisputable that the mandates of the respective authorities should be defined as clearly as possible.

With an allocation of competences based on the principle of *exclusivity* on the one hand, competences can be divided so that, for example, the competition authority is exclusively responsible for the enforcement of competition law and the enforcement of other procompetitive regulation is in the hands of sector regulators. On the other hand, responsibility for all procompetitive measures can lie exclusively with either the competition authority or a sector regulator.

Alternatively, legislatures may rely – across the board or in part – on *concurrent powers* to enforce competition laws and other procompetitive regulation. As mentioned above, in the United Kingdom the FCA has concurrent powers for competition enforcement with the CMA. Certainly, it requires additional resources to keep parallel enforcement structures in place and to avoid inconsistent enforcement activities. However, those costs may be kept within reasonable limits through communication and division of responsibilities between the authorities. With concurrent power regimes come clear benefits: if one authority

[23] N Dunne, 'Pro-competition Regulation in the Digital Economy: The United Kingdom's Digital Markets Unit' (2022) 67 *Antitrust Bulletin* 341, 346 and 349–50.

[24] Art (4) of Law No (4) of 2022 Regulating Virtual Assets in the Emirate of Dubai, available at: dlp.dubai.gov.ae/Legislation%20Reference/2022/Law%20No.%20(4)%20of%202022%20Regulating%20Virtual%20Assets.html.

[25] Defined as 'a digital representation of value that may be digitally traded, transferred, or used as an exchange or payment tool, or for investment purposes. This includes Virtual Tokens [a digital representation of a set of rights that can be digitally offered and traded through a Virtual Asset Platform], and any digital representation of any other value as determined by VARA'. Art (2) of Law No (4) of 2022 Regulating Virtual Assets in the Emirate of Dubai.

[26] Introduction to the Administrative Order No 01/2022: Relating to Regulation of Marketing, Advertising and Promotions Related to Virtual Assets, available at: www.vara.ae/media/administrative-order-01-regulatory-guidelines-18aug2022.pdf.

fails in enforcement, the other may step in. In fact, rivalry among authorities might drive better performance and practice.[27]

Cooperation between authorities should be encouraged not only when they have parallel powers to enforce procompetitive rules, but also between authorities supervising the same market activities for different regulatory purposes. This can be done by facilitating the exchange of information between authorities; through granting a right or imposing an obligation to make submissions in proceedings before each other; or even in a regime that makes intervention by one authority conditional on the approval of the other.[28]

The Digital Clearinghouse is a notable initiative at the European level, initiated by the European Data Protection Supervisor, to achieve coherence in law enforcement in digital markets through closed roundtables for regulatory authorities with a focus on data protection, consumer and competition law.[29] In the United Kingdom, the Digital Regulation Cooperation Forum was set up in 2020 to provide for an institutional framework to foster exchange and cooperation with a view to regulating digital markets between various authorities. The forum was initially established by the CMA, the Information Commissioner's Office, and the Office of Communications, with the FCA joining in 2021.[30]

B. Bureaucracy and the Courts

Looking at the various institutional frameworks of bureaucratic enforcement powers, we see that there is a significant difference between an authority that believes to have identified a breach having to bring a case before a court to enforce the law and it having not only investigatory powers but acting as a first instance decision-maker as it may require that an infringement be ceased and/or to impose behavioural or structural remedies and/or even a fine.

The latter is true for most Member States and the European Union, as competition proceedings there follow what may be called an 'administrative model'.

[27] See WE Kovacic, 'The Institutions of Antitrust Law: How Structure Shapes Substance' (2012) 110 *Michigan Law Review* 1019, 1035–37, posing the effects of rivalry in view of the partly overlapping responsibilities of the Department of Justice and the Federal Trade Commission as enforcers of US antitrust law as a question open to research.

[28] An illustration of the latter regulatory technique in a competition context can be found in the German law on the transposition and implementation of Directive (EU) 2019/633 of the European Parliament and of the Council of 17 April 2019 on unfair trading practices in business-to-business relationships in the agricultural and food supply chain [2019] OJ L111/59. To avoid inconsistencies in the enforcement of the German law transposing the Directive and competition enforcement, the authority responsible for enforcing the Directive's prohibitions (as transposed into German law) may establish infringements and impose remedies only 'in agreement with' the Bundeskartellamt. s 28(2) 1st sentence of the Agri-Organizations and Supply Chains Act (Agrarorganisationen-und-Lieferketten-Gesetz).

[29] See: www.digitalclearinghouse.org/.

[30] See: www.gov.uk/government/collections/the-digital-regulation-cooperation-forum.

In contrast, a 'judicial model' can be observed in Ireland and Austria, where competition authorities investigate cases, yet, where an infringement is found, must bring the case before a court. In Sweden, until 1 March 2021 a separation between investigation and sanctioning applied; since then the competition authority may impose sanctions for infringements. In Denmark and Finland, which for fining decisions follow a 'weakened' judicial model, the authority may render a decision establishing that there has been an infringement, but then must bring the case before court if it wants the infringer to be fined.[31]

The choice among those models, in essence, involves trade-offs between the promptness of decision-making and the quality of control and legitimacy.[32] Moreover, having at its disposal the option to sanction without going to court provides an authority with more leeway for a dynamic enforcement strategy of credibly holding out the prospect of adapting its enforcement activities to the regulatees' attitude in a tit-for-tat manner.[33]

C. Private Enforcement

While the focus here is on the bureaucratic facet of enforcement, possible interrelations with enforcement initiated by private actors and implemented through the court systems need to be mentioned.

i. No Private Enforcement Available

Interrelations between public and private enforcement naturally do not exist where private parties cannot take direct action in court against alleged infringers. Authorities then carry a particularly high responsibility for effective law enforcement. In some jurisdictions, however, private individuals may have the option to file suit against an authority to force it to take enforcement measures. This scenario may be classified as a hybrid between private and bureaucratic enforcement as it involves both private initiative and public enforcement capacities.[34]

A complete absence of private rights of action can have negative repercussions on the effectiveness of public enforcement because it may weaken incentives to provide the authorities with private information about violations of the law. This is because the option of claiming damages may not only incentivise

[31] For an overview of these models, see ECN Working Group Cooperation Issues and Due Process, Decision-Making Powers, Report, 31 October 2012, 5–10.

[32] Kovacic and Hyman (n 11) 535–36.

[33] I Ayres and J Braithwaite, *Responsive Regulation* (Oxford University Press, 1992) 51–52. See also below, text accompanying n 49.

[34] J-U Franck, 'Private Enforcement versus Public Enforcement' in F Hofmann and F Kurz (eds), *Law of Remedies: A European Perspective* (Intersentia, 2019) 108.

direct actions against (possible) infringers,[35] but also create incentives to inform authorities, trusting that they will prosecute the case, which in turn may facilitate subsequent suits for damages (so-called follow-on actions).[36]

ii. Private Enforcement as the Sole Enforcement Avenue

In some regulatory contexts, legislatures do not provide for public enforcement but rely solely on private rights of action. In a procompetitive fintech regulation context this is the case, for example, with the so-called 'Lex Apple Pay' under German law, the right of payment service providers to access 'technical infrastructure' that contributes to mobile and internet-based payment services (including, eg, the Near Field Communication interfaces of Apple's mobile devices).[37] With a view to the big players in the payment services markets, this regulatory choice may appear adequate. However, the availability of only private enforcement seems less convincing regarding (smaller) fintech firms, such as app developers, for whom the prospect of having to bring a case against a big tech player like Apple may appear quite daunting.[38]

iii. Parallel Availability of Private and Public Enforcement

As it is true in general, it is also true in fintech markets that in most cases both public and private enforcement instruments are provided for competition enforcement or for the enforcement of other procompetitive provisions. Ideally, the mechanisms complement each other and compensate for each other's weaknesses.

However, in the real world parallel enforcement mechanisms can weaken each other's impact and lead to inefficiencies. A cartelist may be reluctant to file a leniency application for fear of damages claims.[39] The accumulation of fines and damages can lead to over-deterrence.[40] The availability of private rights of action may thwart a cooperative enforcement strategy[41] – which might serve compliance best in the long run – based on which an authority had (reasonably)

[35] See, eg, a recent class action complaint against Apple, filed on 18 July 2022: *Affinity Credit Union v Apple Inc*, ND Cal, Case 5:22-cv-04174.

[36] Franck, 'Private Enforcement versus Public Enforcement' (n 34) 122–23.

[37] s 58a of the German Payment Services Act (PSSA).

[38] Franck, 'Competition enforcement versus regulation as market-opening tools' (n 9) sub II, subsection 'Second scenario: Private enforcement as the sole enforcement avenue' 18.

[39] See O Bodnar et al, 'The Effects of Private Damage Claims on Cartel Activity: Experimental Evidence' (2023) 39 *Journal of Law, Economics, and Organization* 27.

[40] See on the concept of 'optimal deterrence' and on the possibility of over-deterrence, I Lianos et al, *Damages Claims for the Infringement of EU Competition Law* (Oxford University Press, 2015) 219–35; J-U Franck and M Peitz, 'Toward a Coherent Policy on Cartel Damages' (2017) ZEW – Centre for European Economic Research Discussion Paper No 17-009 13–15.

[41] On enforcement styles and strategies, see below section III.

opted for not pursuing a particular infringement.[42] Trade-offs between public and private enforcement must therefore be considered when designing institutional enforcement. They may be mitigated (eg, leniency applicants can also be privileged when it comes to damages actions)[43] but hardly ever avoided completely.

III. ENFORCEMENT STYLES

A. The Stylised Dichotomy of Adversarial ('Deterrence-Oriented') and Cooperative ('Compliance-Oriented') Enforcement

In the sociological literature on bureaucratic enforcement and regulation, two base models of enforcement strategies are distinguished: the deterrence model and the compliance model. As an analytical tool, these stylised conceptions are useful when reflecting on the institutional design of fintech competition enforcement.

An enforcement style according to which the authority focuses on detecting infringements and identifying, prosecuting and sanctioning those responsible for them[44] has been characterised as 'legalistic' and 'deterrence-oriented'.[45] It will typically lead to a rather adversarial relationship between the authority and the regulated who are (potentially) subject to enforcement measures.

In contrast, a 'compliance-oriented' enforcement strategy has been identified and characterised as follows: 'the style is conciliatory and relies upon bargaining to attain conformity. Enforcement here is prospective: a matter of responding to a problem and negotiating future conformity to standards which are often administratively determined'.[46] This concept thus rests on the assumption that, to ensure an optimal level of compliance, it might be preferable not to pursue each infringement, or, in other contexts, to leave it at a cease-and-desist order where it would also have been possible to impose a fine. This is seen as crucial for effective enforcement as it may avoid strategies of 'minimal' or 'creative'

[42] K Roach and MJ Trebilcock, 'Private Enforcement of Competition Laws' (1996) 34 *Osgoode Hall Law Journal* 461, 485–87, 503; MC Stephenson, 'Public Regulation of Private Enforcement: The Case for Expanding the Role of Administrative Agencies' (2009) 91 *Virginia Law Review* 93, 117–19.

[43] See Art 11(4) and (5) of Directive 2014/104/EU of the European Parliament and of the Council of 26 November 2014 on certain rules governing actions for damages under national law for infringements of the competition law provisions of the Member States and of the European Union [2014] OJ L349/1.

[44] Hawkins and Thomas (n 10) 15.

[45] E Bardach and RA Kagan, *Going by the Book* (Temple University Press, 1982/3rd Printing, Transaction Publishers, 2006) 57.

[46] K Hawkins, *Environment and Enforcement* (Clarendon Press, 1984) 4. See also Hawkins and Thomas (n 10) 5, 15.

compliance and prevent the regulated from becoming entrenched in an attitude of resentment and resistance. The latter is one of the main themes of the work of Bardach and Kagan: rigorous, inflexible enforcement of rules may entail resentment and resistance among the regulated that may in fact undermine the regulatory objectives.[47] Instead, enforcement should aim to make the regulated genuinely aware that it makes good sense to comply with a rule, thus promoting a 'willingness to comply'.[48] This model of enforcement is thus based on a cooperative relationship between authority and regulated.

In 'Responsive Regulation', Ayres and Braithwaite have argued that, in order to translate the awareness of the inconsistencies and discontinuities in the attitudes and actions of real-world corporate actors ('profit-maximising' versus 'law abiding selves') into a robust enforcement policy, one will have to find a sophisticated balance between strategies of persuasion and punishment.[49] Therefore it is crucial to acknowledge and account for the dynamic character of the 'enforcement game'. In this sense, a tit-for-tat strategy may be most appropriate for ensuring compliance: the enforcer waives deterrent responses as long as the regulated firm cooperates. If it becomes apparent that the authority's cooperative attitude is being exploited, enforcement has to switch from a cooperative to a deterrent attitude. For such a dynamic enforcement strategy to work, the authority must first have an armoury of deterrent instruments at its disposal and second it must use them in a skilful manner, tailored to the respective offence. The authority is advised to explicitly display an 'enforcement pyramid' of measures that allow it to escalate enforcement in several stages if defection from cooperation is identified.[50]

B. Financial Markets Authorities' Enforcement Style and Fintech Competition Challenges

There are good reasons to believe that authorities responsible for supervising financial markets tend to take a more 'compliance-oriented' approach to enforcement – compared with, for example, competition authorities. While scholars have identified a broad spectrum of factors that may determine the enforcement

[47] Bardach and Kagan (n 45).

[48] J Black, 'Talking about Regulation' [1998] *Public Law* 77, 87.

[49] Ayres and Braithwaite (n 33) 9–53. The work of Ayres and Braithwaite is particularly well known for their concept of 'enforced self-regulation', according to which the regulatees design their own compliance strategy which the regulatory authority then needs to approve. This and other innovations in the design of regulatory instruments, their interplay with each other and with classical regulatory techniques, and more generally the relationship between forms of state and private social control and conflict resolution in the pursue of regulatory goals, are discussed under the label 'smart regulation'. See N Gunningham and P Grabosky, *Smart Regulation* (Clarendon Press, 1998).

[50] Ayres and Braithwaite (n 33) 35–38.

style of an authority,[51] this assumption is based on the fact that their activities are restricted to one particular sector and that financial service providers, as it has been noted, often 'engage with regulators on a more or less continuous basis in the context of day-to-day supervisory relationships'.[52] Indeed, it has been remarked in the literature on enforcement styles that the adoption of a compliance strategy is more likely where enforcers are dealing only with a 'limited sector of the public'.[53] More specifically, it has been argued that compliance orientation 'tends to be adopted where there is an on-going relationship between regulator and regulated, and particularly where the individuals involved know one another or share a common background or outlook'.[54] Where an authority is monitoring one particular sector and supervising a defined set of firms, and where this goes hand-in-hand with a continuous exchange and the developing of an ongoing relationship with the regulated that will often even entail a personal acquaintance of some type, it seems plausible to assume a tendency for a cooperative enforcement strategy.

Yet, while a compliance-oriented enforcement style might indeed be a rational strategy for the enforcement of financial regulation, it will likely lead to the authority developing a deep understanding of the interests and positions of the incumbent market participants,[55] which may eventually discourage them from tearing down entry barriers through rigorous procompetitive interventions and which may even make an authority more vulnerable to regulatory capture.[56] Certainly, one may well assume that financial market authorities can play tit-for-tat, switching gear and changing into a more adversarial enforcement style if they discover to have been cheated in compliance. However, they will prefer to do so within the framework of an enforcement pyramid tailored to their regulatory

[51] Kagan has grouped these factors into four sets: legal design factors; task environment factors; political environment factors; and leadership factors. RA Kagan, 'Regulatory Enforcement' in RD Schwartz and DH Rosenbloom (eds), *Handbook of Regulation and Administrative Law* (Marcel Dekker, 1994) 390–91. See Black (n 48) 87 ('the nature of the breach … and judgments as to its seriousness … the nature of the regulatees (whether they are well or ill-intentioned, well or ill-informed, and whether the breach was careless, negligent or malicious), and the social and moral legitimacy of the regulation being enforced').

[52] Armour et al (n 18) 561.

[53] Hawkins and Thomas (n 10) 14. In addition, the authors identify two main reasons for the adoption of a compliance strategy: 'rule-breaking behaviour' not consisting of 'clear-cut acts' but being 'episodic, repetitive, or continuous' and victims being 'not dramatically evident to the enforcement agent'.

[54] Black (n 48) 88.

[55] M Hellwig, 'Competition Policy and Sector-Specific Regulation in the Financial Sector' (2018) Discussion Paper of the Max Planck Institute for Research on Collective Goods Bonn 2018/7, 10 ('Specifying and enforcing a desired behavior requires expertise and information, which the regulator can only obtain through constant interaction with the people he supervises. This interaction creates social ties and potential biases as the people involved on the side of the authority come to understand the firms' point of view too well').

[56] On 'agency capture', see below, section V.A.

domain and objectives. Therefore, all in all, it seems plausible that a financial market authority is rather hesitant to take selective confrontational, escalating action for market opening against incumbent market participants such as the traditional banking industry, towards whom they prefer to continue to act in a more cooperative enforcement style regarding financial market regulation.

Things would be different if the financial market authorities had to enforce procompetitive regulation against market participants – for example in the digital industry – whom, incidentally, they do not supervise because they do not offer financial services. In this case, there is no (or at most a quite small) basis for a more 'compliance-oriented' enforcement style that may be generally cultivated by the authority: neither the authority nor the addressee of the regulation has a particular interest in investing in a long-term relationship of trust. However, a financial market authority would have to act then outside its comfort zone and to use an enforcement style it is rather unfamiliar with – a scenario which it will typically try to avoid.

In sum, an authority that has established a participatory, cooperative enforcement style does not seem to be the ideal promoter of fintech competition. This may be a challenge for financial market authorities when they are entrusted with enforcing procompetitive regulation, be it in fintech markets or elsewhere.

C. Competition Authorities' Enforcement Style and Fintech Competition Challenges

Competition authorities are experienced with and tend not to shy away from taking confrontational action against the top dogs in a market. The fact that competition authorities have typically developed a rather adversarial enforcement style may have its roots above all in their fight against cartels. Indeed, cartelisation is precisely the expression of an 'unwillingness to comply', rather than not indicating a compliance-oriented enforcement style. Hawkins and Thomas have observed that 'The deterrence system tends to be associated with *incidents* or *acts* of wrongdoing that by their very nature, are relatively unpredictable, thus allowing no personalized relationships to be established between enforcement agent and rulebreaker'.[57] Given its clandestine nature, cartelisation seems to be exactly the kind of rule-breaking that is included here and which will thus trigger a 'deterrence-oriented', confrontational enforcement style. Moreover, also beyond the prosecution of cartels, competition authorities are typically not involved in the continuous monitoring of specific companies.

With respect to fintech competition, the challenge for the enforcement style of a typical competition authority therefore lies rather in switching to a participatory mode when this appears useful or even necessary for effective intervention.

[57] Hawkins and Thomas (n 10) 14.

As emphasised at the beginning of this chapter, the market entry of fintech firms may depend, inter alia, on access to competitors' facilities, the enabling of data portability, and the possibility of connecting their own offerings with those of their competitors. Consequently, to open up markets, it might for example be necessary to grant access rights to technical infrastructure or to impose obligations to provide for application programming interfaces. Implementing such elaborate and technically ambitious remedies necessarily requires cooperation with the undertakings addressed. An authority that generally pursues a confrontational enforcement strategy may find it difficult to develop the necessary relationship of mutual trust with the regulated base.

IV. EFFICIENT USE OF ADMINISTRATIVE RESOURCES

As with any other form of organisation, bureaucratic enforcement is subject to resource constraints. An essential requirement of its institutional design is therefore to promote the efficient use of resources. An important aspect here is to enable institutions to generate economies of scale and scope. Technical, economic, legal and other expertise should be accumulated to create synergies, be it in the form of employees who are specialised in enforcing a particular set of legal rules or in enforcing the law in specific factual scenarios, or be it in the form of technical devices, such as databases, which allow for an efficient processing of information.[58]

Competition authorities with a broad mandate may realise synergies. If an authority, for example, knows and understands data accumulation, processing and exploitation by BigTech, not only will this know-how be useful for enforcing competition law, but it may also be fruitfully used for implementing privacy law or consumer protection law. However, an expanded scope of responsibilities will only create synergies if, as Kovacic and Hyman aptly put it, 'the functions to be combined are true policy complements and do not consist of a rubbish bin of dissimilar'.[59]

The challenge in promoting fintech competition is to combine sector-specific knowledge with an understanding of a novel business case and the technical innovations behind it. At this point, financial market authorities, which deal with this anyway due to their sector-specific regulatory responsibilities, can be at an advantage. Competition authorities typically try to build up and make use of sector-related know-how through internal specialisation. How effective such special expertise may be developed depends, among other things, on the size of the jurisdiction. Only a certain number of cases justify, for example, entrusting a unit within a competition authority exclusively with financial services, as, for

[58] Franck, 'Private Enforcement versus Public Enforcement' (n 34) 107, 125.
[59] Kovacic and Hyman (n 11) 533.

example, in the European Commission's Directorate-General for Competition.[60] Although the internal organisation is functionally different and thus not readily comparable, it is noteworthy that the Bundeskartellamt (to take one example) has a total of 12 so-called decision divisions (Beschlussabteilungen), one of which is responsible for financial services and insurance, but also for transport as well as tourism and the hospitality industry.[61]

The specific – as it were, 'natural' – advantage of competition authorities lies in their clear focus on the protection of competition, which is why the highest level of expertise – in fact, legal and bureaucratic expertise combined with economic and technical know-how – on the implementation of a procompetitive policy should be found in a jurisdiction's competition authority.[62] It is precisely for this reason that legislatures should consider also entrusting competition authorities with the enforcement of market-opening, procompetitive regulation outside competition law proper.[63] However, competition authorities may have little routine when it comes to the drafting of detailed behavioural instructions and in procedures by which external technical expertise needs to be included. They are also traditionally reluctant to invest resources in the ongoing monitoring of firms' compliance with rules and remedies.[64]

Sector regulators, such as financial market authorities, are also free to pursue internal specialisation and thus concentrate the enforcement of those rules that are intended to promote competition in one unit. This unit could then also act as an 'advocate for competition' within the authority. However, we are not aware of any institution in which such a design has been implemented.

V. REGULATORY OBJECTIVES AND MOTIVATION OF STAFF MEMBERS

Public servants' interests may lie not with optimising enforcement in the general interest but with maximising their own benefit. Such a focus might entail, for example, a tendency to raise those cases that promise public attention or those that promise acknowledgement by superiors if they are handled successfully.[65]

[60] See the organization chart valid as of 16 June 2022, available at: ec.europa.eu/info/sites/default/files/organisation-chart-dg-comp_en_19.pdf.

[61] See the organization chart valid as of 1 September 2022, available at: www.bundeskartellamt.de/SharedDocs/Publikation/DE/Sonstiges/Organigramm.html.

[62] See N Dunne, *Competition Law and Economic Regulation* (Cambridge University Press, 2015) 287; and N Dunne, 'Commitment Decisions in EU Competition Law' (2014) 10 *Journal of Competition Law & Economics* 399, 411–12.

[63] Franck, 'Competition enforcement versus regulation as market-opening tools' (n 9) sub II, subsection 'Third scenario: Enforcement of pro-competitive regulation by competition authorities' 18–19.

[64] ibid, sub II, subsection 'Procedural and institutional limitations' 10.

[65] Armour et al (n 18) 556 ('Self-interested unelected officials … may exploit their delegated discretion with a view to seeking re-appointment, enhancing their current or future career prospects … expanding their power base, procuring additional human and financial resources for their agencies, pursuing pet projects, avoiding disputes with their political masters or the industry they regulate').

Certainly, such agency problems can be minimised through internal organisation, behavioural guidelines and monitoring mechanisms.[66] Moreover, leadership seems to be crucial: the tone from the top is an essential aspect in public authorities, so that each individual staff member does his or her best to ensure that the regulatory objectives are achieved in the best possible way.

While, prima facie, there is no reason to believe that agency problems are in general dealt with more or less effectively in competition authorities compared with financial market or network regulators, in the following we will touch on two aspects that deserve special attention for the institutional design of fintech competition policy: sector regulators are regarded as being more vulnerable to agency capture; and effective procompetitive interventions require a procompetitive mindset from acting officials.

A. Corruption and Agency Capture

Public enforcement is often associated with officers who are under-incentivised for effective and efficient enforcement.[67] Staff members cannot pocket fines they impose on violators and typically have no other (direct) monetary incentive to optimise enforcement. Performance-based compensation is quite a rare phenomenon and difficult to design.[68] This poses a systematic risk of corruption, namely of collusion between infringers and public enforcement agents, which results in a socially suboptimal level of enforcement.[69]

However, one should not be too quick with a critical evaluation of civil servants' incentive structure.[70] First, while civil servants indeed typically receive a fixed salary, in a well-organised public bureaucracy they may rightly expect that doing a good job will pay off through a rise in the hierarchy, which will in turn lead to more power and a higher salary. Second, civil servants might be sufficiently eager to enforce the law encouraged through non-monetary pay-off. They act in the awareness that their work serves the general interest and the public good ('public service ethos').[71] Indeed, it seems plausible that those who

[66] ibid, 567–74 (discussing five institutional arrangements to constrain regulatory failure with a view on financial market regulation: transparency requirements; independent oversight; precommitment mechanisms; compensation; and liability).

[67] Thus, it is a common assumption that private enforcement, compared with bureaucratic enforcement, can be associated with efficiency gains. AM Polinsky, 'Private versus Public Enforcement of Fines' (1980) 9 *Journal of Legal Studies* 105, 107 ('the profit motive might be imagined to lead to lower costs under either form of private enforcement relative to public enforcement'); MA Cohen and PH Rubin, 'Private Enforcement of Public Policy' (1985) 3 *Yale Journal on Regulation* 167, 188–89.

[68] Armour et al (n 18) 571–73.

[69] GS Becker and GJ Stigler, 'Law Enforcement, Malfeasance, and Compensation of Enforcers' (1974) 3 *Journal of Legal Studies* 1, 3–4.

[70] Franck, 'Private Enforcement versus Public Enforcement' (n 34) 123.

[71] Armour et al (n 18) 555, 572, fn 71.

enforce the antitrust laws and other procompetitive regulation draw their motivation (at least in part) from the conviction that they belong to the 'good guys'. It is therefore advisable for a bureaucracy to invest in generating an ethos from which the individual staff member can derive a non-material return.

Where the enforcement activities of an authority are corrupted, one speaks of agency capture: the regulated market participants have acquired a position to influence the enforcement process to their advantage.[72] It seems generally acknowledged that sector-specific supervisory authorities – such as financial market authorities – are more vulnerable to capture.[73] They typically have multiple contacts to representatives of the industry, compared with, for example, competition authorities that exercise cross-industry enforcement powers. Companies that are subject to financial market regulation often maintain a continuous exchange with the authority.[74] What is more, where an industry is subject to sector-specific regulation, industry participants have strong incentives to invest in maintaining good relations with the competent authority. Certainly, we may be hopeful that outright bribery and corruption will remain a (rare) exception in UK or EU Member States. However, it is fair to assume, as learned observers of financial market regulation have remarked, that 'there are a variety of other more subtle ways in which the regulator's agenda may be captured by the industry'.[75] First, it is not uncommon that enforcers, to ensure their expertise, are recruited from, for example, the financial industry, and that they will work (again) for the industry after their tenure. Those 'revolving doors' may tempt enforcers to act leniently in individual cases when they hope for later benefits.[76] Second, the prestige and budget of an authority may be related to the fact that the supervised industry is flourishing, as well as a general consensus that this condition is vital for the wellbeing of society[77] – aligning the interests of enforcers and regulatees. Third, given the natural information deficit that each enforcer faces, regulated firms have strong incentives to coordinate and to strategically bias the information a sector-specific enforcer will get hold of so that the latter gets a systematically distorted picture of the state of the industry and its impact on social welfare.[78]

[72] See GJ Stigler, 'The Theory of Economic Regulation' (1971) 2 *Bell Journal of Economics and Management Science* 3.

[73] T Indig and MS Gal, 'New Powers – New Vulnerabilities? A Critical Analysis of Market Inquiries Performed by Competition Authorities' in J Drexl and F Di Porto (eds), *Competition Law as Regulation* (Edward Elgar, 2015) 108; Hellwig (n 55) 5.

[74] Armour et al (n 18) 561.

[75] ibid, 92.

[76] ibid, 561. Some doubt whether 'revolving doors' result in significant capture effects: T Makkai and J Braithwaite, 'In and Out the Revolving Door: Making Sense of Regulatory Capture' (1992) 12 *Journal of Public Policy* 61, 72 (arguing that 'it would be misguided public policy to put any limits on recruitment from the industry or on leaving the regulatory agency to work for the industry').

[77] ibid, 562 (pointing to the US financial services industry's efforts to foster a widespread belief that a large and sophisticated financial services sector was in the best interests of all Americans and aptly dubbing this 'soft' capture).

[78] ibid, 92.

One may safely deduce from this that – at least in the abstract – the risk that a financial market authority enforces the law with a bias towards the interest of the industry is greater than with a competition authority.[79] The latter may therefore prove to be the more appropriate authority when it comes to enforcing rules aimed at facilitating market entry for fintech firms in the face of resistance from incumbent firms in the financial industry.[80]

B. Procompetitive Mindset

Anyone who wants to understand the functioning of a bureaucracy should also look at how its individual members perceive the world. Their perception of the 'public interest' they are bound to serve is derived from their individual view of the usefulness, reasonableness and legitimacy of the orders they are supposed to enforce, as well as of the interests of the regulated market participants and stakeholders affected by enforcement and non-enforcement of the regulation. Thus, it has been observed that agency policy is driven by 'shared values that, in effect, become ideologies'.[81] The internalised ethos of a public authority should not simply be conceived as an aggregate of the beliefs and policy preferences of all its staff, but as something that can be purposefully guided in a certain direction. Again, leadership and the tone at the top seem to be crucial: studies indicate that the values of key officials in an organisation tend to have a crucial impact on the value system internalised by staff members when pursuing violations.[82]

Members of staff that are entrusted with the enforcement of competition law or other procompetitive regulation should ideally share the conviction that the regulatory objective of lowering entry barriers and enhancing competition is (at least broadly) in the best interests of society at large. For promoting such a procompetitive mindset,[83] it is certainly helpful if an authority's activities are consistent in pursuing one regulatory objective. Herein lies a comparative institutional advantage of competition authorities in enforcing procompetitive interventions.

In detail, however, it may turn out that competition authorities feel uncomfortable with the kind of procompetitive intervention that is called for to open

[79] However, competition law, given its (supposedly) open-ended goals and, at any rate, open-textured provisions, appears to be particularly susceptible to 'intellectual' capture: A Ezrachi, 'Sponge' (2017) 5 *Journal of Antitrust Enforcement* 49, 70–71.

[80] Franck, 'Competition enforcement versus regulation as market-opening tools' (n 9) sub II, subsection 'First scenario: Enforcement of procompetitive regulation by a sector regulator' 16–18; and sub III, subsection 'Where does the complementary role of competition investigations manifest itself?' 28–30.

[81] Hawkins and Thomas (n 10) 17 ('social constructionist view' of the regulatory process).

[82] ibid, 18.

[83] The terminology is borrowed from T Ackermann, 'Excessive Pricing and the Goals of Competition Law' in D Zimmer (ed), *The Goals of Competition Law* (Edward Elgar, 2012) 369.

up the market in favour of fintech. This can be seen, first, in the enforcement of competition law when it proves necessary to impose detailed behavioural requirements on an infringer which are technical in nature, and which have to be negotiated and monitored. A competition authority might well prove reluctant here as it wants to avoid drifting into the role of a quasi-regulator. It may fear for its procompetitive spirit, which rests on the belief that a competition authority should avoid the temptation to engage in market design, but that competition enforcement should be limited to ad hoc ex post control and the prohibition of certain defined elements of market conduct.[84]

For similar reasons and a fear of the consistency of their procompetitive ethos, it may also be that competition authorities are sceptical about expanding their competences to the enforcement of procompetitive regulation. In fact, there is no denying that the enforcement of (procompetitive) sector-specific law follows a different pattern from competition enforcement. While the latter usually requires assessing and weighing up the market circumstances and the likely consequences of intervention in each individual case, infringements of hard rules – simply put – need to be detected and sanctioned. The authority's leeway may then be limited to deciding whether or not to take up a case in the first place, and which sanctions to impose if an infringement is found. This might seem quite unsatisfactory to a competition authority that is used to having the mission and the means to get to the root of an identified competition deficit.[85]

VI. CONFLICTING REGULATORY OBJECTIVES

Fintech markets are subject not only to regulatory interventions aiming at enhancing competition, but also to regulation that pursues other policy objectives: stability of the financial sector, security and technical integrity of trading systems, consumer and investor protection, data (privacy) protection or the fight against money laundering.[86] In individual cases, the pursuit of these policy objectives may directly contradict procompetitive measures. Furthermore, a high level of regulation in terms of consumer protection, data protection, investor protection, etc may in any case favour incumbents over (potential) newcomers as it

[84] Franck, 'Competition enforcement versus regulation as market-opening tools' (n 9) sub II, subsection 'Procedural and institutional limitations' 9–10.

[85] ibid, sub II, subsection 'Third scenario: Enforcement of procompetitive regulation by a competition authority' 19.

[86] All these protective goals can be identified, eg, in the German Federal Financial Supervisory Authority's legal mission profile. Explicit mention is made of these goals, eg, in s 6(4) of the Banking Act Kreditwesengesetz – KWG) ('stability of the financial system'); s 10(2) 3rd sentence PSSA ('high level of technical security'); s 4(1a) 1st sentence of the Financial Services Supervisory Act (Finanzdienstleistungsaufsichtsgesetz – FinDAG) ('Within its legal mandate, the Federal Agency is also obliged to protect the collective interests of consumers'); s 10(2) 3rd sentence PSSA ('high level of … data protection'); s 50 no 1 in conjunction with s 4(1) Money Laundering Act (Geldwäschegesetz – GwG) ('prevention of money laundering and terrorist financing').

creates barriers to entry. In fact, it is not the exception but the rule that enforcement procedures are confronted with policy trade-offs. Institutional design will have implications on how these trade-offs are managed. It will make a difference, for example, whether a sector regulator such as the FCA[87] is entrusted with the enforcement of both competition policy and protectionist regulation or whether separate authorities implement the various regulatory regimes in parallel.

While the expectation of creating useful synergies may speak for the former arrangement,[88] there have been warnings against bundling competences for the enforcement of procompetitive measures and those with conflicting objectives.[89] This may be seen as particularly problematic with a view on the competence portfolio of financial market authorities. Those authorities' priorities will typically lie with the stability of the supervised sector. Rigorous enforcement of rules that are intended to open markets and provoke fiercer competition may be seen as problematic in this respect, as when the traditional business models of the banks or other incumbents are challenged this may entail risks – in part real, in part only perceived[90] – for the stability of the financial sector.[91] The supervisory authority may therefore find itself in a conflict of objectives and might be tempted to take the latter effect into account when deciding how vigorously it will work to enforce rules designed to open markets up to newcomers.[92]

In addition, financial market authorities have to focus on the technical stability of trading platforms or payment systems, for example. The special relationship of proximity between regulators and regulated parties in the financial industry, based on a continuous exchange of information and monitoring – which has been emphasised above with regard to enforcement style[93] – can also have an impact here. There is a risk that sector regulators, who are very familiar with the business models and technical systems of the regulated industry, will at

[87] See above (n 20) and accompanying text.

[88] See above section IV.

[89] Kovacic and Hyman (n 11) 533.

[90] Carletti and Smolenska (n 1) 19 ('However, given the risks perceived to be posed by FinTech, the regulatory framework might lead to raising barriers to entry into the market (eg by introducing licencing regimes)').

[91] See, on the interrelation between financial stability and competition, Dean Corbae and Ross Levine, 'Competition, Stability and Efficiency in Financial Markets' in 2018 Jackson Hole Symposium: Changing Market Structure and Implications for Monetary Policy (Kansas City Federal Reserve, available at: www.kansascityfed.org/Jackson%20Hole/documents/6988/Corbae_JH2018.pdf) 357–409), who conclude at 395: '1. An intensification of bank competition tends to (a) squeeze bank profit margins, reduce bank charter values, and spur lending and (b) increase the fragility of banks. There is a competition-stability trade-off. 2. Policymakers can get the efficiency benefit of competition without the fragility costs by enhancing bank governance and tightening leverage requirements'. See also X Vives, *Competition and Stability in Banking: The Role of Regulation and Competition Policy* (Princeton University Press, 2016) 228. An overview of the economic literature and its ambiguous results on the interrelationship between intensity of competition and stability of financial markets is provided by JK Mendelsohn, *Systemrisiko und Wirtschaftsordnung im Bankensektor. Zum Ende von Too Big To Fail* (Nomos, 2018) 146–66.

[92] Carletti and Smolenska (n 1) 20; Hellwig (n 55) 5.

[93] See above, section III.B.

the same time develop a particularly good understanding of their interests and thus be inclined to give (too high) a weighting to them in the event of trade-offs in the administrative process. With a view to the payment industry, this can be illustrated with some anecdotal evidence.[94] When staff members of the German BaFin discussed the market entry of payment initiation services in an article published in its journal, it focused solely on the technical risks (in particular, the possibility of 'man-in-the-middle attacks'), which were presented, as it seems, in an overly general and exaggerated manner.[95] In contrast, when elaborating on the same issues in a decision on payment initiation services, the Bundeskartellamt put those risks into perspective and pointed to the fact that the banks themselves offered services that entailed exactly the same risks.[96]

In sum, there are indicators that financial market authorities may not be perfectly incentivised to enforce procompetitive regulation and one might doubt, for instance, the wisdom of entrusting the German BaFin with the enforcement of provisions that are meant to facilitate market entry of payment initiation services.[97]

VII. LEGITIMISING ELEMENTS IN COMPETITION PROCEDURES

Where the legislature promotes fintech competition through market-opening intervention, its democratic legitimacy is straightforward: enacted provisions are approved by elected representatives who may be held accountable by the people. Authorities that enforce procompetitive rules and standards and thus put the law into action bear likewise great responsibility for the formation and development of competition policy. Hence, their practice also requires democratic legitimacy and accountability.[98] Robert Baldwin has identified five main arguments that are consistently employed to justify administrative rule-making: legislative mandate, accountability or control, due process, expertise, and efficiency.[99] These rationales also carry persuasive power with a view to competition enforcement: competition authorities act based on competences granted to them by the legislature and with a mandate with a (relatively) clearly

[94] Franck, 'Competition enforcement versus regulation as market-opening tools' (n 9) sub III, subsection 'Where does the complementary role of competition investigations manifest itself?' 30.

[95] J Kokert and M Held, 'Zahlungsdiensterichtlinie II – Risiken und schwerwiegende Folgen für Nutzer und Kreditinstitute' ('Payment Services Directive II – Risks and Severe Consequences for Users and Credit Institutions') *BaFin Journal* (June 2014), available at: www.bafin.de/SharedDocs/Veroeffentlichungen/DE/Fachartikel/2014/fa_bj_1406_zahlungsdiensterichtlinie_II.html.

[96] Bundeskartellamt, 29 June 2016, B4-71/10, *Zahlungsauslösedienste*, paras 351–58, 417–22.

[97] See above (n 21).

[98] Franck, 'Competition enforcement versus regulation as market-opening tools' (n 9) sub II, subsection 'Different modes of legitimation: competition enforcement as the (more) technocratic way of rulemaking' 14–15.

[99] R Baldwin, *Rules and Government* (Clarendon Press, 1995) 42–48.

defined set of tasks. Competition proceedings follow the rule of law and measures imposed on firms are scrutinised by courts.[100] Authorities are considered to have special professional and technical expertise. Consequently, judicial review may be restricted.[101]

The constitutional requirements for the democratic legitimacy of bureaucratic measures may vary considerably among jurisdictions. Authorities may be held accountable for their activities either (directly) by Parliament or by ministries. A distinction must be made between exerting influence and exercising control over financial matters ('power of the purse'), staff and/or substantive orientation of the authority. Analysing those governing constitutional framework(s) is beyond the scope of this chapter.[102] What is of interest here, however, is a functional dimension to legitimacy and accountability: enforcement processes should yield decisions and create norms that are widely accepted among the addressed market players and the relevant stakeholders. This in turn may depend on the institutional design of the enforcement process, which should, ideally, promote a 'willingness to comply'[103] among the regulated and a conviction to intervene legitimately on the part of the bureaucracy.

In practical terms, that appears to be particularly relevant for the regulatory facet of competition enforcement, which may be crucial when it comes to facilitating market access for innovative fintech firms. In fact, competition proceedings against an industry-dominant firm upon which behavioural remedies are imposed or against multiple firms in one industry with the imposition of uniform behavioural remedies may ultimately come close to industry-wide rule-making. It would seem quite conceivable that competition authorities are reluctant to act as quasi-regulatory market openers (even if perfectly within the remedial leeway entrusted by the law) as they do not see themselves as being sufficiently legitimised for this kind of rule-making.[104]

A legislature that wishes competition authorities feel comfortable in an active role to open markets through competition enforcement seems well advised to provide for procedural elements that promote legitimacy and accountability

[100] See above, section II.B.

[101] See, eg, the Commission's margin of assessment regarding economic matters as confirmed in the ECJ's case law. Case C-413/06 P *Bertelsmann and Sony Corporation of America v Impala*, ECLI:EU:C:2008:392, para 69.

[102] Note, however, that the ECN+ Directive sets a harmonised minimum standard for competition enforcement by Member States with regard to essential relevant aspects such as independence of authorities (Art 4) and resources (Art 5). See Directive (EU) 2019/1 of the European Parliament and of the Council of 11 December 2018 to empower the competition authorities of the Member States to be more effective enforcers and to ensure the proper functioning of the internal market [2019] OJ L11/3.

[103] Black (n 48) 87.

[104] This can be different if a cartel authority is granted quasi-regulatory powers – beyond classical competition enforcement. This is the direction taken by the new instrument introduced under s 19a of the German Competition Act. See J-U Franck and M Peitz, 'Digital Platforms and the New 19a Tool in the German Competition Act' (2021) 12 *Journal of European Competition Law & Practice* 513.

of competition remedies. Authorities should have the option to hold public oral hearings where the representatives of the business segment affected – but also stakeholders – can state their case and make their voices heard. Moreover, procedural rules should facilitate the involvement of external experts if considered useful by the authority or the parties. The implementation of such a participatory enforcement style seems indeed a major challenge for conventional competition proceedings. At this point, a significant advantage of rule-making via UK-style market investigation becomes apparent. The UK's Open Banking initiative, for instance, aiming among other things at the promotion of fintech, has shown how this instrument may work particularly well for the opening of markets and where competition enforcement may hit its institutional limitations as a regulatory tool.[105]

VIII. CONCLUDING REMARKS

This chapter has shed some light on various factors that have an impact on 'the way the agency bureaucracy develops and implements enforcement policy'[106] and which may be of relevance with a view on what has been dubbed here 'fintech competition enforcement'. As might be expected, the insights that can be grasped are for the most part quite abstract and general; the aspects elaborated do not necessarily point in one direction and their interaction can prove to be complex. In fact, much depends on the political, social and economic framework into which an institutional design is 'placed'. Crucially, moreover, it also depends on the persons who act within a given institutional structure. In fact, quite different competition policies may be yielded using the very same institutional design.

Does that mean we are none the wiser as to normative implications? The complexity of these institutional design issues should, first, remind us that the best we can strive for are robust second-best solutions. Yet, no jurisdiction is locked into an existing institutional arrangement. Building on the status quo, incremental improvements for better competition enforcement and implementation of procompetitive policies are always possible.[107]

That is true in general but also regarding the promotion of fintech competition. Some detailed suggestions are given. For instance, the institutional design of competition proceedings could be adapted to improve enforcers' capacity to establish market-opening rules. That might include facilitated options of stakeholder and external expert involvement as well as public hearings. Moreover, a

[105] Overview provided by Franck, 'Competition enforcement versus regulation as market-opening tools' (n 9) sub IV, subsection 'Illustration: Retail banking market investigation with open banking remedies' 33.

[106] See above (n 10).

[107] Kovacic and Hyman (n 11) 537.

few cautious statements of a more general type can be made. There are sound reasons to be sceptical about seeing financial market authorities as agile enforcers of a procompetitive agenda, facilitating fintech market entry. In contrast, there are good arguments in favour of assigning the competition authorities, in addition to their original role as enforcers of competition law, competences for the implementation of other procompetitive regulation, including those provisions specifically aimed at enhancing fintech competition.

Beyond the actual enforcement activities, a major challenge for fintech competition is to ensure that possible anticompetitive effects are considered when regulating to protect the stability and technical integrity of financial markets, but also when implementing the law for the protection of consumers and investors, as well as privacy laws and laws against money laundering. Ideally, competition authorities could act here, beyond their actual enforcement powers, as 'advocates' of open and competitive markets.[108] Admittedly, this may be quite delicate as it reaches into the competences of other authorities and into the political sphere. Therefore, the pursuit of an 'advocacy function' could be supported through institutional design, for example if competition authorities need to be informed about certain proceedings and are given a right to submit competitive concerns. In the case of an 'multipurpose' institution, such as a financial market authority that has competition enforcement powers, it may prove beneficial to concentrate competition competences in one department whose staff internalise a procompetitive mindset and can then also take up the cudgels for low barriers to entry with a view to the various fields of protective regulation.

As an observer of legislative processes relating to financial markets regulation and competition policy, one can get the impression that institutional design issues of bureaucratic enforcement are often decided ad hoc and pragmatically, but not reflected upon theoretically. In any case, lawyers rarely bring these theoretical aspects into the debate; this is not surprising, as both legal practitioners and legal academics tend not to deal with these questions in depth. The gap between socio-legal understandings of bureaucratic law enforcement and the rationalities that in practice determine the setting of the legal framework for it seems considerable, to say the least. This chapter has therefore already served a good purpose in stimulating reflection on the institutional design of bureaucratic enforcement among those concerned with fintech competition and regulation. For there is no question that the practical effectiveness of any measure to promote fintech competition will depend on choices of institutional design.

[108] Carletti and Smolenska (n 1) 20.

12

The Role of Sectoral Regulators and Other State Actors in Formulating Novel and Alternative Pro-Competition Mechanisms in Fintech

DEIRDRE AHERN

I. INTRODUCTION

THE CONVERGENCE OF finance and technological innovation continues to provide exciting opportunities for innovators, investors and consumers in the Fourth Industrial Revolution as digital markets both develop and evolve. A vast array of new fintech services and refashioned business models have come to market including challenger neobanks, robo-advisors, crowdfunding platforms, digital wallet services and virtual currencies along with associated business to business (B2B) services. Developments continue apace such as the rise of the decentralised finance (DeFi) ecosystem using distributed ledger technologies (DLT) infrastructure to transform and further disintermediate financial services. The benefits are immense. Fintech businesses can create efficiencies, boost competition and bring down costs for market entry. Alternative finance providers enable low-cost access to digital finance and banking benefiting financial inclusion for the unbanked and underbanked population.[1] Increased competition can also benefit consumers of disintermediated financial services,[2] who benefit from reduced switching and transaction costs as

[1] T Philippon, 'On Fintech and Financial Inclusion' (2019) National Bureau of Economic Research, Working Paper No w26330.

[2] Cambridge Centre for Alternative Finance, *Second Global Alternative Finance Market Benchmarking Report* (2021) 51, 54–55; Federal Deposit Insurance Corporation, 2017 FDIC National Survey of Unbanked and Underbanked Households (2018) 4.

well as ease of use. While the Covid-19 pandemic accelerated fintech market penetration,[3] often relevant markets cannot yet be characterised as established or stable. Access to data and capital are key as is the need to be able to navigate a complex and transitioning regulatory landscape. Although it is impossible to predict how competition in digital markets will evolve, policy discourse often refers to the potential for a 'barbell' market comprising a small number of large players and large numbers of smaller players.[4] In the digital economy start-ups can enter markets with low entry costs while less agile incumbents may struggle to adapt. Traditional financial institutions with legacy systems may struggle to adapt their offerings to the fintech era. There are veritable minnows who want to innovate as small start-ups and other fintechs who want to scale up. Meanwhile there are tech giants whose dominance across multiple spheres seems unstoppable, making it difficult for challenger firms to make headway.

In this global digital environment, the pace of technological innovation and the speed of states to appropriately calibrate the business and regulatory environment places domestic and global competitive pressure on the fintech ecosystem. In a time of exponential and rapid change many countries have consciously set out to provide an enabling environment for fintechs to incentivise innovation and growth while promoting market confidence. Traditionally regulators have been gatekeepers to market entry. However, there is now a common sentiment among governments and regulators that they should also be nurturers of would-be participants in these fledgling markets so as to contribute to effective fintech competition and growth. Behind this is an economic imperative. Fintech activities have huge potential to drive gross domestic product (GDP) growth, inward investment and cross-border trade. Accordingly, this chapter probes innovative methods that qualify as novel or non-traditional that are being employed by state actors in a bid to boost fintech market participation with the overarching objective of encouraging disruptive innovation and economic growth. Not to put too fine a point on it, to realise the value proposition that fintech implies as a force for positive market disruption, state actors across the globe have been bending over backwards to lend their support to intending fintech disruptors, stepping outside traditional perceptions of the role of regulators, and their expected relationships with their regulatory subjects. The associated upending of the traditional vertical regulatory relationship in favour of a less hierarchical one which focuses beyond the 'rulebook' is what makes it so fascinating for observers of fintech markets and regulation to study.

Although there is consensus across states on the need to attract and foster fintech innovation, there is no manual for how that should be achieved. Rather,

[3] World Bank Group, 'Fintech and the Future of Finance: Overview Paper' (2022) 79.

[4] E Feyen et al 'Fintech and the Digital Transformation of Financial Services' (2021) Bank for International Settlements, BIS Papers No 117, v.

state actors are innovating versatile policy initiatives with a view to attract fintech innovators. Regulators, realising that the national interest in securing fintech turf is at stake, have looked at what their international counterparts have been doing, while others have also been cultivating original tools in service of a pro-fintech agenda in their own right. The position taken here is that state actors are generally to be lauded for their efforts to promote competition and market entry. These measures can, however, pose countervailing policy challenges and outcomes in the round may not be fair or transparent. Moreover, it is contended that, consistent with the evolution of market conditions, a re-evaluation of appropriate regulatory strategies is called for.

The nature of competition goals and their role in policy stances in relation to fintech markets is introduced in section II which discusses competition and fintech markets and the role of the state before moving on to discuss the economic rationale behind pro-innovation tools being pioneered by state actors. Section III moves to explore how crucial elements of fintech infrastructure – access to data and interoperability of systems; access to talent; assistance with the cost of research and development and protection of intellectual property; and access to finance – are being bolstered to help the fintech ecosystem develop and mature. Section IV examines how regulators' provision of fintech supports such as incubators and sandboxes fare as alternative competition promotion mechanisms. It also discusses initiatives that help market entrants to navigate the regulatory environment. Section V makes the case for a more nuanced and integrated policy approach on competition promotion to be adopted by regulators as fintech markets become more established.

II. THE ROLE OF THE STATE IN COMPETITION PROMOTION

When exploring novel and pro-competition mechanisms in fintech, it is relevant to consider how and why they exist, both in the early stages of fintech, and as fintech markets begin to mature. The world has reached 'fintech 4.0', characterised by digitalisation, BigTech and the platform economy with its predomination of digital finance platforms.[5] Although technology transcends geographic borders and fuels globalisation, regulatory and other barriers to entry (including access to finance and labour) influence choice of location for fintech businesses at start-up and scale-up phases. Evidence suggests that alternative finance markets globally are most developed in two jurisdictional groups:[6] first, countries with well-developed finance systems such as Singapore, the United Kingdom (UK) and the United States (US); and second, countries that

[5] DW Arner et al, 'Governing Fintech 4.0: Bigtech, Platform Finance, and Sustainable Development' (2022) 27 *Fordham Journal of Corporate & Financial Law* 1.

[6] Cambridge Centre for Alternative Finance (n 2) 64.

have consciously set out to become attractive hubs for alternative finance such as Estonia[7] and Lithuania.[8]

The level of future innovation and number of competitors is not capable of being mapped out, in part because the capacity for innovation and ease of entry by large players to a whole milieu of upstream and downstream markets defies ready prediction.[9] There are different views on the prognosis for technological innovation. As one commentator puts it:

> Are we living in a period of technology exhaustion, where there are too few big breakthroughs and competition is being fought out through small incremental improvements to old ideas? Or are we on the brink of accelerating change, where technical advances on a number of fronts are about to unleash giant new digital markets?[10]

The true picture may lie somewhere in the middle. In competition terms, the state of existing relevant markets is uneven and fintech markets across jurisdictions do not offer anything approximating a level playing field in terms of barriers to market entry.

Regulation functions to establish trust which propels product and market expansion.[11] By contrast, lack of bespoke regulatory frameworks and resultant legal uncertainty inhibit stable market development and encourage regulatory arbitrage.[12] Encouraging competition when regulatory frameworks lag behind is a tricky business. Buckley et al see any threat of a race to the bottom as being trumped by the 'dire need of more competition'.[13] This is complex territory. Questions of appropriate regulatory approach to fintech activities are not the direct focus of this chapter but the push–pull regulatory tension between supporting a burgeoning industry and regulating it forms a salient part of the calculations being made by state actors taking initiatives to promote competition.[14]

[7] Estonia punches well above its weight with 10 unicorns (business valued at more than $1 billion), one for every 130,000 of its population in comparison to one per 7 million in China: John Thornhill, 'Plural Launches €250mn Entrepreneur-led Fund for European Tech Start-Ups' *Financial Times* (28 June 2022), available at: www.ft.com/content/9e3eaca6-5949-4791-931f-7c703f796843.

[8] Lithuania has more regulated fintechs than any other EU Member State based on development of its licensing regime and has benefited from Brexit relocations.

[9] See, eg, Apple's planned entry to the 'Buy Now, Pay Later' merchant space: Ron Shevlin, 'How Apple will Boost the Apple Card with Buy Now Pay Later' (*Forbes*, 28 June 2022), available at: www.forbes.com/sites/ronshevlin/2022/06/28/how-apple-will-boost-the-apple-card-with-buy-now-pay-later/.

[10] Richard Waters, 'Tech Breakthroughs are Still Coming' *Financial Times* (24 March 2022), available at: www.ft.com/content/997e875b-8262-484e-979f-0cd89f2a1874.

[11] Organisation for Economic Co-operation and Development (OECD), 'Refining Regulation to Enable Major Innovations in Financial Markets' (2015) Issues Paper DAF/COMP/WP2, 9.

[12] D Ahern, 'Regulatory Arbitrage in a FinTech World: Devising an Optimal EU Regulatory Response to Crowdlending' (2018) 3 *Journal of Business Law* 193.

[13] RP Buckley, D Arner, R Veidt and D Zetzsche, 'Building FinTech Ecosystems: Regulatory Sandboxes, Innovation Hubs and Beyond' (2020) 61 *Washington University Journal of Law and Policy* 55, 76.

[14] See further D Ahern, 'Regulators Nurturing Fintech Innovation: Global Evolution of the Regulatory Sandbox as Opportunity-Based Regulation' (2019) 15 *Indian Journal of Law and Technology* 345.

Competition law has an instrumental role to play in preventing market failures arising from cartels and abusive market practices by dominant market players. This holds relevance as BigTechs leverage their dominance into payment services and other fintech markets as TechFins.[15] Furthermore, digital platforms may act as defensive gatekeepers guarding access to infrastructure for downstream market entry.[16] The essential facilities doctrine may in certain circumstances act as a lever to require a dominant entity to provide access to an essential resource to enable market entry.[17] However, competition law 'only reacts to [a] particular kind of market failure'.[18] As the Organisation for Economic Co-operation and Development (OECD) notes, '[i]n general, competition policy focuses on cases where market power is durable, rather than a temporary reward for innovation that can be contested by a competitor with novel technologies'.[19] As such, while well suited for addressing abuses of a dominant position or collusion, competition law will typically not provide any basis for intervention in nascent and underdeveloped fintech markets. In short, once competition law rules have been complied with, a more general objective of facilitating market access and scaling lies beyond the classic concerns of competition law. This is in line with the free market approach in open economies that allows markets to develop freely without state intervention subject to compliance with the law. That being the case, this chapter is interested in how the arrival of fintech has motivated regulators to seek to ensure positive competition participation outcomes for fintech freed from any requirement to first establish anticompetitive practices. Regulators, governments and trade promotion bodies are focused on maximising the potential for innovators to use technology and synergies to provide financial services, but also on nudges that make it attractive for them to explore doing so in their jurisdiction.

Global trade policies of states are aligned with fintech trade development goals to ensure a cohesive digital finance strategy. Bilateral and multilateral trade agreements can help to promote inter-jurisdictional trade and build up the fintech ecosystem. These trade agreements often contain provisions that help to promote market entry and digital trade, most notably through provisions surrounding data access and data transfer across borders.[20] Fintech bridges typically involve some element of regulatory cooperation between jurisdictions.

[15] Bank for International Settlements, 'Big Tech in Finance: Opportunities and Risks' (2019).

[16] The EU Commission is investigating whether Apple abused its dominant position by restricting third-party access to technology needed to develop rival mobile wallet solutions to Apple Pay on Apple devices: European Commission, 'Antitrust: Commission Sends Statement of Objections to Apple over Practices Regarding Apple Pay' IP/22/2764 (2 May 2022); Javier Espinoza, 'Apple Charged by Brussels with Abusing Its Market Power in Mobile Payments' *Financial Times* (2 May 2022).

[17] See, eg, Case C-7/97 *Oscar Bronner GmbH & Co KG v Mediaprint Zeitungs und Zeitschriftenverlag GmbH & Co KG*, ECLI:EU:C:1998:569.

[18] J Drexl, 'Designing Competitive Markets for Industrial Data – Between Propertisation and Access' (2016) Max Planck Institute for Innovation and Competition Research Paper No 16-13, 43.

[19] OECD, 'Handbook on Competition Policy in the Digital Age' (2022) 15.

[20] See, eg, Chapter 19 of the trade agreement between the United States, Mexico and Canada (USMCA) in force 1 July 2020.

Both regulators and firms benefit from the exchange of information involved. Although they have become common in the broader fintech global landscape, fintech bridges lack a uniform definition.[21] As described in the Kalifa Review:

> Each fintech bridge is unique, but they typically allow access to events, meetings and networking opportunities, referrals to streamline regulatory approval, introductions to buyers, investors, trade associations and institutions, advice and one-to-one mentoring from fintech specialists and discounted 'soft-landing pads', grants or subsidies.[22]

Free marketism is having inroads carved into it as state actors globally are proactively devising creative strategies to promote and support competition in fintech markets,[23] and doing so in ways that go beyond the blunt tool of regulatory rules. As Drexl writes, '[t]he question is not only how to protect the free market economy against anti-competitive conduct of firms. Rather, the question is what can be done in order to promote the digital economy'.[24] The underlying justification is a broad, economic 'public interest' goal, rather than narrower competition law-based concerns. There are two limbs to this economic agenda – direct market benefits and associated indirect economic benefits to the state. Fintech's ascendancy 'increases the set of viable arrangements for producing financial services'.[25] Undoubtedly, there are associated benefits for business and retail consumers. Fintech services make customer onboarding, payment services and the delivery of banking and other services more secure, more efficient, more frictionless and more cost-effective while revolutionising and expanding access to financial services markets. At a macro level, the economic benefits to the economy at large[26] are at work in how state actors are playing their hand.[27] States want their piece of the fintech action. This economic motivation is prodding states to be creative in adopting novel pro-competition and pro-innovation mechanisms that frequently lie outside the usual range of tools of a regulator.[28]

[21] As of 2021, the United Kingdom had fintech bridges with Australia, China, Hong Kong, Singapore and South Korea. See generally, L Bromberg, A Godwin and I Ramsay, 'Cross-border Cooperation in Financial Regulation: Crossing the Fintech Bridge' (2018) 13 *Capital Markets Law Journal* 59.

[22] Sir Ron Kalifa, *Kalifa Review of UK Fintech* (HM Treasury, 2021) 38.

[23] See, eg, Australian Government, *Economic Benefits of FinTech* (The Treasury, 2016); European Commission, *Shaping Europe's Digital Future* (2020).

[24] Drexl (n 18) 43.

[25] HE Jackson, 'The Nature of the Fintech Firm' (2020) 61 *Washington University Journal of Law & Policy* 9, 11.

[26] In 2020 the largest alternative finance regional market size was the United States and Canada, followed by the United Kingdom, Europe (excluding the United Kingdom), then Asia Pacific (excluding China), Latin America and the Caribbean (led by Brazil), Sub-Saharan Africa, China, and the Middle East and North Africa (MENA): Cambridge Centre for Alternative Finance (n 2) 25.

[27] 'With Fintech, not only is the classic regulatory dilemma between a facilitatory approach and a regulatory approach at play … an economic agenda is also a significant undercurrent at work': Ahern, 'Regulatory Arbitrage in a FinTech World' (n 12) 347.

[28] Broader questions of tensions between economic and other goals in this arena are turned to in section V.

Regulators are taking a broader view of their mandate. As the US Department of the Treasury has observed, '[a] regulatory environment with largely binary outcomes – either approval or disapproval – may lack appropriate flexibility for dealing with innovations'.[29] The Securities and Exchange Commission (SEC) has for some time had an express role in promoting 'efficiency, competition and capital formation' that extends its traditional investor protection mandate.[30] In the United Kingdom, the Financial Conduct Authority (FCA) not only possesses traditional market regulation functions, but its statutory dual mandate also acknowledges competition objectives including facilitating innovation and market entry.[31] Other agencies who lack this formal mandate have sallied forth with a competition promotion approach on a less formal or de facto basis.[32] Thus, within a continuum of what this author has coined 'opportunity-based regulation', financial services regulators are playing 'a critical part in actively nurturing and promoting competition in emerging and nascent FinTech markets, in addition to operating in the traditional regulatory space'.[33] This is evident in the rhetoric employed by these agencies as they contribute to making their jurisdiction competitive on the world stage, thereby delivering economic growth. Malta's Financial Service Authority expressly sets out to 'strengthen confidence in the market and its institutions, thereby fostering a robust and dynamic FinTech sector in Malta'.[34] In the United Kingdom, the FCA sets out its ambition 'to promote competition by supporting disruptive innovation … To remain Europe's leading FinTech Hub, we have to ensure that we continue to be an attractive market with an appropriate regulatory framework'.[35] Supporting the establishment of the elements of a robust infrastructure for fintech is crucial to nurturing the fintech ecosystem and the ability for innovators and their businesses to flourish. We now move to examine what supports for fintech are being put in place.

III. BUILDING THE FINTECH INFRASTRUCTURE

A. Access to Data and Interoperability

We are living in a data economy which up-ends traditional models of production. As the raw material of FinTech markets big data is the foundation for

[29] US Department of the Treasury, 'A Financial System that Creates Economic Opportunities: Nonbank Financials, Fintech and Innovation' (2018) 167.

[30] This was the effect of the National Securities Markets Improvement Act of 1996, § 106.

[31] Financial Services and Markets Act 2000, s 1B(3) (as substituted by s 6 of the Financial Services Act 2012). See further, Independent Commission on Banking, *Final Report: Recommendations* (2011) paras 8.75–8.87.

[32] See generally, Ahern, 'Regulators Nurturing Fintech Innovation' (n 14).

[33] ibid, 356.

[34] Malta Financial Services Authority, *FinTech Strategy*, available at: www.mfsa.mt/fintech/fintech-strategy/.

[35] Financial Conduct Authority (FCA), *Regulatory Sandbox* (2015) 5, available at: www.fca.org.uk/publication/research/regulatory-sandbox.pdf.

the infrastructure of fintech. In this data-driven economy, the role of the state is changing.[36] Digital IDs facilitate entirely digital onboarding by fintechs. Consequently, jurisdictions that have progressed this have a competitive advantage. In the European Union (EU), electronic identification (eID) under the Electronic IDentification, Authentication and Trust Services (eIDAS) Regulation[37] facilitates digital banking and alternative finance services but needs further reform to enable fine-tuning.[38] The United States currently lacks a recognised digital ID[39] although the US Department of the Treasury recommended the introduction of a digital national ID and the development of digital IDs through the public and private sector working together.[40] Meanwhile a key component of the UK's digital finance reform package involves providing for digital IDs.[41]

Ease of data portability is a signifier of a fintech-friendly jurisdiction. The availability of open banking in countries such as the United States is helpful to challenger fintechs in terms of reducing barriers to market entry by facilitating third-party access to client financial data which can be used to develop new fintech services. In the United Kingdom, open banking was driven by the action of the Competition and Markets Authority (CMA)[42] and data standards are planned to create the infrastructure for a secure fintech ecosystem.[43] Data portability ensures that smaller entities can compete with legacy banks by having shared secure access to customer data that will help, for example, to speed up lending decisions and thus improve the competitiveness of banking markets.[44] Open and common APIs[45] and data standards also hold real potential to facilitate market entry. These help to counteract the advantages of incumbents. Jurisdictions that have a concept of open banking that extends beyond

[36] Unsurprisingly this has generated discussion of the appropriate role of competition policy. See, eg, ME Stucke and AP Grunes, *Big Data and Competition Policy* (Oxford University Press, 2016); Drexl (n 18) 10–11; O Borgogno and G Colangelo, 'Data, Innovation and Competition in Finance: The Case of the Access to Account Rule' (2020) 31 *European Business Law Review* 573.

[37] Regulation (EU) No 910/2014 on Electronic identification and trust services for electronic transactions in the internal market [2014] OJ L257/73.

[38] On proposals to improve its operation, see 'Proposal for a Regulation amending Regulation (EU) No 910/2014 as regards establishing a framework for a European digital identity' COM/2021/281 final.

[39] However, the US Department of Commerce National Institute of Standards and Technology (NIST) has issued technical requirements for federal government use: NIST, *Digital Identity Guidelines* (SP 800-63) (2022).

[40] US Department of the Treasury (n 29) 43.

[41] UK Department for Digital, Culture, Media and Sport, 'UK Digital Identity and Attributes Trust Framework' Policy Paper (2022).

[42] Competition and Markets Authority (CMA), 'Retail Banking Market Investigation: Final Report' (2016).

[43] UK Government, Data Standards Authority Strategy 2020 to 2023 (2021).

[44] In the United Kingdom, this was driven by the outcome of the CMA investigation in 2016. See further, CMA (n 42) and www.openbanking.org.uk/.

[45] Application Programming Interface.

data portability to API functionality include Hong Kong, Mexico, Singapore and the United States.[46] Providing for API-based open access to data (as seen in Mexico's Fintech Law) is designed to foster competition. It facilitates financial disintermediation and can increase entry routes, for example, for payment services providers. As Arner et al perceptively note:

> Regulation should aim at securing objective, transparent, and fair risk-based, rather than profit-based, conditions of access. Open interfaces, open-source code of the technology core, fair and non-discriminatory access requirements, and a transparent fee structure enable third-party developers to write proprietary applications for platform clients.[47]

On the other hand, open banking initiatives can also allow BigTechs to increase their dominance[48] and spread its influence across new market segments creating new market concentration issues.[49] As such, it should not be assumed that facilitating market entry through open data and standards will have uniform effects – it may open up markets by reducing barriers to entry but it also facilitates ease of transition of market power to expansion into retail banking markets by BigTechs which can cross-subsidise the costs of market entry and fixed costs such as compliance with complex regulatory requirements.

B. Access to Talent

States that are serious about promoting fintech competition are acutely aware of the need to take action to attract fintech talent: highly qualified data scientists, engineers and others who are vital to developing and scaling up a fintech business. This is very much a global labour market and states are aware that they must compete for talent or face the consequences in terms of ceding competitive advantage. In many cases this manifests itself in special visa and immigration programmes to make entry easier.[50] The success or otherwise of these programmes has huge ramifications for ready domestic access to a pipeline of

[46] M Zachariadis and P Ozcan, 'The API Economy and Digital Transformation in Financial Services: The Case of Open Banking' (2017) SWIFT Institute Working Paper No 2016-001; N Remolina, 'Open Banking: Regulatory Challenges for a New Form of Financial Intermediation in a Data-Driven World' (2019) SMU Centre for AI & Data Governance Research Paper 05/2019, 10.

[47] Arner et al (n 5) 57.

[48] K Stylianou, 'Exclusion in Digital Markets' (2018) 24 *Michigan Telecommunications & Technology Law Review* 181.

[49] These include Meta, Amazon, Google and Apple who have taken steps to enter financial services markets. As an example, before adding 'Buy Now, Pay Later' arm, Pay Later in 2022, Apple was already a presence with the Apple Card credit card, and Apple Pay enabling huge numbers of contactless payments.

[50] See, eg, Australia (Global Talent Programme); Canada (Global Talent Stream); France (Tech Visa). Following the *Kalifa Review* (n 22) 46, the United Kingdom established the Tech Nation visa programme to help fintechs to scale up.

suitably qualified personnel and how welcoming a domestic fintech ecosystem is therefore perceived to be.

C. Research and Development Tax Credits

Availability of research and development (R&D) tax credits assist in driving research and innovation and therefore competition by reducing the costs involved. It is important that the scope of R&D tax incentives is broadly enough defined by states to enable fintech so as to cover not only traditional R&D activities, but also the build-out of new fintech services atop existing legacy infrastructure systems. Similarly, acquiring financial datasets is often a critical component of building and scaling a fintech business model. Thus, it has been argued that the scope of R&D tax credits should extend to covering the costs of the acquisition of financial datasets.[51] The framing of an R&D incentive framework can also be calibrated to positively encourage innovation activities including collaborations. For example, Fintech Australia recommended that large companies should be incentivised to engage in proof-of-concept work with early-stage technology firms.[52] Protection of intellectual property also matters to fintech innovators. Realising this, Singapore scored points for the competitiveness of its regulatory environment by putting in place expedited patent review processes. The SG IP Fast Programme that launched in 2018 was a FinTech Fast Track (FTFT) for fintech inventions followed in 2019 by the Accelerated Initiative for Artificial Intelligence (AI2) for artificial intelligence (AI) inventions.[53]

D. Access to Finance

States are choosing to invest in the fintech ecosystem in order to boost it. These initiatives are targeted at achieving a wide range of defined policy objectives that will enhance competition. Funding has been used to develop tech clusters.[54] In 2017, the Monetary Authority of Singapore (MAS) launched an Artificial Intelligence and Data Analytics (AIDA) fund worth S$27 million designed to boost the development of AI fintech products. It also committed S$225 million under the Financial Sector Technology & Innovation Scheme with the objective of encouraging financial institutions to set up innovation labs in Singapore and to fund interoperable infrastructure for the benefit of the digital economy.

[51] This reform was recommended in the UK's *Kalifa Review* (n 22) 55.

[52] FinTech Australia, 'Submission to the Select Committee on Australia as a Technology and Finance Centre' (2021) 16.

[53] The success of these programmes led to the launch of the SG IP Fast Programme which applies to patent applications for all inventions until 30 April 2024.

[54] See, eg, the C$100 million investment of the Quebec Government in Scale AI as a Canadian AI super-cluster.

More generally, access to capital is not simply being left to the free market. Governments are acutely aware that fintechs need access to capital to transition beyond the start-up phase in order to scale up and to compete at a global level. In many cases there is a funding gap between supply of capital and demand for it up to pre-Initial Public Offering (IPO) phase. This represents an important barrier to entry. Countries are therefore focusing on developing means of providing routes to capital to finance fintech ventures. In the United Kingdom, the Kalifa Review recommended that a £1 billion Fintech Growth Fund would be disbursed over a five-year period to address some of the gap in growth funding to stimulate growth and thus make the United Kingdom more attractive to fintech entrepreneurs at pre-IPO stage.[55] Notably, the policy lever behind this recommendation is on ensuring that UK private institutions participate more fully in extending funding to the fintech sector rather there being over-reliance on overseas investors. This is clearly aimed at making the UK venture capital scene more competitive with that operating in the United States.[56] Increasingly crowdfunding has become a viable way for start-up ventures to raise capital and recognising that, crowdfunding regulatory regimes have been designed to spur economic growth. In the United States, the Jumpstart our Business Startups Act[57] provided a framework for start-up companies and small businesses to raise equity capital using a crowdfunding platform to issue securities. The EU's crowdfunding regulation covers equity and loan-based crowdfunding for businesses.[58]

IV. FINTECH FACILITATORS

States have focused on capacity-building and engagement. Governments and regulators have established a variety of contact points and supports as well as spaces for collaboration and innovation with a view to demystifying the regulatory journey and facilitating fintech innovation and growth. Regulators and countries that have done so develop a reputation for being pro-competition and for nurturing new market entrants.

[55] *Kalifa Review* (n 22) 60. It is anticipated that half of this funding would be provided by large institutions and the remainder from smaller institutions.

[56] Derek Tong and Alexa Williams, 'Fintech Growth Fund: Closing the Funding Gap for Fintechs' (*Linklater's Tech Insights*, 30 March 2021), available at: techinsights.linklaters.com/post/102gubh/fintech-growth-fund-closing-the-funding-gap-for-fintechs.

[57] JOBS Act; PL 112-106. The Act, including Title III (known as the 'CROWDFUND Act') took effect in May 2016. One criticism was that the capital raised was capped at $1 million. This was later increased to $5 million.

[58] Regulation (EU) 2020/1503 of the European Parliament and of the Council of 7 October 2020 on European crowdfunding service providers for business, and amending Regulation (EU) 2017/1129 and Directive (EU) 2019/1937 [2020] OJ L347/1.

A. Centres of Innovation and Building Relationships

Recognising the centrality of innovative research, a number of jurisdictions have established or committed to establishing centres of innovation to drive domestic and cross-border fintech innovation and trade. The Kalifa Review of UK Fintech[59] has propelled plans for the adoption of the establishment of a Centre of Finance, Innovation and Technology which will involve international collaboration 'to ensure that the UK remains a world-leader in fintech'.[60] In the United States, the SEC established its Strategic Hub for Innovation and Financial Technology (FinHub) in 2018 to provide a forum for public engagement on fintech-related issues including digital marketplace funding and use of new technologies.[61] Callaghan Innovation is New Zealand's state-sponsored innovation agency. It adopts a multi-pronged approach in assisting with technology and product development including R&D funding and its Scale-Up New Zealand initiative.

B. Facilitating Partnerships

Many countries have set out to enable the formation of fintech partnerships to facilitate exchange of know-how, encouraging efficiencies and market entry. Long-established banking institutions may seek to become more digitally agile by partnering with fintech start-ups.[62] While incumbent banks may wish to outsource services to fintech start-ups, innovators are drawn to the reputation, customer base and regulatory standing of the incumbents.[63]

Mexico's 2018 Fintech Law permits financial institutions to invest within certain defined ownership limits in fintech companies. This provides capital in return for innovation, facilitating market entry and may also aid financial inclusion and microfinance. In the United States, where many fintech firms would struggle to qualify for a banking licence, they may choose to partner with banks and credit unions.[64] In the United Kingdom, a planned digital scalebox will facilitate incumbent players and fintechs to partner and work together.[65]

[59] *Kalifa Review* (n 22).

[60] Briefing Pack, Queen's Speech (2022) 56.

[61] US Securities and Exchange Commission Strategic Hub for Innovation and Financial Technology (FinHub), available at: www.sec/gov/finhub.

[62] L Hornuf et al, 'How Do Banks Interact with Fintech Startups?' (2021) 57 *Small Business Economics* 1505. While beneficial, these technology partnerships generate new operational risks for banks that require management.

[63] MF Klus et al, 'Strategic Alliances between Banks and Fintechs for Digital Innovation: Motives to Collaborate and Types of Interaction' (2019) 21 *Journal of Entrepreneurial Finance* 1.

[64] AP Scott, *Fintech: Overview of Financial Regulators and Recent Policy Approaches* (Congressional Research Service CRS Report R46333 2020) 3–4.

[65] *Kalifa Review* (n 22) 36.

The provision of tax incentives to encourage partnering has also been suggested.[66] Nonetheless, partnering arrangements must be effectively supervised to ensure that there are no competition concerns or risks to consumers or to financial stability.

C. Incubators, Accelerators and Hubs

Incubators, accelerators and hubs form the backbone of state front-facing infrastructural support for the fintech industry. Although the terms are not terms of art, incubators usually involve mentoring and accelerator hubs which provide a co-working physical space for innovators to experiment and collaborate. As such, they promote and support the creation and growth of innovative start-ups.[67] For example, in Canada, Ontario established a FinTech Accelerator Office to connect fintechs and provide support for their growth. By contrast, innovation facilitators often known as 'innovation hubs' or 'labs' are designed to provide open and friendly informal points of contact with regulators for advice concerning the regulatory framework and its application.[68] The Australian Investment and Securities Commission (ASIC)'s Innovation Hub allows fintechs to receive informal guidance on licensing processes and waivers and other regulatory issues applicable to them as they develop innovative financial products or services. This contrast with a more formal outreach approach as evident in the United States where the depository regulators have set up working groups and offices to understand the impact of technological innovation and to provide an industry point of contact.[69] A step up from these approaches is the hands-on nature of the highly novel regulatory sandbox phenomenon as a catalyst for market entry.

D. Regulatory Sandboxes

The regulatory sandbox has its origins in the United Kingdom where the idea was mooted in 2015 to provide an analogous process to the clinical trials process for the pharmaceutical industry for the financial service industry.[70]

[66] ibid.

[67] A Alaassar, A-L Mention and TH Aas, 'Facilitating Innovation in FinTech: A Review and Research Agenda' (2022) *Review of Managerial Science*, available at: doi.org/10.1007/s11846-022-00531-x.

[68] See further, Ahern, 'Regulators Nurturing Fintech Innovation' (n 14) 350–51: 'Queries generally addressed by hubs include … whether authorisation is needed, how regulatory and supervisory requirements may be applied in practice, anti-money laundering regime issues and the applicability of consumer protection measures'.

[69] The Office of the Comptroller of the Currency established its Office of Innovation in 2017. The Federal Reserve Innovation Program has provided a help desk for banks and non-bank fintechs on financial innovation issues since 2019.

[70] UK Government Chief Scientific Adviser, *FinTech Futures: The UK as a World Leader in Financial Technologies* (Government Office for Science, 2015) 10–11, 52.

The subsequent roll out of the regulatory sandbox by the FCA aimed 'to promote more effective competition in the interests of consumers by allowing firms to test innovative products, services and business models in a live market environment, while ensuring that appropriate safeguards are in place'.[71] The FCA stated:

> A regulatory sandbox has the potential to deliver more effective competition in the interests of consumers by reducing the time and, potentially, the cost of getting innovative ideas to market; enabling greater access to finance for innovators; enabling more products to be tested and, thus, potentially introduced to the market.[72]

This cemented its reputation as a forward-thinking and flexible regulator that welcomed innovation and shepherded it.

Entry to regulatory sandboxes is competitive and the benefits are immense in providing a contained testing with the availability of hands-on free regulatory advice. The FCA earned a reputation that it 'worked hand-in-hand with newcomers, letting start-ups test business models'.[73] The goodwill generated was enormous. Consequently, the regulatory sandbox became emulated the world over by fintech regulators.[74] Within the developed world, regulatory sandboxes are available in a large and growing number of countries[75] and there has been some take-up in emerging and developing economies to promote financial inclusion goals.[76] Consequently, would-be fintech entrepreneurs can weigh up the relative benefits of regulators' sandboxes and their features such as eligibility criteria, duration, available supports, potential for relaxation of relevant regulatory rules[77] and expected reporting requirements.

Sandboxes assist participants with their route to market but impact on barriers to entry and natural selection in fintech markets as they do not seek to level the playing field but rather to extend preferential treatment to a handful of accepted sandbox participants. Sandbox regulators are thrust into actively pursuing a pro-innovation agenda and even a novel 'quasi-market-making role'[78] as they decide what innovations deserve a place in the sandbox for supervised testing.

Being pro-innovation should not come at too high a cost. Pressure on regulators to operate a regulatory sandbox and to do so in a manner that burnishes a

[71] FCA, *Regulatory Sandbox Lessons Learned Report* (2017) para 2.1.

[72] FCA, *Regulatory Sandbox* (2015) (n 35) 2.

[73] Imani Moise and Akila Quinio, 'Why European Fintechs Struggle to Make it in the US' *Financial Times* (14 March 2022), available at: www.ft.com/content/fd1f37a4-4441-42ce-888e-d4a87623ecb0.

[74] Ahern, 'Regulators Nurturing Fintech Innovation' (n 14); and D Ahern, 'Regulatory Lag, Regulatory Friction and Regulatory Transition as FinTech Disenablers: Calibrating an EU Response to the Regulatory Sandbox Stopgap' (2021) 22 *European Business Organization Law Review* 395.

[75] After a slow start, some 10 states in the United States have taken the plunge.

[76] See further Ahern, 'Regulators Nurturing Fintech Innovation' (n 14); Ahern, 'Regulatory Lag' (n 74).

[77] Under its Fintech Law, Mexico allows the narrowing of the regulatory perimeter for up two years during controlled testing.

[78] Ahern, 'Regulators Nurturing Fintech Innovation' (n 14) 358.

domestic and global reputation for being fintech-friendly may lead to regulatory distortions that affect the structure of fintech markets. Furthermore, attention to risk may potentially be downgraded. Brown and Piroska contend that regulatory sandboxes involve the danger of 'riskwashing' whereby 'organisations take actions to make it seem as if an asset class or technology or business model is not excessively risky, whether it is or not.[79] This may be unduly harsh. What is not disputable, however, is that although admission to the sandbox is for beta testing and advice, the competitive selection process for entry to a sandbox means that admission itself has competitive benefits. It is often inaccurately perceived as bestowing a 'coveted regulatory stamp of approval and de facto endorsement of the underlying product or service, which helps to attract customers and venture capital'.[80]

One can see the regulatory sandbox development as integral to states' intention to both attract and nurture fintech innovation. The FCA's review of the regulatory sandbox hailed it as a success in assisting fintech firms to find and in some cases expedite their route to market while reducing costs which would otherwise accrue in obtaining advice on related regulatory compliance issues.[81] While beneficial, the very informality associated with regulatory sandboxes constitutes their Achilles Heel. To maintain credibility, regulatory sandboxes need to be operated transparently, due regard ought to be had to investor protection, and there should be no relaxation of regulatory rules.[82]

E. Proactively Challenging Innovators to Innovate

A variant of the sandbox concept is the digital sandbox. In the United Kingdom, the FCA has used a series of digital sandbox competitions to promote competition in the market. Designed to support new product and service testing and development, one of the benefits is that participants can test using an API digital marketplace. The second phase of the FCA digital sandbox launched in 2021 and was themed around technology for consumers concerning environmental, social and governance data and disclosures. Criteria for selection required genuine innovation providing a new product or solution that was sufficiently differentiated from any existing market developments. However, there also had to be a demonstrated need for participation in the digital sandbox with a view to

[79] E Brown and D Piroska, 'Governing Fintech and Fintech as Governance: The Regulatory Sandbox, Riskwashing, and Disruptive Social Classification' (2022) 2 *New Political Economy* 19, 24.

[80] Ahern, 'Regulators Nurturing Fintech Innovation' (n 14) 362; Jemima Kelly, 'A 'Fintech Sandbox' Might Sound Like a Harmless Idea. It's Not' *Financial Times* (5 December 2018), available at: www.ft.com/content/3d551ae2-9691-3dd8-901f-c22c22667e3b.

[81] FCA, *Regulatory Sandbox Lessons Learned Report* (n 71) para 2.1.

[82] For a development of these arguments see Ahern, 'Regulators Nurturing Fintech Innovation' (n 14).

developing or improving the proposed solution's features – 'proof of concept'. The credibility of the testing plan and post-testing steps was also relevant.

What was interesting was how the regulator used industry engagement to level up the digital sandbox offering. The FCA brought in an Expert Advisory Panel of tech and finance bodies to support the evaluation process. The process was further levelled up by inviting expressions of interest for mentoring, engagement and collaboration from established players with digital sandbox participants and the creation of a dedicated collaboration platform. This showed a regulator going above and beyond to provide a nurturing safe space for seedling new fintech products and services and playing a matchmaking role usually performed by trade promotion bodies.[83] Following the Kalifa Review's recommendation, the FCA plans to establish a new permanent digital sandbox with a view to promoting innovation.[84] This commendable development will 'allow digital collaboration, access to synthetic data sets, design and deployment on open source and open architecture "plug and play" at international, national and sectoral level'.[85] The United Kingdom is expanding its fintech support offering through provision of a 'scalebox' providing support to fintech innovators in their growth phase as they scale or where they fall within identified priority fintech areas.[86]

Also worthy of note is the launch by the ASEAN Financial Innovation Network of a fintech sandbox with the aim of fostering collaboration between financial institutions and fintech firms to enhance financial inclusion in less developed ASEAN markets. Transitioning financial institutions towards use of open architecture is a central part of this sandbox's digital economy proposition.[87] Within the sandbox, APIX represented a global first in creating a cross-order, open architecture platform to power digital transformation in the Asia-Pacific region.

Outside regulatory sandboxes and digital ones, regulators are finding other novel avenues to shape the operationalisation of an innovation agenda. They have organised various competitions and initiatives designed to bring tech innovators together to collectively come up with solutions to societal challenges such as time-limited hackathons[88] and data/tech sprints.[89] Other medium-term

[83] An 'observation deck' allowed regulators to observe the testing and for the process to inform understanding and policy development.

[84] *Kalifa Review* (n 22) 35.

[85] ibid.

[86] ibid.

[87] Monetary Authority of Singapore, 'World's First Cross-Border Open Architecture Platform to Improve Financial Inclusion' 18 September 2018, available at: www.mas.gov.sg/news/media-releases/2018/worlds-first-cross-border-open-architecture-platform-to-improve-financial-inclusion.

[88] A hackathon is an organised public event for group collaborative programming for defined purposes.

[89] A data sprint involves a short set period of time for collaborative completion of a defined programming or coding challenge.

projects have also been launched by regulators to motivate innovation. Launched in 2016, Project Ubin involved collaboration between Singapore's central bank and the international financial industry to test the use of DLT for clearing and settlement of payments and securities. Project Ubin led to a new cross-border payments network by the Monetary Authority of Singapore in partnership with DBS Bank, JP Morgan and Temasek. In the United States, FDIC Tech[90] was created in 2018 to engage with fintech firms to promote competition and economic inclusion, but also to improve safety and risk management for depository institutions.

F. Making Sense of the Regulatory Environment

i. Safe Harbours, No Action Letters and Other Innovations

In the United States, the Consumer Financial Protection Bureau has developed No-Action Letter (NAL) policies for the fintech space creating a safe harbour from enforcement actions provided certain conditions are met. This encourages firms to develop products and services that benefit consumer choice and welfare. The first NAL was issued in respect of a company using alternative data and machine learning in credit underwriting decision-making.[91] Also in the United States, there has been policy discussion of the possibility of providing for a token safe harbour to give developers three years to build a functional or decentralised network with an exemption from registration under federal securities laws.[92] This would see the SEC standing back to allow DLT networks to be established during which time securities laws would not apply. In Australia, ASIC introduced a licence waiver scheme for fintech using its sandbox.[93] Access to it within the Enhanced Regulatory Sandbox includes a requirement that the product or service satisfies an innovation test and a net public interest test.

State actors are aware that regulation may not stand the test of time and that fintechs need time to adapt to changes in the law. In this regard, sunrise and sunset clauses constitute useful mechanisms in promoting market development. A sunrise clause extends its application to events before it becomes operative. By contrast, a sunset clause allows a regime to expire in order to allow a review on its merits after it has been in operation for a time. There is also potential in

[90] Federal Deposit Insurance Corporation (FDIC Tech): www.fdic.gov/fditech/index.html.

[91] Consumer Financial Protection Bureau (CFPB), 'Policy on No-Action Letters; Information Collection' 81 *Federal Register* 8686, 22 February 2016 and revised CFPB, 'Policy on No-Action Letters' 84 *Federal Register* 48229, 13 September 2019.

[92] Commissioner Hester M Peirce, 'Token Safe Harbor Proposal 2.0' (Securities and Exchange Commission, 13 April 2021). On 5 October 2021, Congressman Patrick McHenry, introduced a bill called the Clarity for Digital Tokens Act of 2021 which would amend the Securities Act of 1933 and put into law the Safe Harbour 2.0 Proposal.

[93] First introduced in 2016, this was reworked in 2020.

this arena to use a grandfather or legacy clause that allows entities to adhere to a set of rules that predates the implementation of a new regulatory regime. To be most effective, safe harbours need to be time limited rather than perpetual.[94]

ii. Navigating Multiple Regulators and Regulatory Codes

Regulatory landscapes for fintech are multilayered. Often there is a domestic fragmented approach to fintech regulation with division among a variety of codes policed by individual sectoral regulators such as financial services and data protection regulators. It is understandable that regulators are bending over backwards to guide fintech innovators through the labyrinth of regulation. This speaks again to an underlying competition promotion and economic agenda at work.[95] The UK Kalifa Review emphasised the importance of a streamlined single interface approach whereby the establishment of a Digital Economy Taskforce would present a coordinating face on a digital finance package.[96] New Zealand set up the Fintech Forum to provide a one-stop shop coordinating advice on fintech regulation across regulators.[97] Meanwhile, Singapore has gone further, pursuing a goal of streamlining regulations to encourage fintech innovation. Its much-lauded Payment Services Act 2019 consolidated previously disparate legal provisions governing different forms of payment services making them more accessible to navigate.

iii. Best Practice Standards

Technical and digital standards can act in place of traditional rule-making and facilitate both national and international interoperability. Singapore's MAS has sought to aid governance and development of good practice standards by publishing guidance around the promotion of fairness, ethics, accountability and transparency (FEAT) concerning the use of AI and data analytics in finance. This led to MAS collaborating with industry partners from 2019 on the Veritas project to create a framework for AIDA projects to evaluating compliance with FEAT and to the successful application of the FEAT methodology to credit scoring and customer marketing.[98] In the United States, the SEC issued guidance on the use of robo-advisors to provide automated investment advice which assists fintechs to comply with relevant investor protection regulation.[99] Meanwhile in

[94] J Grennan, 'FinTech Regulation in the United States: Past, Present, and Future' (2022) 4, SSRN, available at: dx.doi.org/10.2139/ssrn.4045057.

[95] 'Governments fear that if their regulators do not come to the aid of FinTech innovators to assist them to navigate the regulatory framework, entrepreneurs may be discouraged from bringing their product to market in that jurisdiction': Ahern, 'Regulators Nurturing Fintech Innovation' (n 14) 347.

[96] *Kalifa Review* (n 22) 9.

[97] Fintech.gov.nz fintech.govt.nz/.

[98] The Legal 500, Singapore: Fintech www.legal500.com/guides/chapter/singapore-fintech/.

[99] SEC, 'Guidance Update' February 2017, available at: www.sec.gov/investment/im-guidance-2017-02.pdf.

the United Kingdom, official policy is to consider non-regulatory measures such as technical standards before regulatory intervention in order to reduce the regulatory burden.[100] International cooperation on standards is crucial and this is a focus in international fora such as at G7 level.[101]

iv. Regtech and the Reporting Landscape

States are very aware that regulatory complexity and opacity serve as powerful deterrents to market entry. Regulators are themselves climbing on board the technological train. The availability of machine readable legislation and RegTech offers the potential to considerably reduce the time and economic costs associated with compliance for fintechs.[102] The future advent of digital regulatory reporting will transform compliance.[103] It is early days but these developments hold real potential to bring efficiency gains from big data automation and machine learning that will radically transform the supervision and compliance landscape, making it easier to navigate on both sides of the regulatory fence. This is important as the complexity of the regulatory environment represents a considerable barrier to entry for fintechs.

V. STRIKING A BALANCE BETWEEN OVER-REGULATION AND UNDER-REGULATION

This chapter has focused on an array of measures that fall outside competition law tools that are being marshalled by state actors to whip up interest in competing. A challenge for assessing their efficacy is that a direct correlation between state actor proactiveness and market entry can be difficult to establish. It is the synergistic effect of a complex web of combined variables forming an overall favourable climate for fintechs that may induce location and/or market entry in a given jurisdiction. States are focusing on GDP contribution and market valuations[104] as crude indicators of fintech success. However, attracting fintech interest is one thing, such businesses thriving and staying afloat, particularly, in a downturn is another.

It is interesting that the language of policy discourse, including competition policy discourse, is observably shifting to expressly encompass furthering

[100] UK Department for Digital, Culture, Media and Sport, *Digital Regulation, Growth and Unlocking Innovation*, 'Our Principles' (2022).

[101] G7, Digital and Technology Ministerial Declaration (2021).

[102] DW Arner, JN Barberis and RP Buckley, 'FinTech, RegTech and the Reconceptualization of Financial Regulation' (2017) 33 *Northwestern Journal of International Law and Business* 371.

[103] The FCA is working on a project to operationalise digital regulatory reporting.

[104] These include the presence of so-called 'unicorn' fintech public companies with valuations of $1 billion such as Ant Technology (China), Klarna (Sweden), N26 (Germany), Revolut (United Kingdom) and Stripe (United States).

effective competition. The Kalifa Review's vision for fintech policy and regulation in the United Kingdom was 'dynamic leadership that protects consumers yet nurtures fintech activity and encourages competition'.[105] This thinking has also motivated the planned establishment of the Digital Markets Unit in the UK CMA with a view to promoting competition in digital markets.[106] The EU Commission has acknowledged that competition policy objectives ought to be broadened to assist market entry and public interest considerations.[107] Thus the development of the contours of innovation-motivated policy goals as they continue to evolve will be enthralling to observe.

A key reflection on competition promotion endeavours is that the execution of well-meaning policies may potentially prove non-welfare enhancing from the perspective of actual and potential market participants in a given market. Some ex post assessment of competition in fintech markets would assist in judging the effectiveness of the role of state intervention in boosting competition. The danger is that market distortions may indirectly result from selective interventions that favour some market operators more than others. The regulatory sandbox provides a prime example. A question worth interrogating is whether all competition leading to market entry is worth promoting provided that competition rules are abided by, or should the bar be higher? The playing field for entry to fintech markets is never level and in a platform economy the potential for oligopolistic markets that are 'not really bad but not really good' in competition terms looms large.[108] As Langley and Leyshon astutely observe, '[p]rocesses of consolidation rather than competition characterise FinTech because, fundamentally, successful platform reintermediation turns on transforming and monopolising *new* market structures of retail money and finance'.[109] Indeed, a study by the Cambridge Centre for Alternative Finance reports that platforms offering balance sheet consumer and business lending were understandably worried about the threat to their business models from increasing competition from market entry by BigTech firms.[110] Furthermore, within a platform economy dominated by BigTech infrastructure, increased competition has the potential to negatively affect both investor protection and financial stability.[111]

While competition may benefit consumers and the wider economy, fintech policy needs to be holistic and not divorced from the broader regulatory landscape

[105] *Kalifa Review* (n 22) 8.

[106] See also the development of the UK's Digital Regulation Cooperation Forum.

[107] European Commission, *Shaping Europe's Digital Future* (n 23) 4.

[108] European Parliament, 'Competition Issues in the Area of Financial Technology (FinTech)' (2019).

[109] P Langley and A Leyshon, 'The Platform Political Economy of FinTech: Reintermediation, Consolidation and Capitalisation' (2021) 26 *New Political Economy* 376, 382.

[110] Cambridge Centre for Alternative Finance (n 2) 58.

[111] F Kaja, ED Martino and AM Pacces, 'FinTech and the Law & Economics of Disintermediation' in IH-Y Chiu and G Deipenbrock (eds), *Routledge Handbook of Financial Technology and Law* (Routledge, 2021).

including the financial services, anti-money laundering, data protection and competition law landscape. Consumer protection and financial stability goals permeate these systems and demonstrate that competition at all costs should not be welcomed. Arrival of new fintech products may give rise to consumer exploitation concerns such as the explosion of heavily marketed 'Buy Now, Pay Later' products.[112] Money laundering and fraud are also proving challenges as regulators and supervisors struggle to get a grip on properly supervising fintech operators that are global rather than simply domestic in nature.[113] Indeed, regulators are becoming more vocal in articulating what activities are not welcome in their jurisdiction. Thus, a multifaceted 'balancing act' is frequently in evidence by states in adopting a policy approach to fintech.[114]

An unfortunate correlation can exist between the laxity of the regulatory environment and the profitability of the underlying business model. A lax or ill-adapted regulatory or supervisory environment may encourage market entrants who then adopt questionable credit risk and other practices.[115] Thus, having incentivised fintech innovation and markets to take off, sectoral regulators now have to consider if and when a more nuanced approach is required. Important issues of regulatory policy arise for financial service markets regulators the world over – when should they take steps to tighten the regulatory reins or leave it to market discipline? This discussion is salient in relation to the risks presented by cryptocurrencies. An adjustment is seen, in Singapore's shift towards a tougher policy stance on the crypto industry after previously heavily courting the industry.[116] The need for this balancing act around a fulcrum of being 'fintech-friendly' is in line with what this author has previously argued:

> The role of expanding competition suggests a public interest mandate in promoting consumer choice, price and efficiency. This is a completely different driver than a risk-reduction regulatory model which typically stems from a regulatory focus on mitigating the potential for systemic harm and harm to the consumer. In the zeal to embrace FinTech, a legitimate and unavoidable question concerns how easily these two mandates can be reconciled. These divergent drivers create the potential for regulatory friction. Clearly, a competition promotion mandate should not come at the expense of appropriate investor protection and concern for market stability.[117]

[112] Patrick Jenkins, 'Buy Now, Pay Later Must be Regulated – Now' *Financial Times* (7 June 2022), available at: www.ft.com/content/c8496683-f7c6-4ac8-9a56-afab237ebcb1: 'Customers tend to use multiple providers and rack up dozens or even hundreds of overlapping purchases. That not only means individuals' finances can spiral out of control; it also makes it hard to grasp the macro effect'.

[113] The large-scale global fall-out of the German Wirecard fraud scandal provides a cautionary example of this.

[114] Bromberg, Godwin and Ramsay (n 21) 59.

[115] eg, in regard to the extension of high-risk marketplace loans at exorbitant rates before regulation of the market. See further, Ahern, 'Regulatory Arbitrage in a FinTech World' (n 12) 197.

[116] Ravi Menon, 'MAS' Approach to the Crypto Ecosystem' speech 27 April 2022, available at: www.mas.gov.sg/news/speeches/2022/mas-approach-to-the-crypto-ecosystem.

[117] Ahern, 'Regulators Nurturing Fintech Innovation' (n 14) 370.

This in turn raises larger questions which merit future study concerning the appropriate competencies and policy stances of competition authorities and sectoral regulators and how they are influenced by trade policy.[118] Reliance on a broad public interest precept for fintech policy in both competition policy and regulatory policy is leading to a morphing of policy boundaries to advance an economic agenda. Relevant to this discussion is the contention that fintech and innovation discourse involves unnecessary 'solutionism'.[119] It is worth exploring the countervailing moral and social costs for investors, consumers and society in actively fostering a triptych of market entry, market development and scaling as stand-alone ends.[120] Thus, it would be wrong not to balance a discussion on novel and alternative pro-competition mechanisms that state actors are pushing with a sensitivity to risk. A level of discernment is needed in developing fintech policy which includes the need to stand back regularly to take a big picture glance at its impact and to make adjustments as appropriate. Doing this well necessitates consultation between the gamut of regulatory agencies governing digital markets on issues ranging from data protection to prudential regulation to competition issues to decide what role competition promotion should continue to play and how it should manifest. Cooperation and dialogue among both national and international regulators are also crucial.[121] Calls for the emergence of all powerful digital regulators also form part of this conversation.

VI. CONCLUSION

Fintech brings opportunities for entrepreneurship, development of new product and service markets and disruption of old ways of doing business by market incumbents. State actors and the states they represent desperately want to be perceived as being 'pro-innovation' to drive fintech inward investment. Many have succeeded in brandishing that calling card and have done so with bravura, devising a daring, agile toolkit of novel strategies other than market regulation to woo fintech innovators to their markets, to help them gain traction and to scale up. Countries have strategically acted to build up the fintech infrastructure through investing capital, in training and in providing hands-on support and advice to fintechs. Sectoral regulators have also taken brave initiatives to directly nurture innovation and bring it to market while invaluably seeking to make it easier to negotiate the application of complex regulatory environments.

[118] On this, see MM Dabbah, 'The Relationship Between Competition Authorities and Sector Regulators' (2011) 70 *Cambridge Law Journal* 113.

[119] Evgeny Morozov, *To Save Everything Click Here: The Folly of Technological Solutionism* (Public Affairs, 2013); Brown and Piroska (n 79) 21.

[120] W Magnuson, 'The Failure of Market Efficiency' (2023) 48 *Brigham Young University Law Review* 827.

[121] One such network is the Global Financial Innovation Network (GFIN).

These initiatives, along with the wider regulatory environment, give each jurisdiction its unique fintech flavour.

And yet there is an undeniable tension between an agile competition promotion mandate and sensitivity to other salient issues such as abuse of market power, risk to investors and the need for regulation. Boundaries are needed. Competition promotion and comparative benchmarking should not lead to a 'race to the bottom' in order to gain fintech business. Nor should competition promotion involve a risk of regulatory capture. This is a risk for state actors deploying competition promotion strategies, where regulatory masks are lowered and regulators may be dazzled by the seeming brilliance of innovators, a risk augmented by informational asymmetries in knowledge which favour innovators over regulators.[122]

A reasonable prediction is that over time some alternative methods of stimulating competition in fintech markets will become mainstream (the regulatory sandbox already has), while others will have served their purpose and will fall by the wayside as markets evolve in terms of their efficiency and welfare outcomes and their regulation. Mastery by regulators, born of careful market study, leading to the provision of legally certain, proportionate regulatory frameworks constitutes the most robust way of assisting responsible market entry by both domestic and international players. As time goes on, the argument that fintech markets need to be given room to develop and that the emphasis should be on fostering dynamic competition ought to yield to a more measured regulatory approach. This would take account of the distinctive features of digital financial services models that are heavily focused on technology, data and platforms. As fintech continues to reshape financial services markets, regulators need to monitor and study evolving digital market developments including market structure and exercises of market power, to address risks and promote integrity and resilience. This should be buttressed by regular inter-agency national and international dialogue about these issues to ensure an informed and joined-up approach. Widening out the discussion, the meaning of 'public interest' in terms of competition needs expanding with the growing focus on sustainability which assesses the impact of market participation in terms which go far beyond the economic potential which underlies state interests in propping up fintech. This lays a whole host of other criteria for assessing public interest, from company culture to green credentials to value chain relationships – factors which are also increasingly being linked to fintechs' reputation and profitability.

[122] C Abbot, 'Bridging the Gap – Non-State Actors and the Challenges of Regulating New Technology' (2012) 39 *Journal of Law and Society* 329, 336–38.

13

The Path from Open Banking to Open Finance

SIMONETTA VEZZOSO

I. INTRODUCTION

THE DIGITISATION AND datafication[1] of financial services are proceeding at a fast and resolute pace. The European Commission's Communication 'Digital Finance Strategy for the EU' leaves no doubt in this regard, as 'consumers and businesses are more and more accessing financial services digitally, innovative market participants are deploying new technologies, and existing business models are changing'.[2] Within the framework of the European Union's (EU) 2020 Data Strategy[3] and building on what EU Commissioner for Financial Stability, Financial Services and the Capital Markets Union, Mairead McGuinness, recently called the success of open banking,[4] legislation on an 'open finance framework' has been announced for mid-2022.[5] While little is known about the details of the future open finance framework, Commissioner McGuinness at a February 2022 conference explained that it is 'about making better and more conscious use of data' with the 'potential to spark new,

[1] V Mayer-Schönberger and K Cukier, *Big Data: A Revolution That Will Transform How We Live, Work and Think* (Houghton Mifflin Harcourt, 2013) 78 ('To datafy a phenomenon is to put it in a quantified format so it can be tabulated and analyzed'); UA Mejias and N Couldry, 'Datafication' (2019) 8 *Internet Policy Review* 4 ('Despite its clunkiness, the term datafication is necessary because it signals a historically new method of quantifying elements of life that until now were not quantified to this extent').

[2] European Commission, 'Communication: Digital Finance Strategy for the EU' COM(2020) 591 final (24 September 2020).

[3] European Commission, 'Communication: A European Strategy for Data' COM(2020) 66 final (19 February 2020).

[4] Mairead McGuinness, Speech delivered at the Conférence Europe des Services Bancaires et Financiers (24 March 2022).

[5] 'A European Strategy for Data' (n 3) 14. A new open finance framework was officially announced in 2021, seen as instrumental to the European Commission's ambition 'to make the most of the data economy for EU capital markets, consumers and businesses', see EU Commission, 'Capital Markets Union – Delivering One Year After the Action Plan' (25 March 2021) 7.

innovative products that are personalised to the individual consumer'. She also stressed that 'consumers will keep control over their data and how it is shared'.[6] The open finance framework is thus likely to enable access to new types of customer-permissioned financial data under certain conditions, thereby enhancing business to business (B2B) data sharing. In the context of a targeted consultation launched in May 2022, the European Commission describes open finance as 'third-party service providers' access to (business and consumer) customer data held by financial sector intermediaries and other data holders for the purposes of providing a wide range of financial and informational services'.[7] Parallel open finance initiatives are currently ongoing outside the European Union, for instance in the United Kingdom[8] and Australia.[9] As to the United States, a July 2021 Executive Order by the Biden Administration on promoting competition in the American economy encouraged the Director of the Consumer Financial Protection Bureau to consider 'commencing or continuing a rule-making under section 1033 of the Dodd–Frank Act to facilitate the portability of consumer financial transaction data so consumers can more easily switch financial institutions and use new, innovative financial products'.[10]

Unlike the first pioneering and isolated initiatives towards opening up banking data, open finance has now become a pillar of the broader policy objective in the European Union to create a single European data space 'balancing the flow and wide use of data, while preserving high privacy, security, safety and ethical standards'.[11] This (industrial) policy goal is promoted as a concrete alternative to the US way of leaving the organisation of the data space to the private sector and the Chinese way of combining government surveillance 'with a strong control of Big Tech companies over massive amounts of data without sufficient safeguards for individuals'.[12] The overarching ambition is to create a single market for data underpinned by suitable rules for access and use of data, clear data governance mechanisms, ensuring trust in data transactions and respect for European rules, in particular within data protection and competition law.[13]

Two years after the publication of the Data Strategy, much awaited horizontal data-sharing rules have been set out in the Data Act Proposal.[14] In line with

[6] European Supervisory Authorities, High-level conference on financial education and literacy (1 February 2022), recording, available at: youtu.be/82j5NIhyuUk.

[7] European Commission, 'Targeted Consultation on Open Finance Framework and Data Sharing in the Financial Sector' (May 2022).

[8] Financial Conduct Authority (FCA), 'Open Finance, Feedback Statement', FS21/7 (March 2021).

[9] *cf* Australian Government, 'CDR Sectoral Assessment for the Open Finance sector – Non-Bank Lending' (15 March 2022).

[10] White House, 'Promoting Competition in the American Economy', Executive Order 14036 of 9 July 2021, Federal Register Vol 86, No 132, 36987, 36998.

[11] 'A European Strategy for Date' (n 3) 3.

[12] ibid.

[13] European Commission, 'Commission Staff Working Document on Common European Data Spaces' SWD(2022) 45 final, 24.

[14] 'Proposal for a Regulation of the European Parliament and of the Council on harmonised rules on fair access to and use of data (Data Act)' COM(2022) 68 final (Data Act Proposal).

recent remarks made by Commissioner McGuinness,[15] this chapter investigates how lessons learned from open banking on the one hand (section II) and the horizontal data-sharing regime as currently proposed by the Data Act on the other (section III) might shape the future EU open finance framework.

II. OPEN BANKING IN THE EUROPEAN UNION: LESSONS LEARNED

Open finance derives from open banking.[16] Open banking refers to consumer-permissioned flow of data from banks to third parties. In the European Union, the second Payment Services Directive (PSD2)[17] enabled providers of account information and payment initiation to access and use payment account data held by banking institutions, with the customer's consent. While open banking within the scope of the PSD2 is currently limited to payment account data, the future open finance framework is likely to cover broader statutory data-sharing requirements for financial service providers.[18] In a call for advice[19] to the European Banking Authority regarding the PSD2, the European Commission asked about perceived opportunities and challenges 'with respect to the potential expansion from access to payment account data towards access to other types of financial data'.[20] While in the days when the idea of open banking was first making its way through the EU, banks could not be counted among its most ardent supporters, the tone of the discussions on open finance is now generally much more positive.[21] Supervisory authorities are also generally supportive, although they do not fail to highlight possible risks relatingd to data protection, cybersecurity, financial exclusion, poor consumer outcome and data misuse.[22] Among the many financial products that could benefit from an open finance approach, the European Central Bank lists retail investment products, pension products and life and non-life insurance products, as well as new financial

[15] McGuinness (n 4) ('Open finance has the potential to spark new, innovative products personalized to individual consumers – while those consumers keep control over their data. This framework will allow for better use of data across the EU financial sector. It will build on the horizontal rules on data sharing provided by the Data Act. And it will reflect lessons learned from PSD2').

[16] SMSG, Advice to ESMA, ESMA22-106-3473 (30 July 2021) 2.

[17] Directive (EU) 2015/2366 of the European Parliament and of the Council of 25 November 2015 on payment services in the internal market, amending Directives 2002/65/EC, 2009/110/EC and 2013/36/EU and Regulation (EU) No 1093/2010, and repealing Directive 2007/64/EC [2015] OJ L337/35.

[18] EIOPA, 'Open Insurance: Accessing and Sharing Insurance-Related Data – Discussion Paper' (2021).

[19] European Commission, 'Call for advice to the European Banking Authority (EBA) regarding the review of Directive (EU) 2015/2366 (PSD2)' (18 October 2021).

[20] ibid, 3.

[21] See, for instance, Dutch Banking Association, 'Towards Data-driven Digital Finance – Options for an Open Finance Framework' (May 2021).

[22] *cf* European Central Bank (ECB), 'ESCB/European Banking Supervision Response to the European Commission's Public Consultation on a New Digital Finance Strategy for Europe/FinTech Action Plan' (August 2020).

products to satisfy the latent needs of consumers, investors and businesses.[23] Similarly, the European Consumer Organisation, is in principle supportive of the idea of a new legislative framework allowing access to all types of financial information in a 'safe and ethical environment … under full control of the consumer' and with '[c]lear protections ensur[ing] data protection and privacy of users'.[24] Respondents to the European Commission's Consultation on a new Digital Finance strategy underlined the importance of having access to personal non-financial data from 'online platforms (eg, social media, e-commerce, and streaming), from public entities (eg tax and social security), utilities (eg, water and energy), telecommunications, retail purchases, mobility (eg, ticket purchases), cyber incident data, environmental data, and IoT data'.[25]

What are the lessons learned from the implementation of the PSD2 regime so far, of relevance also to the future open finance framework? It might be helpful to think of the still rather limited experience with open banking under the PSD2 as a kind of sandboxing of consumer-permissioned, mandated sharing of a specific type of data – something that open finance would create on a greater scale. Arguably, there is no shortage of reasons to look back with some satisfaction at the concrete impact of open banking under the PSD2, especially when compared with the more muted success of other regulatory interventions in the digital sphere thus far. As recently noted by Commissioner McGuinness, '[n]ew business models have emerged, including those based on the sharing of payment account data – so called "open banking"'.[26] A recent report commissioned by the Verbraucherzentrale, the Federation of German Consumer Organisations, covering a period of one year following the last stage of the PSD2 implementation in Germany, provides empirical evidence of the several new financial service providers that have emerged.[27] Within the still sensitive area of stimulating competition between incumbent financial institutions, dedicated services are now available that can facilitate switching between bank account providers.[28] The very imperfections of the PSD2, in particular the lack of application programming interface (API) standardisation, have stimulated the emergence of new business opportunities, such as a new breed of interface providers whose services are used by the banks themselves when accessing account data held by other banks (which is, perhaps, somewhat ironic).[29] The report highlights that consumers resorting to digital financial services enabled by the PSD2 were seeking services to help them plan their finances, gain a better understanding of

[23] ibid, 48.

[24] European Consumer Organisation, 'A New Digital Finance Strategy for Europe/Fintech Action Plan, Response to the Commission's Consultation' (2020).

[25] European Commission, 'Consultation on a New Digital Finance Strategy, Summary' (September 2020).

[26] McGuinness (n 4) ('In many ways, PSD2 has been a success').

[27] Verbraucherzentrale, 'Gutachten zur PSD2-Umsetzung in Deutschland' (28 January 2021).

[28] ibid, 12 f.

[29] ibid, 22.

their spending, create savings goals and stick to them, make recurring payments transparent and easier to manage (eg, making cancellations), enable automated switching of bank accounts, initiate payments, etc.[30] The PSD2-related advantages that were intended for consumers were user-friendliness, enhanced security, more competition in the provision of traditional financial services, as well as the availability of new and secure services.[31] Overall, there has been a good deal of creativity and innovation in imagining new services of interest to bank account holders and others in the banking data value chain.

Despite some resistance from traditional banking actors,[32] open banking has also been widely recognised as a useful litmus test for banks to measure their ability to transform themselves and seize new business opportunities in the digital age. In particular, open banking initiatives have led banks and other financial service providers to embark on collaborative ventures with small and medium-sized enterprises with the required technical capabilities (FinTech), as well as with larger providers of digital services (BigTech). A recent joint report by the European Supervisory Authorities noted that 'the introduction of PSD2 has … contributed to the growth of FinTechs and BigTechs in the payments market'.[33]

However, there is also cause for concern. Consumers often encounter problems, especially in terms of harms arising from the conflicts of interest at the heart of the business models of many of the new services offered (eg, commissions influencing recommendations offered to consumers) and insufficient data protection.[34] A serious issue identified was that PSD2 providers were asking permission to access consumer data far beyond what would have been necessary for the provision of the services they offered. Thus, for instance, a consumer triggering a payment via a payment initiation service had roughly 30 days of her full turnover history disclosed – covering all other payments and revealing her lifestyle, habits, etc.[35] Additional issues were related to third-party data, such as what entities a customer had made payments to. The extent to which such data were successful shielded by employing technical measures and encryption technologies was highly unclear.[36] Secondary uses of data accessed via the PSD2-enabling framework were particularly problematic. Thus, for instance, payment service providers were processing account data to extract additional data such as personal credit ratings.[37] This processing is legally permissible only if there is separate data protection consent, but it was not possible to verify whether this was actually at hand. A broader risk in this respect is that

[30] ibid, 8 ff.
[31] ibid, 26 ff.
[32] See, for instance, the findings of the Autorité de la Concurrence, Opinion 21-A-05 of 29 April 2021 on the Sector of New Technologies Applied to Payment Activities, paras 329–36.
[33] ESAs, 'Joint European Supervisory Authority response, ESA 2022 01' (31 January 2022) 18.
[34] Verbraucherzentrale (n 27).
[35] ibid, 33 ff.
[36] ibid, 34.
[37] ibid, 35.

creditworthiness checks might become a condition for consumer market participation more broadly. Equally questionable were bundling practices combining basic banking functions with further analyses and recommendations, and related privacy-related permissions.[38] The involvement of the financial regulator in the enforcement of the privacy-related requirements enshrined in the PSD2, on top of the General Data Protection Regulation (GDPR) enforcement by data protection authorities, was also considered unsatisfactory.[39]

The PSD2 report from the Verbraucherzentrale concluded by identifying a need for action from the consumer viewpoint, with regard specifically to: (1) tackling the well-known conflicts of interest at the core of PSD2-enabled business models and beyond; (2) providing clear rules specifying what data should be accessed for the provision of the service required by the customer and the employment of adequate technological solutions to implement them (eg, filtering techniques that limit data access via the PSD2 interfaces); (3) promoting more and better cooperation between data protection and financial authorities in the dual enforcement of the PSD2/GDPR, as instances of data protection violations are likely to remain mostly under the radar or unremedied, possibly at least in part due to the relative novelty of the open banking mechanism; and (4) simplifying and streamlining consent/assent management, enabling more granular and truly informed consent and unbundling services (eg, the option to choose a version of an app providing basic multi-banking services, but not additional recommendations based on extensive data processing).[40]

These and other insights gained from the concrete experience with the open banking implementation under the PSD2 are extremely useful in directing a spotlight towards those aspects of the relationships between consumer and data holder and third party, respectively, which the new framework will have to devote particular attention to. It is also evident that open finance, which inspires the mobilisation of larger financial data flows than those currently allowed by PSD2, must be accompanied by technological solutions that aid consumers in making informed, granular and genuinely value-adding choices. From the point of view of the interface regulating data flows, it seems inevitable that regulation will have to intervene in a careful way to indicate which types of data should be used to provide the service expressly requested by the consumer.

Given the extreme dynamism and complexity of the sector, further reports and analyses are required, complemented by comprehensive consumer surveys, as the preparatory work for the proposal of a new open finance framework continues. Importantly, the future EU open finance framework should reflect a much more mature approach to data governance than in the comparatively early days when open banking was conceived, based on our increased understanding

[38] ibid, 35 f.
[39] ibid, 39.
[40] ibid, 37 ff.

of the variety of regulatory options in terms of data access regimes, as well as, more generally, of the possible huge benefits but also manifold risks of a data-driven economy.[41]

III. OPEN FINANCE IN LIGHT OF THE DATA ACT

As the PSD2 was for open banking, the open finance framework will be a sector-specific regulation. The Commission has already made clear that the new data-sharing regime will have to be built on 'the horizontal rules on data sharing provided by the Data Act'.[42] The proposal presented in late February 2022 by the European Commission is very broad in scope, with the underlying ambition being that it will serve as a 'data sharing enabling' regulatory instrument for the whole economy, industrial data included. The proposed Data Act has close links especially to the Data Governance Act,[43] which aims to improve data sharing across the European Union, including by strengthening data-sharing mechanisms (eg, setting out rules on the re-use of public data) and by reinforcing trust in data-sharing intermediaries. Of particular interest here are Chapter II of the Data Act Proposal, which introduces new rights and obligations related to the Internet of Things (IoT) ('co-generated')[44] data created in both industrial and consumer settings, without regard to the specificities of individual sectors (eg, agriculture, mobility, health, etc) and Chapter III, which contains obligations that apply to all situations where data holders are legally obliged to make data available under other Union law or national legislation implementing Union law.[45]

In keeping with the Commission's overarching data strategy, the future vertical (sectoral) open finance framework will be resting on the horizontal plane of the proposed Data Act. In principle, the Data Act does not affect already applicable EU legal regimes regulating data sharing, such as open banking under the PSD2. However, Recital 87 of the Proposal specifies that '[T]o ensure consistency and the smooth functioning of the internal market, the Commission should, where relevant, evaluate the situation with regard to the relationship

[41] Important reflections emerging from the literature on informational and surveillance capitalism include those from, among others, JE Cohen, *Between Truth and Power: The Legal Constructions of Informational Capitalism* (Oxford University Press, 2019); S Zuboff, *The Age of Surveillance Capitalism* (Hachette, 2019).

[42] McGuinness (n 4).

[43] Regulation (EU) 2022/868 of the European Parliament and of the Council of 30 May 2022 on European data governance and amending Regulation (EU) 2018/1724 (Data Governance Act) [2018] OJ L152/1.

[44] *cf* ALI-ELI, Principles for a Data Economy – Data Transactions and Data Rights, adopted by the ELI Council in September 2021, 134 ff, available at: europeanlawinstitute.eu/fileadmin/user_upload/p_eli/Publications/ALI-ELI_Principles_for_a_Data_Economy_Final_Council_Draft.pdf.

[45] Ch III applies only in relation to obligations to make data available under Union law or national legislation implementing Union law, which enter into force after the Data Act enters into force.

between this Regulation and [those earlier data sharing provisions] … in order to assess the need for alignment'.[46] As to safeguarding coherence with future sectoral data-sharing legislation, the Data Act aims to address cross-sectoral issues, while sector-specific needs should be addressed by complementary rules.[47] Needs specific to individual sectors acknowledged by the Data Act Proposal include 'additional requirements on technical aspects of the data access, such as interfaces for data access, or how data access could be provided, for example directly from the product or via data intermediation services' as well as 'limits on the rights of data holders to access or use user data, or other aspects beyond data access and use, such as governance aspects'.[48]

Therefore, the Proposal tabled by the European Commission should be assessed especially with regard to the Data Act's cross-sectoral, horizontal and foundational function in terms of data governance within the European Commission's EU data strategy. With regard to the rules foreseen in Chapter II on the sharing of IoT data, it should be kept in mind that, at least in some sectors, these rules will be complemented by more tailored regimes. The European Commission has already made clear that specific provisions are likely necessary for the automotive sector, setting the conditions for accessing and using in-vehicle generated data.[49] Most remarkably, besides introducing a new data access right for the IoT data, Chapter III of the Data Act contains general rules for B2B data sharing in all economic sectors, including B2B sharing of financial data, and is therefore directly applicable within a future open finance framework establishing new data access rights. Moreover, it is still an open question whether and to what extent the IoT data access right in Chapter II of the Data Act will serve as a model for further EU-level data-sharing initiatives, such as the provision of new financial data access rights. The Commission itself hints at this possible role played by Chapter II provisions when it, in a recent targeted consultation, asks whether new data access rights in the area of open finance should provide an exclusion for financial institutions which are small or medium-sized enterprises holding customer data, thus mirroring Article 6(d) of the Data Act Proposal as it would apply to the new IoT data access right.[50] This is a crucial question, also taking into account that Chapter II rules on IoT access rights might be only a limited fit for data-governance regimes in other areas, depending on the nature of the data involved, the specific data-value chain, different combinations of market failures, etc.

[46] Recital 87.

[47] See 'Accompanying Commission Staff Working Document – Impact Assessment Report' SWD(2022) 34 final (Impact Assessment Report) 65.

[48] Recital 87.

[49] European Commission, 'Access to Vehicle Data, Functions and Resources: Call for Evidence for an Impact Assessment' (29 March 2022).

[50] 'Targeted Consultation' (n 7) 17.

We must now await the Proposal of a data-sharing regime for the financial sector to be tabled by the Commission. The remainder of this section presents some initial reflections on the intersection of the Data Act Proposal and the future open finance framework.

A. Data within the Scope of the New Access Right

Chapter II of the Data Act establishes a new data access right. The provisions contained in Chapter II apply to personal and non-personal data generated through the use of connected devices or related services. Data are defined as 'any digital representation[s] of acts, facts or information and any compilation of such acts, facts or information, including in the form of sound, visual or audio-visual recording'.[51] A connected product is 'any tangible, movable[52] item that obtains, generates or collects data concerning its use or environment, and that is able to communicate data via a publicly available electronic communications service'. The tangible item in question could be anything from huge manufacturing machinery to the smallest fitness tracker. By means of its physical components, the connected device generates data concerning its performance, use or environment. Sometimes, a device can be accompanied by a service, such as the lifestyle advice provided by a fitness tracker. A related service under the Data Act is 'a digital service, including software, which is incorporated in or inter-connected with a product in such a way that its absence would prevent the product from performing one of its functions'.[53] The new access right does not cover free-standing online services such as for instance internet banking. Moreover, data stemming from interactions between the user and the connected device through a virtual assistant and related to the use of the device also fall within the scope of the Data Act.[54]

The Impact Assessment accompanying the Data Act Proposal explains that by granting users new IoT data access and portability rights 'data holders (eg manufactures of data collecting devices) cannot continue to enjoy a "de facto" exclusivity over the data at the expense of users and other companies, as is currently the case'.[55] The clear objective is to avoid lock-in effects as well as to open up more opportunities to generate value from IoT data. The Commission recognises that IoT data are an important input for aftermarket, ancillary and other services. Open banking under the PSD2 serves as a prior example of a sector-specific regulation aimed at tackling a similar problem of de facto data

[51] Art 2(1).
[52] Including where incorporated in an immovable item, see Art 2(2).
[53] Art 2(3).
[54] Recital 22.
[55] See 'Impact Assessment Report' (n 47) 67.

exclusivity with regard to customer bank account data.[56] An incremental policy step along the same lines could extend the open banking mandate to include non-PSD2 accounts, such as savings accounts.[57] The categories of data considered by the Targeted Consultation range from savings and securities accounts to insurance and pension products.[58] In a March 2021 Statement, the UK Financial Conduct Authority (FCA) suggested that the implementation of open finance in the United Kingdom should be 'proportionate, phased and ideally driven by consideration of credible consumer propositions and use-cases'.[59] The choice of the financial data to open up should be made through a multi-pronged assessment of their potential in terms of increased competition, innovation and true value for consumers through for instance improved (eg, less biased) advice, financial inclusiveness and surveillance, decreased cybersecurity risks, etc. Respondents to a 2019 Call for Input from the FCA agreed that 'a transparent approach to data ethics that recognises the benefits and costs to consumers of sharing their data would support the growth of open finance'.[60]

B. Consumer in Control

Building on the data portability right under the GDPR, the Data Act aims to put consumers (data subjects) more in control of their data. The Impact Assessment Report[61] accompanying the Data Act Proposal notes that this enhancement is required for at least two reasons. The first is that Article 20 GDPR does not entitle the data subject to continuous or real-time access to their data. The second is that the recent Final Report on the sector inquiry into the consumer IoT has shown that exercise of the data portability described in Article 20 GDPR is fraught with difficulties.[62] Similarly, Commissioner McGuinness already made clear that 'consumers will keep control over their data and how it is shared'.[63] The Targeted Consultation asks respondents their opinion about the most significant obstacles preventing the portability right under Article 20 GDPR from being fully effective in the financial sector.[64] It is very likely that the answers from the respondents will lead the Commission to conclude that the new open finance framework might be necessary to put consumers more in control of their data. The 'enhancements' to the data portability right at the

[56] See also S Vezzoso, 'Fintech, Access to Data, and the Role of Competition Policy' in V Bagnoli (ed), *Competition and Innovation* (Scortecci, 2018) 32.

[57] FCA, 'Open Finance: Feedback Statement' (March 2021) 24.

[58] 'Targeted Consultation' (n 7) 17.

[59] 'Open Finance' (n 57) 30.

[60] ibid, 19.

[61] 'Impact Assessment Report' (n 47) 4.

[62] See Commission Staff Working Document accompanying the 'Final Report – Sector Inquiry into Consumer Internet of Things' SWD(2022) 10 final (20 January 2022).

[63] McGuinness (n 4).

[64] 'Targeted Consultation' (n 7) 19.

core of the IoT data access right are substantial. Article 20 GDPR foresees a right of the data subject to receive and transmit personal data concerning him or her 'which he or she has provided to a controller', where the legal basis for processing is consent or contract. Instead, under the Data Act, the right of the user to access ('receive') and make available ('transmit') to a third party concerns 'any data generated by the use of a product or related service, irrespective of its nature as personal data, of the distinction between actively provided or passively observed data, and irrespective of the legal basis of processing'.[65] Moreover, contrary to data portability under the GDPR,[66] the user is entitled to access, use and share the data 'where applicable, continuously and in real-time',[67] as is already the case under the PSD2 and might be required also under the open banking framework, depending on the type of financial data falling under its scope.[68] A further difference between the Data Act and the GDPR concerns the technical obligations relating to data sharing. Pursuant to Article 20 GDPR, data subjects shall have the personal data transmitted directly from one controller to another, but only where technically feasible. Recital 68 GDPR clarifies that controllers are not obliged 'to adopt or maintain processing systems which are technically compatible'. Recital 31 Data Act states that unlike Article 20 GDPR, that Regulation 'mandates and ensures the technical feasibility of third party access to all types of data falling within its scope, whether personal or non-personal'. The operational part of the Proposal, however, is silent on the scope of the obligation to guarantee technical feasibility. This could be explained by the fact that the preferred policy option emerging from the Impact Assessment Report accompanying the Data Act Proposal did not contemplate mandatory technical means for data access, instead leaving room for 'vertical legislation to set more detailed rules addressing sector specific technical aspects of data access, for example cyber-security, data formats or covering issues going beyond data access as such'.[69] However, this does not answer the question of how those technical obligations should play out in *non*-sector regulated contexts, which might require further clarification in the Data Act itself.[70] Setting up the appropriate technical infrastructure will be key to the success of the future open finance framework. As the Commission itself acknowledges, 'putting in place such an infrastructure might be costly and involve many steps, including the standardisation of data and the access technology itself'.[71]

[65] Recital 31.

[66] J Cremer, Y-A de Montjoye and H Schweizer, 'Competition Policy for the Digital Era. Report of the Special Advisors to Commissioner Vestager' (2019) 81.

[67] See Arts 4 and 5 Data Act.

[68] 'Targeted Consultation' (n 7) 19 ('machine-readable access and machine-to-machine communication').

[69] 'Impact Assessment Report' (n 47) 67.

[70] Max Planck Institute for Innovation and Competition, 'Position Statement on the Commission's Proposal of 23 February 2022 for a Regulation on harmonised rules on fair access to and use of data (Data Act)' (25 May 2022) 107 f.

[71] 'Targeted Consultation' (n 7) 19.

C. Compensation

The aforementioned 'complements' to Article 20 GDPR that the Data Act introduces might indeed turn out to be true enhancements, empowering the user's access and usage of its co-generated data. However, Article 9 of the Data Act in Chapter III introduces the more 'ambiguous'[72] possibility for the data holder legally obliged to make data available to set a reasonable compensation to be given by third parties for any cost incurred in providing direct access to the data generated by the user's product. The making available of IoT data to a third party should be free of charge to the user,[73] and this is likely to be the case also for consumers or businesses within the open finance framework. The compensation rule falls under Chapter III and it is therefore a general B2B data-sharing rule. Where the data recipient is a microenterprise or a small or medium-sized enterprise, the Data Act establishes that reasonable compensation should not exceed the costs directly related to making the data available to the data recipient and attributable to the request and should not be discriminatory. Moreover, the data holder has to provide the data recipient with information setting out the basis for the calculation of the compensation. At any rate, this rule could be derogated by sectoral legislation where appropriate (ie, no or lower compensation).[74] Recital 43 adds that '[i]n justified cases, including the need to safeguard consumer participation and competition or to promote innovation in certain markets, Union law or national legislation implementing Union law may impose regulated compensation for making available specific data types'. As with the discarded option to impose detailed technical specifications for data access seen above, the Impact Assessment Report to the Data Act Proposal acknowledges that if data holders were to be prevented from requiring compensation from third parties, this would boost innovation through data use.[75] Conversely, the Impact Assessment considers that 'under more stringent technical conditions with less possibilities to recuperate investments, data holders would be disincentivized to invest in data generation'.[76]

By contrast, on the one hand, open banking under the PSD2 is not structured as a data portability right of the bank account holder, but as a right of the payment user to make use of the third-party payment services covered by the legislation. On the other hand, the PSD2 foresees the legal obligation between the bank (the holder of the account data) and the bank account holder not to discriminate payment orders 'other than for objective reasons, in particular in terms of timing, priority or charges vis-à-vis payment orders transmitted directly

[72] For legal and economic arguments against the possibility for a data holder to charge a price for the making available of data to a third party, see, in particular Max Planck Institute (n 70) 28 f.

[73] See Art 5(1).

[74] Art 9(3).

[75] 'Impact Assessment Report' (n 47) 29.

[76] ibid, 47.

by the payer'.[77] In this respect, the bank is not entitled to additional charges from the bank account holder, while it is much debated if the bank could charge an additional fee from the third party.[78]

Whether or not the future open finance framework is going to include a compensation rule remains to be seen. In the Targeted Consultation, the Commission asks respondents if they would support an obligation on third parties to compensate financial firms holding customer data for making the data available in appropriate quality, frequency and format and, if so, how this should be designed.[79]

D. FRAND

Chapter III contains another obligation that will be particularly relevant as part of the open finance framework. Article 8 states that '[W]here a data holder is obliged to make data available to a data recipient under Article 5 or under other Union law or national legislation implementing Union law, it shall do so under fair, reasonable and non-discriminatory terms and in a transparent manner' (FRAND). If a data recipient considers the conditions under which data have been made available to it to be discriminatory, it shall be for the data holder to demonstrate that there has been no discrimination. Both data holders and data recipients have access to certified dispute settlement bodies. Beyond the FRAND obligations, there are other interesting horizontal data-sharing provisions, such as a data exclusivity ban.[80]

E. Derived and Inferred Data

Recital 14 states that the data within the scope of the Data Act representing the digitalisation of user actions and events 'are potentially valuable to the user and support innovation and the development of digital and other services protecting the environment, health and the circular economy, in particular through facilitating the maintenance and repair of the products in question'. However, information derived or inferred from such data is not covered by the Data Act. Thus, for instance, the aggregated data relative to the use of a specific connected machinery would not be within the scope of the IoT data access right. With regard to the IoT context, this restriction has already been much criticised

[77] Art 66(4) lit c) PSD2.

[78] *cf* J Hoffmann, 'Safeguarding Innovation in the Framework of Sector-specific Data Access Regimes: The Case of Digital Payment Services' in German Federal Ministry of Justice and Consumer Protection Max Planck Institute for Innovation and Competition (eds), *Data Access, Consumer Interests and Public Welfare* (Nomos, 2021) 374 ff.

[79] 'Targeted Consultation' (n 7) 19.

[80] Art 8(4).

because, in many instances, it would not allow the third party to provide high quality aftermarket services to the user.[81] Similarly, some financial services provided by third parties to consumers and business might in some instances require access to inferred and derived data, and this is something that should be considered carefully in the context of the future open finance framework. Moreover, there might be instances in which it would appear fair for a consumer to have access not only to the raw data, but also to the individual-level insights that the data holder has generated based on the consumer's financial data.

F. Data Use Limitations

Of particular interest are the provisions of the Data Act Proposal which focus specifically on limitations regarding what the different data stakeholders can do with respect to the co-generated data that they *hold* (data holder), *have obtained/access to* (user) or *receive* (third party) under the Data Act. Thus, for instance, the user cannot use the data obtained to develop a product that competes with the product from which the data originate. Similarly, the third party cannot use the data it receives to develop a product that competes with the product from which the accessed data originate or share the data with another third party for that purpose. Moreover, the third party cannot use the data it receives for the profiling of natural persons within the meaning of Article 4(4) GDPR, unless it is necessary to provide the service requested by the user. There is also a ban to derive specific insights – a farm/user of IoT devices should not see its position in the contractual negotiations on the potential acquisition of the user's agricultural produce undermined by the specific insights that the data holder could gain from the use of the product.[82] It remains to be seen how these provisions can be tailored to the open finance setting. Thus, limits on the use by data holders and third parties of certain insights about the consumer could be adequate in order to avoid unfairly losing out on core financial opportunities (eg, an affordable bank loan for purchasing real estate).

G. Third-Party Eligibility as a Data Recipient

The Data Act contains very few eligibility rules regarding third parties as recipients of IoT data, possibly because of the horizontal nature of the instrument. It is plausible, however, that sectoral regulation will introduce forms of accreditation,

[81] See W Kerber, 'Governance of IoT Data: Why the EU Data Act Will Not Fulfil Its Objectives' (2022), available at: papers.ssrn.com/sol3/papers.cfm?abstract_id=4080436; Max Planck Institute (n 70).

[82] Recital 25.

as already foreseen by the PSD2. Based on Article 5(2) of the Proposal, undertakings designated as gatekeepers pursuant to the Digital Markets Act cannot be recipients of user-permissioned data generated by IoT products or related services.[83] Moreover, a third party receiving data at the request of the user cannot make the data available to a designated gatekeeper (Article 6(2)). It is to be expected that some restrictions on the use of customer-permissioned financial data by designated gatekeepers will be included in the open finance framework. In their joint response to the European Commission's February 2021 Call for Advice on digital finance and related issues,[84] the European Supervisory Authorities[85] provided an in-depth assessment of BigTech's inroads into financial services against the background of the growing digitisation and datafication of the sector.[86] The Targeted Consultation Article 6(d) of the Data Act asked whether large gatekeeper platforms requesting data access should be excluded from being able to benefit from such data access rights.

IV. CONCLUSION

The new open finance framework will build on the experience from open banking, which has been positive, but has also shown that consumers often encounter problems – especially in terms of harms arising from the conflicts of interest at the heart of the business models of many of the new services offered, the lack of adequate solutions empowering them, and insufficient consumer and data protection. The new open finance framework should draw on the lessons learned from open banking, take advantage of its successes, and strive to overcome the difficulties that have arisen along the way. The Commission's plan to introduce new data access rights in the financial sector is ambitious and bound to reflect our increased shared understanding of the possible benefits and risks of a data-driven economy. At any rate, it should be clear that the access and usage right introduced for co-generated data in an IoT setting can only partially serve as a model for financial data access rights. Taking the Data Act as a starting point, substantial efforts are still needed to frame tailored solutions aiming to empower consumers and help them benefit from substantially better financial choices.

[83] Art 5(2).

[84] European Commission, 'Request to EBA, EIOPA and ESMA for Technical Advice on Digital Finance and Related Issues' Ref Ares(2021)898555 (2 February 2021).

[85] Following the European system of financial supervision (ESFS) introduced in 2010, the three European Supervisory Authorities are the European Banking Authority (EBA), the European Securities and Markets Authority (ESMA) and the European Insurance and Occupational Pensions Authority (EIOPA).

[86] ESAs (n 33) 15.

Index

www.ingramcontent.com/pod-product-compliance
Ingram Content Group UK Ltd.
Pitfield, Milton Keynes, MK11 3LW, UK
UKHW020233290926
15470UKWH00002B/518

9 781509 963348